HISTORY MAKERS
of the
Old Testament

History Makers of the Old Testament

Elmer Towns

VICTOR BOOKS®

A DIVISION OF SCRIPTURE PRESS PUBLICATIONS INC.
USA CANADA ENGLAND

Recommended Dewey Decimal Classification: 221.9
Suggested Subject Headings: BIBLE, OLD TESTAMENT, HISTORY

Library of Congress Catalog Card Number: 89-60161
ISBN: 0-89693-744-5

VICTOR BOOKS
A Division of Scripture Press
Wheaton, Illinois 60187

CONTENTS

INTRODUCTION

Certain people make history. They are generals who win wars, explorers who discover new areas, rulers who bring about change in society, or thinkers who write books and/or transform the world with their ideas.

History makers are influential and their places in history are measured by what they accomplish. But that does not mean they are necessarily famous. Some history makers walk obscurely through life, unknown by those around them, but the next generation experiences the results of their influence.

This book is an unusual approach to the Old Testament. It is a study of those people who have influenced the events of the Old Testament. Obviously, I could not include every event in an Old Testament history, nor could I say everything about each person that I discuss. This book follows one of several approaches that historians use to interpret and record the events of the past. Some historians interpret history as a struggle between good and evil, sometimes called a Jewish view of history. Other historians use a cycle view of history; i.e., people struggle from hardship to prosperity, then become lax and lose their attainment and again become captive to adversity. I have chosen to interpret the Old Testament through the influence of great individuals as they improved society or destroyed the quality of life in their culture.

History makers have cast a long shadow over the Old Testament. The spiritual level of society is often measured by the quality of its leadership. What these *History makers* did in the past is the way I interpret the work of God today, that great men build great churches and average pastors maintain them.

This book is not just an Old Testament survey that gives the theme, outline, author, and contents of an Old Testament book. There are many outstanding such books, such as *Willmington's Survey of the Old Testament* (Victor) by my life-long friend Harold Willmington, who teaches with me at Liberty University. *History Makers of the Old Testament* is a history of the Old Testament that places people and events in a sequential order. But it does more than pin incidents on a time-clothesline, it interprets the Old Testament through the sequential influence of history makers.

The average American is not interested in dusty history stories. They want to know about people. And God's people want to know about God's people. So I believe they will love reading about Old Testament people like themselves. The people who lived before Christ were not much different from us today. They have the same desires, family problems, and frustrations. Yet average people, in difficult circumstances, with inadequate means, faced insurmountable obstacles and became history makers. Their lives are worth our study.

This book is more than just a collection of historical data about people in the Old Testament. It attempts to analyze the spiritual principles of history makers and apply them to twentieth-century life. Therefore, practical applications from the lives of Old Testament heroes are made to modern people.

Some of the material in this manuscript is drawn by permission from the course in Old Testament Survey (BIBL 101 and 102, Liberty University School of LifeLong Learning) by Dr. Ed Hindson, D.Phil. We both taught this course at Liberty University. I appreciate his knowledge and insight into the Old Testament.

I want to recognize the work of Rev. Douglas Porter in this manuscript. During his seminary days he lived in my home and we developed more than a teacher-student relationship. We became friends and we share this same philosophy of history. Doug was my graduate assistant. He helped in the research, typed the narrative from my class notes, and helped me think through the issues.

Mr. Garen Forsythe, a graduate student in Old Testament at Liberty University, proofread the Hebrew notations.

Sincerely yours in Christ,
ELMER L. TOWNS
LYNCHBURG, VIRGINIA
1989

ONE

LUCIFER:
The Beginning of the Eternal Rebellion

(Genesis 1:1-25; Isaiah 14:12-17; Ezekiel 28:11-19)

The endless stream of eternity was interrupted when God created the world. A drama of humanity began to unfold on the stage of history. The angels in front-row seats became witnesses to a splendid stage production of the magnificent grace of God.

"In the beginning God created the heavens and the earth" (Gen. 1:1).

Time was divided into compartments described as, "morning and evening." The simplicity of lengthening shadows and the chirping of crickets echoed the details of Creation. The brilliant sunrise of each new day mirrored the majesty of the Creator.

The angels applauded God as He created first land, then water, and next the energy called sun. It is said, "[Angels] shouted for joy" (Job 38:7) because they were overwhelmed by the power and beauty of new things unfolding before them.

"In the beginning God created the heavens." The word *heavens* is plural which includes the whole of heaven and all its innumerable parts. This includes the angels, the throne of God, and everything therein. The heavens were created at the same time as the angels; neither is eternal. As a matter of fact, nothing is eternal but God, even His throne is not eternal. For if anything were eternal it would be equal to God.

"In the beginning God created the heavens and the earth" is a summary statement that includes all that went before the first creative day (i.e., heavens) and all the Creation of the next six days. Time and space begin in Genesis 1:1.

LUCIFER AND THE ETERNAL REBELLION

God created angels along with heaven. An angel is a living being that has the ability to think, feel, and decide. Millions of angels were created instantaneously. They are spirit beings, meaning they do not have a physical body, though later in history they would manifest themselves in human form.

The word "angel" is derived from the Greek word *angelos* which means "messenger." It is always used in the masculine gender in Scripture though it is debated by scholars if sexuality in the human sense is ever ascribed to them. The power of angels is inconceivable (2 Kings 19:35), but not omnipotent. The wisdom of angels is extensive (2 Sam. 14:20), but not omniscient. The number of angels is great (Heb. 12:22), but not limitless. Angels are greater than man because God created man just a "little lower than the angels" (2:7).

These beings were created by God to serve Him and be about His throne perpetually. Only three are specifically named in Scripture: Lucifer, Michael, and Gabriel. There is reason to believe each of the three named angels in Scripture were leaders in the hierarchy of heaven. One of the strongest arguments for this conclusion is the observation that when Lucifer rebelled, he was accompanied by a third of the angels, who were cast out of heaven (Rev. 12:4, 9).

Lucifer apparently was the leader among the other two angels and was even called the "anointed cherub" (Ezek. 28:14). His name means "morning star." There is no reason to believe he was anything like the popular Halloween characterizations of the devil today. In his original state, Lucifer was incredibly wise and perfect in "beauty" (v. 7). He was compared to the beauty of a variety of valuable gemstones (vv. 13-14). Yet Ezekiel records the great indictment against him noting, "Thou was perfect in thy ways from the day that thou wast created, till iniquity was found in thee" (v. 15, KJV).

Lucifer, the highest of angels, was the "anointed cherub." His glory sat as a crown above the head of God. Lucifer created lower than God was not satisfied with his position; he desired something higher.

Lucifer was the most beautiful angel. Though he was wise, his wisdom reminded him of his limitations. He wanted to be like God. Lucifer had feelings of pride because of his exalted position. Lucifer was not satisfied with serving God; he desired equality with God.

THE CHARACTER OF LUCIFER'S RISE AND FALL
The fall of Lucifer occurred before the seven days of Creation. Some have even felt that because God's plan was corrupted by Lucifer, the creation of man was God's second attempt to create a being that would worship Him voluntarily. Lucifer's fall brought the entrance of sin into the perfect Creation of God. The Scriptures attribute his rebellion to his incredible beauty and unbridled ambition (Ezek. 28:17; Isa. 14:12-15). Blinded by pride, Lucifer attempted to take the place of God Himself and rule over the entire Creation.

THE FALL OF SATAN *(Isa. 14:12-15)*

I will . . . take God's place

Ascend into heaven	*Acts 1:9-11*
Exalt my throne	*Revelation 22:1*
Govern heaven	*Isaiah 2:1-4*
Ascend above the heights	*Philippians 2:9*
Be like the Most High	*Genesis 14:19, 22*

Three prominent factors were present within Lucifer's mind as he sought to unlawfully ascend to the highest throne in the heavenlies. The first was pride. The Apostle Paul spoke of "being lifted up with pride he fall into the condemnation of the devil" (1 Tim. 3:6, KJV). His ambitious pride in his God-given splendor convinced him that he was worthy of God's throne and glory. Second, unbelief was also in the mind of Lucifer. As a result he failed to believe that God would really punish him if he committed a sin. As a small child will purposely test his parents' prohibitions in order to find out if they mean business, so Lucifer, deluded by his pride, did not apparently understand the entire nature of God. Third, thoughts of self-grandeur were undoubtedly his enemy. He deceived himself into believing that he could actually wrestle the throne of God away from the Almighty. With blinded confidence, Lucifer and his hosts moved on the throne, only to be met with a barrage of divine judgments.

Ascend into heaven
Lucifer's first attempt involved his ascent into the abode of God. Lucifer wanted to ascend above his position. He moved into the third heaven, the dwelling place of God. This involved more than visiting the throne room of God, for he probably had access to it as the messenger of God. He wanted God's place in the throne room.

Exalt his throne
Lucifer also sought unlawful authority over the other angels. He wanted to be exalted above the stars. The term "star" is often used in Scripture to represent angels (Rev. 1:20; 12:4). If Lucifer was originally one of the three archangels of heaven, this description of his rebellion may mean he sought to expand his sphere of authority to include those angels under the jurisdiction of Michael and Gabriel. This move would make him the ultimate authority in heaven, perhaps taking the place of God over the angels.

Govern heaven
Further, he desired to "sit also upon the mount of the congregation, in the sides of the north" (Isa. 14:13, KJV). The phrase "mount of the congregation" is an expression relating to the central ruling authority in the kingdom of God (2:1-4). Lucifer seemed to be saying, "I want a share in the kingdom." The problem was that he wanted God's share. The "north side" is

a term relating to God's presence in Scripture (Ps. 75:6-7). During the millennial reign of Christ, Christ will rule this earth from the north (48:2).

Ascend above the heights

There can be no question that Lucifer was prepared to attempt a coup in heaven. His desire was not simply to get closer to God but to surpass God. "I will ascend above the heights of the clouds" (Isa. 14:14). Clouds are often used to refer to the glory of God. In fact, 100 of the 150 uses of the English word "clouds" in the Bible have to do with divine glory. Lucifer sought glory for himself that surpassed the glory of God. The Apostle Paul revealed Lucifer's future desire when he wrote, "Who opposeth and exalteth himself above all that is called God, or that is worshiped, so that he as God sitteth in the temple of God, showing himself that he is God" (2 Thes. 2:4, KJV).

Be like the Most High

The title "Most High" describes God as possessor of heaven and earth (Gen. 14:19). Lucifer wanted God's possessions. "The Most High" *(El Elyon)* is a title of God not only emphasizing His possession of heaven and earth, but His sovereign right to exercise the divine authority of God for himself. By becoming like the Most High, he would be the possessor of heaven and earth. By ascending into heaven, he would rule angels and ultimately enjoy his own perverted form of messianic rule.

To be God means nothing is equal to you. There cannot be two Gods for that is a contradiction of terms, an impossible confrontation of authority. For two equally unlimited forces will inevitably collide.

"In the beginning God created the heavens and the earth." To create the earth means the Creator is all powerful or omnipotent. To create matter out of nothing means the Creator is life-giving. Life is energy, and God activated His life into the energy of the atom that holds the molecules in their microscopic orbit, thus making matter.

But the Creator is also a Person. As personality includes intelligence, God intelligently created by a plan so that His Creation reflected His pattern, a harmonious system. But personality is also reflected in will or determination. The Creator decided what to create and spoke the world into existence. If the Creator were only force, the creative process might have continued uncontrolled and undirected. But His will controlled His power. And God the Person also etched His emotions into the blue mountain ridge, the golden grain, and matchless colors of the birds' feathers. God the Person chose to love, and therefore gave life to all His Creation.

But God the Person is sovereign and omniscient. He cannot allow anything in His Creation to go contrary to His nature. God the all-knowing Person knew Lucifer's rebellious desires as he thought them. He knew Lucifer's disobedient actions as he did them. God the holy and just One had to punish that which was contrary to His plan. God cast Lucifer out of heaven. Those angels that followed Lucifer were judged with him. Those angels that obeyed God and repudiated Lucifer were rewarded. They would never again face the temptation to disobey God.

The Bible teaches that God "seeketh such to worship Him" (John 4:23, KJV). But God wanted more than worship from beings who are frozen into righteousness. He does not want men to worship Him as a machine performing a function. God wants communication with those who choose to relate to Him. God wanted worship to spring from a free choice.

The motives of God that created Lucifer would also allow Him to create another person. This person would be lower than the angels. The next created person would be different than angels. Instead of living in the presence of God in heaven as angels, this next person would be placed on earth. Angels are incorporeal beings without physical properties, but this next person would be limited to a body. Angels have access to God and are the messengers of God, but this next person would be limited to a body. The next created person would be less than an angel, yet could do more than the angels. He would be made in the image of God and from his freedom could communicate with God. All that God desired from His creature could be realized in this person called man.

First, God created a new environment for man; it was called earth. As the angels lived in the limitless environs of the nonphysical heavens, man would live in a physical world. He would need physical food to sustain his physical body. He would need to depend on himself to stay alive, while at the same time depend on God who gave him life. Man would need a delicate balance.

The angels existed by the choice of God, and needed nothing. They did nothing to sustain themselves. Man was lower than the angels in many ways. Man had to care for himself, cultivate the garden, name the animals, and take care of himself. But man was above angels in the exercise of his independent-dependency.

Man was given vast responsibility; he was allowed to do that which was originally controlled by God. He was told to "subdue the earth" which meant man could merge elements to make metal, or cut timber to make furniture. As God was the Creator, man was the maker. No one reads of angels who could control their environment or their destiny. Man was told to cohabitate and repopulate, no one reads of angels enjoying this privilege.

Man was given the privilege and responsibility of freedom. By the exercise of his personality he could serve God, or he could eat the forbidden fruit. Freedom rightly exercised has its rewards, and God communicated with man in the cool of the day. But freedom also has its potential hazards. God knew the dangers and warned man that if he disobeyed by eating the fruit, "Thou shalt surely die."

God judged the angels who refused to remain in their state. He created a burning hell for Lucifer and the angels who rebelled against Him. Those angels who obeyed God were frozen in perpetual service. They would never be tempted to disobey.

"What if man rebels?" thought the angels.

There is risk in freedom. God knew when He created free man, that man could not handle freedom. God knew man would rebel and that He would have to punish man as He had punished the fallen angels.

"Is the risk worth it?" asked the angels.

God seeketh such as should worship Him, and worship is nothing when it is forced. God is love and He wanted to have a man who could love Him in return. It was imperative that man have freedom, for love and freedom go hand in hand.

"What if free man chooses not to worship God?" the angels continued.

God will shower His love on man in giving Him rain for food and sun for strength. God will give Him intelligence to provide for his needs.

"Is that enough to get man's loyalty?" again the angels asked.

God will speak to man through his conscience. Man's conscience will let him know what to do and avoid. Then man will see the existence of God through the blueprint of God in nature. Man will intuitively know about God.

"Why will God do all this for man?" finally the angels asked.

No one can fathom the purpose and love of God. God the Creator made man and gave him life. Then God gave man constant opportunities to worship Him. But man continually rebels. The opportunities of freedom became the trap of slavery.

God devised a plan for him. After man rebelled against God, God gave him another opportunity to be saved and worship the Lord. God's Son would be judged in the place of man. He would be the Lamb slain before the foundation of the world (cf. 1 Peter 1:20; Rev. 5:6), because God planned to restore man even before man rebelled. Why? "For God so loved the world that He gave His only begotten Son, that whoever believes in Him should not perish but have everlasting life" (John 3:16).

PERSPECTIVE: THE REBELLION CONTINUES TO THE END

The Scriptures describe the continuing contest between Lucifer and God. When Cain murdered his brother, or David committed adultery with Bathsheba, the rebellion against God continued. When Israel fell down to a false idol or the church accepted the doctrine of Balaam, the rebellion that was first evident in Lucifer is carried on by others. The original conflict between Lucifer and God is seen only faintly in the embryonic scenes of past history, but becomes clearer as the Old Testament pages unfold to the reader.

Though there is no indication in Scripture that Lucifer will ever end his rebellious attitude toward God, the time is coming when God will declare an end to his rebellious acts. "Those who see you gaze at you, and consider you saying, 'Is this the man who made the earth tremble, who shook kingdoms, who made the world as a wilderness and destroyed its cities, who did not open the house of his prisoners?' " (Isa. 14:16-17) The rebellion that once began in heaven will ultimately end in hell.

TWO

ADAM:
The Man Who Had Everything to Lose

(Genesis 1:26–3:24)

The last day of Creation is the greatest in the sense that God created a person who mirrored Himself. The universe with its awesome power and magnificent beauty did not completely satisfy the Creator. "I will make man," determined God. "I will make him like Myself."

God molded man out of the dirt and as he lay prostrate on the ground, the angels who viewed this sight could not have imagined the vast potential that could be wrought by this creature who was lower than them in nature and status. God breathed into this lifeless clay-person and man became a living soul. The word *soul* means breath; man now had the breath or life of God in him. As man arose from the ground, he reflected God who made him, for man was made in the image and likeness of God (Gen. 1:26-27).

The name Adam is actually a Hebrew word for man and is used in that sense some 560 times in the Old Testament. Linguists have suggested his name may mean "creature," "ruddy one," "earthborn," "pleasant," or "social," but none are certain. The word *Adam* comes from the root for "red," suggesting red clay was present when man was created. There seems to be a linguistic relationship between the Hebrew word for *dust* and the word for *man,* which is emphasized in the Creation account (2:7). Adam is identified by his

name eight times in the New Testament, plus other references to him where he is not specifically identified.

Someone has suggested the Bible is a story of two men,
Adam and Christ, and those who follow them. This is certainly
in keeping with the teaching of the Apostle Paul (Rom. 5:12-
21), who identified Christ as the second Adam.

ADAM, THE SON OF GOD *(Gen. 1:26-31; 2:4-25)*

The only reference to Adam by name in the Gospels concludes
the genealogy of Christ, "Adam, the son of God" (Luke 3:38).
This expression reminds the reader that Adam was not born
into a family but rather was created "of God." The Old Testament uses two words for *create* to describe the relationship
between Adam and God. The first term *bara'* emphasizes the
power of God in creating Adam (Gen. 1:27). The second term
yasar emphasizes His artistic creativity in forming man from
the dust much as a potter molds an artistic vessel of clay (2:7).
Adam was the artistic creation of God and what a creation that
was!

One of the principles by which God governs His universe is
the law "like begets like," as seen in the expression "according
to its kind" (Gen. 1:12, 21, 24-25). God created various species of animal and plant life and they reproduce themselves
after their own kind. When God created Adam He continued
the same principle. God highlighted His Creation with a repre-
sentation or mirror image of Himself (v. 26). In a very real
sense Adam was not just another catalog selection of possible
life forms in the mind of God but rather he was a replica of
God Himself. This was Luke's emphasis when he called Adam
"the son of God" (Luke 3:38).

Some Jewish rabbis taught man was created on the sixth day
so that God could keep him humble; the gnat was created
before him. There are many reasons for man's creation on the
sixth day, but one suggestion is that God created the home for
man before He created its occupant. One cannot carefully read
the description of Adam's first home without recognizing the
similarity of it with our final home. Adam was created to live
and work in a place that might rightly be called "heaven on

earth." It was a completely self-sufficient environment with everything Adam could need or want.

THE GARDEN OF GOD

---

1 The river of God flowing *(Gen. 2:10-14; Rev. 22:1-2)*
2 The presence of the tree of life *(Gen. 3:24; Rev. 22:2)*
3 Absence of sin and curse *(Rom. 5:12; Rev. 22:3)*
4 Fellowship with God *(Gen. 3:8; Rev. 22:4)*
5 All things were new *(Gen. 1:1; Rev. 21:5)*
6 Presence of the glory of God *(Gen. 3:8; Rev. 21:22)*
7 No temple or need for a temple *(Gen. 3:8; Rev. 21:22)*
8 Open unguarded gate *(Gen. 3:24; Rev. 21:25)*

In his original state Adam was far more than today's average mortal man. That God gave him the responsibility of naming the animals demonstrates something of his great intellectual ability. The same could be said of his understanding of biology and agriculture as evidenced in his care of the Garden. Further, Adam's moral state differed from contemporary man in that he was in a state of innocence or conditional holiness. He had not yet experienced the difference between right and wrong and though he was created with a will of his own, that will was not naturally inclined to rebel against God.

In an area described as "eastward of Eden," God had planted a garden which was ideally suited for Adam (Gen. 2:8). Further, recognizing Adam's need for companionship, God made the first woman. Jesus described Adam and Eve as an ideal standard for all marriage (cf. vv. 23-24; Matt. 19:4-6). Within the Garden God provided everything that couples would ever need or could ever want. Both Jewish and Christian expositors have often called the Garden "paradise," applying one of the titles of heaven to it.

Adam was given something else which God thought necessary for man to find complete fulfillment—responsibility. The first major covenant which God made with man was made with Adam in the Garden (Gen. 1:28-30; 2:16-17). This Edenic

Covenant required five things from Adam. The first was the responsibility to reproduce, to "be fruitful and multiply" (1:28). This was followed by the command to "subdue" the earth. A third responsibility for Adam was to maintain dominion or sovereignty over the animal kingdom (v. 8). He was also to care for the Garden and to eat of its vegetation; i.e., herbs, fruits, vegetables (v. 30; 2:16). Finally, this covenant prohibited Adam from eating the fruit of a particular tree identified as the tree of knowledge of good and evil (v. 17). Adam was warned that eating of that tree could only result in death.

THE TRANSGRESSION OF ADAM *(Gen. 3:1-19)*
Adam certainly was the man who had everything he needed or could ever want. Yet the tragedy of Adam's life is that he is remembered chiefly for the one day in his life when he lost it all. According to Scripture, Adam lived some 930 years (Gen. 5:5). Yet one day in his life was so significant that the world has never been the same since.

No one is certain just how long that first couple enjoyed the benefits of their Garden paradise. Estimates of various commentators range from a few hours to a few years. Still, the day came when Adam violated the terms of his covenant and sin became a part of human experience.

Though both Adam and Eve ate the forbidden fruit that day, the responsibility for that sin is always placed on Adam in Scripture. The historical record of that first sin of the race records a conversation only between the woman and a serpent, but it is implied that Adam was also present though silent (cf. 3:6). Adam had been given the particular command not to eat the fruit (2:17). Eve was deceived and tricked into eating the fruit but Adam sinned with his eyes open; he knew that to eat the fruit was to transgress the law of God (1 Tim. 2:14). There is never any biblical justification for Adam's actions that day.

Individuals normally fall into sin only after they become tolerant of questionable activities. This appears to have been the case with Adam. Some commentators argue his first sin was not eating the fruit but standing by silently while Eve talked with the serpent. Under the terms of the Edenic Covenant, Adam and Eve had dominion over "everything that creeps on the earth" (Gen. 1:28-30). Though it could be argued that one does not surrender control to talk with a subordinate, it is obvious in this conversation that the subordinate was controlling Eve. At best, Eve's conversation with the serpent was questionable. Had the conversation not existed, the fruit may not have been picked . . . nor eaten.

The serpent was successful in tempting Eve to eat the fruit by appealing to three areas of temptation. She ate only when she "saw that the tree was good for food, that it was pleasant to the eyes, and a tree desirable to make one wise" (3:6). When one compares Satan's later temptation of Christ, it is noted that the Lord was also tempted in these three areas, but without sin. This was due to His fidelity to the Word of God.

HOW SATAN TEMPTED

Strategy (1 John 2:16)	Eve (Gen. 3:6)	Christ (Matt. 4:1-11)
1 Lust of flesh	Good for food	Stones for bread
2 Lust of eyes	Pleasant to eyes	Glory of kingdoms
3 Pride of life	Desire to make one wise	Prove His deity with a miracle

When Adam and his wife ate that fruit, they immediately began losing everything of value in their lives. Their knowledge of evil immediately had a negative effect on the intimacy they had with each other (Gen. 3:7). When they heard the voice of the Lord, they were fearful of God rather than desiring to have fellowship with Him (v. 8). Because of their disobedience, God had to judge their sin. Because of the widespread involvement of various beings, many were immediately judged. These included the serpent, man, woman, and the earth itself.

When Satan tempted Eve, he was embodied in a serpent. He did not form himself like a serpent, nor did he take on qualities of a serpent. Satan used a serpent as a vehicle for temptation. Satan used an actual serpent, so God cursed the serpent for his part in the temptation (allowing Satan to use him). "So the Lord God said to the serpent: 'Because you have done this, you are cursed more than all cattle, and more than every beast of the field; on your belly you shall go, and you shall eat dust all the days of your life' " (v. 14). The actual physical form of the serpent was changed as a consequence of the Fall. We cannot ignore the fact that most people have an unusual fear of snakes, even those that are nonpoisonous.

Eve also was cursed for her part in the Fall. "Unto the woman He said: 'I will greatly multiply your sorrow and your conception; in pain you shall bring forth children; your desire shall be for your husband, and he shall rule over you' " (v. 16). Eve, in particular, and women in general, live with two results of the Fall. First, they have a natural inclination to their husbands which would in some occasions lead to conception. And, secondly, they have increased pain in childbirth.

God also judged Adam for his sin. God introduced a new emotion into his experience—sorrow (v. 17). He was to continue to have dominion over the ground, but now he would till a cursed ground. His labor would be multiplied and he would find himself working harder and producing less. Physical death was also introduced into the human experience. "In the sweat of your face you shall eat bread till you return to the ground, for out of it you were taken; for dust you are, and to dust you shall return" (v. 19). Apparently Adam also lost the complete dominion he earlier possessed over the animals. Man would still rule the beasts of the earth, but with far more difficulty. Some animals would attack and kill man, other animals would resist him, and still other animals would be too dumb to heed man's direction.

THE DAYS OF ADAM *(Gen. 3:20-24; 5:1-5)*

Everything was different for Adam after the Fall. His innocence was replaced with a conscience. His paradise became a burden. A distance came between him and God that had not formerly existed. No longer could he live under the ideal conditions of the Edenic Covenant. God made a new covenant with Adam known as the Adamic Covenant (Gen. 3:14-19). Though much of this covenant was negative, for Adam it offered hope and became the content of his faith in God.

One of the first things Adam did under the terms of the Adamic Covenant was to rename his wife "Eve." The significance of this act is recognized in understanding the meaning of the two names Adam gave his wife. The name "Woman" (Heb. *'ishshah)* conveys the idea of a close relationship with man (Heb. *'ish*—cf. Gen. 2:23). The name "Eve" literally means "lifegiver." God had promised Eve sorrow in childbirth and Adam exercised his faith in the word of God by referring to his wife not as a woman or a wife, but rather the mother of their yet unborn children.

After the first sin, God came walking in the Garden seeking fellowship with man. Since God knows all things, He knew man had sinned. After confronting our first parents with judgment for their sin, God continued seeking man. In response to the faith of Adam, God did what He always does when people come to Him by faith. He restored Adam to fellowship with Him (reconciliation). "Also for Adam and his wife, the Lord God made tunics of skin, and clothed them" (3:21). Many commentators interpret those "tunics of skin" typically as "the garments of salvation" (Isa. 61:10). Since God would have had to kill an animal to provide the skins, it was probably here that God taught Adam of the need for a sacrifice for sin.

Not only did God provide salvation for Adam and Eve, He made their new relationship with Him secure by expelling them from the Garden. There were two trees of significance in the Garden paradise. When Adam ate of the tree of knowledge of good and evil, he plunged the whole human race into sin. Had he also eaten of the tree of life, he would have lived forever in that state. Understanding the eternal consequence of that act better than Adam could ever hope to, God "drove out the man" (Gen. 3:24). It probably seemed at the time to Adam a harsh act on the part of God, but in reality it was a further evidence of "the grace of God that brings salvation" (Titus 2:11).

God forgave Adam for his sin as He forgives all who come to Him by faith, but Adam still had to struggle with the consequence of his sin for the rest of his life. His first son, Cain, followed his example in rebelling against the command of God and it resulted in the murder of the second son, Abel (Gen. 4:1-8). With the birth of his third son, Seth, Adam saw his family degenerate into the practice of calling things by the name of the Lord, probably the first reference to cursing and idol worship (v. 26). Finally, after over 900 years of life, Adam himself died physically as the ultimate result of his sin in the Garden (5:5).

Though Adam had lost everything in his decision to violate the command of God, he did not abandon hope as so many today do when confronted with major setbacks or failures. He realized that even in the judgment of God there was grace. Adam was willing to rebuild his life by faith in God. No man has ever committed sin with such severe consequences as Adam, yet even for Adam there was grace.

PERSPECTIVE: THE LAST ADAM
(Rom. 5:12-21; 1 Cor. 15:45-59)

God promised Adam and Eve a coming Redeemer. If God had to condemn man because of Adam's sin, He would also provide the means of redeeming mankind. The promise of the seed of the woman in Genesis 3:15 is called the "Proto-evangelium," or first mention of the Gospel. Ultimately, there would appear in Adam's race the promised Child who would bruise the head of the serpent and defeat the power of sin. That was the first of many Old Testament messianic prophecies which find their fulfillment in the person of Jesus Christ whom Paul calls "the last Adam" (1 Cor. 15:45). In this sense Adam is "a type of Him who was to come" (Rom. 5:14).

Every evil influence that Adam passed on to humanity, Christ overcame for the race. Because of Adam's transgression, everyone is born with a sin nature, but Christ offers a new nature to those who experience His salvation (2 Cor.

5:17). Everyone will die because of Adam, but Christ's death is a substitute for sin and through the Cross the repentant sinner receives new life. Jesus claimed, "That they may have life, and that they may have it more abundantly" (John 10:10). While the race is "condemned already" (3:18) because of Adam's sin, "there is therefore now no condemnation to those who are in Christ Jesus" (Rom. 8:1). Jesus came as the last Adam to lead a new race of those who were born again into His kingdom (John 1:13; 3:3). Writing to the Romans, the Apostle Paul outlined a comparison between Adam and Christ and their respective "races."

ROMANS 5:12-21

Adam	Christ
Sin entered	Grace entered
Offense transferred	Free gift offered
Condemnation	Justification
Death reigns	Righteousness reigns
Disobedience	Obedience
Makes men sinners	Makes men righteous
Sin abounds	Grace abounds
Death	Eternal life

THREE

CAIN:
A Depressing Story of Failure
(Genesis 4:1–5:32)

No one can imagine the awe that surrounded the conception and birth of the first child in history. Adam and Eve knew they were to "replenish" the earth, but they had never been through the experience surrounding childbirth. They had no parents to guide them during pregnancy, and there is no record of God giving them instructions in the intricacies of bringing forth life. Most scholars think the innate knowledge given to our first parents at Creation included wisdom for bringing a child to maturity.

As we relate to the dreams of joy that surround a new baby today, what about our first parents? They were looking for a "seed" (Gen. 3:15) that would defeat the tempter and deliver them. They probably did not understand the long-range nature of prophecy, so they probably expected their first child to be their redeemer.

The first child born to human parents carried great expectations. Adam and Eve had lost their paradise, and no doubt they told their child of their experience. He should have learned by their mistake. God is quick to judge, but full of mercy. The first child, Cain, should have sought to walk with God as did his parents; but he did not.

One of the unfortunate results of Adam's sin was that it changed the nature of man, and that changed nature was evident in his first child. Sin became not only a part of human experience, it also became a governing factor in human nature. Due in part to the different physical conditions governing the pre-Flood world, men lived long lives, each person living almost a thousand years. But they were long evil years for the most part. The first man born into this world rejected God, murdered his brother, and established an evil society. Ultimately the world became so wicked that God destroyed all but a single family by means of a Flood.

If history revolves around the lives of men and their influence, this early era of world history revolved around the influence of Cain. Remembered primarily as a man of great sin, he became the father of a civilization which is also today remembered chiefly for its wickedness. Many years later some of the final books of the New Testament described a sinful society and "the way of Cain" (Jude 11) and "Cain who was of the wicked one" (1 John 3:12).

THE WAY OF CAIN *(Gen. 4:1-7)*

The life of Cain is in many senses an irony. Here is a man who could have been remembered as a great man of God, but chose rather to follow his own selfish way. In this sense, he is an example of the truth of the proverb: "There is a way which seems right to a man, but its end is the way of death" (Prov. 14:12; 16:25). His name means "acquisition" and he was so named by his mother because of her belief that she had received the promised seed, "a man even Jehovah" (Gen. 4:1, literal translation). Some commentators believe that Eve's later naming of Abel (the name could mean "breath" or "vanity") suggests a sense of disappointment on her part because Cain as a child was not living up to her expectations as "the God-Man."

In the early life of Cain there were a number of positive "firsts" by which he would probably have been remembered had it not been for the murder of Abel. The first recorded offering to the Lord was by Cain (v. 3). Further, though God probably provided a sacrifice for sin in the Garden for Adam, the first recorded example of a sacrifice for sin was God's command to Cain (v. 7). Most Christians do not realize that the Scriptures record the Lord speaking more with Cain than with any other man in the pre-Flood world. Yet none of these positive influences were of any benefit to Cain who was committed to being his own selfish authority in life.

The tragedy of Cain is the tragedy of a man who lives his own life his own way. He brought an offering to God, but he did it his way (Jude 11). His brother Abel also brought an offering, but he did it by faith (Heb. 11:4). Cain's offering was "an offering of the fruit of the ground" (Gen. 4:3) whereas "Abel also brought of the firstlings of his flock and of their fat" (v. 4). Abel's offering was accepted; Cain's was not.

Several reasons have been suggested as to why Cain's offering was rejected. It is widely believed that the difference between these offerings is a difference of blood. Those who hold this view point out Abel offered a blood sacrifice and it is the shedding of blood that is a propitiation to reconcile man to God. While this may be the case, others note that God made allowances for a non-blood offering in the grain offering (Lev. 2:1-16) and suggest the difference between Cain and Abel was one of attitude. That the Scriptures describe Abel as choosing the first and finest in his flock may imply Cain did not. Cain's attitude may have been, "Anything will do for God." This conclusion is contrary to the biblical prohibition of offering to God defective sacrifices. A third view argues the difference was in the object of worship. While all agree Abel was a worshiper of Jehovah, some interpreters believe Cain's offering and later murder of Abel was a part of the worship of pagan deity; in which case Cain's example may have been the precedent on which other human-sacrifice cults later developed.

The result of Cain's unacceptable sacrifice was evidenced in his reaction when God rejected him. Rather than repenting of his self-centeredness and responding positively to God, Cain got angry to the extent that it soon became evident in his physical appearance. Even though Cain was mad at God, God did not abandon Cain. Rather the Lord came to Cain and asked him a series of three probing questions that should have helped him understand his real problem. "Why are you angry?

And why has your countenance fallen? If you do well, will you not be accepted?" (Gen. 4:6-7)

As Cain began to think through this series of questions, he was being forced to recognize his own failure. His countenance was fallen because he was angry. He was angry because he thought God had unjustly rejected his offering. But deep down inside he must have known that God would have accepted him and his offering if he had done what was right.

God offered Cain another chance. God told Cain, "If thou doest well, shalt thou not be accepted? And if thou doest not well, sin lieth at the door" (v. 7, KJV). There is a question concerning the word *sin*—what was at the door? There are two ways this word has been interpreted. First, the Old Testament uses the same word for *sin* and *sin offering*. God could have told Cain there was an animal at the door that he could use for a sin offering. This first view emphasizes the grace of God. Even though Cain brought the wrong offering, now God was giving him a second chance to bring a blood offering. The second view interprets *sin* to be the imminent judgment that is on the other side of the door of opportunity. The Scriptures are silent concerning any response to the Lord's questions on the part of Cain.

When a man chooses to live life his own way, his ability to communicate with God or others is greatly influenced by his decision. When one directs anger toward God, it is not long before he does not feel like engaging in prayer and Bible study and begins to find it difficult to get along with others. That was the experience of Cain. Not only did Cain have difficulty responding to God, he soon could not communicate with his brother. "Now Cain talked with Abel his brother" (v. 8), but the word used to describe that conversation is significantly different than one would expect. The word *'amar* used here is almost always followed by the statement which was spoken. Here there is nothing recorded that Cain said, implying he had nothing to say. Some ancient versions recognized the significance of this word and added the phrase, "Let us go out to the field" (Samaritan Pentateuch, LXX, Syriac, Vulgate). The emphasis of the statement here is "Now Cain said to Abel his brother . . . " but the words just didn't seem to come.

RESPONDING TO GOD

The Way of Cain	The Way of the Lord
1 Offering of anything to God	Giving God the first and finest
2 Anger toward God for personal sin	Repentance toward God for personal sin
3 Fallen countenance	The joy of the Lord
4 Ignoring God	Obeying God
5 Hating (murdering) his brother	Loving God and others, even your enemies
6 Denying personal responsibilities	Accepting personal responsibility
7 Accusing God of injustice	Accepting God's judgment and confessing sin
8 Cutting oneself off from God	Seeking to please God by faith and growing into a greater intimacy with God

---

THE WICKEDNESS OF CAIN *(Gen. 4:8-15)*
Cain is best remembered by most Christians today not for his sacrifice to the Lord, but rather his slaying of Abel. But why would a man like Cain kill his own brother? The Bible answers this question of motive noting, "Because his works were evil and his brother's righteous" (1 John 3:12). When a man allows his own "desperately wicked" heart to be the sole authority in governing his way, his works will also be characterized as wicked.

We cannot be certain how long Cain continued to harbor his anger against God. Finally Cain erupted. "And it came to pass, when they were in the field, that Cain rose against Abel his brother and killed him" (Gen. 4:8). His anger toward God was directed against the man of God. He could not exterminate God so he attacked his godly brother instead.

Even after he had murdered his own brother, Cain was still not abandoned by God. Again the Lord came to Cain with a probing and convicting question. But now Cain's discouragement and despondency had turned to defiance. As far as Cain was concerned, God had no right to interfere in his life with His convicting questions. He was not the only one who could ask questions. With a rebellious attitude Cain blurted out, "I do not know. Am I my brother's keeper?" (v. 9)

Cain continued on the road to destruction, the way that apparently seemed right to him. He had refused to worship God according to whatever light he had. When God had refused to accept his compromise, Cain had gotten angry. Some would say his anger had become madness. Without motive he had attacked his brother, pouring out his brother's blood into the earth. Now when confronted with his sin, he chose to tell a deliberate lie to God, "I do not know." The very holiness of God demanded that Cain be held accountable for his evil act. Now it was God's turn to respond, "What have you done? The voice of your brother's blood cries out to Me from the ground" (v. 10).

Cain probably did not realize this would be his final appeal from the God of grace. Of the generations to come from this man, God would in the future say, "My Spirit shall not strive with man forever" (6:3). Cain had one more chance to repent before he would learn experientially what it means to suffer the consequences of sin. God would give Cain one last chance to repent. When the Bible describes those whom "God gave . . . over," it was because they rejected God. "And even as they did not like to retain God in their knowledge, God gave them over to a debased mind, to do those things which are not fitting" (Rom. 1:28). The encounter between God and Cain was a moment that would have eternal consequence. God had earlier explained to Cain's father the consequences of sin. He was now explaining the same thing to Cain. Would he like Adam even now respond in faith?

"And Cain said to the Lord, 'My punishment is greater than

I can bare!' " (Gen. 4:13) When Martin Luther came to translate the response of Cain, he wrote, "My sin is greater than can be forgiven." But it was not God who was refusing to forgive sin; Cain was refusing to have his sin forgiven. The defiance was still there. He was accusing God of injustice. Though confronted with the just and natural results of his own sin, Cain chose to exaggerate the severity of the penalty and blame it all on God.

Once again the Lord spoke with Cain, but this time it was different. There was no appeal in His voice. He simply reminded Cain he still had his life, a life that would still be protected by God. "Then Cain went out from the presence of the Lord" (v. 16). Never again would the Lord be mentioned in Cain's lifetime or in the generations to come in the Cainite civilization. If God ever cries, tears must have come to His eyes that day as He watched Cain finally walk away.

THE WORLD OF CAIN
(Gen. 4:16-24; 5:21-24; 6:1-8; Rom. 1:18-31)

Every society tends to revere its founding father and in so doing, reproduce something of his character in their lives. The society which began with Cain was no different. Unfortunately, it too reproduced the rebellious character of Cain, becoming a race committed to their own destructive way.

When Cain determined to abandon the Lord, he appears to have determined to create his own utopia. Perhaps he remembered his parents talking about how wonderful life was when they had lived in the Garden of God. For whatever reason, Cain chose the region of that garden paradise for his new home. But when he arrived east of Eden, all he found was the land of Nod which literally means wandering. He began his family and determined to settle down in a great city he would build and name after his son Enoch. But the use of the imperfect tense in the verb "built" (Gen. 4:17) suggests he never completed that task; the city remained unfinished.

Cain's failure to accomplish his objectives was also characteristic of his descendants for several generations. In fact, there were no significant recorded accomplishments for six generations. It was the children of the seventh generation from Cain that existed before the Flood which washed them from the face of this earth.

But there was another darker side to this advanced godless society. It is typical of every society which rejects God to the point of being abandoned by God, a society where "the wickedness of man was great in the earth, and that every intent of the thoughts of his heart was only evil continually" (6:5). So prevalent was evil in the world of Cain that "the Lord was sorry that He had made man on the earth, and He was grieved in His heart" (v. 6). It was a world so calloused that it could for 120 years reject the preaching of Noah and ignore the recorded warnings of Enoch.

The poet has rightly observed, "The saddest words of tongue or pen, are these four, 'It might have been.'" By this standard the failure of Cainite society was indeed sad. No man sins unto himself and when a man removes God from his life, he also robs future generations of their potential spiritual heritage. This principle is particularly evident in the experience of Cain when the lives of representatives of the seventh generation are compared.

The seventh from Adam in the line of Cain was a man named Lamech. His name means "powerful" and he appears to have been obsessed with his own strength. In his song to his wives he boasted, "I have killed a man," using a continuous present tense of the verb to be (4:23). He was the first recorded to violate God's law of monogamy and marry two wives. Throughout the Old Testament plural marriages are normally closely related to turning after false gods. Further, we know that Lamech was proud of his association with Cain. He chose in his song to identify with Cain personally (v. 24) and named one of his children after Cain (v. 22).

The only other man of the seventh generation identified in Scripture was Enoch. Enoch was the seventh generation through the line of Seth. Enoch was a man who had power with God and walked with God. While Lamech might talk of his great accomplishments, Enoch was the first to tell others of God's accomplishments (cf. Jude 14-15). Enoch was a preacher of righteousness. While others boasted of their great superiority, Enoch declared something of the majesty and grandeur of God Himself. In a world that constantly worshiped a variety of pagan deities (Gen. 4:26), "Enoch walked with God three hundred years" (5:22). Others might be proud of their family heritage, but Enoch was humbled in his association with God. He was the second great man of faith in history recorded in Hebrews 11—God's Hall of Fame. One can only wonder if Cain had at any point responded to the Lord's gracious appeals, could Lamech have been another Enoch?

THE SEVENTH GENERATION

Lamech	**Enoch**
1 His name means powerful	He had power with God
2 He boasted of his accomplishments to his wives	He preached to others concerning what God would do
3 He emphasized the superiority of Lamech	He declared the majesty and grandeur of God
4 He was the first to practice polygamy	He was the first to walk with God
5 He was proud of his association with Cain	He was humbled in his association with God

---

PERSPECTIVE:
THE DARK SIDE OF HUMANITY CONTINUES

Cain was a man of great potential for good who, in rejecting God, came to be known as a great influence for evil. He was a man who chose to govern his life by his own standards rather than the standards of God. When things began to fall apart in the life of Cain, he became angry and rejected any help. He set a precedent for worshiping God with a non-blood offering and became the forerunner of all who feel they can approach God by good works. Cain's mother first thought of him as the God-Man, the one who could resolve her own problems with sin, but he rejected any opportunity to serve God. He was one who could recognize the audible voice of the Lord, but his life is a depressing story of rejecting what he heard. Cain could have been remembered as a man who walked with God and served God, but Cain denied God's rightful place in the society he founded.

"There is a way which seems right to a man, but its end is the way of death" (Prov. 14:12; 16:25). There is nothing particularly wrong in making one's own plans in life as long as it is understood that one's life is governed by God's principles (16:1). That was the problem of Cain and is the problem of many today like him. If people would heed His warning they could "enter by the narrow gate; for wide is the gate and broad is the way that leads to destruction, and there are many who go in by it" (Matt. 7:13).

FOUR

NOAH:
The Man Who Was Scared into Action

(Genesis 6:1–8:19)

So degenerate did the world become that within ten generations after Adam there was little remaining worth salvaging. As Enoch warned the people of the ultimate judgment accompanying the coming of the Lord, he used the word "ungodly" four times in a single verse attempting to describe the conditions of that day (Jude 15). Lamech, the eighty-two-year-old grandson of Enoch, commented at the birth of his son, "This one will comfort us concerning our work and toil of our hands, because of the ground which the Lord has cursed" (Gen. 5:29). The people of that day knew of the relationship between evil and the curse of God, but chose evil anyway. The birth of the son of Lamech was significant for it marked both the end and the beginning. Six hundred years later it would be that son, Noah, who sailed on the waters of a flood which destroyed the world that then existed and became the genetic father of the present world.

Noah lived in a world not too unlike contemporary society. Jesus spoke of that society as "eating and drinking, marrying and giving in marriage, until the day that Noah entered the ark" (Matt. 24:38). It was a time "when the sons of God came in to the daughters of men and they bore children to them" (Gen. 6:4). Some interpreters suggest this involved sexual relations between fallen angels (or demons) and the human race. They argue that: (1) the term "sons of God" always means angels in the Old Testament; (2) the results were giants (v. 4); (3) the Flood was not a natural consequence but was a universal judgment of such vast devastations that eliminated any trace of sin and the unnatural offspring of the cohabitation between angels and women; (4) the angels were locked in hell (Tautarus) till judgment (2 Peter 2:4) and that the context suggests the Flood; (5) early Hebrew and Christian tradition held the "sons of God" were fallen angels.

Others argue the statement records the breakdown of separation between the world and God's people; i.e., the godly line of Seth intermarrying with the ungodly line of Cain. They argue that (1) the previous two chapters list the godly and ungodly genealogies separately so that this cohabitation grows out of the context; (2) Jesus said angels do not reproduce (Matt. 22:30).

A third view interprets the "sons of God" as a military title referring to the practice of soldiers finding wives among the women of a captive city. Whatever that activity may have actually involved, the biblical record suggests that it, like all of society, was permeated with evil. It was in this evil world that "Noah found grace in the eyes of the Lord" (Gen. 6:8).

THE FAITH OF NOAH *(Gen. 6:8-22; Heb. 11:7)*

Noah is listed in the New Testament Hall of Faith chapter as one of those who demonstrated faith (Heb. 11:7). He is further identified as one of only two antediluvians of whom it was said he "walked with God" (Gen. 6:9; cf. 5:24). In contrast to the wickedness of his age, Noah was one to whom God could entrust saving humanity and salvaging the world, or at least that part of the world worth salvaging.

The Scriptures note of this man, "Noah was a just man, perfect in his generations" (6:9). Here was one who understood the need for both faith and works. That he could be described as a "just man"; i.e., one who was justified by God, suggests he had already expressed faith in God for it is by faith that a man is justified (Rom. 5:1). On the other hand, his life was exemplary in that he was "perfect in his generations." His faith was evident in his works. He warned others of the coming judgment. A New Testament apostle described Noah as "a preacher of righteousness" (2 Peter 2:5). He certainly had a lifestyle that gave authority to his message.

There is some difference of opinion as to the duration of Noah's pre-Flood ministry. Some commentators believe it lasted 120 years assuming Noah began his ministry warning the people of a coming end to the race (Gen. 6:3). On the other hand, Noah's sons were only a hundred years old when they entered the ark and appear to have been married before God assigned Noah the task of building it (v. 18). Regardless of the duration of his ministry, all are agreed as to its results. Apart from his wife, sons, and their wives, Noah was apparently unsuccessful in convincing others of the danger.

The greatest evidence of faith in the life of Noah was his building of an ark. Two particularly significant facts help to better understand the extent of Noah's faith. First, it had never before rained on the earth. Noah himself was apparently not told of the rain until the final week of loading the ark (7:4). He simply believed God would flood the world without understanding the means God would use to produce the water.

The second unusual fact about the ark is its size. Scholars debate the size of a cubit described as either eighteen or twenty-two inches long. By these standards the ark was 450/550 feet long, 75/91.6 feet wide and 45/55 feet high. In the history of navigation only within the last 150 years have men begun building ships that large. Some writers suggest that Noah's ability to build such a large seaworthy vessel is an indication as to how advanced the pre-Flood civilization must have been.

According to an ancient legend, Noah learned carpentry from a book on that subject written by Adam. However he acquired his construction abilities, the blueprint for this job came from God Himself. The ark was to be a three-story vessel with a large door in the side and a window around the top. It had rooms or cages for the animals. It was sealed with a "pitch" covering on both the inside and outside, giving the ark a large black effect. The lumber used for construction was limited to the tightly grained gopherwood. There were to be areas to store food supplies, keep the livestock who would live in the ark with them, as well as living quarters for Noah and his family. God gave the details to Noah directly and "thus Noah did; according to all that God commanded him, so he did" (6:22).

From time to time the Scriptures reveal God giving men specific detailed instructions concerning the performance of a duty; i.e., the building of the ark, the tabernacle, the offering of sacrifices, etc. In addition to being certain men understood how to accomplish their divinely commissioned tasks, these detailed instructions are often given because of the typical significance of the object built or task performed. The ark in this sense is a type of salvation. This is emphasized even in the Genesis account by two first usages of significant words related to the doctrine of salvation. The first term is the Hebrew word *kaphar* translated "cover" and "pitch" (v. 14). This term is used most often in the Book of Leviticus where it is consistently translated "atonement." The second usage is the word "come" which is the invitation of the Lord to Noah to enter the ark (7:1). Typical of the many invitations to salvation found in Scripture, this "come" is extended by God to man and urges him to take advantage of God's provision for preservation in light of impending judgment. The following chart illustrates several other similarities between Noah's ark and our salvation.

THE TYPICAL SIGNIFICANCE OF NOAH'S ARK

1 Gopherwood speaks of death; a tree cut down; i.e., the cross *(Gen. 6:14; Rom. 5:8)*.

2 The covering of the ark illustrates the Atonement, Heb. *kaphar (Gen. 6:14; Lev. 16)*.

3 The size of the ark illustrates the sufficiency and greatness of Christ and salvation (cf. *Heb. 2:3, 14; 1 John 2:2)*.

4 The divisions of the ark and separation of the clean and unclean illustrates the law of separation *(Gen. 6:14,*

16; 7:2; 1 Cor. 6:17).
5 The window of the ark through which Noah could only
look up illustrates the place of prayer in the Christian
life *(Gen. 6:16; Ps. 5:3).*
6 The single door of the ark points to Christ—the only
way to God *(Gen. 6:16; John 14:6).*
7 The ark itself illustrates the salvation experience of
the believer *(Heb. 11:7).*
8 The Flood which followed the entering into of the ark
illustrates baptism which follows salvation *(1 Peter
3:21).*

THE JUDGMENT WATERS *(Gen. 7:1–8:19)*

After the ark was completed, God invited Noah and his family
to come aboard. Apparently it took a full week to get everyone
and everything aboard. Assuming the food supplies were already aboard, there were still two of every unclean animal and
seven of every clean animal that came aboard the ark (Gen.
7:2; 8:9). According to the estimates of Morris and Whitcomb
(The Genesis Flood, Baker, 1961) this involved about 35,000
individual animals representing all of the known species of animals today. Because many of these were small, they suggest
there was no difficulty holding all of them in the ark. The care
of these animals on the ark may have been greatly simplified if
the animals engaged in hibernation as do many species of animals today.

When the ark was completely loaded, "the Lord shut him in"
(Gen. 7:16). That same day it began to rain. The resulting
Flood was caused not only by the rain but also by the release
of subterranean bodies of water described as "the fountains of
the deep" (v. 11). The eruption of the fountains of the deep
seems to imply an explosion. The tremendous pressure of
water on the face of the earth would cause mud slides and
changes in its terrain. All human life except Noah and his
family was destroyed. All animal life disappeared. The horren-
dous results gave evidence of the judgment by God.

Many creation scientists believe the world was surrounded

by a heavy atmosphere, just as the Planet Venus is covered with thick clouds today. They call this the "Canopy Theory"; however, the term could convey the idea of a plastic shield which is misleading. They believe in the thick atmosphere idea because: (1) there was no rain before the Flood and the ground was watered by mist (2:5); (2) archeology reveals vegetation in all parts of the planet implying the earth had a tropic arctic effect; (3) it accounts for dinosaurs which were primarily plant-eating animals; (4) it accounts for long life, if among other things ultraviolet rays were shielded; (5) the source of the waters that were used in the judgment of the earth; and (6) when God "divided" the atmosphere on day two into the sky and waters, He did not say it was good as He said on the other days of Creation, because He would finish dividing the atmosphere in the Flood. Another implication of the "Canopy Theory" is that seasons were introduced after the Flood (8:22), and that the Flood was more than a gigantic natural flood of the Tigris and Euphrates Rivers, but that it was a judgment of God on mankind and creation.

When the rain stopped, the waters continued to rise for another 110 days. Noah and his family would spend over a year aboard the ark before returning to dry earth.

Sin had so dominated the antediluvian world that it required a catastrophic judgment from God. The Flood was successful in destroying all life on earth which remained outside the ark. So thorough was the destruction of the world that then existed, that archeologists have yet to find traces of that former civilization. Unbelievers have suggested the story of the Flood in the Bible came from the several legends in ancient civilizations. The opposite is obviously the case. So memorable was this event in the minds of Noah and his descendants that virtually every civilization remembers among their legends the story of a great universal flood.

HOW LONG WAS NOAH ON THE ARK?

40 It began raining the day Noah and his family entered the ark and rained for forty days *(7:11-13)*.

110 The waters prevailed for 150 days. This number includes the 40 days of rain *(7:24)*.

74 The waters continually decreased from the 17th day of the 7th month and mountain peaks began appearing by the 1st day of the 10th month *(8:5)*. This amounts to 74 days if one assumes a 30-day month $(13 + 30 + 30 + 1 = 74)$.

40 Forty days later, Noah sent out the raven *(8:6)*.

7 Seven days later, the dove was released for the first time (implied in *8:10*—"yet another 7 days").

7 Seven days later, the dove was released for the 2nd time *(8:10)*.

7 Seven days later, the dove was released for the 3rd time *(8:12)*.

29 The covering of the ark was removed 29 days later (cf. *8:13*).

57 Noah appears to have waited an additional 57 days before he and his family left the ark *(8:14)*.

371 Total days on the ark are 371 by this reckoning. But if Noah's dates are based on lunar months of 29½ days rather than 30-day months, the above numbers would need to be adjusted accordingly. The difference in this case would amount to 6 days or a total of 365 days, exactly one solar year.

God did not forget Noah in the midst of the destruction, but rather "God remembered Noah, and every living thing, and all the animals that were with him in the ark" (8:1). By cutting off the supply of water and sending a wind to speed up evaporation, God began the long process of drying the flood-soaked world. Nine months after the invitation to enter the ark, its first occupant was released, a raven. This bird of prey did not return to the ark but "kept going to and fro until the waters had dried up from the earth" (v. 7). No doubt this bird found plenty of food as the floodwaters descended exposing the decomposing remains of those who had not been in the ark.

A week later Noah released a second bird from the ark, a

dove. Though the ark had been grounded on Mount Ararat for more than four months by this time, it had been less than seven weeks since the first mountain peaks had been visible to the occupants of the ark. Noah released the dove to determine how low the waters had fallen. When the dove returned, he knew there was still some water covering the ground. He repeated this experiment a week later and the dove returned with a freshly plucked olive leaf indicating that vegetation had begun to grown on the land. When the dove was released a third time a week later, it did not return. Presumably it found the outside world a more suitable living environment.

Within a month of the final release of the dove, Noah removed the protective covering of the ark and was able to gaze out at a very dry world. Still, Noah and his family remained on the ark another fifty-seven days. They had entered the ark at the invitation of God and apparently decided to remain on the ark until God told them to leave. The day finally came when God announced it was time for their departure. Again Noah obeyed God. "So Noah went out, and his sons and his wife and his sons' wives with him. Every beast, every creeping thing, every bird, and whatever creeps on the earth, according to their families, went out of the ark" (vv. 18-19).

PERSPECTIVE:
BELIEVING WHAT WE'VE NEVER SEEN

Sin seems to be stronger than the influence of righteousness. Cain and those who followed him plunged the world into a downward cycle that led to the judgment waters of the Flood. Sin always leads to judgment. But Noah, one man, made a difference. He was a man of faith who walked with God. Through one man humanity was preserved. "By faith Noah, being divinely warned of things not yet seen, moved with godly fear, prepared an ark for the saving of his household, by which he condemned the world and became heir of the righteousness which is according to faith" (Heb. 11:7). Just as Noah believed in a coming judgment he had never seen, we should also realize there is judgment coming and live accordingly.

FIVE

NOAH TO NIMROD:
From Sin to Sin
(Genesis 8:20–11:26)

The first thing Noah did when he left the ark was to build an altar and offer God a sacrifice. Many of the reported sightings of the ark made during the last 150 years claim the door of the ark is missing. It is generally believed that the door was used as wood for this sacrifice. It involved the offering of one of every clean animal or bird that was placed on the ark. It was in response to Noah's sacrifice that God established the conditions of the new world.

First, God promised never to destroy the world again as He had in the Flood. It was in connection with this promise that God established the seasons. Some scientists believe this involved a tilting of the earth's axis which caused the season's climatic changes. It is assumed climatic conditions before the Flood were more uniformly tropical and the polar caps probably nonexistent. Life for Noah in this new world would be different. "While the earth remains, seedtime and harvest, and cold and heat, and winter and summer, and day and night shall not cease" (Gen. 8:22).

Twice before God had entered into a covenant relationship with man and twice before man failed to meet the conditions of the covenant. Now God made his third covenant with the race He had created, the Noahic Covenant (9:1-17). While reestablishing the responsibility of man to provide for himself and live by his conscience, this covenant also involved the institution of human government. Prior to this, man lived in an extended family which was ruled by a family head. But now, in preparation for the years to come when society became larger, man was responsible to live also under the authority of corporate government.

This part of Scripture has many illustrations of men attempting to begin a city (i.e., city-state) or to establish a nation (i.e., family ethnic groups). Just as the twentieth century sees many people attempting to establish their own company or industrial corporations, so many patriarchs had an internal drive to begin a nation. The Noahic Covenant either motivated or reflected that desire. During this time, nations were technically city-states, or like the fifes of the Dark Ages.

The covenant with Noah involved the principle of government which would apply to a larger group of people than just one extended family. The core of the Noahic Covenant was the judicial taking of life (v. 6), which is the ultimate expression of government. Since the death penalty is the ultimate exercise of justice, all other laws of government lead up to that judicial decision and find their credibility in the death penalty. Human government is a divinely appointed institution together with the institutions of the family and church.

The sign of the Noahic Covenant is the rainbow. God promised, "I set My rainbow in the cloud, and it shall be for the sign of the covenant between Me and the earth" (v. 13). This may or may not have been the first time a rainbow was seen, but from now on it would have new meaning. It was a symbol of hope in that it represented a promise by God that He would never again destroy the world with a flood. In light of this promise of Noah, it is interesting to note that the North American Indians interpreted the presence of a rainbow in the sky as a sign of dry weather believing the arch of the bow held back the waters stored behind the vault of the sky.

Tied to the Noahic Covenant was a third distinct era in human history sometimes called the dispensation of Human Government. God no longer allowed the conscience of individuals to be the sole basis of human life. The universal Flood punished individuals because God had dealt with people individually in the earlier period of conscience. Since all men failed, then all were punished. However, in this new era, God also confirmed elements of the previous covenants, man was to fill the earth and provide for his necessities (v. 1).

God was under no delusion when He made His new covenant with Noah. He knew "the imagination of man's heart is evil from his youth" (8:21). Despite the fact man had already violated the conditions of two prior covenants, God was prepared to offer yet another opportunity for man to live in a harmonious relationship with Him. Still, it was not surprising to God when within a few generations, mankind was again in a state of rebellion to God.

FAILURE UNDER THE NEW ORDER *(Gen. 9:18-29)*
One might think spending a year aboard the ark while God destroyed the rest of the human race for its wickedness might have a life-long effect on Noah, but such was not the case. Rather than dispersing over the whole earth as directed by the Lord, Noah and his sons appear to have chosen to live together as an extended family. After the Flood, Noah became a grandfather as his three sons had sons of their own. Probably at this point, Noah and his sons became ranchers slowly traveling south with their herds and flocks as they grazed in the open pastures. Perhaps Noah was beginning to feel old with all his grandchildren running around or maybe he was just tired of the constant traveling involved in a nomadic lifestyle. For whatever reason, the time came when Noah settled for a somewhat tranquil lifestyle, and again changed his occupation from being a carpenter. "And Noah began to be a farmer, and he planted a vineyard" (Gen. 9:20).

The Scriptures record Noah's farming career in one tragic harvest season. It began when "he drank of the wine and was drunk" (v. 21). Over the years both Jewish and Christian commentators have tried to be kind to Noah noting this is the first mention of wine in the Scriptures and suggesting Noah may not have known the beverage would have an alcoholic content that produced drunkenness. But in light of the New Testament revelation of drinking in the days of Noah before the Flood (Matt. 24:38), this excuse hardly holds water. Noah was the patriarch of his family and as such should have known what Solomon later learned on the knee of Bathsheba: "It is not for kings, O Lemuel, it is not for kings to drink wine, nor for princes intoxicating drink" (Prov. 31:4). But over the years there had been an apparent change in Noah. He had drifted from God. His gradual wandering from God may have been imperceptible to the casual observer, but now years later it was evident that the Noah who raised the wineskin to his lips was not the same Noah who "was a just man, perfect in his generations" (6:9).

As Noah lay naked in a drunken stupor, "Ham, the father of Canaan, saw the nakedness of his father, and told his two brothers outside" (9:22). Because Noah later cursed Canaan, it was probably Canaan who first "saw" Noah and told his father Ham what happened. Just what happened in the tent is not certain. Traditionally, Jewish rabbis held Noah was castrated either by Ham or Canaan. Other commentators suggest Noah was abused homosexually while in his drunken state. Still others argue it was the act of looking on a father's nakedness that constituted the sin. When Shem and Japheth learned of Noah's state, they grabbed a garment, perhaps Noah's own garment that Ham had presented as evidence of his claims, apparently walked into the tent backward, with his coat held to their eyes, "and covered the nakedness of their father" (v. 23).

When Noah finally recovered from the effects of his wine and realized what had happened, he cursed Canaan and blessed Shem and Japheth and their descendants. Under the conditions of Noah's statement, the descendants of Canaan, the Canaanites, were designated the servants of the descendants of Shem. Canaan lived in the land of Canaan which became the Israel of our day. They did not become part of the black peoples of Africa and the curse has nothing to do with the servitude of black races. Canaan became servant to Shem when Joshua conquered the Promised Land and defeated the Canaanites.

NIMROD AND THE REBELLION OF BABEL
(Gen. 11:1-9)

Despite the fresh start offered to the human race, sin would again have its destructive effect on mankind. In the generations after Noah, descendants of Adam's race would continue to rebel against the principles of God. The chapters following the Flood trace the ethnic backgrounds of many people groups elsewhere named in the Old Testament and in particular describe the character of Babel, that one particular city-state which throughout history represents man's futile attempts to rebel against the Lord.

The fourth of the eleven "generations" recorded in the Book of Genesis (Gen. 10:1) demonstrates the unity of the human race through the sons of Noah. However, the listing of seventy tribes is not an exhaustive list of the nations, because there are other groups who later develop who are named in Scripture; i.e., Moab, Ammon, Edom, etc. But the listing is exhaustive enough to demonstrate the fundamental relationship between all peoples in the world today. The number seventy in biblical numerology often is representative of completeness. There were seventy elders selected by Moses and later seventy men served in the Sanhedrin. In both cases, these represented at least in theory the sum of the nation. Significantly, Jesus chose seventy disciples to preach the Gospel, perhaps symbolic of the later missionary efforts of the whole church to reach the whole world (Luke 10:1). These seventy nations listed in Genesis 10 therefore are representative of all nations.

The genealogical listing of Genesis 10 is not naturally divided into three groupings, each including the descendants of a particular son of Noah. The first group, the sons of Japheth (vv. 2-5), seems to include most of the Indo-Aryan linguistic group. The sons of Ham (vv. 6-20) are then noted as including primarily those nations south of Canaan including many African nations. The third group, the sons of Seth (vv. 21-31), represent the semitic tribes of the Near East. This is the racial group which produced Abraham, and a later genealogy of Shem and Terah serves to introduce the life of Abraham (11:10-32).

Sin, which entered the human race through an act of rebellion by Lucifer, again had its impact on Adam's race through another act of rebellion. Nimrod, the great grandson of Noah, may have only been a young child when Noah got drunk in his tent, but he matured, earning himself the reputation of being "the mighty hunter before the Lord" (10:9). His entire personality was characterized by rebellion. His name is built on the Hebrew verbal root *marad* and means, "We will rebel" or "Come, let us rebel." The Hebrew expression "the mighty hunter before the Lord" suggests Nimrod was bold in his defiance against the Lord. He was a hunter in the sense that he hunted men in the establishing of his kingdoms. This designation became a proverb of his day and of later ages also. His success in this area is evidenced in that he is the recorded father of as many as nine city-states, Babel (Babylon), Erech, Accad, Calneh, Nineveh, Rehoboth Ir, Calah, and Resen (vv. 10-12). Of these, Babel was his first and best known.

The name of the city, Babel, is unusual in that it has two different meanings in two of the languages of the Near East. In Akkadian, it means "the gate of the gods." This is probably more reflective of Nimrod's original intention in establishing this city. It was in this place the people decided, "Come, let us build ourselves a city, and a tower whose top is in the heavens; let us make a name for ourselves, lest we be scattered abroad over the face of the whole earth" (11:4).

The "Tower of Babel" was in all likelihood a ziggurat similar to those pyramids among the ruins of that area today. It was not a round tower that reached into the clouds of the atmosphere similar to towers drawn in children's storybooks. It was a pyramid similar to those found in Egypt. These were man-made "sacred mountains" normally equipped with a temple at the base which served as the religious center of the city, and an astrological chart on the top by which the astrologers made their predictions as it related to the life of the city and its ruler. Within the theological framework of these primitive astrologers, Babel and its tower were a "gate to the gods." It was built "toward" the heavens to interpret the heavens. It did not literally reach to heaven.

The second meaning of Babel is based on its relationship to the Hebrew verb *balal* meaning "he confused" (v. 9). This meaning is related to the miraculous confusion of tongues which took place as the tower was being built. God knew something concerning the extent of what men could do in their united rebellion against Him. He decided to "confuse their language, that they may not understand one another's speech" (v. 7). As a result, the tower was left unfinished and families scattered over all the earth in linguistic groups. According to the ancient records of Nebuchadnezzar (605–561 B.C.), a sixty-foot ziggurat was found in this region unfinished which he himself finished. There is a tradition repeated today by the natives of the area that identifies a ziggurat at Borsippa, about seven miles southwest of the ruins of Babylon, called Birs Nemrod as the original Tower of Babel. This tradition warns tourists not to go near it or they will lose their memories just as the original people of the tower lost their memory of the original language of the world. The first reference to tongues was *judgment* (Gen. 11:9), next given in *grace* (Acts 2:4), finally united in *glory* (Rev. 7:9)."

The city of Babel, later called Babylon, is a consistent symbol of a godless society in rebellion against God throughout Scripture. Babylon (a name for the city and the nation) would be later identified for its sins and superstitions (Isa. 47:8-13). Babylon is the nation into which Israel would enter as captives for seventy years (Dan. 1:1-7). Later still Babylon will be noted for its immense wealth and eventual doom (Rev. 17–18). During the Roman persecutions of the early church, the early Christians began using the name Babylon as a code word for the Roman Empire which at that time was the focus of the rebellion against God. Nimrod sought to build a pyramid to reach the heavens, but it was the embryonic sin of his empire which will eventually bring its destruction (18:5).

The division of the peoples of the earth into ethnic, linguistic, and territorial groups is described in Scripture with three distinct Hebrew verbs. The first is *palaq* (Gen. 10:25) meaning to cleave. While some writers believe this division refers to the linguistic separation of families at the tower of Babel, the use of this verb both to describe the division and as the verbal root of the name Peleg suggests it may refer to a physical and cataclysmic division of the earth on a large scale. God may have "divided the earth" to insure the separation of the various linguistic groups to prevent a revival of Babel. This could account for the North American Indians, South American Incas, and some inhabitants of the sea islands. Some commentators believe that it was at this time that the Americas and the Australian land masses were separated from Eurasia and Africa, perhaps the historical event on which the later legends of Atlantis were based. When God created the world, the waters were gathered "together into one place" (1:19). Now a physical separation of the land mass resulted in continents and oceans isolating groups of people to develop their own unique cultures.

The second Hebrew verb used to describe this division is *parad* (10:5, 32) meaning to divide in judgment. The separation of the peoples at Babel was an act of judgment on the part of God. It was His "disruption" of man's rebellion. The languages and dialects spoken around the world today are a constant reminder that God has discerned and judged the sin nature of Adam in all of us. "Therefore, just as through one man sin entered the world, and death through sin, and thus death spread to all men, because all have sinned" (Rom. 5:12).

The third Hebrew verb used by Moses to describe the division of Babel is *nachal* (Deut. 32:8) meaning to divide for an inheritance. This is reflective of the character of God who even in judgment is gracious. Even when dealing with the rebellion of Nimrod at Babel, He offered the rebels an inheritance which was theirs for the taking. Similarly today, the God who judged sin on the cross offers the life and home of His Son as an inheritance for all who come to Him by faith.

PERSPECTIVE:
SEEDS OF REBELLION CONTINUE TO GROW

How then did the descendants of a common parentage come to have the varied racial features so evident in the world today? The solution to this nagging question is probably found in the environmental influences on relatively isolated societies throughout history. Most creationists today would argue that the genetic pool was complete in Adam including all of the potential characteristics of each race. But there's more to it than that. When the peoples of the earth finally were divided after the Flood on linguistic grounds, it was most natural for them to build societies among themselves. They traveled to different regions in their family groups and began new societies. Because of the genetic inbreeding which naturally resulted, certain physical features naturally became increasingly dominant in the group. Further, the conditions of their new homeland would, over generations, also have an effect on the descendants of those pioneers of the race. These environmental influences would include such things as harsh winters, tropical sun, and to some extent, even the characteristic diet of the region. In some cases, these racial features were further developed by cultural practices such as the binding of feet or the stretching of the neck.

In the midst of a degenerate world, "Noah found grace in the eyes of the Lord" (Gen. 6:8). His faith in the revealed Word of God was the motivating force of his life resulting in the building of "an ark for the saving of his household" (Heb. 11:7). When confronted with the major crisis of his life, the Flood, Noah believed God and was saved. But like so many today, when the crisis was over, his faith began to waver. Before his days were over, Noah was found drunk, the same sort of activities that characterized those who were destroyed by the great Flood.

Even under the new covenant, man was destined to fail God. It was more than obvious that man was "evil from his youth." The seeds of rebellion had been planted in the heart of man as Adam had bitten into the forbidden fruit in the Garden. Now it would always be a part of fallen human nature. In fact, Noah's great grandson became a leader of the people best known for their rebellious attitude against God. His actions led to the dispersion of the people at the tower of Babel. This event marked the end of the age of human government as God prepared to deal with man under the terms of yet another covenant.

SIX

ABRAHAM:
Called to Begin a Nation
(Genesis 11:27–12:9)

The judgment of Babel reflected the failure of the descendants to begin nations and the dispersion into all the earth reflected God's plan for nations. God called Abraham to begin a "chosen" nation among the nations of the earth. The emergence of Abraham unfolds the drama of God's relationship to His people. God begins a new "people group," a new relationship of faith, and the line through whom the Deliverer would come.

Apart from Jesus Christ, Abraham is in many respects the greatest man in Scripture. Moses, David, and Paul would certainly be recognized as great in the minds of those who know their stories, yet all of these would point to Abraham as their father and speak his name with respect. Christians, Muslims, and Jews identify Abraham with the coveted title, "Friend of God" (2 Chron. 20:7; Isa. 41:8; James 2:23). To this day the Arab world also calls Abraham *El Kahil,* meaning "The Friend"; i.e., the friend of God.

Abraham holds a prominent place also in the New Testament. Apart from Moses, no other Old Testament character is identified by name as many times. When one realizes that many of the references to Moses are found in statements introducing citations from the Law, the life of Abraham is clearly the most often Old Testament life referred to in the

New Testament. He is there identified as the Father of Israel (Acts 13:26), the levitical priesthood (Heb. 7:5), the Messiah (Matt. 1:1) and all Christian believers (Rom. 4:11; Gal. 3:16, 29).

Abraham's life is also discussed in terms of being a type or Old Testament illustration of the Christian believer (John 8:56), justification by faith (Rom. 4:3), justification by works (James 2:21) and living by faith (Heb. 11:8-17). While the life of Abraham teaches many important principles, his life is above all else the story of a man who lived by faith. He did not have Scripture to guide him, nor did he have the examples of others who lived for God, yet Abraham walked by faith. Abraham learned experientially that even when he failed God, God was faithful. The story of Abraham is the story of a man who experienced the growing pains in a life of faith until the times of his greatest testings when he demonstrated he was not "weak in faith . . . but was strengthened in faith" (Rom. 4:19-20). This study of the life of Abraham will be concerned primarily with learning the principles of faith from the greatest man of faith who ever lived.

THE FIRST CALL OF ABRAM
(Gen. 11:27-31; Acts 7:1-4) (2092 B.C.)

Abraham would not have been remembered as the greatest man of faith and the friend of God if he was judged by his family. Many Christians look at great faith as some type of inherited blessing reserved for the children of ministers, missionaries, or a few deeply spiritual Christian laymen. Terah, Abraham's father met none of these qualifications. Terah, whose name means "traveler," was a worshiper of idols (Josh. 24:2), probably involved in the worship of the moon god. When years later the Prophet Isaiah wanted to remind the Jews of their humble beginnings, he said, "Look to the rock from which you were hewn, and to the hole of the pit from which you were dug. Look to Abraham your father, and to Sarah who bore you" (Isa. 51:1-2).

Though the Scripture explains, "Now Terah lived seventy years, and begat Abram, Nahor, and Haran" (Gen. 11:26), it appears that only the oldest of these sons was born that early in the life of Terah. By comparing other references to dates in the lives of Abram and Terah, Abram appears to have been the youngest son of Terah born some sixty years later (cf. 12:4; 11:32). When this son of his old age was born, Terah gave him the name Abram based on the words *ab* meaning "father" and the verb *raham* or its Babylonian equivalent *remu* meaning "he loves." Literally the name means "he loves his father." Because of the later greatness of Abraham, some have suggested his name should be understood as "beloved father" or "exalted father."

Abram was raised in a place identified as "Ur of the Chaldeans." The name Ur was a common name for a city in that the Babylonian word for city was *uru*. Because of this there may have been many cities of that day identified as Ur. The most famous of these today is the archeological site of "the Babylonian Ur" at Mugheir near the Persian Gulf. Many contemporary scholars identify this Ur as the Ur of the Chaldeans in which Abram was raised. Others disagree with this conclusion for one or more reasons. Even if the Babylonian Ur was not Abram's hometown, what archeologists have discovered there gives us some insight into the nature of cities in that day.

REASONS FOR A NORTHERN LOCATION OF "UR OF THE CHALDEANS"

---

1 Traditionally, until 1850, Urfa near Haran in southern Turkey was considered the Ur of Abram. Geographic references in Scripture seem to support a northern location for Ur.

2 The social-legal traditions of the patriarchs tend to point to a northern origin.

3 Babylonian Ur never referred to as Ur of the Chaldeans in the cuneiform records found there.

4 Lower Mesopotamia was not called Chaldea until 1,000 years after Abraham. Abraham lived in Mesopotamia before coming to Haran (*Acts 7:2*).

5 When Abraham sent his servant to the land of his

birth to find a wife for Isaac, he went to Haran *(Gen. 24:4)*. Jacob later fled to Paddan Aram in the same area when fleeing from Esau. The family of Abram appears to have established themselves in the north.

6 The ancient designation of a northern area as "Holdai" is thought to be related to the expression "of the Chaldeans."

7 The patriarchs are described as Arameans suggesting identification with a northern race (Jacob, *Deut. 26:5;* Laban, *Gen. 31:47)*.

8 The Babylonian Ur is on the wrong side of the Euphrates River according to Joshua's description *(Josh. 24:2-3)*.

9 A tablet from Elba reportedly refers to an Ur of Haran.

10 Chaldea is described in the context of several northern cities *(cf. Gen. 22:22; Isa. 23:13)*.

The city of Ur was a prosperous city during the time of Abram's childhood. Excavations at that site have uncovered an abundance of both public buildings and comfortable private homes. It was a city of law and order and appears to have been both a producing and trading center. It was a center largely devoted to the moon god Nauna(r)-Sin. Many of the names associated with the cult of lunar worship including Terah, Sarah, Milcah, Nahor, Haran, and Laban.

Terah himself was involved in worshiping and serving idols (Josh. 24:2). According to Jewish legend, Terah made idols until his son Abraham convinced him of the folly of worshiping a powerless idol. Terah's decision, however, to leave Ur and dwell in Haran suggests he never abandoned his idol worship. Haran was one of the centers for the worship of the moon god. If the conversion of Terah was the reason for the family's departure from Ur, one would think he would have chosen somewhere other than Haran for his new home.

Two other reasons might be suggested for the family move. The first may have been associated with the death of Haran

(Gen. 11:28). The Hebrew expression *'al pene* literally means Haran died "upon the face" of his father. The expression emphasizes that Terah saw and survived his son's death. According to the customs of Ur, the body of Haran would have been placed in a baked ceramic coffin and kept in the family home. The death of Haran in this way would be continually remembered by the family.

The significance of this becomes apparent with the discovery by Sir Leonard Wooley of an anti-Semitic racial prejudice which was becoming increasingly common during the time of Abram. Tablets found at Ur reveal a general northerly migration of the Habiru tribe (cf. 14:13, Abram the Hebrew) which was usually the result of these Aramaean settlers attempting to escape economic and other forms of oppression. The death of Haran may have been the result of an anti-Semitic attack; i.e., a mob lynching or riot.

A second reason for Terah's departure has been suggested in the politics of the day as it related to Terah's economic interests. Abraham's possession of camels (12:16; 24:10) suggests Terah may have been involved in international trade to some degree. About the time of Terah's departure from Haran, Hammurabi was engaged in blocking the overland trade routes north of Ur. Moving to Haran would insure greater freedom to move his goods to other cities.

The third reason is that God had called Abraham and he would not desert his family, so Terah went with Abraham. Terah's reasons for leaving Ur are not known. In his address before the Sanhedrin, Stephen reminded his listeners: "The God of glory appeared to our father Abraham when he was in Mesopotamia, before he dwelt in Haran, and said to him, 'Get out of your country and from your relatives, and come to a land that I will show you' " (Acts 7:2-3). When he was called of God, Abram left Ur for the nomadic life of the wilderness. The shores of the Great Sea (Mediterranean Sea) were called the edge of the world. When Abraham met the "God of glory," he was ready to follow Him to the edge of the world.

"The God of glory" is one of the eight characteristic names of God in Scripture. The Sanhedrin which Stephen was addressing had a high respect for the temple largely because it was thought to be the dwelling place of the Shekinah glory, the essential presence of God Himself long before a temple or tabernacle had been raised by the Jews. This same God of glory appeared to Abram in Ur. Later, James, the pastor of the Jerusalem church of which Stephen was a deacon, ascribed the title "the Lord of Glory" to Jesus (James 2:1). Stephen may have been claiming it was Christ Himself who appeared to Abram in Ur. Jesus on one occasion had told some religious leaders, "Your father Abraham rejoiced to see My day, and he saw it and was glad" (John 8:56). This was the first of many meetings between God and Abraham.

THE EIGHT CHARACTERISTIC NAMES OF GOD

The God of Glory *(Ps. 29:3; Act 7:2)*
The God of Comfort *(Rom. 15:5; 2 Cor. 1:3)*
The God of Hope *(Rom. 15:13)*
The God of Love *(2 Cor. 13:11)*
The God of Patience *(Rom. 15:5)*
The God of Peace *(Rom. 15:33; Phil. 4:9)*
The God of All Grace *(1 Peter 5:10)*
The God of Truth *(Deut. 32:4)*

The first call of Abram involved three things on his part. First, he was to separate himself from his country. Second, he was to separate himself from his family. Finally, he was to separate himself unto God traveling to the place God would show him. In response to this first call, Abram obeyed only the first of the three commands. His failure to separate from his family as instructed by God resulted in his stopping short of Canaan and wasting precious years in Haran.

Haran (Heb. *Charan*) was a leading frontier settlement of the Sabians in northwestern Mesopotamia (name means land between the rivers). Abram and Terah would have arrived here about the time of the building of a major temple dedicated to the worship of the moon. Archeologists who have compared the religions of Ur and Haran generally conclude they are so closely related that the moon god worship may have been brought to Haran from Ur by the migrating Habiru tribe of which the family of Terah may have been a part.

How long Abram remained in Haran the Scriptures do not state. Swiss reformer, J.H. Bullinger, argues the stay in Haran was 25 years but that opinion is based largely on his perceived significance of the number 25 in the 175-year life of Abraham $(175 = 7 \times 25$ or 7×5^2, five being the number of grace and seven the number of completion). Matthew Henry suggests a stay of 5 years without offering any clue as to how he arrived at that figure. However long the stay at Haran, it was a time of both life and death. Though Sarai, Abram's wife, was herself barren, children were born to their servants during the years they remained at Haran. It was also toward the end of this period that Terah, Abram's father, died.

Haran represented for Abram the middle ground between partial and full obedience to the call of God. For every call of God there is a "Haran," a place somewhere short of absolute surrender to the plan of God. Many times a Haran may appear to others as a time of blessing, but the blessing one might occasionally experience in his "Haran" falls short of the blessing God intends to give in the place of obedience. Abram overcame Haran only when Terah died. The Christian overcomes his "Haran" and enters into the place of obedience when he recognizes the death to self accomplished by Christ on Calvary (Rom. 6:6).

THE RENEWED CALL OF ABRAM
(Gen. 12:1-5) (2091 B.C.)

While at Haran, God again issued His call to Abram. The Hebrew word *wayom'er* though translated "had said" is a qal imperfect and should probably be translated simply "said." There is no pluperfect tense in the original Hebrew and in light of Stephen's claim (Acts 7:2, 4), this should probably be viewed as God's second attempt to secure complete obedience from Abram. This is not at all inconsistent with the way God dealt with others in the Old Testament (cf. Jonah 3:1).

Under the terms of this second call, God again required of

Abraham the same thing He called for in the first call. There was, however, this time a greater sense of urgency in the commission. The verb *led-leda* is a qal imperative form meaning "go." Implied is the idea of departing with all speed; i.e., escaping for your life. It is the same form used by the angels who later urged Lot to quickly leave Sodom before the city was destroyed.

With this renewed call on the life of Abram, God added a sevenfold promise. God promised: (1) to make Abram a great nation, (2) to bless Abram, (3) to make his name great, (4) to make Abram a blessing, (5) to bless those who bless Abram, (6) to curse those who curse Abram, and (7) to bless all the families of the earth in Abram. When Abram obeyed and arrived in the land, God added an eighth promise, to give the land to Abram's descendants. Because of God's promise to Abraham, it is called "The Promised Land."

Many commentators point to this call of Abram and his subsequent obedience as the beginning of a new era in God's dealings with man. Some speak of it as the beginning of the dispensation of promise, others the beginning of God's dealing with individuals and groups on the basis of grace. In one sense that marked the beginning of the nation Israel, though that nation would more properly trace their "birth" to the Exodus from Egypt under Moses. The numerological significance of these promises has not been overlooked by many writers. Seven is the number of perfection or completion whereas, God added an eighth promise, eight being the number of the Holy Spirit, and the number of new beginnings.

One of the new principles relating to God's dealing with man introduced in this promise is the idea of God treating mankind on the basis of how they treat Abram. Applied to his descendants today, the promise insures those who bless Israel will be blessed of God, whereas those who curse Israel will be cursed of God. It is interesting to note that the plural verbs are used when God speaks of blessing (them) but singular verbs are used when God speaks of cursing (him). It is as though the promises were given in anticipation there would be many to bless and few to curse. Further, two different verbs are here

translated "curse." The first is a form of *kalal* meaning "to
treat lightly, view as insignificant, or despise." It denotes "the
blasphemous cursing on the part of man." The second is a
form of *'arar* and identifies "the judicial cursing on the part of
God."

The seventh of these promises is also uniquely expressed in
the Hebrew language. The expression translated "of the
earth" is the Hebrew word *ha'adamah* meaning "of the
ground." This is also the term used by God to identify the
ground which he cursed because of Adam's sin (Gen. 3:17).
Further, many linguists have noted the relationship between
the name Adam which is also used throughout the Old Testament as a generic designation of the human race, and the
Hebrew word for ground *'adamah*. In this blessing of Abram,
God intends to reunite all the families of the cursed earth and
overcome the effects of the curse on the human race. This is
further emphasized by the verb tense and grammatical construction which might better be translated, "and by you all the
families of the earth will bless themselves." This aspect of the
promise focuses not on the descendants of Abram but rather
on the Descendant of Abram "who is Christ" (Gal. 3:16). All
the nations of the earth bless themselves when they accept
Abram's Seed as Messiah.

In response to this renewed call of God, Abram left Haran
and began a spiritual pilgrimage that would last 100 years. The
fact that Abram was 75 years old when he began to live by
faith has over the years been an encouragement to older
Christians that one is never too old to begin following God.
Abram's faith was expressed in his obedience to God. The
influence of his faith is evidenced even as he began to live by
faith in that Lot also determined to go with him. Some commentators believe Abram and Sarai may have adopted Lot as
their own son when his father Haran died. If Haran had been
the firstborn son of Terah, it may be that Lot was actually
older than Abram. Some Jewish interpreters sought to identify
Abram's wife Sarai with Iscah, the daughter of Haran. Old
Testament theologian, H.G.A. Ewald suggests Iscah was really the wife of Lot, but neither view has any biblical support.

Abram and his company "departed to go to the land of Canaan. So they came to the land of Canaan" (Gen. 12:5). In traveling from Haran to Shechem, their 430-mile journey would have taken them through the city of Damascus. French archeologist Andre Parrot suggests the trip through Damascus may have been when Abram secured one of his principal servants Eliezer of Damascus (cf. 15:2-3). When Abram arrived in Canaan, he continued traveling south until he came to Shechem.

EXPRESSING FAITH AMONG THE CANAANITES
(Gen. 12:6-8)

Abram's first stop in Canaan was near Shechem at a landmark identified as "the terebinth tree of Moreh" (Gen. 12:6). This tree was apparently a significant local landmark, probably a particular oak tree used in some kind of pagan worship. The difficulty in specifically identifying the particular kind of tree is evidenced in the varieties of oaks present in Israel. The Hebrew word *alon* is used to identify as many as nine species of oak and as many as twelve other subvarieties. These are among the largest trees in the region which is probably why they were chosen as shrines for the worship of pagan deities.

Identified simply as *alon Moreh,* some identify this tree as belonging to a man named Moreh. The name Moreh has been translated "teacher" or "soothsayer" and it may have been the name was really a title for the priest of some local Canaanite cult. If this is true, it is interesting to note that God revealed Himself to Abram and promised him the land of the Canaanites at the very place where they would come to worship their false god and perhaps practice divination in an effort to determine the will of their gods. Abram's faith in God was in this way demonstrated to be more effective than the pagan worship of his neighbors.

When Abram arrived, the Scripture notes, "And the Canaanites were then in the land" (v. 6). Some five centuries would pass before the descendants of Abram would under Joshua conquer the Canaanites and take the land God had given them. The presence of the Canaanites was yet another test of Abram's faith. God promised to give his descendants an already-possessed land. To make matters even worse, from all appearances the cursed Canaanites seemed to be better off than the blessed Abram. For one who had been raised in Ur and had lived in Haran, the lifestyle of a bedouin shepherd must have at times seemed less attractive than that of city dwellers in Canaan. This may be one reason why Lot eventually abandoned his tents for a home in Sodom (14:12).

The Canaanites were the descendants of Canaan, the cursed grandson of Noah. Following the dispersion after the Tower of Babel, the Canaanites came to settle in the general region between the Jordan River and the Mediterranean Sea. When Joshua conquered the Canaanites and occupied the "Promised Land," he carried out the curse on Canaan, son of Ham. He was made a servant at that time. The religious attitudes of the Canaanites centered around the worship of *Baal* and a hierarchy of gods including one called *El.*

The *El* of the Canaanites was not the same god as the *Elohim* of the Old Testament which is sometimes abbreviated *El.* The worship of the Canaanite *El* involved human sacrifice, usually children, though sometimes adults, whereas the worship of God in the Old Testament forbade human sacrifice. When Abram "built an altar to the Lord, who had appeared to him" (12:7), he was worshiping the God whose attributes included justice (18:25), righteousness (v. 19), grace (19:19), wisdom (20:6), mercy (v. 6) and faithfulness (24:27). No pagan deity in Canaan ever possessed so high a moral character.

The worship of God in Abram's life normally involved the building of an altar. The verb translated "built" is a form of *banah* which was usually reserved for the building of something out of stone blocks. In this way Abram was demonstrating his faith differed from the Babylonian worship of the moon god Nauna(r)-Sin. In Babylon, altars were made of baked or unbaked bricks. In Canaan, two kinds of altars were built, the altar of earth and the altar of stone (cf. Ex. 20:24-25). While little else is known of the construction of Abram's altars, it is unlikely that they involved the selection of twelve stones as the significance of that practice was connected with the number of the tribes of Israel and represents a later development in the worship of the Lord.

One of the keys to recognizing the spiritual state of Abram is the tent and the altar. When Abram lived in tents and worshiped at altars, he was expressing his faith in God. When he abandoned the tents and altar, he was lapsing in his faith in God. There was no tent and altar in Egypt when Abram lied about his wife Sarai. The writer to the Hebrews recognized the importance of the tent as an expression of the patriarch's faith (Heb. 11:9).

The tent and the altar were symbols of separation in the life of Abram. By living in a tent, Abram was separating himself from the Canaanite who dwelt in cities. When Abram worshiped at the altar, he was separating himself to God. In this way the tent and the altar together represent the life of the believer. The Christian who lives by faith today will be a separated Christian. Biblical separation always involves a separation from the world and to the Lord. Some Christians adopt a legalistic approach to the Christian life concentrating on what the Christian must separate from, but there is no joy in legalism. On the other hand, some Christians are frustrated in their Christian life because they emphasize their separation to the Lord in prayer and Bible study without their separating themselves from sin and the world. The key to fulfillment and a deeper walk with God is not the tent *or* the altar, but the tent *and* the altar.

PERSPECTIVE:
FAITH IS OBEDIENCE TO THE WORD OF GOD

Faith in God necessarily involves obedience to the call of God. God is faithful and obeying the call of God involves recognizing His faithfulness to do what He says He will do. "He who calls you is faithful, who also will do it" (1 Thes. 5:24). When God calls us to salvation, we are saved when we respond by faith depending on Him to save us. Our sanctification is the result of our obedience to that call knowing He is able "to present [us] to Himself a glorious church, not having spot or wrinkle or any such thing, but that it should be holy and without blemish"

(Eph. 5:27). So the key to effective Christian service is a faith-obedience to the call of God to serve Him.

When God calls, faith responds in complete obedience. Abram's initial hesitancy to obey the call of God may have been in part due to family loyalties which were at that time stronger than his loyalty to God. Only the death of Terah could result in conditions where Abram would obey God. Sometimes a believer's loyalty to the things of the world prevent whole-hearted obedience to the call of God. A death is necessary for separation. It is then when the Christian should recognize his identification with Christ in death and resurrection (Gal. 2:20). Only when the believer reckons himself dead to self and the things of the world is he then free to completely obey the Lord (cf. Rom. 6:11).

Finally, obeying the call of God initially must be followed by a continued faith-obedience to the call of God. This involves a separation to God from the world. There is often a waiting period between the time God promises and the time we receive, and that is the time God expects us to express our faith before "the Canaanites" through the symbols of separation and faith; i.e., "the tent and the altar."

SEVEN

ABRAHAM:
Lapse of Faith: Reasoning with God

(Genesis 12:10–13:4)

When God called Abram to separate himself from his family and country, He did so with the purpose of producing from Abram a great nation. As the founder of the Jewish nation, Abram was appointed by God to be a witness to the rest of mankind concerning God (Isa. 44:8). Further, that race was to be a depository of divine revelation (Rom. 3:2) and a channel of blessing to the world (15:8-12). The ultimate objective in God's choice of Abram was to prepare the world for a coming Messiah and Saviour of that world (Isa. 53). Such was the tremendous responsibility associated with the privilege of being called "the friend of God."

If the Old Testament were nothing more than the patriotic history of Jewish scribes, the story of Abram would be an account of a never-failing patriarch who excelled in every challenge he faced. But because the Old Testament is part of the Scriptures identified as "the Word of Truth" (2 Tim. 2:15), it records an accurate account of his growth in faith. That growth not only included the continual process of trusting God for bigger and better things, it also included times when Abram failed to trust God completely only to learn of God's unfailing faithfulness.

The man of faith was also at times a man of failures. Perhaps it is in the record of his failures that we can best identify with Abraham. That being the case, we can take heart in the fact that every mention of Abram in the New Testament is positive. Just because there is a time in the past, or even the present, when you found it difficult to trust God does not eliminate the possibility of becoming a great man or woman of faith in the days to come. Perhaps understanding why Abram fell and how he came back to the place of communion with God will help us in our own struggle of faith.

ABRAM AND THE FAMINE *(Gen. 12:9-13)*

After worshiping God in the land his descendants would inherit, Abram continued to travel south. The verb translated "journeyed" (Gen. 12:9) is a form of the verb *nasa'* literally meaning to break up a tent or to remove. Used in this context with Abram, it vividly describes the nature of a nomadic lifestyle in the Near East with repeated "breaking camps" to travel. Because of the significance of the tent and the altar in the life of Abram, this act of taking down his tent and removing himself from his altar may be the first hint of the problems to come. More than one commentator has noted that God never directed Abram to make the journey to Egypt nor is there any evidence of Abram having communion with God while in Egypt.

As his camp traveled south in the land of promise toward the Negev (desert), Abram encountered a famine, the first of thirteen famines recorded in Scripture. This famine is described as "severe in the land" (v. 10). The Hebrew word *kaved* here translated "severe" literally has the idea of being heavy, or that of being multiplied, lengthened, or extended. It was apparently not just the famine but the severity of the famine that moved Abram to make the journey to Egypt. It was customary for Egyptian border officials to grant refuge to those seeking to escape from famines (cf. 26:1; 43:1). When confronted with a severe problem and finding circumstances advantageous to leave the land of promise to find refuge in Egypt, Abram did what must have at the time seemed the most reasonable course of action available, he "went down to Egypt" (12:10).

While not disputing the severity of the famine, two things should be noted concerning Abram's interpreting that problem as a directive to journey to Egypt. First, the famine was apparently not severe enough to drive the Canaanites from the land. They remained while Abram departed. Second, the same word used to describe the severity of the famine is later used to describe the wealth of Abram (13:2) suggesting that even in going to Egypt, Abram had not escaped what was essentially his problem.

The combination of broken fellowship with God and severe problems in life was followed by a third condition in the life of Abram that resulted in his lapse of faith, a willingness to accept a temporary solution alleviating the symptoms rather than searching for a more complete answer to his real problem. Abram's intent when traveling to Egypt was "to sojourn there" (12:10). The Hebrew verb *qur* means "to dwell as a stranger" or to live in a place temporarily. Abram never intended to live in Egypt continually, but he didn't leave under his own volition either.

A fourth characteristic was Abram's willingness to lie concerning his relationship with his wife. Abram feared the Egyptians would kill him in order to take Sarai into a harem. His fears may not have been entirely unreasonable. Written on the pyramid of Unas, a Pharaoh of the Fifth Egyptian Dynasty is a magic formula which states concerning that Pharaoh, "Then he takes away the wives from their husbands whither he will, if desire seizes his heart."

It is interesting to note the timing of Abram's appeal to Sarai, "when he was close to entering Egypt" (v. 11). Perhaps Abram had thought he could trust God to take care of him in Egypt, but as he left the land of promise he may have been plagued with a nagging doubt. Some have suggested that the wives of Egyptians were generally ugly and faded early. The women of Chaldea held their youth and beauty longer than other cultures. Others have noted that Egyptian women do not wear veils as is customary in other parts of the Near East. As the couple got closer to Egypt, the contrast between Sarai's physical beauty and the Egyptian women would have become increasingly obvious to Abram.

The grammar of Abram's statement to Sarai (vv. 11-13) suggests a pleading on the part of Abram. The statement begins with a demonstrative participle of entreaty which would be literally translated, "Behold, please." Abram then described his wife using the expression *yepheth-mar'eh* literally meaning "beautiful to behold." The word *yapheh* was used not only as an adjective meaning "beautiful" or "fair," but also conveyed the idea of the "fairest one," or "most beautiful." Part of Abram's success in convincing Sarai to agree to his plan may be attributed to the fact he appealed to her vanity with tenderness.

Abram may have explained to Sarai that she didn't have to lie, but only that not elaborate on the truth. In identifying herself as Abram's sister, she was telling the truth, but not the whole truth. She was the biological half-sister of Abram (cf. 20:12). Further, sisterhood was a legal status which could be achieved under law by a wife, particularly if she had been given in marriage by her brother. Sarai may have also been a sister in this sense as well. In identifying herself as Abram's sister, Sarai was telling the truth, but she was telling the truth with the intent to deceive and therefore was lying.

Abram was looking for the road of least resistance which is not always the best path. He was rewarded with a comfortable lifestyle in Egypt, even if that meant undermining his relationship with his wife (12:13). Many of the later struggles and conflicts in the life of Abram find their root in this period when Abram temporarily abandoned the pioneering life of faith for the more comfortable lifestyle of the world in Egypt. From this point on in Scripture, the land of Egypt most often represents the world and sin in typical interpretation.

ABRAM AND THE PHARAOH *(Gen. 12:14-20)*

When Abram arrived at the Egyptian border, the response of the Egyptians to Sarai's beauty confirmed Abram's fears. "The Egyptians saw the woman, that she was very beautiful. The princes of Pharaoh also saw her and commended her to Pharaoh" (Gen. 12:14-15). In all probability, the princes of Pharaoh were border officials similar to contemporary customs officials. The word "pharaoh" is not a name but rather a title given to rulers of Egypt meaning literally "the king." The particular Pharaoh who took an interest in Sarai may have been a local ruler over part of Egypt rather than the king over the whole nation.

At first, everything seemed to be going well for Abram. His plan had worked. As he had suspected, the Egyptians were enamored with his wife's attractiveness. By passing her off as his sister, Abram had access to a life of luxury in Egypt. "He had sheep, oxen, male donkeys, male and female servants, female donkeys, and camels" (v. 16). Sarai too was enjoying a more comfortable lifestyle than that with which she had been accustomed. She was now living in Pharaoh's home (v. 15) and according to Jewish tradition was also the recipient of the symbols of wealth. Like the daughter of Pharaoh, Sarai was apparently given a maid, a girl named Hagar.

Some contemporary Christians have the mistaken idea that God always blesses obedience with abundance and judges sins with hardships. Abram could certainly have used that kind of erroneous logic to justify his spirituality during this lapse of faith. In reality, he experienced famine in the will of God and an abundance of material wealth out of the will of God. But the absence of two spiritual symbols illustrates Abram's spiritual state at this time. There was no tent or altar in Egypt.

When the Lord intervened in this period of Abram's life, He did so indirectly by afflicting "Pharaoh and his house with great plagues because of Sarai, Abram's wife" (v. 17). The exact nature of these plagues is not here identified, though some commentators have speculated they may have involved barrenness as was later the case when Sarai became part of the harem of Abimelech (cf. 20:18). Whatever the nature of the plagues, Pharaoh soon identified the true relationship between Abram and Sarai as the cause of these plagues. He responded by confronting Abram with his sin and sending him out of Egypt. Despite the fact Pharaoh asked questions, there is no recorded response of Abram. Some interpreters regard this silence as the result of deep conviction in which Abram realized his sin and could offer no justification for it.

Pharaoh ended his relationship with Abram and Sarai by commanding "his men concerning him; and they sent him away, with his wife and all that he had" (12:20). The Hebrew verb *wayeshallechu* implies not only the idea of dismissing one but also that of Pharaoh's men escorting Abram out of the land of Egypt (cf. 18:16; 21:27). It does not necessarily denote an involuntary dismissal but definitely implies the appointing of men to conduct Abram out of the land together with his wife and possessions. We have no clue as to how long Abram remained in Egypt. It may be that he would have continued in Egypt much longer had he not been thrown out of the country.

In Egypt Abram learned the problems we run from in one place are usually greater at the next place. He would have been better off to suffer hunger in the Promised Land than to be rich in Egypt. Further, his experience in Egypt illustrates the truth that backsliders usually don't take the initiative in getting out of their "Egypt." God had to plague Pharaoh who then expelled Abram from the land.

ABRAM AND THE LORD *(Gen. 13:1-4)*

The absence of a tent or altar in Egypt suggests the absence of a close communion with God in Egypt. In order to restore that fellowship he had formerly with God, Abram had to return himself to that place of fellowship. Just as years later the Lord urged the church at Ephesus, "Remember therefore from where you have fallen; repent and do the first works" (Rev. 2:5) so that they would once again return to their first love, so Abram had to return to the place where he departed from God before he could renew again the intimacy in fellowship he once had with the Lord. That which disrupts the communication between the Christian and God must be dealt with before the communication can be restored. Normally the Lord does not call the backslider to a general repentance, but rather to repent of the particular sin that initiated the backsliding. The following chart illustrates how Abram had to retrace his steps back to the place of communion after his lapse of faith and journey to Egypt.

Just as "Abram went down to Egypt" (Gen. 12:10), now "Abram went up from Egypt" (13:1). The words down and up refer to more than a geographic direction. They imply his spiritual direction. When he left Egypt, he took with him not his "sister" (12:11-13), but his wife (13:1). The route taken on both occasions was the same route through the Negev in southern Palestine, only the direction was different. When he had approached the Negev from the north, Abram's problems

---

ABRAM—RETRACING HIS STEPS
(Gen. 12:9–13:4)

Steps in Backsliding	Steps in Restoration
1 Removing his tent and abandoning his altar— broken communion with God *(12:10)*	1 Leaving Egypt *(13:1)*
2 Focusing on his problems as problems of the famine *(12:10)*	2 Recognizing Sarai as his wife *(13:1)*
3 Calling Sarai his sister *(12:11-13)*	3 Identifying his problems *(13:2)*
4 Entering Egypt—becoming at home in the world *(12:14-16)*	4 Returning to the place of the tent and altar— restored communion with God *(13:3-4)*

---

were interpreted in light of a *kaved* famine (12:10). Now, coming from the south, it was Abram who was very *kaved* in his wealth (13:2). He continued on his journey, repeatedly breaking up his camp and moving on until he arrived at the place he had begun his journey from God (vv. 3-4; cf. 12:8-9). "And there Abram called on the name of the Lord" (13:4).

At this point in his commentary on Genesis, Matthew Henry observes, "All God's people are praying people. You may as soon find a living man without breath as a living Christian without prayer." In light of this, it is significant to note the absence of prayer in the life of Abram during his lapse of faith. Prayer is an expression of faith in the life of the believer, "for he who comes to God must believe that He is, and that He is a rewarder of those who diligently seek Him" (Heb. 11:6). When Abram again pitched his tent between Bethel and Ai, it was more than another stop on his seemingly endless pilgrimage. It marked the renewal of his spiritual life which had been suffocating in Egypt.

PERSPECTIVE:
RETURNING FROM A LAPSE OF FAITH

When Abram began his pilgrimage of faith, he apparently did so after making provisions for himself in terms of an alternate plan to be used if living by faith didn't work (Gen. 20:12). At first all went well for Abram and he could trust God without having to resort to plan "B." But as Abram began to wander from that place of intimate communion with God, he was by nature increasingly more problem conscious than power conscious. The result of a greater independence from God was his ultimate dependance on plan "B." In Egypt, the man of faith was the man of failure.

But such a lapse in faith need not be permanent nor does it necessarily prevent one from maturing his faith into "strong faith." Like Abram, when we lapse in faith, we must return to the point of our departure from God if we desire once again to enjoy the joy of communion we once knew. Abram is today remembered as the man of faith in part because he returned "to the place where his tent had been at the beginning" (13:3).

EIGHT

ABRAHAM:

His Choice of Faith

(Genesis 13:5-18)

When God called Abram into his pilgrimage of faith, He required of Abram that he leave his country, kindred, and father's house (Gen. 12:1; Acts 7:3). Abram's obedience to both the first and second call of God was only partial, he did not leave his kindred. Initially he left his native country of Ur of the Chaldeans to travel to Haran with his father and family. After the death of Terah in Haran and in response to the second call of God, Abram left his father's home but took with him his nephew Lot. When Abram returned from his lapse of ✳ faith in Egypt into the place of fellowship with God, God brought yet another crisis into his life to effect a more complete obedience in the man of faith. The strife between the herdsmen of Abram and Lot was the means which God used to effect Abram's separation from his kinsman.

Sometimes the full effects of sin are not realized until much later in life. When Abram lapsed in faith and went down into Egypt, he appears to have benefited financially. He not only survived the famine which affected Canaan, but because of his lie, also increased his wealth in terms of both herds and servants. It was not until he returned to the land of promise to continue his life of faith that the full impact of sin was realized. First, his wealth was largely responsible for his conflict with Lot, and second, one of the servant girls acquired in Egypt would be involved in the birth of Ishmael. In Lot's case, it seems that even when Lot was removed from Egypt, Egypt was not removed from Lot.

RESOLVING A CONFLICT *(Gen. 13:5-13)*

When Abram and Lot settled at the site of their former camp "the land was not able to support them, that they might dwell together" (Gen. 13:6). Several reasons could be suggested for this problem. The famine which had affected the land during Abram's sojourn in Egypt may not have completely ended. Also, the Canaanites had apparently expanded their holdings in the land as evidenced by the presence of "the Perizzites" (v. 7). But the chief reason for this problem suggested in the biblical text is that "their possessions were so great that they could not dwell together" (v. 6).

The inabilities of verse 6 are emphasized by the negation of two different Hebrew verbs. The first verb *nasa'* means "to support." The second verb *yachol* means "to master or comprehend." Both verbs are negated with the same Hebrew adverb of negation *lo'*. The strength of this negative is evidenced in that when used in a question, the question always assumes an affirmative response. The emphasis here is that the land was certainly not able to master or comprehend the situation; i.e., they certainly could not dwell together. The reason for both these problems is suggested in their possessions. The land had supported them and they had dwelt together before acquiring their additional wealth in Egypt.

The believer needs to be careful with what is acquired while outside of the will of God. The riches of Egypt hindered the relationship between Abram and Lot and eventually became a snare to Lot. Normally, the problem in human relations is an indication of a deeper problem. The strife between Abram and Lot might have been settled if they had had a proper attitude toward their possessions; but this appears to be a case where possessions were placed before people. In times of revival and persecution, people with great differences seem to get along together, but in times of affluence and ease, the same people will divide over comparatively minor issues.

Two different words are used in this passage to describe this strife. The Hebrew word translated strife in verse 7 is *riyb*, most often used to refer to a personal or legal contest. Included in this general term are the ideas of an adversary, cause, chiding, contending, controversy, pleading, strife, and suit. When Abram made reference to the strife in the next verse, he used the word *meriybak* which emphasizes the effect of the strife in provoking anger and ill feelings. The suggestion seems to be that what began as a series of minor disputes was beginning to ignite the emotions of those involved and was perhaps about to explode.

One of the complications of this family feud was the presence of both the Canaanites and the Perizzites in the land (v. 7). Though mentioned several times in Scripture, there is some question concerning the exact identity of the Perizzites. Indeed, it is easier to know who they are not than who they are. They are probably not another ethnic tribe or nation in the Old Testament as the Hebrew word is on at least one occasion used to describe the Jews living in villages in Elam (Es. 9:19). Some have suggested they were those who lived in the lowlands or plains based on the supposed etymology of the word; however, the problem with this conclusion is that they are in several places described as living in the hill country (cf. Josh. 11:3; Jud. 1:4ff). Perhaps the title is best understood in the context of Canaanite society. According to the tablets found by archeologists at Ugarit, the Canaanites lived in city-states surrounded by villages or suburbs. Some commentators believe it is best to view the Perizzites as the villagers or suburbanites of the day. This would also explain how an otherwise unknown people could be so widely scattered as to be associated with the Canaanites, Jebusites, and Jews.

Abram appealed to Lot in a hope to bring an end to the strife. He called for an end of strife between Lot and himself and their respective herdsmen noting "for we are men, brethren" (Gen. 13:8, literal translation). Abram's twofold appeal to bring an end to the strife was based on an appeal to their humanity and family. Of the various Hebrew words for men, Abram chose *'anashim,* a generic term referring to humanity.

The subtle suggestion behind the use of this word was, "Let's not act like animals. Let's be human about this matter." Beyond this, Abram reminded Lot of their family ties. In the Near East, family ties are strong throughout the extended family. This is evidenced in the next chapter when in spite of their strife and separation, Abram went to war to rescue Lot.

On this occasion Abram suggested they divide the land between them and gave Lot first choice. It has been more than once noted that first choice belonged to Abram, the patriarch of the family. His willingness to yield his right to the best in order to resolve the strife suggests the degree to which Abram was committed to developing an adequate solution to the problem. Lot's choice of the Jordan Valley also reflects something of his character. He chose the land because "it was well watered everywhere (before the Lord destroyed Sodom and Gomorrah) like the garden of the Lord, like the land of Egypt as you go toward Zoar" (v. 10). The garden of the Lord is an Old Testament type of paradise or heaven. In contrast, the land of Egypt is an Old Testament type of the world. In the mind of Lot he may have begun to think of worldly success as his paradise. Perhaps this explains why he began drifting toward the city of Sodom in spite of the fact "the men of Sodom were exceedingly wicked and sinful against the Lord" (v. 13).

Lot's selfish choice opened the door to compromise. Perhaps the reason Lot began dwelling in the cities of the plain can be explained in terms of the supposed benefits the world offered his children. The Hebrew word *yashav* means to dwell, in the sense of remaining in a place. The cities of the plain, including the home of the "exceedingly wicked and sinful" men of Sodom, was to become Lot's home. The same word is used of the man of faith later in this chapter when Abram "dwelt by the terebinth trees of Mamre, which are in Hebron, and built an altar there to the Lord" (v. 18). Lot chose the affluence of Sodom over the altar of the Lord. Though he himself "was oppressed with the filthy conduct of the wicked (for that righteous man, dwelling among them, tormented his righteous soul from day to day by seeing and hearing their lawless deeds)"

(2 Peter 2:7-8), his children were very adaptable to the nature of life in Sodom and some of them refused to leave when the city was destroyed. Even the two daughters who did escape with their dad were eventually involved in an incestuous relationship with him, a practice more characteristic of the city of Sodom than the camp of Abram.

The character of Lot's new home is described in the statement, "But the men of Sodom were exceedingly wicked and sinful against the Lord" (Gen. 13:13). Two of the several Hebrew words for sin are used in this verse to describe the nature of the sinfulness of Sodom. The first is *ra'im* translated "wicked." The root idea behind this term is that of being evil in disposition. This implied meaning is captured in the translation, "The men of Sodom were wicked in nature." The second term is *hatta'im* translated "sinful." The root idea behind this term is that of "missing the mark," similar to the Greek term *harmartia*; i.e., missing the mark (cf. Rom. 3:23). The implication of this term is that they were sinful in their activities which fell short of God's standard of holy perfection. The activities of the men of Sodom were evil because their fundamental disposition was wicked.

RENEWING A COVENANT *(Gen. 13:14-18)*

The Scriptures note significantly, "And the Lord said to Abram, after Lot had separated from him" (Gen. 13:14). This is the first mention of the Lord speaking to Abram since the famine in Canaan and Abram's subsequent sojourn in Egypt. Even though Abram had retraced his steps back to the original campsite between Bethel and Ai, and had restored his altar and prayed, God had apparently chosen to remain silent throughout the dispute with Lot. It was not until after the separation with Lot that the Lord spoke to Abram. This is particularly significant in light of Abram's responsibility to leave his kindred (12:1). Full obedience to the known will of God always results in a deeper relationship with the Lord, particularly where that obedience involves the practice of biblical separation (cf. Isa. 52:11; Ezek. 20:34, 41; 2 Cor. 6:17).

The purpose of the Lord's meeting with Abram on this occasion appears to have been to encourage Abram by renewing or confirming His covenant with Abram. He began by instructing Abram to "lift your eyes now" (Gen. 13:14). This command provides an opportunity to contrast Abram and Lot. When earlier "Lot lifted his eyes" (v. 10), he was attracted to that which reminded him most of Egypt; i.e., the world. The result of Abram's lifting up his eyes was that he saw the land of promise. A man's vision reveals a great deal concerning his character. Later in the Old Testament, the man of God would be called a seer (1 Sam. 9:9, KJV). Notice the role of vision in the life of Abram.

THE VISION OF ABRAM

1 He saw the earth   *(13:14)*
2 He saw the heavens   *(15:5)*
3 He saw the Lord   *(18:2)*
4 He saw the substitute *(22:13)*

The recital of God's covenant with Abram in this context varied significantly from the earlier promise. Now the land is not only promised to the descendants of Abram, it also now belonged to Abram (Gen. 13:15). Further, this covenant was made eternal by the addition of the Hebrew expression *'ad-'olam* literally referring to endlessness in time and normally translated as here by the English word "forever." The implication why the covenant is repeated to Abram is that the heirs of Abram would be his physical descendants; i.e., Israel. This conclusion is also in keeping with the New Testament distinction between Israel and the church (cf. 1 Cor. 10:32). The eternal nature of this covenant makes the Jews a unique ethnic group in that they alone are guaranteed a perpetual existence.

Some commentators have looked for a special significance in the twofold description of Abram's descendants as "the dust of the earth" (Gen. 13:16) and "the stars" (15:5) suggesting the former refers to his physical descendants whereas the latter refers to his heavenly or spiritual descendants. In all probability both expressions should be viewed as idiomatic expressions emphasizing the immense number of Abram's physical descendants.

The Lord concluded His remarks to Abram on this occasion with the double imperative, "Arise, walk in the land through its length and its width, for I give it to you" (v. 17). The practice of walking through the land appears to have been a symbolic legal practice related to the idea of staking a claim on a piece of real estate (cf. Josh. 1:3; 24:3). The Lord was encouraging Abram by faith to claim his title deed to the land. As Matthew Henry observes, "Though Lot perhaps had the better land, yet Abram had the better *title*. Lot had the paradise such as it was, but Abram had the promise; and the event soon made it appear that, however it seemed now, Abram really had the better part."

The man of God is not damaged when he yields himself to the circumstances of God. Lot's choice of the better land did not hurt Abram but rather resulted in Abram's receiving a greater blessing. The man of faith can trust his decisions to God because he knows that God holds the future. When Lot chose by the eye of sight, he eventually lost everything. Abram chose by the eye of faith and gained eternity.

In obedience to the command of God Abram traveled south and established a new base camp "by the terbinth trees of Mamre, which are in Hebron" (Gen. 13:18). The use of the verb *yashav* here translated "dwelt" denotes the idea Abram settled down in this place as the central point of his subsequent stay in Canaan (cf. 14:13; 18:1). This grove apparently belonged to a man named Mamre whose name means firmness or vigor and who later became an ally of Abram (cf. 14:13).

PERSPECTIVE: THE LIFE OF FAITH INVOLVES SEPARATION

Living by faith sometimes involves difficult situations and hard choices. There are times when God is silent and seems to have abandoned us even when we pray. It was at such a time that Abram was called on to resolve a crisis with Lot that eventually led to their separation. To abandon one's family at a time when it seems one has been abandoned by God is certainly a difficult choice to make. Yet that was part of the lonely path of faith to which God had called Abram. It was only after Abram had been faithful to God in making that difficult decision that God revealed His greater faithfulness to Abram.

Separation is a choice of faith which must be made in the life of every believer if he would live by faith. That separation is essentially a separation to God and His purposes for one's life, but it also necessarily involves separation from sin and the world. We are never really separated to God until we are also separated from that which is opposed to God. Also, to separate from the world without separating to God produces no lasting spiritual benefit.

NINE

ABRAHAM:
The Fighter
(Genesis 14:1-24)

Often faith in God is defined passively. Faith is thought of exclusively in terms of waiting on God or resting in His promises. While this is true of some aspects of the life of faith, there is also that active side of faith which calls for decisiveness and courage. As the carnal mind is at war with God, there will always be battles to be fought by the believer. Abram, the man of faith, learned the lessons of a victorious faith when he accepted his responsibility to fight an enemy.

Genesis 14 is unique in Scripture, first because it records the first war recorded in Scripture and recounts Abram's only military conflict in his pilgrimage of faith. Second, this chapter introduces the mysterious king-priest Melchizedek who though rarely mentioned in Scripture is significant because of his relationship to Christ. Third, the chapter also records the first mention of tithing in Scripture emphasizing its significance with particular reference to a new name for God, *El Elyon.*

THE CAPTURE OF LOT *(Gen. 14:1-12)*
This chapter begins with the expression, "And it came to pass in the days of " (Gen. 14:1). These two Hebrew words, *vayehi bemeyi*, occur six times in the Old Testament, always introducing a time of trouble ending with a blessing (cf. Ruth 1:1; 2 Sam. 21:1, 14; Es. 1:1; Isa. 7:1; Jer. 1:3). What follows

here is the identification of several rulers with names typical of
the period (2000 B.C.). Over the years various attempts have
been made to identify these names with known characters of
that period.

Amraphel, king of Shinar, was for years identified with the
famous Hammurabi of Babylon. Supporting this view is the
identification of Nimrod's city-state Babel in the land of Shinar
(cf. Gen. 10:10; 11:2, 9). More recently, archeologists have
learned of kings named Hammurabi in Aleppo and Qurda. This
appears to be a common title of that period and there may
have been other rulers by that title or throne name. If this
Amraphel (pronounced Hammurabi in other semitic languages)
was the ruler over Nimrod's kingdom, this would also explain
why he is named first.

The second king, Arioch of Ellasar, was formerly identified
with Rim-Sin or Larsa but more recent archeological discoveries have resulted in a probably more accurate designation. An
equivalent form of the name Arioch has been found in both
Mari and Nuzi documents. The son of Zimri, Lim, king of Mari
is called Aruwuk(u) and may be the Arioch mentioned here.

The third king, Chedorlaomer of Elam, is virtually unknown
outside of Scripture. Some scholars attempt to identify him
with Katir-Nakkauti I of Elam assuming both a later date for
this event and a scribal error in the text. Few commentators,
however, have adopted this conclusion. The name is typical of
Elamite names and means "servant of Lahamar"—an Elamite
goddess. Ironically, though we know so little about this king,
he may have been the dominant leader of the invading force.
The Elamite dynasty was particularly strong at this time. Perhaps as archeologists uncover the ruins of Elam in the years to
come, more will be learned about the actual rulers of this
period.

Tidal has been identified with Tudhaliya, one of five known
Hittite kings. He is described here as "king of nations." This
English translation may suggest more than the Hebrew word
goyim necessarily implies. Old Testament scholar, Franz
Delitzsch, argues this term should be identified as an old name
for Galilee (cf. Josh. 12:23; Jud. 4:2; Isa. 9:1). This suggests

the Hittite kingdom dominated Galilee and that Abram's attack at Dan (Gen. 14:14) occurred when the invading army thought their campaign was over and they were safely into their own territory.

The combined strength of these four invading kings is evidenced in the nature of their military campaign. They appear to have been primarily concerned with clearing a trading route through the Jordan Valley to the Gulf of Aqaba. The biblical account of this campaign emphasizes the spirit of rebellion on the part of the five kings of the plain of Sodom. It may be that others had also rebelled, not only failing to send tribute but also interfering with the commercial trade of the invading nations. The attack against the king of Sodom and his allies appears to be the conclusion of the campaign.

Several groups are specifically identified as victims of this extended military campaign. The first of these mentioned is the Rephaim (v. 5). All that is known of this group is their notable size. The name means "long-stretched" and they were known as a tribe of giants. Some have suggested they may have been descendants of an unknown patriarch named Rapha. Others argue they were a kind of genetic mutation caused by the crossbreeding of angelic fathers and human mothers, a practice which may have occurred both before and after the Flood (cf. 6:4). However, this is probably not the case.

The second group mentioned, the Zuzim (14:5), are probably to be identified with those whom the Ammonites called Zamzummin and appear also to be among the Rephaim (cf. Deut. 3:11). The third group named the Emim also are in other places identified as part of the Rephaim (cf. 2:11). Their name literally means fearful or terrible, perhaps referring to the fear or terror they would normally put into the hearts of their enemies.

The fourth group here named are the Horites. Their name is probably based on the Hebrew word *chori* meaning dwellers in caves. They were the original inhabitants of the area between the Dead Sea and the Gulf of Aqaba, but were later conquered and exterminated by the Edomites.

The attack on the Amalekites and Ammorites by the invading army drew their allies into the battle. Some writers believe the name of the invader's base of operation suggests the real nature of this battle. They invaded from the city of Kadesh, which is called En Mishpat (Gen. 14:7). While the name Kadesh means "sanctuary," the name En Mishpat translates "the spring of judgment." Some falsely believe this battle may have been a preliminary judgment of God against the cities of the Sodom valley and suggest the battle was intended to warn Lot.

Though the invading army represented the empires of four kings and they were in battle against five kings in addition to the Amalekites and Amorites, still they were victorious. This was due in part to their superior military expertise and the bungling of the kings of Sodom and Gomorrah. Under the ancient rules of war the victor had the right to all the people and wealth of the captured city. Among those taken by the victorious army was Lot, Abram's nephew.

The appearance of this battle in Scripture has resulted in many asking why it was significant enough to be included in the inspired account. One reason suggested is that it records the capture of Lot, thus giving a background to Abram's subsequent actions. A second possible explanation, however, interprets this battle in the context of Abram's experience with God. Abram had just been given the land by the Lord and in obedience to the command of the Lord, had claimed it as his possession (13:14, 18). Abram's recognition of the Lord as El Elyon (14:22) suggests he understood the land still belonged to God and that it had been given to him to exercise stewardship over the resources of God. While the battle of these verses may have had commercial and/or political motives, Abram would have recognized the armies had invaded the land of Jehovah. In that Abram had sworn allegiance to the Lord (v. 22), he had to defend the Lord's interest. Had his actions been motivated only to rescue Lot, he would probably not have surrendered Lot later to the king of Sodom.

THE RESCUE OF LOT *(Gen. 14:13-16)*
For the first time in Scripture the term "Hebrew" is used, here as a description of Abram. Historically, most conserva-

tive scholars have interpreted this title as a designation of a descendant of Eber (Gen. 10:24-25; 11:15-17). In more recent years, however, there have been various attempts to find a relationship between Abram the Hebrew and a group of that time known as the Habiru or Hapiru. Scholars are not agreed; some argue the term "Hebrew" is the same as the Babylonian term *habiru*, others claim the two words are unrelated. Probably a more accurate conclusion is to recognize the Hebrews as part of a much larger group known as the Habiru. The Habiru were known at that time for their raids on cities similar in nature to Abram's successful raid on the invading armies.

Abram accomplished the rescue of Lot relying on his 318 trained servants and the assistance of 3 friends and their forces. It was the custom of that day for a patriarch to have trained servants who could defend his interests in a military conflict. That Abram had 318 of these suggests something of the size of Abram's household. These were joined by Aner, Eschol, and Mamre, three men who dwelt near Abram and who probably also had trained servants like Abram.

By the time Abram caught up with the invading army, they were already at Dan in northern Palestine. By dividing the forces into several smaller raiding parties and launching a surprise night attack, Abram was able to gain the advantage. The foreign armies were pursued as far as Hobah, north of Damascus, and the captive persons and wealth of Sodom recovered.

The conquering of the four kings and their armies was only the first of two battles Abram would have to fight in this chapter because of his sworn allegiance to the Lord. His next enemy, the king of Sodom, would be much more subtle in his attack on the authority of God. Often, the most dangerous time in the Christian life is right after some great victory of faith. Understanding the potential weakness of Abram's strength, God arranged for Melchizedek to meet Abram and prepare him for his encounter with the king of Sodom.

ABRAM AND MELCHIZEDEK *(Gen. 14:18-20)*
Melchizedek is one of the most mysterious of all individuals in the Bible. Like Balaam, he appears to have been a Gentile king

who had come to faith in the true God and had committed himself to serve God as a priest. Unlike Balaam, every biblical reference to Melchizedek is positive. Still, there is some disagreement over just who Melchizedek was. At least four possibilities have been suggested.

Some have argued that Melchizedek should be identified with Shem, the son of Noah and father of the Semitic race of which Abram was a part. Supporting this view is the genealogical data of Genesis 10 suggesting the lives of Abram and Shem overlapped for some years. The weakness of this view is that it is highly unlikely that Shem would be identified with the title Melchizedek and not be identified as Shem if that was who he was in fact.

A second view suggests Melchizedek was a Christophany; i.e., a preincarnate manifestation of Christ. This view is based largely on the misinterpretation of the New Testament claim that Melchizedek was "without father, without mother, without genealogy, having neither beginning of days nor end of life, but made like the Son of God, remains a priest continually" (Heb. 7:3). This claim, however, only argues that the ancestry, birth, and death of Melchizedek are unknown and that in this way he is similar but not the same as the Son of God.

A third view of Melchizedek is that of the *Arabic Catena*. That book describes him as the son of Heraclim, grandson of Peleg and great-grandson of Eber. His mother is identified as Salathil, daughter of Gomer, granddaughter of Japheth and great-granddaughter of Noah. Though this theory has the advantage that it is promoted by a document of antiquity, it also conflicts with the New Testament claim that the ancestry of Melchizedek is unknown.

The most probable view involves recognizing Melchizedek not as a name but rather as the title of the king-priest of Jerusalem. Supporting this view is the use of this title in the Amara letters and its application to a later Jebusite king (Josh. 10:1, 3). Also, the New Testament seems to view this name as a title meaning "king of righteousness" (Heb. 7:2). When David conquered the Jebusites and made Jerusalem his capital, he and his descendants became heirs of this dynasty of king-priests. This was particularly true of the Son of David, Jesus (cf. Ps. 110:4).

Melchizedek is described as the priest of *El Elyon*, God Most High. As with other titles of Deity in Scripture, this title is a revelation of the nature of God. This name is used to identify God particularly to polytheistic Gentiles. The idea in this name is that the true God of Israel was above all other false gods of the Gentiles. By way of implication, this name identifies God as the "possessor of heaven and earth" (Gen. 14:19, 22). This name is frequently applied to Christ by demons, perhaps in recognition of the failure of Satan to overthrow *El Elyon* in his initial rebellion (cf. Isa. 14:14).

Abram's meeting with Melchizedek occasioned the first mention of the practice of tithing in Scripture, and for many embryonically teaches the doctrine of storehouse tithing. In the Old Testament there was a particular emphasis placed on "the place" (cf. Deut. 12). The tithe was brought to the "place" which was the tabernacle and later the temple in Jerusalem. This place was characterized by the presence of the symbols of redemption and the central worship of God. Also, it was the place where the man of God served. When Abram paid tithes to Melchizedek, "the priest of God Most High" (Gen. 14:18), the symbols of redemption; i.e., bread and wine, were present. Also, Melchizedek was king of Salem (Jerusalem) which was "the place" God later established as the location where God could be worshiped in His temple (cf. Ps. 74:2).

The meeting of Abram and Melchizedek occurred "at the Valley of Shaveh (that is, the King's Valley)" (Gen. 14:17). The actual location of this valley is thought to be in the area of the Brook Kidron. At that place Melchizedek blessed Abram, using both a style and words characteristic of Hebrew poetry. "Blessed be Abram of God Most High, Possessor of heaven and earth; and blessed be God Most High, who has delivered your enemies into your hand" (vv. 19-20). This blessing was the preparation of Abram for his next battle and subsequent renunciation of the wealth of Sodom. It was a reminder to Abram of his commitment to the Lord and the fellowship

Abram enjoyed with the Lord. The believer's daily communion with God is the preparation necessary for the crises which one encounters in the Christian life.

ABRAM AND THE KING OF SODOM
(Gen. 14:17, 21-24)

Melchizedek was not the only king who came to meet Abram in the Valley of Shaveh. He was also approached by the king of Sodom. This may have been Bera who fled in battle earlier or a successor to that throne if Bera had been a casualty of the battle. While the Scripture notes the fleeing of the king of Sodom, his death is not specifically recorded (Gen. 14:10).

Bera's approach to Abram was intended to result in the formation of an alliance between the man of faith and the king of Sodom. His name means "gift" and he was willing to make a gift of the wealth of Sodom in exchange for the return of his people. Such a proposal was typical of the culture of that time. Under common rules of war, Abram was permitted to retain all the spoils of war. Also, Abram may have been able to justify keeping both the captives and wealth of Sodom by claiming they were a fulfillment of the Lord's earlier promise (cf. 13:17). However, to form a pact of this nature would have involved an allegiance that recognized the king of Sodom as authoritative over at least some part of the land of Palestine. Because Abram had sworn allegiance to *Jehovah El Elyon*, he necessarily had to withdraw from any opportunity that would have compromised his earlier commitment.

Abram explained, "I have lifted my hand to the Lord, God Most High, the Possessor of heaven and earth" (14:22). The Hebrew expression *harimothi yadi*, literally translated "I have lifted my hand," conveys the idea of raising one's hand in surrender and hence the idea of taking an oath of allegiance. In essence Abram was saying, "I have already pledged allegiance to *Jehovah El Elyon* and cannot, therefore, serve another." This principle is stated in the New Testament when Jesus warned, "No man can serve two masters" (Matt. 6:24) and James asked, "Do you not know that friendship with the world is enmity with God? Whoever therefore wants to be a friend of the world makes himself an enemy of God" (James 4:4).

Though Abram accepted both the bread and wine offered by Melchizedek, he would accept nothing "from a thread to a sandal strap" (Gen. 14:23) from the king of Sodom. While both Abram and Melchizedek worshiped the same God, *El Elyon*, Abram had nothing in common with Sodom and her king. According to Jewish legend God later destroyed Sodom at the moment both the sun and moon were in the sky because they were the two principal objects of worship in that city. In so doing God demonstrated His superiority over both false gods.

Though Abram's personal commitment to the Lord forbade him from making an alliance with the king of Sodom, he was careful not to impose his personal convictions on others who did not share his commitment to God. His refusal to accept the offer of the king of Sodom was accompanied by his claim that his neighbors and allies, Aner, Eschol, and Mamre, were free to accept the offer if they so desired.

PERSPECTIVE: FAITH INVOLVES STRUGGLES

Faith is not only passively trusting or waiting on God, it is also actively obeying the implied commands of faith. When discussing the Christian's spiritual warfare, Paul stressed the importance of having the "shield of faith" (Eph. 6:16). Because the world is in a state of war against God, the spiritual Christian will have occasions when he will be engaged in the fight of faith.

If one is to consistently experience the victory of faith in these conflicts, he must realize the two distinct battle strategies of the enemy. Sometimes the enemy of faith will take the form of an outright attack against the authority of God. More often, however, the approach will be more subtle, requiring only a minor compromise in some seemingly insignificant area. Abram's fellowship with God at Hebron prepared him for the battle against the five invading kings. His fellowship with God before Melchizedek prepared him for the more dangerous battle with the king of Sodom. The only way a believer can adequately prepare for the necessary battles of faith in his Christian life is to continually deepen his fellowship with Christ.

TEN

ABRAHAM:
Justified by Faith

(Genesis 15:1-21)

The fifteenth chapter of Genesis records a signficant day in the life of Abram. It was a day not only marked by a revelation of God, the fifth of nine such manifestations in the life of Abram, but also a day when God confirmed an unconditional covenant with the man of faith. That day of fellowship with God began early in the morning while the stars were still visible (15:5) and did not end until the sun had set that evening (v. 12). This may have been the longest meeting of Abram with God in his pilgrimage of faith.

The account of this meeting is also important theologically as it introduces a number of important theological concepts. Among these are the ideas of revelation, faith, and the imputation of righteousness. Also, the content of and manner in which God confirmed His covenant with Abram has important soteriological and eschatological implications.

THE AFFIRMATION OF FAITH *(Gen. 15:1-6)*
The events of this chapter come immediately after Abram's successful military campaign and his renunciation of the wealth of Sodom. It was in this context that "the word of the Lord came to Abram" (Gen. 15:1). This is the first of many occurrences of this phrase in the Old Testament and emphasizes some special revelation of God to Abram. Most often this

phrase was used by the prophets to introduce their divinely inspired message from God. While there were many means of revelation in Scripture, the use of a vision is prominent here. This "vision" most probably relates to the entire chapter and not just this initial introduction.

God's message to Abram on this occasion begins with the expression, "Do not be afraid" (v. 1). This is the first of eighty-four occurrences of this phrase in the Old Testament. The verb *yare'* here is in the imperfect tense suggesting Abram was somewhat afraid of the circumstances in which he found himself before this manifestation of God. The further revelation of the character of God here provides a hint as to what Abram may have feared.

God first reveals Himself to Abram as his "shield." The Hebrew word *maqen* is used several times in the Old Testament as a descriptive title of God. It occurs most often in the psalms of David and always in the context of some military campaign. Some have suggested Abram may have been fearing a retaliation from the conquered kings of the previous chapter and needed this reassurance from God. Others suggest God revealed Himself here as a shield simply to remind Abram that He was responsible for Abram's military victory (cf. 14:20).

The second aspect of God's self-revelation here is the phrase "your exceedingly great reward." In the context of the previous chapter, this is an obvious contrast to the wealth of Sodom which Abram had renounced because of his allegiance to the Lord. It was customary for a vassal ruler to be rewarded by his superior when he fought on behalf of his master. God here honors that custom by giving Himself as Abram's exceeding great reward.

Abram's response to this new revelation of God was to ask the question, "Lord God, what will You give me?" (15:2) This question has been interpreted both as an expression of faith and despondency. Those who see it as an expression of faith argue that Abram asked for a gift believing God was his exceeding great reward. Those who recognize it as an expression of despondency argue Abram asked because he felt God had not fulfilled a previous promise concerning Abram's descendants. Perhaps the faith of Abram here was like the faith of the disciples which Jesus called "little faith." Little faith is faith in God mixed with a measure of unbelief.

According to the custom of his day, Abram was prepared to appoint one of his household servants as his legal heir. He had in this regard appropriated Eliezer of Damascus whom he described as "one born in my house" (v. 3). The Hebrew expression *ben-bethi* literally translated "a son of my house," is an expression found in the adoption contracts of that day. It does not mean Eliezer was born into his house as a servant (cf. 14:14 where a different expression is used). The meaning here appears to be he is adopted as "a son of my house"; i.e., as though he were my son born in my house. Abram had already appointed Eliezer heir before this vision occurred. The verb *yoresh* is a qal active literally meaning "he is taking possession of " my affairs.

God corrected Abram here by reminding Abram of His promise, now emphasizing that Abram would be the biological father of his heir. The adoption contracts of that day stipulated that a natural son born after a legal adoption always replaced the adopted son as a legal heir. God drew Abram's attention to the stars still visible and announced, "So shall your descendants be" (15:5).

Abram's response to the word of God was faith. "And he believed in the Lord" (v. 6). The Hebrew word translated "believed" is *'aman*. In a typical covenant ceremony this was the actual response of one party to another in expressing agreement. It may have been that Abram expressed his faith by saying *'aman* at the appropriate place in a covenant ceremony. In Scripture the word "amen" is always a strong affirmation of faith. Some writers have translated this phrase, "Abram said, 'Amen' to the Lord." This is the first specific mention of faith in Scripture. Though others before had believed God (cf. Heb. 11:1-7), the word "believe" first occurs here.

These early verses of Genesis 15 are filled with first references. Another first mention here is that of imputed righteousness. "He accounted it to him for righteousness" (v. 6). Righteousness refers to the state or condition of being right with God. Just as the sin of Adam is imputed to everyone born physically, so the obedience or righteousness of Christ is imputed to everyone who by faith is born again spiritually (cf. Rom. 5:12-21). In expressing faith in God, Abram received the imputed righteousness of Christ (4:3) and became the friend of God (James 2:23). Abraham was declared righteous through his unconditional trust in the Lord, because he believed the word of God and was willing to act on it.

FIRST REFERENCES IN GENESIS 15:1-6

The word of the Lord came *(vv. 1, 4)*
Do not be afraid *(v. 1)*
Believed *(v. 6)*
Imputed *(v. 6, KJV)*
Righteousness *(v. 6)*

THE CONFIRMATION OF FAITH *(Gen. 15:7-21)*

In the remaining verses of this chapter God used the customary means by which men formed contracts or covenants in Abram's day to form an eternal covenant with Abram. He began by first identifying Himself noting, "I am the Lord, who brought you out of Ur of the Chaldeans, to give you this land to inherit it" (Gen. 15:7). The foundation of this covenant was God's character and revelation of Himself to Abram. On this foundation alone, everything else rested.

Abram then responded to God with a natural question, "Lord God, how shall I know that I will inherit it?" (v. 8) This was not an expression of doubt but rather a request for some confirmation of the promise. God confirmed His promise to Abram by committing Himself in a blood covenant. These blood covenants were customary among the peoples of Canaan even before God gave it a special significance here. Typically, several animals were severed and laid out on either side of a path. The two parties entering into the covenant would then pass together through the rows of dead animals as a demonstration of their commitment to fulfill their covenant obligations (cf. Jer. 34:18). The implication of this act seems to be the suggestion that if the party failed to fulfill his covenant obligation, he should die like the animals.

Abram's obedience to God in preparing the animals for the covenant service is a demonstration of his faith in God. It is interesting to note that one of every acceptable sacrificial animal was used in this ceremony. It is noted that the birds of prey, representing the enemies of Israel, consistently tried to destroy Israel. Second, it is noted that when extreme darkness came on them, the glory of God passed through their midst.

Notice the time element involved in making this covenant. When God first spoke with Abram, it must have been very early in the morning as most of the stars were still visible (Gen. 15:5). Before God appeared to confirm His covenant with Abram, however, the sun had begun to set in the west (v. 12). As Bible commentator Matthew Henry observes, "God often keeps His people long in expectation of the comforts He designs them, for the confirmation of their faith; but though the answers of prayer, and the performance of promise comes slowly, yet they come surely."

When the covenant was confirmed, God alone passed through the animals in the form of "a smoking oven and a burning torch" (v. 17). Because only God passed through, the covenant becomes an unconditional covenant of God. If Abram had passed through with the Lord it would have meant Abram would have had to keep his half of the covenant, hence it would have been a conditional covenant.

It became unconditional when God went through by Himself. The smoking oven and burning torch are Old Testament emblems of the consuming wrath of God (Ps. 18:7-9). The Hebrew word *thannor* suggests the "oven" was a cylindrical firepot typically used in Eastern homes of that day.

PERSPECTIVE: THE PROMISE OF FAITH

In the confirming of this covenant, God promised Abram the largest possession ever promised in a covenant to Israel. The

Hebrew word *nakar* meaning "river" (i.e., the Nile) is used rather than the term *nachal* which is used in Numbers 34:5 and means "brook." There is the "Brook of Egypt," probably referred to in the Numbers reference, at the southern boundary of Palestine, but the "River of Egypt" can mean none other than the Nile. The territory included in this covenant includes everything from the Nile River to the Euphrates River. Historically, Israel has never possessed all of that territory. This area is further described as the homeland of ten Gentile tribes of peoples then inhabiting Palestine. Various lists of these heathen tribes occur in the life of Abram identifying eleven different groups. It is interesting to note that this territory takes in all of the area in which Abram had lived and traveled.

ELEVEN

HAGAR:
Source of Contention
(Genesis 16:1-16)

One of the most difficult lessons to learn in the life of faith is waiting on God. Someone has defined success in ministry as being God's person, in God's place, doing God's work, in God's timing. Perhaps the hardest part of that equation is discerning and acting in accordance with God's timing. Particularly in Western society which is plagued with the tyranny of the urgent, waiting on God for His timing can be an agonizing experience in the life of faith.

But waiting on God is a necessary part of the life of faith. As the hymn writer noted, it takes time to be holy. A calm assurance comes when a believer's faith has had time to mature.

The events of Genesis 16 record another lapse in the faith of Abram, a lapse which occurred as a result of his failure to continue waiting on God for the promised seed. After waiting for ten years he gives up and listens to his wife. From a human perspective, we might tend to justify Abram's actions because he yielded only after waiting for the promised seed for ten years. He might have been able to rationalize his behavior in the light of contemporary customs of taking a servant girl into a harem, or having a child by a servant girl.

The central character in the biblical record of this lapse of faith is not Abram, but rather Hagar, a female Egyptian slave in his household. According to Jewish legend, Hagar was a daughter of Pharaoh given to Sarai during an earlier lapse in the faith of Abram while they were in Egypt. Though the Scriptures make no reference to her relationship to a Pharaoh, it is clear she was an Egyptian (Gen. 16:1). In biblical typology, Egypt is often a type of the world. The relationship between Abram and Hagar can represent the ungodly marriage of a believer to the world. Later, the son born of that relationship would be used to illustrate the spiritual conflict between the old man and the new man, the flesh and the spirit. It will be the conflict between Ishmael and Isaac.

HAGAR AND ABRAM *(Gen. 16:1-3)*

Despite the repeated promise by God that Abram would be the father of a nation, his wife Sarai was barren. Barrenness in the East is considered among the greatest tragedies which might befall a family. Children were considered the heritage of the Lord and a sure sign of the blessing of God (1 Sam. 2:20-21). Even in the New Testament, Elizabeth spoke of the Lord taking "away my reproach among men," when she realized she was bearing a child (Luke 1:25). A couple was suspect who had been married for any length of time and did not have children. Usually those suspicions were directed toward the woman and it was assumed she had some great sin that God was judging. It is no wonder that after ten years in a new land, and probably many years of marriage before that, Sarai was concerned about her barrenness and attributed it to an act of God, "The Lord has restrained me from bearing" (Gen. 16:2).

Sarai proposed a scheme whereby an heir to the promise could be born. According to the widely practiced custom of the day, a wife could give one of her maids to her husband as a slave-wife, and any child of that union could be a legitimate heir. Later, several of the twelve sons of Jacob (Israel) were actually sons of slave-wives given to him by his wives. This was probably Sarai's intent as she made her offer of Hagar to her husband.

Perhaps Sarai found herself growing discouraged and even depressed. No doubt she longed for a son, but it was physically impossible. Her culture and upbringing convinced her of her failure to give her husband an heir.

Significantly, the Hebrew verb *'ibbaneh* is used here translated "I shall obtain children by her" (Gen. 16:2). A more literal translation of this verb would be, "I shall be built up." Sarai viewed the birth of a male heir, by whatever means possible, as the key to raise her spirits.

The Scriptures note significantly, "And Abram heeded the voice of Sarai" (v. 2). By divine plan, the chain of command in marriage appointed the husband as a ruler over the wife. While this does not justify wife abuse, physical or otherwise, it does suggest that the leadership in the decision-making process in the home normally requires the husband to fulfill his responsibility as a leader. For the second time in Scripture, a great man follows the carnal suggestion of his wife with disastrous results (cf. 3:6, 12).

Apparently, Hagar was not consulted in this arrangement. Sarai "took" Hagar and gave her to Abram, probably against the will of Hagar and without her consent. The Hebrew verb *wattikach*, here translated "took," is a verb which was normally reserved to describe the violent taking of captives in battle, and is in other places translated with such verbs as to seize, to lay hold of, to take from, to take away, to capture, and to conquer. While the practice here described was widely practiced, it did not minimize the human tragedy.

HAGAR AND SARAI *(Gen. 16:4-6)* (2080 B.C.)
As planned by Sarai, Abram had relations with Hagar and a child was conceived. It is interesting to note Hagar's response toward Sarai when she learned she was pregnant. "Her mistress became despised in her eyes" (Gen. 16:4). The Hebrew verb *yattekel*, here translated "despised," literally means "to be small" or "to be lessened." Whatever respect Hagar may have had for Sarai before her marriage to Abram was lessened. Counselors observe that a common effect of abuse results when the abuser literally is viewed much smaller in life by the abused. Apparently, Hagar viewed Sarai as the one responsible for her abuse, and responded accordingly.

Sarai responded to her new relationship with Hagar by finding someone else to blame, her husband. Her action is not too unlike the normal response of a carnal Christian not willing to assume responsibility for his own actions. She blamed her husband for the sort of problems that are involved when a man has two wives. Abram turned Hagar over to Sarai's authority. He wrongly wiped his hands of any responsibility.

Under the legal code of Hammurabi, a maid who had been elevated to the status of slave-wife could be returned to her status as maid, but not expelled from the household. Abram was apparently observing this custom when he returned Hagar to Sarai's control. Sarai responded by venting her own inner frustrations directly against her pregnant maid. "Sarai dealt harshly with her" until Hagar fled from the camp of Abram. The name Hagar means "flight" and serves not only as a name, but a characterization of her temperament. By today's social norms we might sympathize with Hagar and justify her actions. But under the legal codes of the day, her actions were clearly illegal and could not be justified regardless of the circumstances. The silence of Scripture concerning any efforts on the part of Sarai or any other member of the camp of Abram to find and return Hagar suggests Sarai was content to overlook Hagar's illegal act as long as she remained far away.

HAGAR AND *EL ROI* (Gen. 16:7-14)

Despite Sarai's contentment to ignore Hagar's flight, God did not overlook the situation. For the first time in Scripture, an individual identified as "the Angel of the Lord" makes an appearance in Scripture. A survey of the various appearances of this Angel in the Old Testament indicates He is more than an angel; He is called God. This is one of several forms of Christophanies or preincarnate appearances of Jesus in the Old Testament. Significantly, this appearance is made to a Gentile woman in distress rather than to the man of faith. The Lord is always ready to meet people with problems at their point of need regardless of their pedigree or background.

The Lord met Hagar "by the spring on the way to Shur" (Gen. 16:7). The name *Shur* means "wall" and refers to an Egyptian border town. In her confusion and distress, Hagar was running home to Egypt. Apart from the intervention of God, Hagar would have returned to Egypt.

God asked two questions designed to bring conviction. "Hagar, Sarai's maid, where have you come from, and where are you going?" (v. 8) Despite the relationship between Abram and Hagar (v. 3), God here addressed Hagar only as Sarai's maid. The first question was designed to force Hagar to identify her sin (flight from a master was wrong under any circumstances according to the laws of the day). The second question was designed to force Hagar to reconsider her actions before going farther. The questions were effective. Hagar's response, "I am fleeing from the presence of my mistress Sarai" (v. 8), demonstrates she understood her rightful relationship to Sarai and is an implied confession of her crime of running away.

It was not God's intent to condemn but rather restore the fallen. His advice to Hagar emphasized two of the most important attitudes prerequisite to the blessing of God, repentance and submission. Hagar was to "return" to Sarai and "submit yourself under her hand" (v. 9). The biblical idea of submission is to get under another to support another. If Sarai had been wrong in her treatment of Hagar, the maid had also been wrong in her attitude toward her mistress. The key to the blessing of God in Hagar's life required her to repent and submit to Sarai. Twenty years later, God would arrange the circumstances of Hagar's life so that she could leave the camp of Abraham without forfeiting the blessing of God.

In this circumstance God revealed His attributes in three significant names. First, He named the son of Hagar *Ishmael*, meaning "God hears." Second, He revealed Himself to Hagar as *El Roi*, meaning "God sees." Third, He met her at a well named *Be'er Lahai ro'i*, meaning "the well of life and vision." God was reminding her that He heard her cry, He saw her situation, and He was alive and active in resolving her problems. That trinity of divine attributes will encourage Christians today if constantly remembered. For the next few years under the hand of Sarai, Hagar would be reminded of these promises every time she called the name of her son.

HAGAR AND ISHMAEL *(Gen. 16:15-16)*

As instructed by the Lord, Hagar returned to the camp of Abram and gave birth to her son. As prophesied by the Lord, Abram named the son Ishmael. The Scriptures note Abram was eighty-six years old when Ishmael was born, and ninety-nine before he again heard directly from the Lord (16:16; 17:1). For thirteen years, Abram raised Ishmael as his son and the promised seed. For thirteen years, Abram enjoyed the fruit of the flesh. For thirteen years Abram assumed he had adapted the plan of God by fathering a son by Hagar. Abram probably thought that Ishmael was the seed promised by God. For thirteen years Abram was self-deceived. In biblical numerology, thirteen is the number of rebellion. For thirteen years, Abram lived outside the perfect will of God. His life was wrapped up in the fruit of his flesh, Ishmael. There is no mention of a tent or an altar during that period.

But the birth of Ishmael had a more far-reaching effect than would be evident in the life of Abram. Ishmael would become the father of a nomadic nation which has perpetually opposed the physical heirs of Abraham, Israel. A later descendant of Ishmael named Mohammed would be the father of Islam, a major world religion which has historically opposed the spiritual heirs of Abraham, the church of Jesus Christ. All this because of the failure of the man of faith to wait patiently for the Lord's timing. There are no real shortcuts in the life of faith.

PERSPECTIVE: THE FRUIT OF THE FLESH

When one enters into a personal relationship with Jesus Christ, his sin nature is not eradicated. He will still struggle with the influence of the flesh from time to time in his walk with God. His experience may not be much unlike that of the Apostle Paul, who admitted, "For what I am doing, I do not understand. For what I will to do, that I do not practice; but what I hate, that I do" (Rom. 7:15). The apostle confessed his growth in faith was characterized by a constant struggle with an inner nature (the flesh) warring against his spiritual motives and goals for his life.

The life of faith has both positive and negative ramifications.

Positively, the life of faith is an active response to the known will of God. Negatively, the life of faith is a struggle against the natural carnal instincts of humanity. The believer grows in faith not when he has the sinful flesh nature removed but when he understands and applies the victory over that ever present nature which he has in the death, burial, and resurrection of Jesus Christ.

TWELVE

ABRAHAM:
Faith Confirmed

(Genesis 17:1-27)

The Apostle Paul uses the expression "weak faith" only a few times in his writings and only in the Epistle to the Romans. On one occasion he described Abram as "not being weak in faith . . . but was strengthened in faith" (Rom. 4:19-20). This strong faith was evident in the events surrounding the announcement of the birth of Isaac. This strong faith is characterized by Paul when he wrote, "Who, contrary to hope, in hope believed, so that he became the father of many nations, according to what was spoken, 'So shall your descendants be' " (v. 18). The Apostle Paul defined faith in the following terms: "And being fully convinced that what He had promised He was also able to perform" (v. 21).

The strong faith of Abram was a faith that believed in hope even in an apparently hopeless situation. It was a faith grounded on the revealed Word of God. It was a faith that could rest on the promises of God because he was "fully persuaded," intellectually, emotionally, and volitionally, that God was indeed able to accomplish that which He promised to do. It is that kind of faith toward which every Christian should strive.

When Ishmael was born, Sarai was barren, physically unable to have children, but Abram's reproductive organs were functioning. Now thirteen years after the birth of Ishmael, both Abram and Sarai were "dead" physically; i.e., in their reproductive capacities (v. 19). This makes the birth of Isaac not only spectacular as a son of Abram's old age, but indeed miraculous, as one born from the dead (cf. Heb. 11:19).

THE REVELATION FROM GOD *(Gen. 17:1-16)*
The events of this chapter occur thirteen years after those of the previous chapter. For thirteen years, heaven had been shut up to Abram. During that time, there was apparently no communication from God to the man of faith. Ishmael was the fruit of Abram's flesh, and the eighty-six-year-old Abram was busy playing with the fruit of the flesh. Abram had no doubt come to think of Ishmael as his heir and the promised son of the covenant. Thirteen is the number of rebellion and Abram had probably passsively forgotten God. Now after all those years, God again appears to Abram with a renewed revelation, a new responsibility and a promise of the imminent fulfillment of the covenant.

Concerning El Shaddai (vv. 1-3)
Some commentators see the covenant God made with Abram as typical of the suzerainty treaties common to that day. When a king made a covenant with a lesser king or vassal, the covenant always began with the title of the king. When the Lord appeared to Abram to confirm His covenant with him, He revealed Himself to the ninety-nine-year-old man of faith as *El Shaddai,* Almighty God. Linguists are not agreed as to the etymology of this title and usually suggest one of three possibilities. Some link the word to the Hebrew *shadad* meaning "to devastate" and argue the title lays emphasis on the irresistible power of God. Others believe the word is related to the Akkadian word *shadu* meaning "mountain" and argue the title means something like "God of the Mountains." The third and most probable meaning of this word is based on its relationship to the Hebrew word *shad* meaning "breast."

El Shaddai is by nature a tender title of God. It is used exclusively in Scripture of God in relation to His children. Some writers have spoken of "the Mother-love of God" when trying to explain more fully the nature implied in this name. To the child held to his mother's breast, the mother is the all-sufficient one providing both physical necessities and emotional support. Similarly *El Shaddai* is the all-sufficient One in the believers' experience. He has been accurately described as "the God who is enough."

This was the favorite name of God used by Job. For Job in the midst of his suffering and despair, *El Shaddai* was enough. The character suggested by this title is that of supplying the need and comforting the hurt. Over the years, many Christians have discovered the true nature of *El Shaddai* only in their darkest hours. When one understands this name of Jesus, he can grow in his Christian experience knowing the tenderness that characterizes Christ till he can confess with Job, "Though He slay me, yet will I trust Him" (Job 13:15).

The revelation of this new name to Abram carried with it a continued responsibility. The Hebrew verb *hithehalleche* is the second person hithpa'el imperfect and is better translated with the emphasis "continue to walk" before Me. There are four descriptions of the walk of the believer with God in Scripture. First, we are to wait before God as children (Gen. 17:1). Also, we should walk with God as friends in fellowship (5:24). Third, we walk behind God as servants in obedience (Deut. 13:4). Finally, we walk in God as members of His body (Col. 2:6).

Abram was further instructed here to "be blameless" (Gen. 17:1). The Hebrew word *tamim* may mean "perfect, wholeheartedly, or blameless." The word has the sense of wholeness when used of attitudes and is translated "without blemish" when used in the context of sacrifice. Abraham was here being called to maturity that he might be genuinely and unreservedly committed to God's service. When the Scriptures talk of perfection, they speak of three things. First, one is "perfect" if to the best of his ability he is walking before God with Him. Second, perfection is sometimes viewed as not offending one's conscience. Finally, perfection is being fully conformed to Jesus Christ. When we walk by faith, we must have a perfect heart with God as its object (cf. Heb. 12:2).

Each revelation of God in the life of Abram had a specific purpose. Here the revelation related to the covenant that God had made with Abram at least thirteen years earlier. Now when God says, "And I will make My covenant" (Gen. 17:2), He was not planning to establish a new covenant but honor the prior covenant. The Hebrew expression *wa'ettenah berithi* signifies not so much to make but rather to give or put; i.e, to realize the covenant and set in operation the things promised in the covenant. Twenty-four years earlier, God had called Abram to follow Him and now He is announcing His intention to honor His promise and give His servant the promised seed.

In response to this announcement, Abram fell on his face humbling himself before God. His posture reflected the attitude of his heart. It is interesting to note the construction of verse 3. When "Abram fell on his face," then "God talked with him." Only when we humble ourselves before God is the communion we once had with God restored completely. This simple act reflects a change in Abram which ended at least thirteen years of dryness in his relationship with God.

Concerning Abraham (vv. 4-8)
Notice the growth of the covenant as it relates to Abraham and his descendants. First, God promised to make Abram "a great nation" (12:2). Then his descendants are compared to "the dust of the earth (13:16—physical Israel), and the stars of heaven (15:5—spiritual children of Abraham by faith). Now God speaks of Abram's descendants as "many nations" (17:4).

With the announcement concerning the fulfillment of the covenant, God also changes his name from Abram to Abraham, noting he would be "a father of many nations" (v. 4). This name change involved the addition of the fifth letter of the Hebrew alphabet to the name of the man of faith which added the phonetic sound *ha* to his name. This is the same basic change which was later made to the name of his wife. The significance of this name change has been variously interpreted.

Linguistically, the name Abraham has a meaning in keeping with the expanded promise of the covenant. It is a compound of the word *'ab* meaning "father" and *raham* which like the Arabic word *ruham* means "multitude," hence the father of

multitudes or many nations. Some writers see a special significance in the addition of the letter to the name of the patriarch
and his wife, in that it is the only letter common to the two
principle names of God in the Old Testament. Also, it is the
fifth letter of the Hebrew alphabet which has special significance to some who interpret the number five as representing
grace. It has even been suggested that there is a phonetic
significance to the names Abraham and Sarah. The change
involves the sound *ha ha* or *ah ah* which is reminiscent of
laughter. The name Isaac means laughter and, when his birth
is announced, both Abraham and Sarah laugh. Some commentators suggest God also laughs, rejoicing with Sarah in the
birth of her son (cf. 21:6).

Though Abraham was at the time ninety-nine years old and
the father of only one son not recognized by God, the Lord
promises here to make him "exceedingly fruitful" (17:6). The
Hebrew expression used here is *bime'od me'od,* literally "exceedingly exceedingly" fruitful. When one considers the sheer
numbers of those ethnic groups who today trace their cultural
and racial roots to Abraham, it is evident that the promise
given here was not exaggerated.

The covenant God made with Abraham was an everlasting
covenant (v. 7). It was a covenant made by God alone (15:17)
and therefore was not dependent on Abraham or his descendants at all. It was a promise not only to Abraham but also to
his "seed." The Hebrew word *zer'ach* is a collective noun and
may be singular or plural depending on the context. The context here suggests the noun is plural referring to Israel as the
seed of Abraham. The Apostle Paul's argument of Galatians
3:16 concerning the seed (singular) is based on Genesis 21:12
where the context demands this same word be understood as
singular. The land of Abraham's sojournings is the eternal possession of his descendants, the nation Israel (17:8).

Concerning circumcision (vv. 9-14)

A third feature of this fresh revelation from God was the
introduction of circumcision as the sign of the covenant. This
was not the first time circumcision was practiced by primitive

peoples. It was widely practiced by the Egyptians before this and there is some evidence it may also have been practiced in Ur. Normally, the pagan practice of circumcision is associated with an initiation rite into manhood and is therefore usually performed around puberty. Circumcision as practiced by the Jews was unique in that it was practiced on the eighth day. It is here given a special covenantal meaning. It implied a commitment both to the nation (v. 14) and to God Himself (Jer. 4:4). This commitment to God involved the ideas of belonging to God, being separated to Him, being pure in Him, and being possessed by Him. It also came to symbolize the abandonment of heathen ways (Josh. 5:9) and the natural will of self (Deut. 10:16).

Characteristic of the contemporary covenants of Abraham's era, there is a reference to the one who fails to keep the sign of the covenant being cut off from the people (Gen. 17:14). The practice of circumcision was the token or sign of the covenant (v. 11). The Hebrew word *'oth* may be translated "sign, mark, token, badge, standard, monument, memorial, or symbol." In both the Old and New Testaments, God established certain symbols as an outward evidence of an inward reality. Symbols are important to God. Some Christians argue certain symbolic acts like baptism and the Lord's Supper are not important as long as you know the reality they represent. Others faithfully observe the symbol without experiencing the reality. Both positions are contrary to the teaching of Scripture. Keeping the symbols of our faith does not create spirituality, but does reflect our faith in the Word of God, and should be practiced in that light.

The command to circumcise was a command to circumcise on the eighth day (v. 12). There have been several explanations offered as to the significance of the eighth day. Dr. S.I. McMillen, M.D., himself an advocate of the practice of circumcision for perceived health reasons, argues the eighth day after birth is the safest time to perform the operation because vitamin K, an important blood clotting element, is not manufactured in an infant's intestinal tract until the fifth to seventh day after birth and a second element important to blood clotting, prothrombin, is available in a greater concentration on the eighth day than at any other time in life.

A second explanation offered by some to explain the significance of the eighth day is based on numerology. Eight is the number of resurrection, and new life, or new things in Scripture. Though the Jews held the Sabbath or seventh day as holy, it was always on the eighth day that the greatest of Jewish festivals was celebrated. The Feast of Firstfruits, the Day of Pentecost, the climax to the Feast of Tabernacles, and the beginning of the Feast of Unleavened Bread all fell on the eighth day, Sunday. These were the greatest feasts in the Old Testament and had typical significance concerning the relationship between Christ and believers today. In keeping with the significance of the eighth day on Israel's festive calendar, circumcision was also commanded on the eighth day.

Concerning Sarah (vv. 15-16)

For the first time since God called Abraham from Ur of the Chaldeans to follow Him by faith, Sarai is included in the covenant. It is easy to be critical of Sarai's unbelief in the Hagar incident, but in her defense it could be argued that God had not given her a specific promise. It was of course always implied because of God's established pattern for the home (2:24), but for almost two and a half decades, Sarai walked by faith, being yielded to Abram and God's will for his life.

As with her husband, Sarai was also renamed here. Her name is changed from Sarai to Sarah. This represented a change in meaning from "princely" to "princess."

THE REQUEST OF ABRAHAM *(Gen. 17:17-18)*

A rejoicing of faith (v. 17)

When Abraham heard the renewed promise of God, he "fell on his face and laughed" (v. 17). His first response was that of gratitude to God. He fell on his face before God in appreciation. When God promised Abraham a son, his laugh was a laugh of gratitude. Though at times it seems like gratitude is the least remembered of all virtues, the life of faith is the life of gratitude. The man of faith takes time to thank God and others for what they have done for him.

But Abraham's laugh was also a laugh of faith. The Hebrew word *wayyitsechak* means he laughed or laughed repeatedly. French reformer and theologian, John Calvin, explains this laugh: "Not that he either ridiculed the promise of God, or treated it as a fable, or rejected it altogether; but, as often happens when things occur which are least expected, partly lifted up with joy, partly carried out of himself with wonder, he burst out into laughter."

A request of the flesh (v. 18)

No sooner had Abraham expressed his faith in laughter than he made a request of the flesh. Ironically, at the highest moment of spiritual experience, at a moment when Abraham was truly "strong in faith," he still prayed for the flesh. It is a reminder that we can appear fleshly at the moment of our greatest spiritual experience. Several times it seems Abraham was willing to accept a "halfway" blessing of God when God had promised full and complete blessings. He would have been satisfied with Haran, but God wanted to give him Canaan. He seems here to be satisfied with Ishmael, but God wanted to give him Isaac. As we learn faith from the positive example of the man of faith, we ought also to learn from his mistakes. Do not go halfway with God, get His very best.

Abraham prayed, "Oh, that Ishmael might live before You!" (v. 18) Terms such as living and killing had particular significance in the covenantal terminology of that day. A man was "killed" when rejected in his claims to authority by a rival and made to "live" if the superior reestablished him on the throne. Abraham is here praying that God would allow Ishmael to be the seed notwithstanding the birth of another son.

THE REPLY OF GOD *(Gen. 17:19-22)*

Concerning Isaac (vv. 19, 21)

God responded to Abraham's prayer of the flesh by first reiterating the terms of His covenant. Isaac would be the seed, not

Ishmael. This is one of the few times in Scripture when a child is named by God before his birth. The name Isaac is significant in that it is based on the verbal root for laughter. There is usually a lot of laughter surrounding the announcement, birth, and weaning of a little "bundle of joy." Some commentators prefer to translate the name, "May He smile (upon him)." In the Old Testament the smile of God was an anthropomorphism of the blessing of God on the one who was the object of that smile.

That Isaac should be the chief heir was in keeping with the culture of that day as reflected in laws of Hammurabi and the laws of Lipit-Ishtar. Legally, a natural son was always the chief heir over the son of a slave woman even when born later. Abraham's affection for his thirteen-year-old son caused him to desire something not only contrary to the will of God, but conflicting with the normal custom of society also.

Concerning Ishmael (v. 20)
Still, God chose to answer Abraham's prayer and bless Ishmael with a dynastic status as the patriarch over twelve princes. He had no part with Israel but is the father of several Arab groups and the spiritual father of Islam. This may not have been part of God's original intent as the blessing of Ishmael is prefaced with the remark "as for Ishmael, I have heard you" (v. 20). In light of the historic animosity between the Arabs and the Jews evident even today in much of the contemporary terrorist activity, and considering the difficulties of evangelical Christians in predominantly Moslem countries, we should learn from Abraham's mistake again and be careful how we pray when we are in the flesh. It may be there are some prayers better left not only unanswered but also unspoken.

PERSPECTIVE: THE RESPONSE OF ABRAHAM
(Gen. 17:23-27)
In obedience to God, Abraham again demonstrated his faith in and faithfulness to the Word of God quickly. The same day (Gen. 17:23, 27), all the men of Abraham's household were circumcised. In the sense that Pentecost is sometimes called

the birthday of the church in the New Testament, this day has been called the birthday of the covenant people in the Old Testament. To get the blessing of God, the people of God must quickly obey.

The Scriptures also note that Ishmael was thirteen years old when he was circumcised (v. 25). To this day, Ishmael's Arab descendants still circumcise their sons at age thirteen. Some writers see a numerological significance in this circumcision at age thirteen. Thirteen in Scripture is the number of rebellion whereas part of the significance of circumcision was in one's submission to God.

THIRTEEN

ABRAHAM:
The Intercessor

(Genesis 18:1-33)

There is a relationship in the Christian life between fellowship with God and ministry for God. This was certainly true in the life of the man of faith, Abraham. This chapter illustrates the nature of faith as both communion and intercession. The chapter begins with Abraham the friend of God enjoying fellowship with God, and concludes with him praying on behalf of the city of Sodom.

When God renewed his covenant with Abraham, He changed the name of Abraham and his wife. On the basis of Sarah's response to the Lord's announcement concerning the forthcoming birth of Isaac, some commentators believe Abraham had not told Sarah of God's intentions. If this was the case, one of the purposes of Jehovah's visit with Abraham may have been to communicate the promise to Sarah. Second, He had to communicate to Abraham that the Judge of all the earth was about to judge and destroy the cities of the plain including the principal cities of Sodom and Gomorrah.

COMMUNION WITH GOD *(Gen. 18:1-21)*
Though we do not know the exact time lapse between Genesis 17 and 18, it could not have been more than a few weeks or months. Abraham was 99 years old when God confirmed the covenant (17:1) and 100 years old when Isaac was born the

next spring (21:5). The events of this chapter must have occurred just a short time after chapter 17. After over fourteen years of silence, this would be the second visit of God to Abraham within a few weeks or months. The desert period in Abraham's life was being replaced with a time of fellowship and communion with God.

Communion with God is the basis of intercession with God. As Bible expositor, C.H. MacIntosh, noted, "The soul that can draw near to God in the assurance of faith, having the heart and conscience perfectly at rest with God, being able to repose in God as to his past, the present and the future, that soul will be able and willing to intercede for others."

The appearance of the Lord (vv. 1-8)

As Abraham sat in the door of his tent at midday, he noticed three men arriving. His camp was established at a place identified as the Oaks of Mamre. The trees for which this place was named were probably what would today be called "scrub oaks." Though they were not the towering oaks coveted by lumbermen today, their presence would provide some limited shade from the scorching desert sun and protection from windstorms. The name Mamre means fatness, and the presence of the oaks would also suggest an available source of fresh water. Even with the shade of the oaks, midday temperatures in that region would probably reach about 110°F or 43°C.

Some commentators have identified the three men who visited Abraham as the three Persons of the Trinity. There can be little doubt that one of them identified as Jehovah in this chapter is a preincarnate appearance of Christ, but the other two are only angels (cf. 19:1). Also, as God is Spirit, it is doubtful if the Father or Holy Spirit ever have or will possess physical bodies. While Abraham prayed to Jesus, the two angels traveled to Sodom to investigate the evils of that city and justify the judgment of God on it.

The hospitality shown by Abraham to these three "strangers" is very typical of Eastern hospitality. First, he invited them to remain with him. That he addressed the men with the title *Adonai,* translated "Lord," suggests he did not at first recognize Jesus. This was a common greeting of respect which one used to address an honored friend or even stranger. There is some textual dispute over the actual title used here, but the context suggests *Adonai* is the correct title. The word exists in the Massoretic Text but is marked as "holy" by the Massoretes here and in three other places in this chapter (18:3, 27, 30, 32). Some argue this means the text was changed by the Sopherim or official editors of the Old Testament and the word should be *Jehovah*. Others claim the original word was *Adonai* and that the Massoretes marked it because the One called by this title in this context is God who is "holy." Supporting this latter view is the Samaritan Pentateuch which reads *Adonai* plural; i.e., "my lords." It is doubtful that Abraham identified one of his guests as Jehovah until later, perhaps verse 9 where Sarah is called by the name God gave her or verse 13 where *Jehovah* is first used in conversation.

Abraham invited his guests to wash their feet and rest in the shade while he prepared the meal. Footwashing was a common practice before meals demanded by both the climate and style of shoe worn (cf. 19:2; 24:32; Luke 7:44). The verb *wehisha'anu* here translated "rest yourself," means to recline, leaning upon the arm. It is unlikely Abraham expected the three men to rest under a single tree but used the expression much as one might today invite someone to "lie in the shade" (cf. Gen. 18:8).

While his guests relaxed, Abraham proposed to prepare "a morsel of bread" with which the guests could "refresh your hearts" (v. 5). The verb *wema'adu* means to refresh and sustain with eating and drinking; i.e., strengthening the heart. Describing the meal as a *fath lechem,* "morsel of bread," is a typical way in which such a lavish banquet might be described in the East even today, much as a Southerner might invite a guest in for "a biscuit" and serve an entire meal.

Being hospitable is important in the East even more so than in other parts of the world. This explains the sudden action which characterizes the preparation of the meal and the great quantities involved in the menu. The verb *mahari,* translated "make ready quickly" (v. 6), is a pi'el imperative and the mood of the moment might better be caught with the translation, "Quick! Three measures of meal! Knead! Make cakes!" No doubt that is very representative of both the content and mood of Abraham's conversation as he passed through the tent on his way to the field to find a calf.

The menu for this "morsel of bread" included *'egoth,* a small cake or biscuit baked in the hot ashes of the fire and so named because of its round form; veal; butter; and *leben,* a dairy product very similar to yogurt. The three measures of fine meal used to bake the biscuits is slightly more than an English bushel and would probably produce over 750 dinner rolls even after burnt ones unsuitable for serving company were removed. Depending on the breed of cow, the calf butchered for the meal could produce up to 100 pounds or more of tender veal. It may be safely assumed similar amounts of butter and yogurt were also provided. Obviously, the banquet was more than three men could eat, but the amounts mentioned in this context are typical of such hospitality. After the guests had eaten all they could, other members of the household would be invited to participate in the dinner. Even Abraham the host would not eat until his guests ate (v. 8). Though the menu served both beef and dairy products, something not kosher by Jewish standards today, the Scriptures record "they [i.e., Jesus and the two angels] ate" (v. 8).

The assurance of the Lord (vv. 9-15)
After the meal, the visitors inquired about Abraham's wife asking, "Where is Sarah your wife?" (v. 9) This may have been the moment Abraham began to recognize the presence of Jehovah among his guests, though Abraham himself never addresses Him by this title in the chapter.

The Lord then repeated the promise concerning the birth of Isaac, adding the specific time of his birth. The expression *ka'eth hayyah* literally means "the time of life or reviving" (v. 10). It is the expression which was used to identify the spring season when the plants and animals dormant in winter "came to life again." The promise here is that Sarah herself would give birth to a new life in the time of life; i.e., next spring.

Like Abraham, the initial response of Sarah to this promise was laughter. Unlike Abraham, however, hers was not the laughter of faith but the laughter of doubt. She immediately focused on the problems and ridiculed the expectation of child-bearing. Both she and Abraham were old and Sarah's reproductive organs were no longer functioning. Even when she was younger and healthier, she had been barren. To these problems may be added the New Testament revelation that Abraham's reproductive organs were no longer functioning (Rom. 4:19). With these known factors in mind, it is not surprising Sarah laughed the laugh of doubt. This is even more likely to have been the case if this was the first time she had heard of Isaac's birth. She probably meant no malice and certainly did not mean to insult the guest. She merely laughed within herself.

Jehovah omnisciently responded to the silent laugh of Sarah by asking why she laughed. Next, Jehovah asked the penetrating question twice asked in the Old Testament and once answered, "Is there anything too hard for the Lord?" (Gen. 18:14; cf. Jer. 32:17, 27) Actually the Hebrew word *hayippale'* here translated "Is it too hard?" literally means "Is it too wonderful?" In the Old Testament, a miraculous work is sometimes called a wonder. The translation of the word is revealing of perspective. When looking to the impossible situations of life, men too often focus on the problems and soon come to think of them as "too hard." On the other hand, the Lord invites us to focus on the prospects and His power and comprehend the wonder of the extraordinary works of God. It is not beyond the power of God to bless those who need blessing or judge those who need judging.

When confronted with her unbelief, Sarah denied she laughed (Gen. 18:15). Later in faith she would confess her laughter and invite others to laugh with her a laughter of rejoicing, gratitude, and faith (21:6). But unbelief makes cowards of us when it comes to testifying to what God is doing for us.

The announcement of the Lord (vv. 16-21)
Good friends do not keep secrets from friends. That was the

kind of relationship Abraham enjoyed with God. All believers have the same relation to God, but not all take advantage of the same fellowship with God. Three times in Scripture Abraham is called "the friend of God" (2 Chron. 20:7; Isa. 41:8; James 2:23). He is the only man who is so identified, suggesting the uniqueness of his relationship. The offer of such a close relationship with God is made available to every believer today (John 15:15).

The intimacy of the relationship that existed between Abraham and God is hinted at when the Lord says, "For I have known him" (Gen. 18:19). The expression *ki yeda'ettiw* means "to know a person thoroughly and so after becoming well acquainted with him, to choose or select him" (Isa. 41:8). Someone once defined a friend as someone who knows all about you and likes you anyway. This is the type of friend God was to Abraham.

Because of their relationship, God chose to reveal His intention concerning the destruction of Sodom and Gomorrah. This destruction is hinted at and implied by the Lord when He says, "I will go down now, and see whether they have done altogether according to the outcry against it" (Gen. 18:21). The expression *'asu kalah* is elsewhere used in Scripture to express the utter destruction of a city (Nahum 1:8; Zeph. 1:18).

INTERCESSION BEFORE GOD *(Gen. 18:22-33)*
As the two angels made their way to Sodom, Abraham began to intercede for the city. The Massoretes list this text as a scribal correction and it may mean either "Abraham stood yet before the Lord" or "The Lord still stood before Abraham" (Gen. 18:22). Regardless of the correct textual order, the verse introduces the rest of the chapter in which God waits for Abraham to speak or waits while he speaks. The whole account portrays the approachability of God by His servant in prayer.

Earlier Abraham was the savior of Sodom (14:13-16) and now he was to become Sodom's intercessor. Some writers argue Abraham prayed as he did to perserve the life of Lot his nephew who was then living in the city, but it is noteworthy that Lot is never mentioned by name in this prayer. Perhaps Abraham prayed for Sodom because of the genuine love for the people he had as a result of his fellowship with God and earlier rescue of the people. True love for people springs from an abiding faith in God.

Prayer is the means by which faith intervenes in the apparent plans of God. Oswald J. Smith called intercessory prayer "the highest form of Christian service." Charles Haddon Spurgeon once called prayer "the slender nerve that moves the arm of the Omnipotent." God Himself testifies of the influence and power of intercessory prayer alluding to the prayer of Moses. "Therefore He said that He would destroy them, had not Moses, His chosen one stood before Him in the breach, to turn away His wrath, lest He destroy them" (Ps. 106:23). But because intercessors are human, their prayers are often limited. It has often been noted Abraham quit asking before God quit giving. Notice the six requests on Abraham's prayer list for Sodom.

ABRAHAM'S PRAYER LIST

---

1 Would You also destroy the righteous with the wicked? Would You also destroy the place and not spare it for the fifty righteous that were in it? Shall not the Judge of all the earth do right?

2 Suppose there were five less than the fifty righteous, would You destroy all of the city for lack of five?

3 Suppose there should be forty found there?

4 Suppose thirty should be found there?

5 Suppose twenty should be found there?

6 Suppose ten should be found there?

Abraham had a better understanding of Sodom than did Lot and was therefore more qualified to intercede on behalf of the city. We have a better understanding of the world at a distance in the presence of God. Abraham walked a separated life and understood Sodom better than Lot who went down and experienced all that city had to offer. His greater insight concerning the sin of Sodom is evidenced in the terms both he and Lot used to describe the city. Abraham used the expression *'im rasha'*, translated "with the wicked" (Gen. 18:23) referring to wickedness in the sense of the restless activity of a fallen nature. Lot also referred to the sin of Sodom using the term *tare'u*, translated "do so wickedly" (19:7), referring to that which breaks up all that is good or desirable. Lot saw the sin of Sodom as evil because of the effects of that sin. Abraham understood the sin as evil because of its radical nature.

Abraham's prayer for the city was not just for the preservation of what existed but for the salvation of the people. Therefore he asked God to "spare" the city (18:24). The Hebrew verb in the expression *wel' thissa'* means to take away and bear the guilt. It is used often in the Old Testament to describe the idea of forgiveness. Because the prayer of Abraham was conditional, God responded in the same way. This is one of the few times God prefaces His remarks with the word "if."

PERSPECTIVE: PERSISTENCE IN PRAYER

Abraham quit praying for the city when God offered to spare it for the sake of ten righteous in it. Several reasons have been suggested as to why he quit asking at this point. First, if Lot had only reached his family and the spouses of his married children, there would have been ten righteous in the city. Also, in a city the size of Sodom, Abraham may have simply assumed there were at least ten righteous people living there. Third, it has been suggested Abraham feared he was getting close to his "credit limit" with God and therefore quit while he was ahead. A fourth suggestion offered is that Abraham believed if there were not ten righteous in the city, the city didn't deserve to exist. A final explanation assumes Abraham suddenly realized at this point there were in fact not ten people in Sodom who could be called righteous and that the shock of that realization caused him to quit praying. Based on the subsequent action of the angels, who dragged Lot and his family out of the city before they could judge the city, and preserved Zoar because they could not get Lot out, God would have spared the city for one righteous man (cf. Ezek. 22:30).

FOURTEEN

LOT:
The Destruction of Sodom

(Genesis 19:1–20:18)

The story of Lot tells of a man who utterly failed to understand the devastating effect that evil associations can have in one's life. Though the wickedness of the city of Sodom was generally known, Lot chose to make his home there because of some apparent advantages of the region (Gen. 13:11). Earlier, Lot's capture by the kings under Hammurabi's alliance should have been warning from God, but it went unheeded.

Lot sat in the gate, suggesting a degree of involvement in the civic affairs of the city (19:1). His reluctance to leave demonstrates the grip that the city had on him (v. 16). Though the New Testament affirms Lot was a righteous man (2 Peter 2:7), the last record of Lot in the Old Testament portrays him drunk and in an incestual relationship with his daughters (Gen. 19:30-38). The example of Lot demonstrates just how far a just man can fall when he backslides.

Perhaps the saddest effect of a backslider is not on his own life, but rather his effect on others. Lot's failure in Sodom had a negative effect on the growing faith of Abraham. Perhaps as a result of Lot's failure, Abraham was influenced to compromise so as to almost risk the promised seed. Something happened in the heart of Abraham as he watched the destruction of Sodom and before long, Abraham was again engaged in lying about his wife (20:1ff). Had it not been for a dramatic intervention of God, the son of Sarah might have been a Philistine, the son of Abimelech.

THE RESCUE OF LOT *(Gen. 19:1-16)*

"Lot was sitting in the gate of Sodom" as the angels entered the city (Gen. 19:1). Sitting in the gate of a city in ancient times suggested a judicial office in the city. Jewish legends claim Lot was chosen chief among the judges of the city because he had ceased to reprove them for their sin. From a biblical perspective, the ineffectiveness of righteous Lot in the wicked city of Sodom stands in direct contrast to the examples of both Joseph and Daniel who remained faithful to God in the wicked societies in which they lived.

Knowing the character of the city intimately, Lot pled with the angels to be his guests rather than spend the night in the street as they suggested. The New Testament reveals Lot was "oppressed with the filthy conduct of the wicked (for that righteous man, dwelling among them, tormented his righteous soul from day to day by seeing and hearing their lawless deeds)" (2 Peter 2:7-8). Homosexuality was the particular sin which seems to have been so predominant on its city streets at night. Even today homosexuality is identified with that city under the broader designation of sodomy.

Perhaps because of the growing acceptance of homosexuality as an alternative lifestyle in Western society today, it has become increasingly popular in some circles to dispute the idea that Sodom was destroyed for its sin of homosexuality, or that the angels were endangered by the men of the city. Several weak arguments are used to support this view. First, they argue the Hebrew verb *yara'* refers to a sexual or carnal knowledge in only 15 of the more than 900 occurrences of the term in Scripture. While this observation is correct, those places where the secondary meaning of *yara'* is noted are places where the context so demands that interpretation.

Second, they argue that intercourse as a path to personal knowledge depends not on the physical act but rather sexual differentiation and complementation. Assuming that presupposition of psychology, it is concluded that it is incorrect to speak of "knowing" one through a homosexual act as suggested in the usual interpretation of Genesis 19:5 and Judges 19:22. While that may or may not be the case, the weakness is that it would be denied by most homosexuals. As the term is attributed to such individuals in both of the above noted passages, the psychology of knowing has little application to the context.

A third argument of the pro-homosexual interpreters relates to an apparent violation of the rights of a *qer* (stranger). This term appears to have had certain technical significance in identifying what might today be called a landed immigrant ot resident alien. The argument is that Lot failed to have the credentials of the men approved before receiving them as overnight guests in the city. Accordingly, it is argued the men of the city wanted "to know" the strangers in the sense of inspecting their credentials. The problem with this alternate interpretation is again found in the context. It is doubtful Lot would have invited the men to "inspect the credentials" of his daughters to satisfy their desire (Gen. 19:5, 8). Further, it is questionable that Lot would have described such an act as wickedness (v. 7). Ultimately, the New testament revelation leaves no question as to how this passage should be interpreted (Jude 7).

When Lot resisted, the men of the city responded by turning their attack on him. The angels came to Lot's defense by blinding his attackers. The Hebrew word *bassanewerim,* here translated "with blindness," is a rare word and probably refers to some sort of confused or dazzled state (cf. 2 Kings 6:18). The angels told Lot to contact other members of his family so that the entire family would be preserved. The Hebrew participles of Genesis 19:14 suggest the sons-in-law were in reality only engaged to marry his daughters and were not yet members of his family. They mocked and refused to leave the city.

THE DESTRUCTION OF THE CITIES OF THE PLAIN
(Gen. 19:17-29)

When Lot was finally dragged out of the city by the angels, he was warned to escape to the hills to avoid becoming a victim of the imminent destruction. Some writers have suggested the reason for this warning was to escape the radiation which may have been a part of the destruction of Sodom. Others suggest he was to avoid the explosion of molten sulfur which eventually claimed his wife as a victim. But still Lot was reluctant to obey these messengers of God completely. Even in the last moments of Sodom, Lot pled for a concession from the angels. He asked to go to a nearby city. Apparently the thrill of city life was in his blood.

One of the cities apparently scheduled for destruction was Zoar. The Hebrew word *tso'ar* literally means "a little one." In his appeal to the angels, Lot defended the city as an acceptable place to live, noting "is it not a little one?" (19:20)

The angels granted Lot sanctuary in the city of Zoar and preserved that city from destruction for his sake. This demonstrates the commitment of the Judge of all the earth to do right and not condemn the righteous with the wicked (vv. 21-22; cf. 18:23-25ff). The angels revealed their motive for constantly hastening Lot when they claimed, "for I cannot do anything until you arrive there" (19:22). Probably in answer to the real intent of Abraham's prayer, God had designated the safe rescue of Lot as a prerequisite to the destruction of Sodom.

The Scriptures record, "The sun had risen upon the earth when Lot entered Zoar" (v. 23). According to Jewish legend, the early morning time of the destruction of Sodom was significant because it fell at a time when both the sun and moon were in the sky. The presupposition is that the citizens of Sodom prayed to the moon for preservation during the night and to the sun for preservation during the day. The destruction of Sodom is therefore said to come at a time when both sects would have been engaged in prayer to their false gods.

God destroyed Sodom with fire and brimstone (i.e., burning sulfur) falling on the city. So great was the sin of Sodom, God burned the deepest hole on earth as His wrath was poured out on Sodom. With the exception of a couple of oceanic valleys, the southeast corner of the Dead Sea has the deepest hole in the earth. This is that area formerly known as the Valley of Sidim, or the Valley of Sodom. So severe was the destruction of Sodom, archeologists have yet to find ruins of the city. It is widely believed this is in part due to the flooding of the destroyed valley by the overflow of the Dead Sea. One of the effects of this destruction is the high mineral concentration of this region which may have been exposed and released from other elements by the intense heat of the burning.

As the destruction of Sodom was in progress, Lot's wife paused to look back on the city which had for so long been her home. The Hebrew word *wattabbet* implies a longing associated with her look. She paused to look at Sodom as they entered Zoar, wishing rather that she was still in Sodom. She was rewarded for her act by becoming a pillar of salt, which probably means she was covered with ash and molten salt that was thrown throughout the area as a result of the explosions of fire, sulfur, and salt. She probably did not become a statue of salt as most imagine but became entombed with a pillar (pile) of salt as the materials crystallized around her. She had not gotten out of the danger zone. In the New Testament, the warning, "Remember Lot's wife" (Luke 17:32), stands as a warning to those who linger and quibble with God, thus endangering themselves as they turn back to a life of sin.

But Lot's wife was not the only one who witnessed the terrible destruction of the cities of the plain. Abraham, the man of faith, could also see billowing clouds of smoke rising out of the valley as he looked over the valley from his vantage point near the Oaks of Mamre. Standing in the place where only the day before he had prayed for the preservation of Sodom, Abraham saw the city's destruction. The Hebrew verb *wayyashekef*, here translated "and he saw" (Gen. 19:28), implies looking down on something with amazement and grief. The context of this word suggests Abraham may have thought he had insured the preservation of Sodom through his intercession of the previous day. Seeing the cloud of smoke rising from the valley, Abraham was probably grief stricken, assuming Lot also had perished in the city's destruction. It is interesting to note Abraham was apparently never informed of Lot's rescue. As he stood in the place where he had prayed for the city, now he watched its destruction. Perhaps he concluded God had destroyed his righteous nephew with that wicked city. His false conclusion about the character of God, based on his own ignorance, was no doubt a factor in his subsequent lapse of faith at Gerar. When confronted with similar confusing problems of faith in our Christian life today, it would be good to learn from the example of Abraham. We should realize the key which might resolve our crisis of faith may lie outside our understanding of the facts.

THE CONTINUED BACKSLIDING OF LOT
(Gen. 19:30-38)

Though Lot escaped the destruction of Sodom, the damage had been done to his family. His fear became so overpowering he eventually moved what remained of his family out of Zoar into a mountain cave (Gen. 19:30). His daughters, perhaps thinking the whole world was destroyed with Sodom, planned to repopulate the earth. They plotted to have sexual relations with their own father to carry on the family name. After getting him drunk, each on successive nights "lay with her father" (vv. 33, 35). Drunkenness is often associated with immoral sexual practices in Scripture. The result of these relationships was the birth of Moab and Ammon. The nations which developed from these two sons were later enemies of Israel. These nations were responsible for the worst carnal seduction in the history of the nation (Baal-Peor—Num. 25) and the cruelest expression of religious perversion (worship of Molech—Lev. 18:21).

ABRAHAM'S LAPSE OF FAITH AT GERAR
(Gen. 20:1-18)

Following the destruction of Sodom, Abraham moved his camp to Gerar (Gen. 20:1). It was there that he would again fail to trust God and lie about his relationship to Sarah. The incident is very similar to his previous lapse in Egypt. The coming disaster in Abraham's life is hinted at even in the name of Gerar, which means "the halting place." It was probably so named because it was a popular rest stop along the caravan route. But for Abraham, it became a halting place in his walk with God.

Abraham lied about his relationship with Sarah because he

concluded, "Surely the fear of God is not in this place" (v. 11). However, Abimelech listened to God and obeyed Him, proving Abraham wrong. Abraham was probably still confused over the destruction of Sodom; therefore, he himself was having difficulty trusting God and assumed others responded the same way. It is common for a backslidden Christian to assume others are also guilty of their own hidden sin.

As he had lied earlier to Pharaoh, so now he lied to Abimelech. Abimelech is a throne title rather than a personal name. The title means "father-king." Only when God confronted Abimelech, who then confronted Abraham, did Abraham repent of what had become his besetting sin. The existence of this sin in the life of Abraham should encourage Christians today that they can begin their walk of faith before they gain victory over their besetting sin. It should also be remembered, however, that the full blessing of that walk of faith, i.e., Isaac, was not given until Abraham confessed and repented of this sin. This was the first time Abraham repented of the sin which he had practiced even though it was the second time he was caught engaged in it. After this repentance, there is no record of Abraham again lying concerning the identity of Sarah.

An interesting postscript to the account is Abimelech's response to Sarah. In releasing her to Abraham, he still referred to him as her "brother" even though he was then aware of their marriage (v. 16). The verse concludes, "Thus she was reproved."

PERSPECTIVE: THE HIGH COST OF BACKSLIDING

This final chapter in the life of Lot demonstrates something of the high cost of wandering from God's perfect will for one's life. In his willingness to identify with the citizens of Sodom rather than with Abraham, the man of faith, Lot forfeited not only his intimacy with God but his material wealth and family. Even though he maintained personal religious convictions, he was unable to communicate those values to his wife and family.

But Lot's backsliding may have affected more than his wife and daughters. When Abraham saw the destruction of Sodom, he was overcome with shock and grief. He probably did not realize the life of his nephew had been preserved. As he saw the destruction of Sodom, he may have jumped to false conclusions about God that led to his own failure to trust God in a difficult situation. One of the highest costs associated with the backsliding of a Christian is the negative influence of that act in the lives of those who may be watching from a distance. Often the backsliding believer may not realize the individual concerned is even aware of the problem.

FIFTEEN

ISHMAEL:
The Fruit of the Flesh

(Genesis 21:1-21)

What seems like such a simple story in this chapter is really the basis of some important theological implications for us today. The casting out of Hagar and Ishmael was used by the Apostle Paul to explain the nature of the conflict between the new nature we have in Christ and the old or Adamic nature sometimes called the flesh (cf. Gal. 4:21-31). It is the story of the man of faith overcoming the flesh.

Isaac was born when Abraham was 100 years old, after he had been promised a seed 25 years earlier. Fourteen years earlier, Hagar had given birth to Ishmael and for most of the intervening period, Abraham had treated Ishmael as the heir. After the birth of Isaac, Ishmael was seen mocking Isaac, just as faith and flesh often coexist until a choice must be made between the two. Abraham was then faced with the difficult task of casting out his son Ishmael, the fruit of the flesh. His example implies several important truths concerning being victorious in overcoming the flesh.

CARING FOR THE FRUIT OF FAITH
(Gen. 21:1-8) (2066 B.C.)

The birth of Isaac was a celebration of the fruit of faith in the life of Abraham and Sarah. Giving birth to her son is specifically mentioned in the New Testament as Sarah's great act of faith. It was only possible "because she judged Him faithful who had promised" (Heb. 11:11). The close relationship between Sarah's faith and the word of God is evident in the opening verses of this chapter. Three times in the first two verses, there is a reference to the word of God. The Word of God is the source of life. "By faith we understand that the worlds were framed by the word of God, so that the things which are seen were not made of things which are visible" (Heb. 11:3). Just as the spoken word of God is the source of life for Abraham, the Bible which is the inscribed Word of God is our source of life. Jesus is also the incarnate Word of God because "in Him was life, and the life was the light of men" (John 1:4). The Word of God is both the source and object of our faith.

Sarah gave birth to Isaac "at the set time of which God had spoken" (Gen. 21:2). The Hebrew word *lammo'ed* may be translated fixed or appointed time, season, epoch, or appointment. God has a time for His appointments. We need to learn something about God's timing. Faith and patience are the twin powers to propel us over the trials of life. Trials will prevent one from becoming overly optimistic and faith will keep one's trials from making one pessimistic. Faith is not developed because of trials. The Bible develops faith (Rom. 10:17). Trials only reveal the faith that is already there. One of the most important lessons of faith one can learn is to wait for God's timing.

The need to wait for God's timing is emphasized in the great Old Testament affirmation of faith, "The just shall live by his faith" (Hab. 2:4). The previous verse emphasizes this principle of timing. "For the vision is yet for an appointed time; but at the end it will speak, and it will not lie. Though it tarries, wait for it; because it will surely come, it will not tarry" (v. 3). One of the most difficult lessons of faith to learn is that of the times of God. Abraham waited twenty-five years for the promised seed, but Isaac arrived right on time according to God's calendar and clock.

Isaac was a miracle baby. He was given to Abraham and Sarah by omniscient grace and received life through resurrec-

CHILDREN NAMED BEFORE BIRTH IN SCRIPTURE

Ishmael *(Genesis 16:11)*
Isaac *(Genesis 17:19)*
Cyrus *(Isaiah 44:28)*
John the Baptist *(Luke 1:13)*
Jesus *(Luke 1:31)*

tion power. He had a supernatural birth and in this way was a type of Jesus Christ. His birth was the product of grace. Grace is receiving the exact opposite of what you deserve. In keeping with the covenant, he was circumcised on the eighth day, representative of the new thing God was doing and the new beginning of the family of Abraham.

Again the Scriptures record Sarah laughing (Gen. 21:6). This time her laughter was the laugh of faith, a testimony to her faith. She encouraged others to rejoice with her in her great joy. The Hebrew expression *yi'echak liy* here translated "laugh with me" refers to the laugh of astonishment or rejoicing rather than the laugh of derision. This is in keeping with the surprise or astonishment of Sarah at the birth of Isaac. All of the verbs in the next verse are expressed in the perfect tense which when used in questions expresses astonishment at that which appears to the speaker as having the highest degree of improbability.

In keeping with Eastern custom, Abraham hosted a festival at the weaning of his son. The Bible does not specifically state the time of Isaac's weaning and various commentators have speculated from several months to five years. Eastern mothers tended to breast-feed their children longer than do Western mothers today. It was not uncommon for the child to be walking long before he/she was weaned in such societies. Swiss reformer, J.H. Bullinger, suggests Isaac was not weaned until he was 5 years old. His argument is based on the chronological figures used in Scripture concerning the time from Abraham to the Law. There were 430 years from the call of Abraham at age 75 to the giving of the Law (Gal. 3:17) and

400 years from the confirmation of the promise at the weaning of Isaac (Gen. 21:12) to the Law (Acts 7:6). As Abraham was 100 years old at the birth of Isaac, the above figures may be harmonized if Isaac was weaned at age 5.

CASTING OFF THE FRUIT OF THE FLESH
(Gen. 21:9-21)

At the feast celebrating the weaning of Isaac, Sarah saw Ishmael "mocking" her son (Gen. 21:9). The Hebrew word *metsachek* translated "mocking" is a pi'el participle and intensive form of the verbal root of Isaac's name. Ishmael was fourteen years older than Isaac; therefore it must be viewed as intentional mocking rather than mere childish quibbling. A sense of maliciousness is implied both here in the context and by Paul's use of the word "persecuted" in Galatians 4:29. Even the RSV which here translates the word "playing" elsewhere translates it "jesting" (Gen. 19:14) and "to insult" (39:14, 17). Isaac had the promise of being next in line to be the "Father of nations." Yet Ishmael was motivated by unbelief, envy, and pride to attack Isaac. Isaac, the source of his father's holy laughter, was now the object of carnal laughter. Isaac was the object of ridicule. God had said, "Is anything too wonderful for the Lord?" Ishmael disagrees in unbelief.

Ishmael's actions on this occasion offended Sarah not only because they were directed at her son, but because they were reminiscent of her own treatment of Hagar. The trampling of Hagar by Sarah was imitated by Ishmael's trampling of Isaac. Most parents discover too late how their children pick up their prejudices as well as their blessings.

Sarah responded to the mocking of Ishmael by calling on Abraham to "cast out this bondwoman and her son" (21:10). Two different Hebrew words are translated by the single English word "cast" or "placed" in this chapter (vv. 10, 15). The first is *qaresh* meaning "to drive away, to expel," or in the context of casting off a wife, "to divorce." The second verb is *shalache* meaning "to throw, cast off, away, or down," or in the context of Hagar casting Ishmael under a shrub, "to drop." When Hagar cast off her son, she probably dropped him from exhaustion (v. 15). Here, however, the verb must be understood as a formal request from Sarah that Abraham divorce his slave wife and expel both her and her son from the household.

What Sarah requested was not the normal cultural proceeding but was permitted in the legal statutes of the day. According to the code of Hammurabi, the sons of a slave wife could share in an inheritance equally with the sons of a free wife only if the father legitimized them at his own initiative. While the status of the son of a slave wife given by a free wife for the purpose of producing an heir is unclear, it would appear from the biblical record that Abraham had in fact treated Ishmael as his legitimate heir. According to the code of Lipit-Ishtar, about 150 years earlier than that of Hammurabi, the son of a slave wife would relinquish any inheritance claim in return for his freedom. Ishmael was apparently a legitimized son and secondary heir after Isaac, but Sarah here called on Abraham to give him his freedom and so force him to give up his rights as heir.

While the whole account of the divorce of Hagar and casting out of Ishmael is set in a context 4,000 years old, it is characteristic of the conflict tearing apart many families today. Second marriages, particularly those in which each spouse had children of a former marriage, are often characterized by the "my son" (v. 10) "his son" (v. 11) type of dispute Abraham and Sarah here had. For Abraham it was "very displeasing" even to think of casting out his son. Had God not intervened, Abraham may not have done so. It is hard to cut off the flesh.

God was in this context using Sarah to reveal His will for Abraham. Abraham was instructed to obey Sarah's request "for in Isaac your seed shall be called" (v. 12). The Hebrew word *zara* (seed) is a collective noun in which the context must determine whether it is singular or plural. The context here demands the noun be understood as singular. This is further demonstrated by Paul's use of this statement to demonstrate that Christ is the Seed (singular) of Abraham (cf. Gal. 3:16).

Characteristic of Abraham's walk of faith is his ready obedience to the clearly revealed will of God. "So Abraham rose early in the morning" (Gen. 21:14), probably the next morning. There is an urgency in making one's break with the flesh. It becomes increasingly more difficult to do so the longer we wait. Abraham filled a bottle of water, probably a resewn goatskin holding five to seven gallons, and placed it on Hagar as he sent her and her son off. Depending on how well the water was conserved and how much one drank, the supply could last two to four days in the desert. There is an interesting contrast in this passage between man's provision, a bottle of water, and God's provision, a well of water.

Some writers have questioned the historicity of this account on the basis of Ishmael being referred to as a child carried by his mother. Actually the Hebrew word *yeled*, a term of relationship, means "child" only in the sense of one born to a parent. It is often used in Scripture to refer to a young man, regardless of his age, who is the child of his parent. Also, as noted above, the verb *shalache* translated "cast" (v. 15, KJV) would be better translated "dropped." If the mother and son, both weary from thirst and hunger, had been leaning on each other supporting each other as they walked, she would have "dropped" him when unable to support his weight any longer. Neither of these words implies a specific age contrary to that implied in the historic setting of the account.

Unable to support her son any longer, Hagar managed to get him at least into the shade, but generally viewed the situation as hopeless. She left her son "at a distance of about a bowshot" (v. 16). The distance of "a bowshot" refers to the distance an archer would shoot an arrow during practice, about fifty feet. While Hagar cried without hope, Ishmael apparently prayed. The LXX translation of verse 16 adds the words "the boy lifted up his voice and wept." God heard the prayer of Ishmael and answered it (v. 17).

God showed Hagar a well of water she had not before noticed where she got water to revive both herself and her son. Again God promised to make Ishmael "a great nation" (v. 18), a promise which has been more than kept. The passage ends noting Ishmael grew and lived on a desert plateau south of Canaan, became an archer, and married an Egyptian wife. The Kedarenes, descendants of Ishmael, were later celebrated bowmen (25:13-15; Isa. 21:17). The brief account of his later life here is rich in typical truth. He lived outside of the land of promise and married a woman of Egypt, typical of being married to the world.

PERSPECTIVE: OVERCOMING THE FLESH

Many Christians today can more readily identify with Ishmael than Isaac in their Christian lives. Just as Abraham was called of God to cast out the son of the bondwoman, so today must we cast off the flesh. The old and new natures struggle within the man of faith for supremacy. This was the experience of even the Apostle Paul (Rom. 7:15-25). The solution to this problem is also offered by Paul. We must "put off . . . the old man" and "put on the new man" (Eph. 4:22-24). The Greek verbs in this passage imply a continuous action. There is no guarantee against backsliding. Abraham discovered the sins of the past will always crop up again if they are not judged (cf. Gen. 20). "That which is born of the flesh is flesh, and that which is born of the Spirit is spirit" (John 3:6).

Regeneration does not mean we change the old man but rather add the new man. The old nature is not eradicated (1 John 1:8), nor is it improved. The new nature consists of new thoughts, new desires, and new power which are radically different from those of the old man. One of the two is going to control you, the choice is yours. The old nature (Ishmael) shall not be heir together with the new nature (Isaac). God has judged the old nature, and it should be treated as dead.

The key to experiencing continuous victory over the flesh in the Christian life is to continually apply the four significant verbs of Romans 6 to your personal experience. First, *know* that the old man is dead and we have a new nature as a result of our union with Christ (Rom. 6:3, 6, 9). Second, we are to *reckon* or count on, rely on this to be so in our lives (v. 11). Third, we must once and for all present ourselves to God (vv. 13, 16, 19). Finally, we must continuously *obey* the leading of the Lord through the Word of God (vv. 16-17).

SIXTEEN

ISAAC:
Sacrificed to God

(Genesis 22:1-19)

Four times in his pilgrimage of faith, God came to Abraham to make a request that must have severely tried his faith. First, he called this son of a moon god worshiper to leave his country and family to see a land God wanted to show him (Gen. 12:1). Later, it was necessary for Abraham to separate from his nephew Lot who was probably more like a son to him than a nephew (13:1-18). The third great trial involved the casting out of Ishmael who for thirteen years was thought to be the promised seed of Abraham (21:14). The fourth and greatest crisis of his faith is the offering of Isaac as a whole burnt offering on Moriah which is recorded in this chapter. This account is sometimes referred to as the *Akedah* story, a word based on the Hebrew verb for binding.

To the oriental mind, everything is wrapped up in the seed. When God required of Abraham his son, He was asking for everything—his future, his line, his heir. To not have a son is viewed as to be next to death itself. Yet when God made the supreme request of Abraham, Abraham said yes. Abraham was one of several parents who was willing to give his child back to God.

PARENTS WHO GAVE THEIR CHILDREN TO GOD IN SCRIPTURE

Abraham gave Isaac
Amram and Jochebed gave Moses
Jephthah gave his daughter
Hannah gave Samuel

If a soldier serves his country faithfully and records great victories in the battle, he is honored with medals and offers of less strenuous work during his declining years. But for the soldier of the cross, there are always more battles to be fought and won. And the battles which follow great victories are often more severe and trying than the former battles. The important thing about *'emunah* (faith) is that it finds its fullest expression in the realm of action. In what may be the most Hebraic epistle of the New Testament, James brings out this emphasis behind the Hebrew word for faith noting, "faith without works is dead" (James 2:20). It is interesting that James should point to the events of this chapter to prove his point concerning an active and living faith (v. 21).

A TRIAL OF FAITH PROPOSED *(Gen. 22:1-9)*
(2051 B.C.)

Genesis 22 begins with the phrase *wayehi 'achar haddebarim ha'elleh* translated, "Now it came to pass after these things" (v. 1). This phrase is a summary expression referring not only to Abraham's past experiences, but also to his growing experience of faith. And it came to pass after Abraham's obedience to the call of God, after his lapse of faith characterized by reasoning with God, after his choice of separation, after fighting the enemy of faith, after having a faith based on Christ, after waiting patiently for the Lord, after learning the importance of symbols of faith, after learning the relationship between communion with God and intercession for man, and after overcoming the flesh, God still had lessons of faith to teach the man of faith.

Of the four trials of faith in Abraham's life, this was no doubt the most severe. The Hebrew word *nimmah* is a pi'el perfect intensifying the emphasis of the verb; i.e., he completely tried or he tested thoroughly. Like its English counterpart "tempt," the verb originally had the same emphasis as the word test or try (cf. English "attempt") and only later came to have its negative connotation. God was testing to affirm Abraham's faith rather than tempting to destroy it. Charles Haddon Spurgeon observed the severity of this trial when he noted, "There is scarce a single syllable of God's address to him, in the opening of this trial, but seems intended to pierce the patriarch to the quick. . . . Oh, trial of trials! Contemplative imagination and sympathetic emotion can better depict the father's grief than any words which it is in my power to use. I cast a veil where I cannot paint a picture."

There are apparently three sources of trials in Scripture. The first of these comes from Satan and must be permitted by God. This was certainly the experience of Job. A second source of trials is circumstances. While there is some dispute over the exact nature of Paul's thorn in the flesh, it probably fits into this category. The third source is God. Here Abraham was being tried directly by God Himself. The most troublesome thing about this is that it is difficult in the midst of the trial to discern the source or purpose of the trial. Just as Job seemed to think the attack of Satan was from God directly, it is doubtful if Abraham could have understood the purpose of God in this trial.

God only tests those who are closest to Him. Abraham had been following God for fifty years when this great crisis came. In all those years, it is interesting that God never once tested Lot in this way.

The Lord did not test Abraham to hurt him or disallow him but to approve him. Across America there are testing companies like Underwriters' Laboratory involved in the testing of thousands of patented products each year. In the process of testing a product, it may be exposed to extreme temperatures, hazardous chemicals, even fire and explosions. This severe testing procedure is not designed to learn how to destroy the product, but rather to show how strong and safe the product is. Similarly, the testing of God is the means whereby He measures our faith and approves it.

God called for the sacrifice of Isaac on a mountain He would show Abraham in the land of Moriah. The name Moriah means "shown of Jehovah" or "vision of Jehovah." It was the mountain which was later the temple site for Solomon's temple (2 Chron. 3:1). When translating this verse in the Vulgate, Jerome translated the meaning *terram vissionis,* "land of vision," rather than transliterating the name. Some commentators believe Moriah was originally a descriptive phrase of an area and only later became a proper name.

The offering Abraham was to offer was a burnt offering of his son. The burnt offering was one of the five major offerings in the sacrificial system of Israel and was sometimes called the holocaust because it involved the whole sacrifice being burned on the altar. This offering is twice emphasized in God's instruction to Abraham (Gen. 22:2). The Hebrew *'alah* translated "offer" and the name of the sacrifice, *'olah,* are both based on the same Hebrew root meaning to cause to ascend as the flame and smoke ascended by burning. Abraham would not have understood God wanting him to give Him Isaac by killing him on an altar and burning his body completely with fire. He was being called to a course of action which would seem to jeopardize his highest hopes in life. It must have seemed that obedience to the request of God would totally destroy his future usefulness, especially as it related to the covenant.

God, who is by nature immutable, forbad the offering of human sacrifice in the Law, so even at the beginning of the command, it was not the intent of God to kill Isaac. That was not known by Abraham, however. From his perspective, it was God's intent that Isaac die. God did not want the sacrifice of a son but rather the surrender of a father. What the Lord desired was not Isaac's life but Abraham's loyalty. The Lord does not want things when He asks for sacrifice. He wants our complete obedience. Sacrifice is a surrender of the will. Abraham understood that even if God does not want something, if He asks for it, it must be offered.

It is approximately a sixty-mile journey from Abraham's

camp at Beersheba to Mount Moriah. Making the journey in three days suggests Abraham did not waste any time in keeping the command of God. Still, during the trip he had seventy-two hours to think about the command to kill his son. While the reference to time here is correct in the geographic context, it is also emphasized in this account because of the nature of the protracted test and Abraham's sustained obedience. Some writers believe the reference to the third day is a symbolic reference to the resurrection of Christ. Much of this account has typical significance to the offering of Christ by God the Father on Mount Moriah (Calvary) at a later date (cf. Heb. 11:17-19).

When the mountain came in view, Abraham told his servants to remain with the animals while he and Isaac went to worship, adding "and come back to you" (Gen. 22:5). The Hebrew verb *wenishubah* has a first person plural ending. There is no way to escape the conclusion that Abraham and Isaac would together worship God; i.e., in the burnt offering, and that Abraham expected they would together return from the mountain. In light of the action of Abraham on the mountain and the revelation of Hebrews 11:17-19, Abraham apparently planned to kill his son, burn the body of his son on the altar as a whole burnt offering to God, and watch God raise his son back to life out of the ashes left on the altar. No wonder the faith of Abraham is defined in terms of Abraham being fully persuaded God is able to keep His promises (Rom. 4:21; Heb. 11:19).

It was not until Abraham and Isaac were climbing the mountain together that Isaac raised the issue of a lamb for a sacrifice. Abraham responded, "My son, God will provide for Himself the lamb for a burnt offering" (Gen. 22:8). Interpreters argue over the translation and meaning of this statement. The Hebrew word *yire'eh lo* may be translated "He Himself will provide" or "He will provide Himself." One's basic presupposition as to what the Bible is all about, will to a certain extent, determine how one translates this word. Still, within the context, there are indications that the translation of the *King James Version* is most likely the correct one. The Hebrew word *haseh* translated "a lamb" includes the definite article

GOD IS ABLE

Able to give much more *(2 Chron. 25:9)*
Able to deliver His people *(2 Chron. 32:14-15)*
Able to deliver from the fiery furnace *(Dan. 3:17)*
Able to abase the proud *(Dan. 4:37)*
Able to deliver from the lions *(Dan. 6:20)*
Able to raise up children from stones *(Matt. 3:9)*
Able to graft Israel in again *(Rom. 11:23)*
Able to make him stand *(Rom. 14:4)*
Able to make all grace abound *(2 Cor. 9:8)*
Able to do exceedingly abundantly above all we can
   ask or think *(Eph. 3:20)*
Able to subdue all things unto Himself *(Phil. 3:21)*
Able to keep that which I have committed unto Him
   against that day *(2 Tim. 1:12)*
Able to help them that are tempted *(Heb. 2:18)*
Able to save Him from death *(Heb. 5:7)*
Able to save to the uttermost *(Heb. 7:25)*
Able to raise him up *(Heb. 11:19)*
Able to save and to destroy *(James 4:12)*
Able to keep you from stumbling, and to present you
   faultless before the presence of His glory *(Jude 24)*
Able to open the scroll *(Rev. 5:3, 5)*

and can be translated "the Lamb." If the statement were included here only to the effect that Abraham expected God at the last moment to provide the sacrificial lamb, certainly a more fitting conclusion to the story would be the offering of a lamb rather than a ram. It is far more likely that Abraham was looking forward to that distant day when on that same mountain God in human flesh would offer Himself as the ultimate whole burnt offering and sacrifice for sin.

The expression "God will provide Himself" almost has the ring of the lifelong motto of Abraham. This was the essence of the mottos which characterized the China Inland Mission and the life of the founder of that mission, J. Hudson Taylor. Some people rest in the Lord and enjoy the blessing of God, but there are a few who rest in the Lord and enjoy God Himself. There is a great difference between enjoying the blessing of God and enjoying God Himself. Abraham had learned to enjoy God during the years of his pilgrimage.

While the chief lesson of this chapter concerns the trial of Abraham's faith, it is also revealing concerning the character of his son, Isaac. Isaac was about 30 years old at this time and no doubt able to overcome his father physically if he so desired. Yet there is no indication of any reluctance on the part of Isaac to cooperate with his father in the sacrifice. He was a son who willingly submitted himself to his father much as Jesus also later willingly submitted Himself to God on the cross.

THE TRIAL OF FAITH PASSED *(Gen. 22:10-19)*

Abraham passed the trial of faith when he raised the knife to kill his son (Gen. 22:10). As far as Abraham was concerned, at that moment the decision had been made and the intent was established to kill his son. God accepted the settled decision of Abraham as though the knife had been lowered and Isaac actually slain. By deciding to obey God and kill his son, Abraham demonstrated his wholehearted allegiance to God. What God required was to be the supreme object of affection in Abraham's life, therefore He demanded of Abraham the sacrifice of that which was most valued by Abraham. His act of sacrificing Isaac proved the genuineness of his faith in God (James 2:21). The binding and offering of Isaac was a symbolic confession of an indwelling faith (Rom. 10:9-10).

The appearance of the Angel of the Lord to prevent the actual physical killing of Isaac was a preincarnate appearance of Jesus Christ in the Old Testament also called a Christophany. This is evident when the "Angel" acknowledged He was the One to whom Isaac was being offered (Gen. 22:12).

When the sacrifice of Isaac had been called off, Abraham noticed that "behind him was a ram caught in a thicket by its horns" (v. 13). The capture of the ram is significant for three reasons. First, if the ram had been trapped in the bush any other way, he might have been blemished and therefore inadequate as a sacrifice animal. Second, the horn of an animal is the symbol of strength in the Old Testament suggesting more than the thicket was holding the ram in place. Third, the ram was offered in the stead of Isaac emphasizing the substitutional nature of sacrifice.

Out of this experience of faith, Abraham learned yet another name for God which is really the name of a place. The name *Jehovah Jireh* literally means "Jehovah will see." But the idea of sight assumes a provision for those needs which are seen by Jehovah. The inspired translation of the name is, "In the mount of the Lord it shall be provided" (v. 14). Over the years, Christians have held to this name of God as a reminder that "the Lord shall provide" (cf. v. 8). Together with the name Ebenezer implying "Thus far the Lord has helped us" (1 Sam. 7:12), this name often appeared in the publications and on the buildings of the China Inland Mission.

The Angel of the Lord spoke a second time to Abraham after the offering of the ram. Again the covenant is emphasized and Abraham is reminded that his descendants would be "as the stars of the heaven" (heavenly seed of Abraham) and "as the sand which is on the seashore" (earthly seed of Abraham). The fact that this covenant is unconditional and not dependent on either Abraham or his seed is emphasized by the expression *bi nishebbe'etti* translated, "By Myself I have sworn" (Gen. 22:16). This is the strongest possible oath God could take to honor His covenant.

TWO CALLS FROM THE ANGEL OF JEHOVAH

A Call for Substitution *(22:12)*
A Confirmation of Revelation *(22:16-18)*

PERSPECTIVE: SACRIFICE AND COMMITMENT
Abraham learned to give up visible things because he saw by the eye of faith Him who is invisible. It is a hard thing otherwise to give up the security of what you can see for the apparent insecurity of that which remains unseen. This vision was foundational to the faith of Abraham, "for those who say

such things declare plainly that they seek a homeland" (Heb. 11:14). Had the focus of Abraham been allowed to dwell on the things of this life, he would *not* have been faithful to God (v. 15). So today, keeping our focus on Jesus is the key to the life of faith (12:2).

When Abraham and Isaac returned from the mountain, they made their way back to Beersheba. The name *Beersheba* means the "well of the seven or the well of the oath" (Gen. 21:31). Typically, it is the well of commitment. After demonstrating their faith in a very special and unique way on Moriah, they returned home to the well of commitment. Some Christians today point to times when they expressed great commitment to God, forgetting that a faith commitment to God is more than an event, it is a lifestyle. Others misunderstand the nature of their salvation and see no need to live a consistent Christian life after being saved. But Abraham and Isaac left Calvary (Moriah) to dwell at Beersheba, the place of commitment.

While the focus of our study of this chapter has concentrated on the faith of Abraham, it should be remembered that the events on Moriah were a type or figure of the essence of the Gospel. Most conservative scholars agree Moriah and Calvary should both be identified near the city of Jerusalem. Isaac, like Christ, was the son who was obedient unto death (Phil. 2:5-8). Abraham is typical of God the Father who did "not spare His own Son, but delivered Him up for us all" (Rom. 8:32). The ram which was offered in Isaac's stead is typical of Christ offered in our stead (Heb. 10:5-10). Finally, the preservation of Isaac is viewed as typical of the resurrection in the New Testament (11:17-19).

SEVENTEEN

SARAH:
A Burial of Promise
(Genesis 23:1-20)

The faith with which Abraham faced the trials of life was the same faith with which he faced the reality of death. The New Testament states concerning the patriarchs of Israel, "These all died in faith" (Heb. 11:13). The Greek word translated "in" is *kata,* meaning "according to or controlled by." Even though they did not realize the fulfillment of the promise in their lifetimes, they believed. Had their minds been set on the land of their origins, they might have gone back. But these great men and women of faith were so set on following God by faith they were still controlled by that faith.

The faith of Abraham and Sarah was more than the expression of an overoptimistic couple. It was the confident assurance that the unseen promises of God would be fulfilled. It was that which was necessary in approaching the opportunities of life, and it was that which made a difference when they were forced to face death. The faith of Abraham made a difference in the way in which he approached his wife's death.

THE DEATH OF SARAH *(Gen. 23:1-2)*
Sarah was 127 years old when she died. She is the only woman in the Bible whose age is revealed. For 62 years she followed her husband in his pilgrimage of faith. For 37 of those years she had been the mother of the promised seed. Because

of her fidelity to her husband in the unusual course of his life, she had several unique opportunities to see God at work and became the matriarch of the people of God, Israel, and an ancestress to the Messiah. Yet despite all this, when she died there was a certain emptiness in the home. Her husband and son both mourned her loss (Gen. 23:2; 24:67).

The man of faith must meet death as all men must meet death. It would be wrong to deny death's existence or treat it as though the loss is not there. He must see death as God sees death. Death is a terrible thing often referred to in Scripture in the context of the most severe of warnings. Death is the inevitable result of sin. But it is only temporary, an intermission. The Scriptures liken death to sleep; i.e., body sleep rather than soul sleep. For the believer, to be absent from the body is to be present with the Lord. This is possible only because Jesus has the key to death. Still, even when the most spiritual Christian dies, despite our eschatological knowledge, there is still a sense of loss. Abraham experienced both grief and tears over the deceased.

Sarah died in Kirjath Arba, later called Hebron. The name Kirjath Arba means the City of Arba (35:27). Arba was one of the original inhabitants of the town and the father of a race of giants (Josh. 14:15; 15:13; 21:11). When Caleb conquered the city he renamed it Hebron meaning place of fellowship. The reference to both names here is a reminder that Sarah died in the midst of the world, yet she was still in fellowship with God.

Abraham's response at the death of his wife would not sit well with some misguided Christians today. The Scriptures describe him with the phrase *liseppod . . . welibekkothah*, "to mourn . . . and to weep for her" (Gen. 23:2). Some Christians believe it is wrong to mourn or weep for a deceased Christian, citing 1 Thessalonians 4:13. But that verse does not teach Christians do not sorrow at the loss of a loved one, only that their sorrow is not as severe as one who is without hope. When Sarah died, Abraham experienced the two common feelings of grief all men encounter at such times. First there were the immediate tears which come as a natural physical response to the shock of the sense of loss. This was followed by a longer period of mourning. The Scripture does not reveal the length of the mourning period, but as it was concluded before Sarah was buried, it was probably not more than a few days. Later Joseph mourned for his father seventy days in Egypt before returning to bury his father and then remained there an additional week. Depending on a variety of factors, the mourning period of a person following the death of a loved one may last from a few days to sometimes several years.

THE PURCHASE OF A GRAVE *(Gen. 23:3-16)*

It took the death of Sarah for Abraham to realize the beginning of the fulfillment of another aspect of the promise of God. In purchasing a grave for Sarah, Abraham held title to his first piece of Canaan. For over fifty years he had lived with the promise knowing he would eventually inherit all of Canaan, though he did not know how or when. The purchase of ground was another step of faith that God would give him the Promised Land.

Just as there is a time to mourn and weep over the loss of a loved one, so there is a time to depart. At death there must be a detachment from the deceased. The Bible records, "Then Abraham stood up from before his dead" (Gen. 23:3). The Hebrew verb *wayyakam* paints a vivid picture of what probably took place. The verb literally means "and he rose up from." It is common for those mourning the dead in the East to fall prostrate before the body of the deceased or to sit before it in mourning. Yet as the time of mourning came to an end, Abraham got up from his place of mourning to deal with the matter of a burial.

The place of burying was no small matter to Abraham. The grave he would purchase for Sarah would also serve as the family grave for at least four generations.

Abraham referred to himself as "a foreigner" in the land as he made his appeal to buy a grave (v. 4). The Hebrew word *qer* is a technical term meaning he was a resident alien with some kind of relation to the community but also having restricted rights. In Israel, such a stranger could not own land. It is not known what restrictions were applied to the stranger in the Hittite society.

Abraham's stated purpose in wanting to purchase a grave was "that I may bury my dead out of my sight" (v. 4). It was customary in Ur to place the bodies of the dead in clay containers and store them in a room or basement of the family home. The effect of such a practice must have been to prolong the grief of those living in the home as the sight of the casket was a constant reminder of the past. Abraham had grown in his life of faith and knew there was a time to go on with his life. The practice of placing a cremation urn on the mantle or establishing a "memory shrine" in the home will often hinder the necessary adjustments to life after the death of a family member.

When Abraham made his appeal to buy a burial place, the children of Heth offered him the choice of graves. The Hebrew word *bemibehar* translated "in the choicest of " (v. 6) is a term used to designate the most select, the best quality. Some commentators believe the offer of a burying place may have been an attempt to prevent Abraham from owning the land. But Abraham did not want outsiders involved in his faith relationship with God. As an act of faith, he dealt honestly in his business transactions as Christians are instructed to do so in the New Testament (Rom. 13:8; 2 Cor. 8:21; 1 Thes. 4:12).

Abraham was offered the best available because he was viewed as "a mighty prince" (Gen. 23:6), literally the prince of God. The emphasis of this title probably implied he belonged to God, was under God's protection, blessed by God, and so a mighty or distinguished prince (cf. Ps. 36:7). Though there was a Canaanite god named *El,* the title for God in this title is *Elohim* suggesting this is a reference to Abraham's God rather than the Canaanite god.

Abraham's selection of a grave was the cave of Machpelah then owned by Ephron ben Zohar (Gen. 23:8-9). Both the LXX and Vulgate translate the name Machpelah here as "the cave with two entrances or compartments." Probably the name was originally a descriptive phrase which came to be the name used in the legal description of the property (cf. v. 17). With the purchase of this cave, Abraham owned his first piece of the land promised to him by God.

According to the real estate provisions in Hittite legal codes, the landowner was financially responsible for the taxes on a piece of property unless he sold it in its entirety. Some commentators believe Abraham tried to avoid the transfer of these obligations by requesting a severance in which he would purchase the cave only, but Ephron insisted on selling the property as a whole, both field and cave (vv. 17, 19-20). All was done in a businesslike way at the entrance or gate of the city.

One might question if Ephron was not taking advantage of Abraham's grief in this real estate transaction. Without records of other purchases of a similar nature, it is impossible to be certain, but 400 shekels of silver seems a little expensive (v. 15). Jeremiah paid 17 shekels for a field (Jer. 32:9) and David paid 50 shekels for a threshing floor and oxen for a sacrifice (2 Sam. 24:24). More expensive pieces of real estate purchased in the Old Testament include the temple site which sold for 600 gold shekels (1 Chron. 21:25) and a Samarian hill purchased by Omri for 2 talents (6,000 shekels) of silver (1 Kings 16:24). Supporting the idea that Abraham may have overpaid is the absence of any bartering over the price of the land which would seem more characteristic of a commercial transaction in the East.

The purchase was made with "currency of the merchants" (Gen. 23:16). As there were no coins issued by the state, pieces of metal of fixed weights were to be used in trade. It is possible that these shekels had been weighted and marked by traders as a kind of legal tender in an effort to establish some sort of standardization and minimize the occurrence of fraud.

PERSPECTIVE: BURIAL TO POSSESS THE LAND
The description of the grave in which Sarah was buried may have come from the actual title deed of the property (Gen. 23:17-18). The particular reference to trees is characteristic of Hittite land transactions. The whole chapter seems to reflect the Hittite laws current in the times of the patriarchs. When the field was legally purchased, Sarah was the first of four generations to be buried in the cave of Machpelah.

152 History Makers of the Old Testament

Abraham experienced the death of Sarah knowing there will be a resurrection day. Some of the strongest affirmations of a resurrection faith were made by Job, believed to be a contemporary of Abraham by some writers. When Abraham earlier offered his son as a whole burnt offering on Moriah, he began to do so knowing God would raise Isaac up from the ashes of the altar. Yet despite the fact he looked forward to a resurrection day, he was careful to address the need to bury the dead. Christians today should not attempt to minimize their responsibilities in facing death by simply affirming their faith in the resurrection.

It took the death of Sarah before Abraham began to possess the land of Canaan. Similarly, we begin to possess the riches of God by death, the death of Christ. His death was the means whereby we were reconciled to God and united with Christ so as to be able to claim the promises of God. All that we receive from God cost Jesus His life.

EIGHTEEN

REBEKAH:
A Bride for the Promised Son

(Genesis 24:1-67)

The final chapter in Abraham's life of faith is the story of his calling out a Gentile bride for the promised son. Most commentators agree Genesis 24 is typical and though it records an actual historical event, it should be interpreted as a type. A type is an earthly picture with a heavenly meaning. In this chapter, several characters seem to be representative in their role as types of the Trinity, the church, and the world. Similarities are evident between Abraham and God the Father. Isaac is elsewhere been established as a type of Christ. The unnamed servant is generally viewed as a type of the Holy Spirit. Rebekah, the Gentile bride is seen as a type of the church, the bride of Christ and her brother Laban is typical of the world from which that church is called. These types will be examined more closely as they appear in this chapter.

In many respects, the unnamed servant is the key to the progress of this chapter. Though he is not named, it is generally thought it is Eliezer who is described here. He is specifically named in the Targum and described here with the expression *hammoshel bechal* meaning "who ruled over all" (Gen. 24:2; cf. 15:2). Each large household would have a principle servant of this nature like Eliezer in Abraham's household or Joseph in Potiphar's household (39:4). Later in Israel's history, this was an important office in the royal court (1 Kings 4:6;

Isa. 22:15). There are several similarities between this servant and the Holy Spirit.

THE SERVANT AS A TYPE OF THE HOLY SPIRIT

1 Both are sent.
2 Both come bearing gifts.
3 Both come teaching about the Son.
4 Both come to woo and convince.

THE SERVANT AND THE FATHER *(Gen. 24:1-14)*

The first part of this chapter contains the last recorded words of Abraham the man of faith as he sent out his servant to find a Gentile bride. It describes a man who had for many years walked by faith and was now enjoying some of the fruits of that lifestyle. The Hebrew verb *berach* is a pi'el perfect conveying the idea of intensity in the verb; i.e., "He [the Lord] had greatly or abundantly blessed" (Gen. 24:1). This is not contradictory at all to the reference to Abraham's age in the same verse. The translation of *ba' bayamim*, "well advanced in age," is unfortunate in its negative connotations. The Hebrew implies only advanced age without reference to the state of health or evidence of decay. Abraham lived about thirty-eight years after the marriage of Isaac.

As Abraham commissioned his servant to find the bride for his son, he called on him to place his hand under his thigh (v. 2). This custom of placing one's hand under another's thigh appears to have been an act associated with swearing an oath. It is only referred to in one other place in Scripture (47:29). Some Jewish commentators believed the act had reference to circumcision which was the sign of the covenant. If this were the case, it would indicate the seriousness of the vow in that one swore by the covenant of God. Others believe it symbolically committed the descendants of the oath makers to maintain the terms of the oath and/or avenge any infraction of it. Jewish commentator Ibn Ezra argued the act was a symbolic placing of oneself under the authority of another. Whatever the specific meaning of the act, it was apparently associated with making a covenant or taking an oath of special significance.

Abraham called on his servant to swear by both Jehovah and Elohim, the covenant or relationship name of God and the strong or mighty name of God (24:3). In the years of his pilgrimage, Abraham had come to know God as both Jehovah who could be trusted and Elohim who was able to do as He promised. The use of both names of God in this context demonstrates both Jehovah and Elohim were the same God and that he did not worship several gods as did his pagan neighbors. He was different from his neighbors and therefore separated from them. His major concern on this occasion was that his son would not violate that separation by marrying a Canaanite. The life of faith is a life of separation—separation from sin, separation to God, separation for service (cf. 1 Thes. 1:9).

This chapter contains the last recorded words of Abraham in Scripture (Gen. 24:7). These words serve to illustrate the tremendous growth in the faith of Abraham over the years of his sojourn, especially when compared with the first recorded statement of the man of faith to God (cf. 15:2). The earlier statement is an expression of doubt, this a strong affirmation of faith. A lot more than his name changed over the years of his pilgrimage.

Though camels were not used for military purposes until much later, there is archeological evidence that they were domesticated even before the time of the patriarchs. Abraham's servant took ten of his master's camels and samples of his master's wealth and began the journey. The Hebrew phrase *wechal mubh 'adonayw beyado* is better translated, "taking all sorts of choice gifts from his master in his hand" (24:10). While it is true Eliezer had control of his master's wealth, the emphasis here is that he took samples of that wealth with him as he went out to find the bride. In the same way, the Holy Spirit has all the riches of God and shares samples of that wealth with the bride of Christ today.

The servant left the camp of Abraham and made his way "to Mesopotamia, to the city of Nahor" (v. 10). The Hebrew words *'el 'aram naharayim,* translated "Mesopotamia," literally mean "Aram of the two rivers," or "between two rivers." The two rivers referred to in the expression are generally assumed to be the Euphrates and the Tigris. The "city of Nahor" may refer to Haran where Abraham left his family; i.e., the city where Nahor lived, or to another city by that name. Evidence of the existence of a city named Nahor at this time is found in the numerous references to that city in clay tablets discovered at Mari. Though archeologists have not yet found the city of Nahor, every indication suggests it is in the region of Haran.

Arriving at the city well, the servant prayed for divine direction in the choice of a bride. The city was built close to a natural spring and it was customary for the women of the city to draw water from the well and carry it back to their home in the city. The Hebrew word *'ayin* translated "well" (Gen. 24:13) was generally reserved for a spring of water. As the

---

ABRAHAM AS A TYPE OF GOD THE FATHER

1 Both are rich and characterized by wealth.
2 Both have a supernatural "only begotten" son.
3 Both fathers give all to their sons.
4 Both offered their sons as an offering on Moriah.

---

servant prayed by the well, he asked God to "show kindness" to Abraham by helping him find the bride. The Hebrew word *chesed* is a covenant term meaning kindness or steadfast love. The servant interpreted God's answer to his prayer as an evidence of God's love for Abraham.

THE SERVANT AND THE BRIDE *(Gen. 24:15-28)*
God sometimes has the most unique sense of timing. Even as the servant finished his prayer outlining the sign whereby he could recognize the bride of Isaac, Rebekah came out to the well for water. She was the appointed bride for Isaac. As the servant met and talked with her and her family, and later traveled back to his master with her, he must have been impressed with the character of this girl. The following chart

lists several of the qualities particularly noted of Rebekah in this chapter.

THE QUALITIES OF REBEKAH

1 Good looking (attractive) *(24:16)*
2 Friendly *(24:18)*
3 Gracious *(24:18)*
4 Hard worker *(24:19)*
5 Hospitable *(24:25)*
6 Respectful *(24:64)*
7 Modesty *(24:65)*

Rebekah is twice referred to in this chapter as a virgin (Gen. 24:16, 43). Actually, two different Hebrew words are used in these verses both translated into the same English word. The first word is *bethulah* meaning a virgin in the sense of a woman who has not had relations with a man. The second word is *'almah* referring to a young woman of marriageable age. Every *bethulah* was an *'almah,* but not every *'almah* was a *bethulah.* The application of both these terms to Rebekah suggests she was mature enough to be considered for marriage and still morally pure.

Rebekah proved herself to be a hard worker in offering to water the camels. It is estimated the camels could drink up to 150 gallons of water. As he watched Rebekah in action, the servant tried to decide if this was the bride. The Hebrew word *mishetta'eh* translated "wondering" (v. 21) is based on the root for desert and is used to describe the feeling of being inwardly laid waste; i.e., totally confused. It was not until he gave her the gold jewelry and learned who she was that he was satisfied he had found the right girl. His initial gift to Rebekah was about ten and a half ounces of gold.

Typically in this chapter, the servant takes time to thank God for every indication of success (vv. 26-27, 48, 52). Sometimes it seems that gratitude is the least remembered of all virtues. The success which would inflate the natural man with pride and arrogance, humbles the man of God. His first thought is to thank God for what He has done. His success was understood in terms of the *chesed,* the condescending love of God, and the *'ameth,* the truth of God, both displayed in the fulfillment of His promise (v. 27).

Rebekah responded to the unusual scene at the well by going to her mother's house (v. 28). As a virgin, Rebekah would have lived apart from the men among the female members of the family. In most homes, this would be a restricted wing of the house in which only the women lived.

REBEKAH AS A TYPE OF THE BRIDE OF CHRIST

1 Both are Gentile brides.
2 Both are called out by the Servant (Holy Spirit).
3 Both are recipients of the gifts of the Servant.
4 Both are called to make their own decision.

THE SERVANT AND THE WORLD *(Gen. 24:29-53)*
Laban, the brother of Rebekah, seems to have been the spokesman for the household. This may have been due to the death of his father or possibly the result of a polygamous relationship. According to records uncovered at Nuzi, the institution of fratriarchy where a brother was the authority in the home existed in Hurrian society. It was customary for a father to marry other wives and in doing so, abandon the children of the one for whom he cared least (cf. Gen. 34:5, 11, 25; Jud. 21:22; 2 Sam. 13:22). Laban may have been acting according to the custom of his society in this chapter, though here and later in Genesis, he seems to be motivated by greed. Characteristic of Laban is the phrase, "when he saw" (Gen. 24:30). Rebekah on the other hand showed kindness before she saw.

Laban addressed the servant as "thou blessed of the Lord" (v. 31). Even though they lived outside the revelation of God, they had some understanding of the God of Abraham. Some commentators believe this was simply a title. Maybe that was all it was, but perhaps it was also more than a title. Later, they would identify the servant's intent to take Rebekah as Isaac's bride as proceeding from the Lord (v. 50). The servant was welcomed. Laban was probably the one who unsaddled the camels as it would be viewed as extremely inhospitable to expect a guest to care for his own animals (v. 32).

The servant refers to Abraham rather than Abram. Just as the Holy Spirit witnesses to us concerning the Father, so Eliezer witnessed to them concerning the father of multitudes (v. 34). All that the father possesses, he has given to the son (v. 36), and implied in that is the realization that she who marries the son can be joint heirs with the son. As members of the bride of Christ, we are heirs of God and joint heirs with Christ. Marriage is a biblical picture of our commitment to Christ.

Abraham's servant described his own relationship to the Lord with the expression *'asher hathehallaketti lefanayw* translated "before whom I walk" (v. 40). The use of the hithpa'el implies the idea of consistency; i.e., "before whom I walk habitually." One of the reasons God blesses the servant with success may be related to his consistent walk with God.

LABAN AS A TYPE OF THE WORLD

1 The bride is called out from both.
2 Both are indecisive to the appeal of the Servant.
3 Both are recipients of secondary blessings/
  common grace.
4 Both are concerned with material over spiritual riches.

When the family indicated a willingness to allow Rebekah to be the bride of Isaac, the servant distributed more valuable jewels and clothing not only to Rebekah, but also to Laban and the mother of the bride. These gifts to the family may have been the formal bride price and a means of concluding the matter finally (cf. 29:18).

THE SERVANT AND THE GROOM
(Gen. 24:54-67) (2026 B.C.)

When the servant planned to leave the next morning, the family sought for a delay (Gen. 24:55). The expression "a few days, at the least ten" is similar to a contemporary vague reference to time; i.e., "a week or so." They were in essence asking the servant to wait awhile so that they could make their final decision. When the servant refused to agree to the delay, they consulted with Rebekah.

It is an unusual thing in a primitive society that a woman should be consulted and her opinion considered before an important decision would be made. But the events of this chapter are in harmony with the apparent relative independence of Hurrian women according to Nuzi tablets. The Hurrian marriage contracts specifically required the consent of the bride. When she agreed to go, the family supported her decision and sent her off with a typical blessing for a young bride (v. 60).

The Scriptures give no indication how long the 900 mile journey of the servant took, but when he arrived in the region of Beer Lahai Roi (the well of life and vision), Isaac had already arrived at his father's camp. Some commentators argue that the servant's reference to Isaac as "my master" (v. 65) suggests Abraham had died. That is unlikely if the events of the next chapter are assumed to be in its correct chronological order. It is more likely that Abraham had appointed Isaac as coregent of the household, perhaps even dividing his flocks and placing Isaac over the herd grazing in the Negev (v. 62). The Hebrew verb *ba'* translated "came" (v. 62) is a qal perfect and would be better translated "had come." This would explain how Isaac was at his father's camp when the bride arrived.

Isaac was returning from an evening walk in the direction of Beer Lahai Roi meditating as he walked. The Hebrew verb *suach* occurs only here in Scripture (v. 63). Some translators argue the word means mourning and note Isaac was later comforted by Rebekah. But the LXX translators understood the verb to refer to meditation and translated it that way. Isaac may have been meditating about his flocks, but if he had been summoned to his father's camp to prepare for marriage, then it is more likely he was meditating over his approaching marriage or praying for the servant as he sought the bride or praying for the bride as she returned to Canaan.

As Isaac was seen, Rebekah "dismounted from her camel"

(v. 64). The Hebrew verb *wattippol* means "to jump off or spring from quickly." It is an oriental custom for a woman to show respect for a man by bowing and greeting him. When the servant identified the stranger in the field as Isaac, she covered her face with a veil (v. 65). It was thought to be immodest for a man to look on the face of his wife before marriage.

ISAAC AS A TYPE OF CHRIST

1 Both had a supernatural birth.
2 Both were the objects of their father's love.
3 Both were rich in their inheritance.
4 Both were Hebrews with a Gentile bride.

PERSPECTIVE:
LEAVING ALL TO GAIN EVERYTHING

All that belonged to the son was shared with his bride, but Rebekah had to leave all to gain all. It is the same today. As the bride of Christ, we make certain sacrifices of this life which are more than repaid as we enjoy the riches of the Son. The marriage of Isaac and Rebekah is a picture of our relationship to Christ as His bride.

NINETEEN

ISAAC:
The Well Digger

(Genesis 25:1–26:35)

Abraham lived thirty-eight years after the death of his wife Sarah. During the interim years, he married a wife named Keturah and fathered six sons. While Abraham cared for all of his sons and gave them gifts out of his immense wealth, there was never any question which son would be the heir of the family covenant. Isaac was supernaturally born when Abraham and Sarah were too old for children. Isaac was the son of promise and heir of the covenant promises of God. Even during his latter years, Abraham was careful to separate "the sons of the concubines" from Isaac, his son (Gen. 25:6).

When Abraham died, Isaac was accompanied by his half-brother Ishmael as they buried their father in the cave of Machpelah (v. 9). Machpelah had been bought by a grieving husband to bury his deceased wife Sarah. The cave was destined to become a patriarchal family tomb. This is the last friendly relationship between these two sons of Abraham or their descendants recorded in Scripture.

The covenant promise of God did not end with Abraham. After his death, God blessed Isaac. The Scriptures hint at the source of that blessing in the identification of his home. "And Isaac dwelt at Beer Lahai Roi" (v. 11), the well of Him that lives and sees. And so would be the relationship with Jehovah in the life of Isaac as it had been with his father. As long as

Isaac would obey the heavenly vision, God would be both the source and fullness of his life.

Often the children of a great man are not recognized for their own greatness because they are so easily compared to the strength of their father. Perhaps that is one of the reasons few Christians seem to recognize the true greatness of Isaac. The high character of this man is hinted at in the New Testament when Isaac is not only identified by name as a patriarch of faith but also as a type of Christ (Heb. 11:17-20). The brief account in Scripture concerning his life after the death of his father should not be misinterpreted by the reader to suggest he was insignificant in the plan of God. As we shall see, Isaac too was an important part of God's covenant plan. But because Isaac was only a man and Scripture records his life accurately, we know also that as great as Isaac was, he too stumbled at times in his pilgrimage of faith.

A FATHER OF TWINS *(Gen. 25:19-34)* **(2006 B.C.)**
Isaac and his wife Rebekah were soon faced with what amounted to a tragic situation in the family life of the Near East; Rebekah proved to be barren. As noted earlier, barrenness was almost always considered an evidence of the judgment of God on a wife or couple. Children are always described in Scripture as a blessing from God. In light of this, it is rather surprising to note how many principal women in the Old Testament were barren. In the case of Rebekah, it moved Isaac to pray for his wife (Gen. 25:21). The Scriptures are not clear as to when the need for an heir became a family concern or when Isaac went to the Lord in prayer, but twenty years would pass between his marriage to Rebekah and the birth of his first son. At that time, it became evident his prayer was more than answered.

Though it would be the only time in her life when Rebekah would carry a child, Rebekah suspected things were not normal. It was more than the discomfort she had heard other women describe that was characteristic of being pregnant. It seemed as though there was a war going on inside her. Puzzled, perhaps even confused, she prayed to the Lord (v. 22).

God's answer must have been surprising to the expectant mother and any others who may have learned about it. First she learned she would be the mother of fraternal twin boys. These two boys would differ greatly from one another, so much so as to father two distinct nations with their own unique ethnic characteristics. But perhaps the most surprising thing was the servile situation that would exist between the two boys. "The older shall serve the younger" (v. 23). When the boys were born, the second to exit the womb held the heel of the first, and even in birth Jacob was struggling with Esau for preeminence (v. 26).

Traditionally, a number of distinct privileges belonged to the firstborn son in a family. Called a birthright, this gave the oldest son, the firstborn, a special claim on the inheritance left by his father and the unique privilege of carrying on the family name to future generations. In the patriarchal family, this birthright had a special spiritual significance. The possessor of the birthright was the one who (1) became heir of the covenant of God, (2) received the promises given to Abraham, and (3) offered sacrifices for the family.

It is not uncommon in the Old Testament for God to select a son other than the physical firstborn to be the recipient of the firstborn privileges including the birthright. The three greatest men in the history of Israel, Abraham, Moses, and David, were all apparently the youngest sons of their fathers, having older brothers. Even Isaac should have realized that principle; he was chosen the heir of his father over Ishmael, who was fourteen years his senior. Isaac and Rebekah let the children separate them and become an issue of contention. "Isaac loved Esau . . . but Rebekah loved Jacob" (v. 28). Perhaps in fairness to Isaac, it should be noted that the prophecy that his younger son would receive the birthright was given to Rebekah, and there is no indication it was ever communicated to her husband.

The first was born covered with hair and appropriately named Esau, meaning "hairy or thick-haired." His brother was apparently not as dark or hairy and was named Jacob. Traditionally, evangelical writers have argued the name means "supplanter" and note Jacob was born grabbing at the heel of his brother, trying to supplant his brother. Additional support for this interpretation is found in Esau's linking of the name Jacob with his brother's actions of supplanting or deceiving him (27:36). Jewish commentators and some evangelicals disagree, arguing the interpretation of the name Jacob to mean supplanter is an expression of anti-Semitism, which began with a bitter brother and has continued to this day. This second group argue the name Jacob is based on the verbal root, "he leads," and suggest the meaning of his name is that "he is led by Jehovah" or "he follows Jehovah."

As the two boys matured in the same home, their distinctiveness became even more apparent. Esau was everything his father could have hoped for in a son. He quickly caught on to the secrets of hunting and became popular with his father by hunting and preparing one of Isaac's favorite meals, venison. Jacob, on the other hand, was more content to remain in the tents. While his brother went out to test his skill against whatever game may be in the fields surrounding the camp at Beer Lahai Roi, Jacob might be found involved in one of any number of activities necessary to the efficient maintenance of the camp.

The first hint as to the character of the two boys was revealed in an account of an incidental meeting and discussion about the birthright. As Esau returned from the field tired, he met Jacob busy boiling "pottage," which means to cook in a pot rather than roast over an open flame. The Scriptures describe the contents of the pot as "stew of lentils" (25:34) which was a pot of "red stew" (v. 30). When Esau, probably a meat eater, saw the bean soup, he longed for some. It would be a spiritually expensive bowl of soup. Jacob agreed Esau could have all he wanted in exchange for the birthright. The attitude of these two boys revealed their spiritual priorities. Most commentators agree Jacob probably had the right desire of faith in seeking the birthright, but his "devious" method revealed his character, supplanter or deceiver. In contrast, before agreeing to his brother's proposition, Esau remarked, "What profit shall this birthright be to me?" (v. 32) The grammar of the question demonstrates he expected or assumed the birthright was of no real value to him. The Scriptures evaluate this attitude, "Thus Esau despised his birthright" (v. 34). As a result, Esau became a type of the profane man (Heb. 12:16-17), while his brother Jacob was listed among the great men of faith (11:21).

This simple event formed the basis for the identification of the future descendants of Esau. Because of his willingness to give up his birthright for a bowl of red lentils, he was nicknamed Edom, which means red. The beans in the bowl were probably red. Later, his brother Jacob would also have his name changed from "supplanter" to Israel, meaning "Prince with God." In both cases, their descendants would identify with the changed named. In the years to come, the nations of Edom and Israel would engage in what would seem to be an ongoing war against each other.

A LAPSE OF FAITH *(Gen. 26:1-16)*

As one reads the account of the sale of the birthright, one wonders at Esau's extreme statement, "I am about to die" (Gen. 25:32). Certainly that is a melodramatic response to a poor day of hunting in the fields. But the poor day in the fields may not have been the first or even an isolated event. "There was a famine in the land" (26:1) which no doubt affected the size of wild herds long before affecting the state of the domesticated herds. While it is still doubtful Esau was at the point of physical death, the severity of this famine was such that Isaac had given thought to going to Egypt. He had already begun to move his camp from Beer Lahai Roi to Gerar when God intervened.

On this occasion, the Lord confirmed His covenant with Isaac. Though Isaac probably heard the voice of the Lord to his father Abraham on Mount Moriah, this is the first recorded appearance of Jehovah to Isaac in Scripture. Isaac was specifically commanded not to go to Egypt but rather to remain a sojourner in the land of promise. Also, Isaac was promised the unique presence of God and the blessings that were part of the covenant. The oath God had sworn to Abraham could now be claimed by Isaac. His descendants would be multiplied and include the source of blessing to all nations.

Like his father before him, Isaac obeyed the call of God on his life, but only in part. A comparison of the verb describing Isaac "dwelling" at Gerar (v. 6) and that commanding him to "sojourn" in the land (v. 3) reveals the limits of Isaac's obedience. The Hebrew verb *qur* translated "sojourn" is a qal imperative meaning "to dwell as a stranger." But the Hebrew verb *yashav* translated "he dwelt" is a qal imperfect based on the idea of sitting down or settling into a community. Some might argue God had permitted Isaac to "dwell" in the land, but the Hebrew verb *shachan* translated "dwell" in verse 2 is another verb expressing the idea of laying down and possessing. God commanded Isaac to possess the land by faith but live as a stranger, but Isaac was beginning to get comfortable enough with the world around him to sit down and become a part of their system.

It is not surprising, therefore, that like his father his faithless attitude was soon expressed in a faithless action. What is remarkable is the similarity of their sin. The weakness of the father became evident in the son. Both men lied about the identity of their wives so as to protect themselves from perceived danger. Both men were willing to allow their wives to be taken by a foreign ruler to preserve their lives. And in both cases, it would appear the men would not repent of their acts without the intervention of the Gentile they had wronged in the process. Only when confronted by Abimelech, the Philistine leader, after he had seen Isaac caressing his wife did Isaac admit his relation to his wife.

This Abimelech should not be confused with the Abimelech who had been involved in the similar sin of Abraham. Abimelech was a dynastic title carried on from generation to generation. The name means "my father the king" and may have been a form of addressing the supreme ruler of a Philistine city-state.

Despite the failure of Isaac, God honored His covenant. Isaac sowed and received a rich harvest of grain the very year his sin was exposed. The Lord also blessed him beyond the hundredfold harvest. His flocks and herds also grew abundantly and before long he was described as "great" and then "very great." He soon became the envy of the Philistines, who tried to provoke him by filling in his father's wells. Perhaps fearing for Isaac's security, should the anger of the Philistines erupt in a more violent attack, or that Isaac himself should respond with violence, Abimelech asked him to leave. "Go away from us; for you are much mightier than we" (26:16).

A SOJOURNER OF FAITH *(Gen. 26:17-35)*

Though Isaac left the city, he did not go very far away. He again pitched a tent, but initially there is no evidence of an altar. He dug wells, a necessity of life in a nomadic camp, but the names of his wells reveal the poverty of his spiritual life.

As the first well was completed, it was claimed by the herdsmen of Gerar and named Esek, which means "contention" (Gen. 26:20). A struggle was waged over the second well which Isaac dug also, and that well was named Sitnah, meaning "hatred" (v. 21). Though the wells were named in the context of conflict with the Philistines, they might also have described Isaac's own spiritual conflict. He was trying to have the best of both worlds. He was once again living in tents, a symbol of the faith of the patriarchs, but he was still "dwelling" (v. 17) rather than "sojourning." He had chosen to dwell in the Valley of Gerar where he could count on the defense of the city, rather than depending on the Lord to be his defense. Those who try to satisfy two worlds are torn apart inside with the contention that results from the enmity between the carnal and spiritual mind.

The digging of a third well apparently coincided with a change in Isaac. The well was named Rehoboth, meaning "enlargement," because there was no struggle associated with this well (v. 22). The naming of this well includes Isaac's first mention of the Lord since he began dwelling in Gerar. Also it is followed by his decision to return to the Promised Land, where he built an altar to the Lord. It was there that the Lord also appeared to Isaac to encourage him again with the promise of His presence and continued blessing. And it was there that Isaac stopped "dwelling" and "pitched his tent." Finally,

Isaac was leaving Gerar, the halting place. The journey was not only physical; it was a refreshing spiritual experience.

When Isaac had completed his separation from the world, he found the world was coming to him. Abimelech traveled to his camp with a friend named Ahuzzath and the chief captain of his army, Phicol. The Hebrew word *mere'ehu* translated "friends" (v. 26) was also the title of the counselor to a political leader. The visit to Isaac was apparently an official "state visit" in which Abimelech sought to establish a treaty with Isaac. Understandably, he was accompanied by his chief military and political advisors.

According to their testimony, the leaders of Gerar attributed the success of Isaac to the blessing of Jehovah. This does not mean they necessarily had adopted the worship of Jehovah themselves or even had a clear understanding of who Jehovah was. They probably used the term loosely to refer to the "god" of the camp of Isaac much as an unsaved person might make an occasional positive reference to "the good Lord" in an effort to demonstrate his respect for a Christian friend's personal religious beliefs. The Philistines were willing to believe the gods of other tribes would bless those tribes as their own gods would bless them.

Isaac agreed to some sort of treaty before he sent them away the next morning. It was later that day that water was struck by those digging a well. Isaac named it Shebah, meaning "oath or commitment." It was now known as Beersheba, the southern limit of the Promised Land. It was a reminder of his agreement with the leaders of Gerar, but it was more than that. It was also a reminder of his greater commitment to the Lord.

Still, all was not well in the household of Isaac. His failures as a father bore fruit in the rebellion of a son. Just as Isaac had married Rebekah at age forty, so his favored son Esau married. But Esau's choice of a wife was Judith, the daughter of a Hittite. Separation was supposed to characterize all members of the household of faith and that vow of separation was clearly violated by Esau in the taking of Judith as his wife. The Scriptures reveal something of the tremendous family tension which must have surrounded this rebellious act in the record of the "grief of mind" experienced by both Isaac and Rebekah (v. 35). But it was only the beginning of sorrows. Later this same son would add a daughter of Ishmael to his growing harem primarily to cause his parents added sorrow (28:8-9). But before that occurred, it was Jacob, their other son, who would take advantage of his father's failing eyesight and with the help of Rebekah, deceive him and create yet another family tension.

PERSPECTIVE

While there is a place for respecting and honoring the faith of our fathers, the Scriptures are more concerned with our experiencing a personal vital faith in God through our Lord Jesus Christ. Often those raised in godly Christian homes or in a church setting characterized by the clear systematic teaching of the Scriptures tend to adopt the faith of those around them and become "Christian" in their thinking and approach to life without ever becoming a Christian. Isaac appears to have mimicked the faith of his father Abraham until a personal crisis in his life brought him to a place where he entered into a personal relationship with God. It is imperative today that each of us examine ourselves to insure we are of the household of faith; i.e., have a personal and vital relationship with God and not depending on the faith of others in our church or family.

TWENTY

JACOB:
The Deceiver

(Genesis 27:1–35:29)

God had promised that Jacob would be heir even before his birth, but it was obvious that Isaac liked Esau better (Gen. 25:28). Esau was more inclined to do things fathers and sons enjoy doing together. On the other hand, Jacob was perfectly content to spend much of his time helping his mother with the sort of chores normally accomplished by women in the culture in which they lived. Just as Abraham argued with Sarah over their two sons (21:9ff), so Isaac and Rebekah fell into the trap of having a favorite one splitting family unity.

The selecting of favorites was tragic in the family of Isaac. It was a case of acting in opposition to the clearly revealed will of God. But Rebekah, rather than reasoning with her husband or allowing God to intervene directly, had another idea. In an effort to give preferential treatment to her son, she established a situation which would ultimately separate him from her for the rest of her life. But for Jacob, the journey from his mother was just the beginning of a very long journey back to a place called Bethel.

THE JOURNEY TO BETHEL *(Gen. 27:1–28:22)*
(1929 B.C.)

As Isaac grew older, he began experiencing some of the common physical problems many older people experience even today. Many people adapt to these problems and age gracefully, but that was not the response of Isaac. As he began his second century of life, Isaac was certain he was near death. His eyesight was failing him and he found himself confined to his sickbed. Perhaps as he thought of the death of his own father twenty-five years earlier, he saw similar symptoms of aging in his own life. What Isaac interpreted to be the end of his life was in reality a sickness from which he would recover. He would live eighty years longer. But as his son Esau began a family of his own while he lay sick in bed, he was certain the end was near. Isaac felt it was time to pass the family blessing to Esau. Whereas the birthright included the special privilege of carrying on the family name and had special spiritual significance, the blessing included the financial inheritance. Jacob had stolen the family name but would not get Esau's money.

The theft of a blessing (27:1-33)
Isaac had determined to bless his firstborn son Esau notwithstanding the problems the son had caused the family in his marriage. Esau was still his favorite son and preferred as a "real man" over his brother Jacob. Calling Esau to his bedside, Isaac asked him to go hunting and prepare a venison dish he enjoyed. It seems clear that Isaac viewed the meal as a sort of last meal to be followed by the bestowal of the family blessing and his imminent death.

But as the father and son talked, another became aware of the conversation. "Now Rebekah was listening when Isaac spoke to Esau, his son" (v. 5). As Esau went out on a hunting expedition, Rebekah herself had things to do and do quickly.

Rebekah called Jacob and told him of the plan of his father. It was then she added her own plan. Jacob was to go to the flock and find two of the finest kids, which she would prepare as Isaac's favorite dish. No doubt the sickness of Isaac had affected his taste to some extent and with the addition of the appropriate spices, it was doubtful he would be able to distinguish between venison and goat. Then Jacob would serve the meal to his father posing as his brother, and receive the family blessing himself.

It was at this point that Jacob expressed his doubts. He and his brother were so different he suspected he would be caught in the act. While Esau was hairy, Jacob was smooth. How could "fair" Jacob convince his father he was his "weather-beaten" brother?

Rebekah had an answer for that problem. She took the skins from the kids and sewed them for the hands and neck of Jacob. Though Esau's skin would be weather-beaten due to his constant exposure to the sun and dry wind, it is doubtful that it was as course as that of an untanned hide or that his hair was as thick as that of a goatskin. But if the sickness of Isaac was affecting his sight and taste, it was reasonable to assume his touch would also be affected. If Isaac would feel the goat hair, it would be enough to distinguish Esau from Jacob. Rebekah dressed Jacob in the finest clothes of Esau which she could find. Now he not only felt like Esau, he even smelled like him.

The plan of Rebekah worked to accomplish what she wanted. Isaac identified the voice of Jacob (v. 22), but was convinced not to trust his hearing. Thinking he was addressing his son Esau, Isaac blessed his son. But the deception did not last long. No sooner had Jacob left than Esau arrived with his venison. Yet as Isaac realized he had been deceived, he also recognized God wanted him to bless Jacob rather than Esau. "And indeed he shall be blessed," Isaac confessed (v. 33).

The threat of Esau (vv. 34-46)
If Isaac was prepared to accept the deceptive act of Jacob as effecting the will of God in blessing his sons, Esau certainly was not. His contempt for his brother was expressed in his slander of his brother. He claimed Jacob had been just as deceptive in "taking away" the birthright as he had in stealing the blessing. In his anger, he failed to recall his own despising of the birthright when he so willingly exchanged it for a bowl of his brother's soup.

When hurt feelings are harbored, they always turn to bitterness, which is often the root of violence. Before long Esau's contempt for Jacob turned to hatred; and as with the brothers Cain and Abel, Esau's hatred was willing to express itself in murder (v. 41). Out of respect for his father, he decided to wait until his father had died before enacting his plan. But as soon as the period of mourning for Isaac had passed, Esau planned to kill Jacob. No one expected Isaac still had another eighty years to live.

As Esau expressed his plan to others, word soon got back to Rebekah and she feared for the security of Jacob. Mothers tend to minimize the negative aspects of their children, but she sensed danger. Esau was merely venting steam, she concluded, and if given time, he would cool off. Still, there was an immediate danger if the two boys crossed paths before Esau calmed down. Rebekah had another plan. She would send Jacob off to live with her brother Laban for "a few days" (v. 44). Perhaps Jacob would find himself a wife in the process rather than bring another Canaanite into the family as Esau had done. Little did she realize how long "a few days" could be. By the time Jacob would return, she would be dead.

The confirmation of the covenant (28:1-9)

If Jacob was going to run from his brother, he was going to be given the privilege of running with his parents' blessing. After Rebekah shared her fears with Isaac that Jacob might marry a daughter of Heth, Isaac called Jacob to himself to command him not to marry a Canaanite but rather find a wife among the daughters of Laban. Confirming the blessing of the Abrahamic Covenant to Jacob, Isaac sent his son on his way to Paddan Aram with the blessing of *El Shaddai*.

When Esau learned his brother had been sent away to find a wife, he realized Jacob was escaping his reach. But by now Esau was so filled with bitterness that he had to express his anger. If he couldn't get Jacob, he would get his parents. Knowing how much they opposed their sons marrying Canaanites, Esau decided it was time to marry another wife. This time it was Mahalath, the daughter of Ishmael.

The promise of Bethel (vv. 10-22)

Jacob was running from Esau and running as fast as he could. It was more than fifty miles from Beersheba to the first recorded stop on his journey. The sun had set and he was tired. Jacob was not used to traveling across the mountainous terrain and knew he was tired enough to sleep on anything. Instead of a soft place to rest his head, he took several stones and arranged them as pillows. And as he rested his head on his pillow-stones, he slept. And as he slept, he dreamed.

He dreamed an unusual dream that night. He saw a ladder set up on earth which stretched up to the gate of heaven. And on the ladder he saw angels, some ascending, others descending. And in the midst of everything was the Lord Himself. And the Lord spoke directly to Jacob.

The Lord confirmed the promise that had been given to Abraham and Isaac before him, and now God was extending it to Jacob. He was the heir of the covenant. He had deceived his father for a blessing. Later his father had willingly blessed him as he sent him for a wife. But now the Lord God Himself confirmed to Jacob the terms of the Abrahamic Covenant. As Jacob awoke from his sleep, he knew he was on holy ground.

"Surely the Lord is in this place, and I did not know it," he concluded. The place where he had spent the night was Luz, but hereafter it was to be known as Bethel, which means "the house of God." Bethel would be more than a geographic point of reference in the life of Jacob. Bethel was the place where the Lord God became the Lord *my* God for Jacob (v. 21). It was the place where Jacob made a sincere commitment of his life to the Lord. That commitment was to be expressed by his willingness to tithe to the Lord. And it would be the place to which he would someday return in a more mature faith than that which led to the building of his first altar.

THE YEARS AT HARAN *(Gen. 29:1–30:43)*

Jacob's twenty years at Haran began with his arriving at the city well about the time his cousin Rachel came to water her father's sheep. Jacob was immediately attracted to her and uncovered the well so as to help her water the sheep. Then he kissed her and identified himself as "her father's relative" (Gen. 29:12). Technically, they were kissing cousins.

Rachel took the news to her father Laban who came to the

well to welcome him to their home in typical Eastern fashion. Laban agreed to house Jacob and pay him for his work. Jacob had been sent to find a wife, and already he had made his choice. He agreed to work for Laban seven years in exchange for the privilege of marrying Rachel. Though he may not have been accustomed to the kind of work given him, he was faithful in his labors. The seven years "seemed but a few days to him" because of the love he had for her" (v. 20). After seven years of work, it was time for Jacob to claim his bride. There was a marriage.

However, it was not until the morning following their wedding that Jacob realized he had met his match. The deceiver had been deceived. Laban had substituted brides on the wedding night and when Jacob woke up the next morning, he was lying next to Leah rather than her sister Rachel. Immediately he was off to register his complaint with Laban.

Laban saw nothing wrong in his actions and sought to justify himself by appealing to a local custom that the eldest daughter had to marry first. Laban agreed to give him Rachel also at the end of the week, probably seven days were spent with Leah as an official "honeymoon." A week later Jacob was given Rachel, but it would cost Jacob another seven years labor.

Polygamy is never endorsed in Scripture and without exception, every recorded instance is an account of domestic trial. Obviously Jacob favored Rachel over her older sister. "Leah's eyes were delicate, but Rachel was beautiful of form and appearance" (v. 17). But the Lord intervened in the reproductive systems of the two wives so that Leah bore children and Rachel was barren. Before long Leah found herself in a struggle with her sister for the love of her husband. Like many women since then, Leah thought she could resolve their domestic problems if only she could bear a son for her husband. Six sons later, she was still longing for the love of her husband (29:31-35; 30:15-20).

The success of Leah in bearing children prompted Rachel to insist on having children also. Because she was barren, Rachel offered Jacob her maid Bilhah. As Bilhah began bearing the sons of Jacob, Leah reentered the competition offering her husband her maid Zilpah. During the years in Haran, twelve children were fathered by Jacob, borne to these four women in his life.

THE FAMILY OF JACOB IN HARAN (1922 B.C.)			
Leah	**Zilpah**	**Rachel**	**Bilhah**
Reuben	Gad	Joseph	Dan
Simeon	Asher		Naphtali
Levi			
Judah			
Issachar			
Zebulun			
Dinah			

Jacob's years in Haran produced more than children. After paying for his wives, he continued working for Laban for wages to be paid in livestock. Though an agreement was struck, the wages were changed by Laban ten times in six years. Still, God blessed Jacob and the size of his herds and flocks grew. Jacob practiced a strange mixture of selective breeding and local superstition to insure his herds and flock would not only increase in number but also in the quality of the animals. Later he recognized God had overruled in his efforts to insure the desired results (31:9-12).

THE LONG ROAD BACK TO BETHEL
(Gen. 31:1–35:15) (1909 B.C.)

The call to Bethel (31:1-16)
The increased size of Jacob's herds and flocks was accompanied by a weakening in the herds and flocks of Laban. Eventually, Jacob overheard the grumbling of Laban's sons and realized his own relationship to Laban was deteriorating. Jacob only had one way to deal with a problem, so he prepared to run away. But to where would he run? God appeared to Jacob twice with the answer (vv. 3, 13). It was time to go back to Bethel.

The stolen idols (vv. 17-55)

Jacob and his family left secretly for Bethel so as not to risk a confrontation with Laban, but Jacob was not the only one with secrets. Unknown to anyone else, Rachel stole the family idols from her father and hid them in a saddlebag. According to documents found at Nuzi, the possession of the household gods of a father-in-law by a son-in-law was legally acceptable evidence that the son-in-law should be recognized as the principle heir of his father-in-law. This explains why Laban was so anxious to have them returned and Jacob was so incensed that he should be accused of having taken them. Jacob and his camp had traveled three days before Laban caught up with them in Mount Gilead.

It is not known what Laban's intention was outside of recovering his idols. He had with him enough of an army to cause serious harm to Jacob's family, but was warned by God the night before to be careful how he spoke to Jacob. The next day he searched for his idols without success (Rachel sat on them and was not suspected). Laban returned home, but not before heated words were exchanged on both sides. Before the two groups split up, a covenant of sorts was struck and a stone pillar erected and named Jegar Sahadutha by Laban, Galeed by Jacob. Called the Mizpah Benediction, both names mean "the heap of witness" in the mother tongues of the two men. In that context, an often quoted statement was made for the first time. "The Lord watch between you and me when we are absent one from another" (v. 49). Though this statement is often repeated today as a benediction, the original context of the statement was that of a threat or a curse. It might be paraphrased today similar to the expression, "God help the one who crosses this line first."

The meeting at Mahanaim (32:1-32)

Having dealt with the danger of Laban's chasing him from behind, Jacob soon heard about the coming of Esau, whom he thought might be chasing him from ahead. When Jacob came to a place he named Mahanaim, he saw a host of angels. The name *Mahanaim* means "double camp" and suggests he viewed himself as sharing the camp with angels. When he sent messengers ahead to greet Esau on his behalf, they returned with news that Esau was coming to meet him and was accompanied by some 400 men. It was enough to cause Jacob to forget about the angels. Once again he was distressed and afraid.

If there was one thing Jacob was good at, it was developing a scheme. On hearing of Esau's imminent arrival, he organized his entire camp in groups that would be offered to Esau, beginning with that which was least important to Jacob. If Esau had a destructive purpose in mind when the brothers were at last reunited, it was hoped he would begin destroying the first part of the camp, giving Jacob and his family time to escape. But Jacob was taking no chances. Before the night settled on the camp, he had made certain a river separated him from the rest of the camp, and he found himself alone.

But Jacob was not alone. God appeared to him. He found himself wrestling with a Man until daybreak. And it was no ordinary man with which Jacob was wrestling. It was another in a continuing series of Christophanies or preincarnate appearances of Christ in the Old Testament. When Jacob realized who he had met, he named the place Peniel meaning "the face of God."

Jacob was never the same after that meeting with God. The change was recognized when God changed his name to Israel meaning "Prince with God." And the change was evidenced in the walk of Jacob. During the conflict, the Angel of the Lord had touched the thigh of Jacob shrinking some sinew in the hollow of his thigh. Thereafter he walked with a limp. The physical injury became Jacob's unique expression of faith (Heb. 11:21).

The meeting with Esau (33:1-16)

As Jacob left Mahanaim, he was ready to meet his brother because he had met God. Jacob saw his approaching brother. Twenty years had changed both of them, and Esau was not coming for revenge, but reunion. He was happy to see his long departed brother and insisted he wanted no gift. But on the persistent urging of Jacob, Esau accepted what was offered. Further he insisted that Jacob and he travel together to Seir. Jacob convinced Esau to return and promised the family would make their way to his brother's home at a more leisurely pace.

Sidetracked to Shechem (33:17–34:31)

Despite the friendly greeting offered by Esau, Jacob was not convinced. Perhaps he remembered how angry Esau had been twenty years earlier and could not accept what must have seemed like a sudden change in attitude. Whatever the reason, Jacob changed direction on his journey and traveled to Succoth and then Shalem. In the course of his travels he built an altar and named it *El Elohe Israel,* meaning "God, the God of Israel." This was an act of faith on his part in that he worshiped God and claimed the promises associated with his changed name. But it was an act of faith which fell short of what it should have been. The altar should have been built in another place and called El Bethel, "the God of the house of God." Jacob did not go back to Bethel as he promised God.

Jacob's compromise in ownership was not without its own price to pay. During his stay in the region of Shechem, Dinah, his daughter, was raped by the prince of the region. Then the heathen prince wanted her for his bride. Her brothers responded to the news by developing a plan by which they could slaughter all the men of the city. First they convinced the men to voluntarily circumcise themselves in the city gate. Then, three days later when the men were in too much pain to even defend themselves, Simeon and Levi went through the city killing every man. The actions of his sons caused Jacob embarrassment and some concern. He was afraid of retaliation by those around in other cities. Once again Jacob was on the move.

Finally to Bethel (35:1-15)

"Then God said to Jacob, 'Arise, go up to Bethel, and dwell there; and make an altar there to God, who appeared to you when you fled from the face of Esau your brother" (v. 1). This time, Jacob was ready to obey.

Before Jacob could return to his Bethel, he had to get rid of the idols he knew had no rightful place in his house. No doubt by now he knew he was in possession of the idols of Laban, but other idols may also have found their way into the household of Jacob. Regardless of their nature, anything having to do with the worship of false gods was surrendered to Jacob, even jewelry, and was buried by him under the oak near Shechem. Only then did the family move to Bethel.

Years prior he had arrived alone, now he returned with his family. God had honored His promise and blessed him abundantly. This time he built an altar and named it not for the place, but the God who made the place what it was. He named it El Bethel, "the God of the house of God."

Bethel became a place of death and blessing. Deborah, Rebekah's nurse, died as they arrived and was buried under an oak named Allon Bachuth meaning "the oak of weeping." Jacob also died spiritually and became Israel. And once again God appeared to confirm His covenant with His people.

PERSPECTIVE

It has often been noted, "There is nothing so permanent as a temporary solution to a problem." That principle is certainly true when it comes to running from problems. Jacob ran from a problem with his brother "for a few days" and when he returned twenty years later, the problem was still enough to cause him to continue running. In the process of trying to escape from his troubles, he kept himself from Bethel, the place of intimate fellowship with God. The scared young man who had met God at Bethel as he ran from Esau was a lame old man with a mature family when he finally returned to the place of that meeting. In his wandering, his family was raised under the influence of the gods of his father-in-law Laban rather than that of the God of Bethel. Jacob should not have been surprised when his sons adopted a value system foreign to that of *El Bethel.* As one ponders the life of this patriarch, two questions ought to probe our conscience. First, what is it that is keeping us away from our own individual Bethel? Second, what is it costing our family?

TWENTY-ONE

JOSEPH:
The Dreamer

(Genesis 37:1–50:26)

Though the Book of Genesis records the lives of several great men, none is described more completely than Joseph. Because he was one of the youngest sons of Jacob, the first-born by Rachel, he was the favorite of his father. But favoritism creates unique problems. Joseph had ten older brothers who resented the special relationship that existed between Jacob and Joseph, and it resulted in their selling him into slavery. In the course of his life, Joseph was an honored son, a common slave, a trusted prisoner, and a leading minister in the government of the Egyptian Pharaoh.

Joseph was a man with a special ability to interpret dreams. This ability manifested itself early in life. But it also aggravated an already tense situation in his own family. His ability to interpret dreams was not only a factor in his being sold as a slave in Egypt, it was the primary factor in his eventual exaltation as the prime minister of that land. Throughout his widely varied experiences of life, Joseph discovered God was faithful in accomplishing His purpose in the world through Joseph. Despite the unfortunate experiences of his life, a key phrase from the mouth of Joseph explains, "God meant it for good" (50:20).

But perhaps the most unique feature of Joseph's life is the quality of his life itself. While the Bible never makes a claim-that Joseph was sinless, it is interesting to note it also never identifies sin in his life. This is one of the reasons that several commentators view him as a type of Christ. Ironically, several generations later, another "Joseph, son of Jacob" would be the adopted human father of Jesus.

JOSEPH AND HIS FAMILY IN CANAAN
(Gen. 37:1–38:30)

Joseph was the eleventh son of Jacob, probably born within a few years prior to the family's departure from Haran. Though little is known about the boy's earlier childhood, he was apparently his father's favorite son. This attraction was probably due in a large part to the preference of Jacob to Rachel, and Joseph's similarity in appearance to his mother. The Hebrew phrase *yepheh-tho'ar wipheh mare'eh* translated "handsome in form and appearance" (Gen. 39:6) describing the physical appearance of Joseph is only used of one other person in Genesis, his mother Rachel (cf. 29:17).

Because of the great love he had for this "son of his old age," Jacob made him a special garment. The Hebrew words *kethoneth passim* translated "a tunic of many colors" (Gen. 37:3) literally refers to a long-sleeved garment, or a coat of many pieces. The coat is significant as the garment of the heir. His brothers would have worn sleeveless garments as sleeves interfered with their responsibilities in the field. A long-sleeved garment signified Jacob was exempting Joseph from the usual work of a son in the field and also designated him as the heir of the household.

His brothers were understandably negative. In selecting Joseph for this honor, Jacob rejected his ten older sons who would generally have had a prior claim. There is some evidence the boys may have already been involved in the domestic dispute between the two principal wives in the family (cf. 30:14-16). The coat only aggravated the situation.

There was a third factor in the dispute between Joseph and his older brothers: it was the dreams of Joseph. Joseph had related to his family that the sun and moon (Jacob and Rachel) and the eleven stars (the brothers) would bow down to him.

The meaning of the dreams was unmistakable. Someday, the rest of the family would honor Joseph and bow down before him. To his brothers who already thought the worst of Joseph, his recounting the dreams must have impressed them as little more than an expression of his arrogance. It was not long before his brothers had a new nickname for their despised brother, "this dreamer" (37:19).

While the seventeen-year-old Joseph remained in the camp of his father, his brothers tended the flocks and herds. Because of the prosperity of their father, caring for the animals often meant herding them to another part of the country so as not to exhaust the area supply of feed and yet still fatten the herds and flocks. Normally, such a journey would be taken without much concern on the part of their father, but on at least one occasion, their father was concerned about their safety.

Two reasons have been suggested for Jacob's decision to send Joseph to check on his brothers at Shechem. There was a marked difference in the character of Joseph and his older brothers (cf. v. 2). Some commentators argue Jacob sent his son to learn of the evil deeds of the brothers. A more probable reason for sending Joseph was the father's concern for their safety. It was at Shechem two of Jacob's sons had killed all the men of the city prompting Jacob to flee the area (34:1-31). Knowing his sons had returned to the area would naturally cause him some degree of anxiety. This may also explain why the boys themselves moved on to Dothan after arriving in Shechem (37:14-17).

As Joseph found and approached the camp of his brothers, they realized they had an opportunity to deal with Joseph once and for all. They conspired to kill him. Had Reuben not spoken on Joseph's behalf, it is probable the others would have done it. Reuben convinced them to throw Joseph in a pit. He probably hoped to later rescue him. Twenty years later, the brothers were still haunted by the memories of Joseph's anguish as he was cast into the pit (42:21).

Christians are sometimes guilty of determining the will of God largely by extenuating circumstances, but sometimes circumstances can result in opportunities for evil men as well as saints. As the brothers ate their food, the opportunity of a lifetime arose. A caravan of Midianites (Ishmaelite merchants) passed by their camp on their way to Egypt. Seizing the opportunity, the brothers sold their brother as a slave for twenty pieces of silver. Based on mid-twentieth century exchange rates, the net profit to each brother in the sale was $1.28 U.S.

In selling their brother to the traders, they thought they were getting rid of Joseph once and for all. What they failed to understand at the time was that God was sending Joseph to Egypt to prepare for the family's migration in fulfillment of the covenant to Abraham. The family of Abraham was beginning to adopt some of the evil values of their neighbors, the Canaanites. This was about to become very evident in the life of Joseph's oldest brother, Judah (38:1-30). God moved the family out of Canaan so they would not degenerate and fall under the severest judgment of God. Also, God would allow the course of sin to run its natural course in the inhabitants of the land before He judged them (15:13-14).

Like their father Jacob before them, the brothers were masters of deceit. They kept Joseph's coat, staining it with the blood of an animal. Later they showed it to Jacob without explanation. Immediately Jacob jumped to the conclusion, "It is my son's tunic. A wild beast has devoured him. Without doubt Joseph is torn to pieces" (37:33). Jacob the deceiver was self-deceived. The family went immediately into mourning. Despite the efforts of others in the family, Jacob continued to mourn and did so for fifteen years (45:27). And as Jacob mourned the death of his son, Joseph was alive and being sold as a slave to a man named Potiphar, a leading officer of the Pharaoh.

JOSEPH AS A SLAVE IN EGYPT
(Gen. 39:1–41:40) (1892 B.C.)

Joseph was purchased in the slave market by Potiphar, "an officer of Pharaoh and captain of the guard" (Gen. 37:36). The name Potiphar means "belonging to the sun god" which was the most powerful of the gods of Egypt. Some commentators conclude Potiphar served his Pharaoh as personal bodyguard.

Though he was only a slave in Egypt, the Bible emphasizes the importance of Joseph even during this period of his life with the repeated observation, "the Lord was with Joseph" (39:2-3, 21, 23). Because of the presence of the Lord, Joseph was blessed and those around Joseph also shared in the blessing of the Lord. Translating the phrase "he was a successful man" (v. 2) in his early English translation of the Bible, Wycliffe wrote, "He was a luckie felowe." Wycliffe used a phrase that Christians would not use today, "luckie felowe" to describe not the rich man but the slave.

As Joseph proved himself faithful, his responsibilities were increased. Eventually he was assigned as the slave-manager of the household. In this position, he was responsible for carrying out his master's wishes and had liberty to act without consultation so long as he felt his actions were in the best interest of his master. And in this he also was to a greater degree in touch with other members of Potiphar's family.

His physical attractiveness was noticed by the wife of his master. As he was the property of her husband, Potiphar's wife no doubt felt at liberty to do as she pleased with what was little more than "living chattel." She approached Joseph inviting him to engage in sexual relations.

Joseph refused her appeal on two grounds. First, as renowned scholar W.H. Griffith Thomas puts it, "The perfect faith of the master called for the perfect faithfulness of the servant." Second, Joseph concluded that engaging in such a relationship as an affair with his master's wife would involve him in "great wickedness, and sin against God" (v. 9). It is interesting to note that in his refusal, Joseph spoke of his own responsibilities to his earthly master and God his heavenly Master. He did not accuse his temptress.

Potiphar's wife refused to accept Joseph's refusal as final. "She spoke to Joseph day by day" (v. 10), or as the Hebrew expression *yom yom* might be translated, "day after day." Despite her persistence, Joseph continued to refuse.

On one occasion, Joseph entered the house to work alone. Normally, a slave of Joseph's caliber would be accompanied by others, but for some unexplained reason, that was not the case on this occasion. Seizing her opportunity, Potiphar's wife grabbed Joseph and again made her appeal. In his effort to escape, Joseph left the room leaving his outer garment in her hands.

Perhaps humiliated by Joseph's repeated rejections, Potiphar's wife became vindictive. First, she accused Joseph of having tried to force her into a compromising position arguing her case before the men of the household. Later she told her husband the same story. "When his master heard the words which his wife spoke . . . his anger was aroused. Then Joseph's master took him and put him into the prison, a place where the king's prisoners were confined" (vv. 19-20).

Did Potiphar believe his wife? Opinions are divided on this question. Some believe Potiphar was angry when he heard his wife's charge and imprisoned his most trusted slave. Others argue Potiphar was angry with his wife and the publicity she had given the alleged attack which forced him to act. They argue that the decision to only imprison Joseph rather than kill him suggests Potiphar was not wholly convinced of his wife's innocence in the matter.

Even in prison, "the Lord was with Joseph" (v. 21). Despite the seriousness of the alleged crime, Joseph was given a remarkable degree of liberty by the jailer. As a keeper of other prisoners, Joseph was again elevated to an administrative role. And in this position, he would meet two men who would lead to greater changes in his life in the years to come.

The chief butler and baker of Pharaoh offended their king on one occasion and as a result were both cast into prison. While the nature of the offense is not identified, it may have been something as insignificant as serving their master an inferior meal, or they may have been charged with an attempt to poison Pharaoh. In prison, they were assigned to Joseph.

In the prison, each man dreamed a dream and was puzzled as he tried to discern the meaning of the dream. Noticing their sadness, Joseph asked about their problem. As the men recounted their dreams, Joseph interpreted them. In three days, the butler would be restored to his service to Pharaoh, but the baker would be executed. Three days later, on Pharaoh's birthday, Joseph's interpretations were confirmed. Despite the butler's promise to remember Joseph when he was restored to service, he forgot about Joseph.

Two years later circumstances in the palace caused the butler to remember Joseph, his former keeper in jail. The Pharaoh dreamed two dreams which his advisers could not interpret. In an effort to help, the butler recounted his experience in prison. Immediately, Pharaoh sent for Joseph.

When Joseph was commanded to appear before Pharaoh, he first shaved and changed his clothes. Facial hair was considered offensive to the Egyptians yet was common among Hebrews. Realizing his beard would hinder him in his ability to communicate with the king of Egypt, Joseph shaved it off. Only then did he appear before Pharaoh.

The interpretation of the dream of seven fat cows followed by seven skinny cows related to seven coming years of prosperity to be followed by seven years of famine. After warning Pharaoh as to what he could expect, Joseph offered his own suggestion as to a recommended course of action. Joseph told Pharaoh to store the excess in the years of prosperity and distribute it during the famine years. Further, Joseph suggested the king appoint a trusted servant to administer the project similar to a minister or secretary of agriculture in the cabinet of a democratic government.

Pharaoh was impressed with the advice of Joseph and his wisdom not only in discerning the dreams but suggesting a strategy by which Pharaoh should govern his national affairs during that time. He decided not only to follow Joseph's advice, but after consultation with other advisers, appointed Joseph to that high position. Joseph was given the ring of Pharaoh, a symbol of the king's authority and declared second only to Pharaoh in Egypt. This promotion was probably not so broad as to include anything outside of the responsibilities which typically would fall under a ministry or department of agriculture. But during the years of prosperity and famine, agriculture was a principal concern of Egypt, therefore Joseph was a principal minister in the government of Pharaoh. According to available Egyptian records, this promotion of Joseph appears to have been the second such case in the history of that Egyptian dynasty to that date.

JOSEPH AS A PRIME MINISTER IN EGYPT
(Gen. 41:41–45:28) (1885 B.C.)

Pharaoh named Joseph "Zaphnath-Paaneah," probably meaning "giver of bread." He was married to the daughter of an Egyptian priest and traveled throughout the land of Egypt preparing for the famine. Thirteen years had passed since he had first arrived in an Egyptian slave market, and now he was one of the most influential men of the land. During the years of plenty, God continued to bless Joseph. Two sons were born during those years and were named Manasseh meaning "forgetting" and Ephraim meaning "fruitful." As abundant harvests were realized in Egypt, Joseph built storehouses and filled them with the excess.

Just as Joseph had said, the seven years of plenty were followed by seven years of famine. An Egyptian hieroglyphic records a seven-year famine about that time but attributes the cause of the famine to the failure of the Nile to rise and overflow its banks in the spring. This may have been a local factor in the severity of the famine in Egypt, but the famine reached far beyond the banks of the Nile and the boundaries of Egypt. When people of other lands began feeling the effects of the famine and heard there was grain in Egypt, Joseph began receiving requests to purchase Egyptian grain. One of the most influential men in Egypt was rapidly becoming one of the most influential men in the world.

Among those desiring to purchase grain from Egypt was the family of his father Jacob. Joseph's ten older brothers were sent to Egypt with money to purchase the needed grains. What they did not realize as they bowed before a high Egyptian official to buy grain was that they were addressing their own brother.

Some people have objected to the historicity of the Joseph story, arguing brothers would certainly have recognized their own brother when they first met or before Joseph is said to have revealed himself. This presupposition overlooks several key factors. First, if Joseph resembled his mother as has already been suggested, and his mother was long dead by this time, it is not likely the brothers would notice any "family resemblance" when they met Joseph. Also, more than thirteen years had passed since they had sold their teenage brother to slave traders, and even if they had assumed he was still alive and in Egypt, they would certainly not have expected him to be such a prominent leader in the land. In addition to the change in his appearance due to age, Joseph was also clean shaven and probably looked more like an Egyptian than a Hebrew. His bearded brothers would not suspect the man who spoke to them in Egyptian was really a Hebrew.

As his brothers bowed before him, Joseph remembered the dream he had as a boy. He questioned his brothers indirectly to learn the state of his father's family. Accusing them of being spies, he imprisoned them for three days. At their release, he agreed to let nine return with grain for their families on the condition they returned with Benjamin. Simeon was held as a hostage in Egypt while the others were allowed to return. This is probably because more than thirteen years earlier, Simeon first suggested killing Joseph instead of putting him in the pit.

The treatment of Joseph toward his brothers caused them to remember their abuse of Joseph more than thirteen years earlier. This may have been the intent of Joseph in "trying" his brothers, but even if that was not his intent, he was learning of his brothers' change of heart without their realizing he understood what they were saying. The brothers were even more disturbed when on their way home they discovered their money in their sacks of grain.

Jacob was not at all pleased with the agreement to take Benjamin to Egypt. Only when the supplies of grain were exhausted did he consent out of need. Reuben promised to protect Benjamin, offering the lives of his two sons in exchange if he failed. Later Judah also offered to be surety for his brother. Finally, the remaining sons of Jacob were sent to Egypt to purchase grain with twice as much money as was needed and instructions to offer to pay for the grain they had already received. A gift of spices and nuts was also sent by Jacob to appease "the man."

When Joseph saw his brothers approaching, he ordered his chief servant to kill an animal and prepare a banquet for the sons of Jacob. The men tried to return the money but were told by a servant that was not necessary. According to their records, no money was missing. When the sons of Jacob learned they would lunch with Joseph (who was probably identified only by his Egyptian name), they prepared the gift they had brought for him. As Joseph arrived at noon, he was met by his brothers who bowed before him. Seeing Benjamin after so many years was too much for Joseph, and he left the room to weep. Then after washing his face, he returned to be with his brothers.

The banquet was conducted with due respect of the two distinct cultures represented. Egyptians were served at different tables than the Hebrews because it was beneath the dignity of an Egyptian to eat with a Hebrew. The sons of Jacob were seated and served with respect to their birth order which was of particular importance to the Hebrews. The general exception to the rule was Benjamin. Joseph saw to it that he received five times more food than his brothers.

The next morning, Joseph's brothers were off with their grain. Joseph had instructed again that their money be returned in the grain and had planted a silver divination cup in the bag belonging to Benjamin. There is some dispute as to how this cup was used by the Egyptians. Some believe gold coins were cast into the cup to call on the spirits. Others argue the cup was filled with water and taken out into sunlight where the effects of the sun on the water would be interpreted as a good or evil omen. The presence of this cup suggests Joseph was to some degree involved in the divination practices of Egypt. The cup may have been a gift from his father-in-law who was an Egyptian priest.

Shortly after the brothers left the city, Joseph sent out his servants to have the men arrested for stealing the cup. By the time the Egyptians had caught up with the brothers, they had discovered their returned money. Though they offered to return it, the Egyptians were only interested in finding the stolen cup. When it was found in Benjamin's bag, the others were free to leave but Benjamin was to return. Remembering their commitment to protect the life of Benjamin with their own, all the brothers returned to Egypt.

When they arrived back at the home of Joseph, Judah spoke on behalf of his brothers. He explained their family history arguing any harm to Benjamin would mean the death of their father. Judah offered to remain in Egypt as a slave to the Egyptian official if only the life of Benjamin be spared.

The time had come for Joseph to reveal himself to his brothers. The offer of Judah demonstrated a dramatic change in character on the part of the brothers. Commanding his servants to leave, Joseph was left alone with his brothers in an emotionally charged atmosphere. Then he made a simple statement, probably in Hebrew whereas to this point he would have spoken Egyptian. "I am Joseph; does my father still live?" (Gen. 45:3)

At first, his brothers were filled with fear, probably suspecting Joseph was about to take revenge on them. To convince them of his good intentions, he explained his plan further. The famine would last an additional five years and Joseph wanted his father's household to move to Egypt during that time where he could take care of them. He urged his brothers to convince their father to move the family and sent some of his own wagons to help. After an emotional reunion with his brothers, Joseph sent them on their way. When Pharaoh heard of Joseph's plan, he was pleased and urged Joseph to help his family make the move by supplying whatever was needed. But in Canaan, Jacob was not as easy to convince. Not until he saw the wagons of Joseph was he prepared to believe his son was even alive (v. 27). Then he was ready to go to Egypt.

JOSEPH AND HIS FAMILY IN EGYPT
(Gen. 46:1–50:26) (1876 B.C.)

Jacob and his family moved to the land of Egypt. The family of Jacob numbered seventy when he arrived in Egypt. This number includes Joseph and his sons who were already in Egypt.

Some critics have disputed the reliability of this number noting the LXX records the number as seventy-five (cf. Acts 7:14). The difference of five in the two texts appears to be the inclusion of five grandsons of Joseph identified in the LXX but not in the Masoretic text. The number seventy here is representative of the entire nation of Israel as the seventy names are representative of the whole world in Genesis 10. Because the brothers of Joseph were shepherds, an occupation considered barbaric to the Egyptians, Joseph arranged for them to live in Goshen. This region was not only cut off from other parts of Egypt, it also included abundant pastures for the herds and flocks.

The devastating effect of the famine destroyed the economy of Egypt and the rest of the world. With the failure of the economy, the men of Egypt agreed to purchase grain with their land. During the remaining years of the famine, Joseph was engaged in buying up the land of Egypt, except the temple lands, and setting up a new Egyptian economy based on state ownership of property and a 20 percent tax on the gross national product. During this time, the Pharaoh apparently directed the family of Jacob should be given the prime lands and be exempt from the national taxation system. As a result, Israel and his family prospered during an international economic crisis.

When Jacob became ill toward the end of his life, Joseph presented his sons to their grandfather. Jacob blessed them and in essence adopted them as his sons in the place of their father. In the process of blessing the sons of Joseph, Jacob followed a common pattern in the Book of Genesis in passing over the firstborn for a younger. Then he called his other sons to his deathbed and blessed them also. His address to them on that occasion was in part a prophetic revelation of things to come in Israel. It records the first use of the significant prophetic phrase "the last days" (49:1). His descriptions of his twelve sons are characterizations of the twelve tribes that make up the nation.

Jacob insisted he be buried in the cave of Machpelah (with Abraham and Isaac) and not in Egypt. His death marked a time of sorrow not only for his family but for the entire land of Egypt. According to the custom of Egyptian embalmers, the body of Jacob was prepared for burial. Scientists today are still unsure of the nature of the embalming practices which preserved the bodies of Pharaohs so remarkably well. The national period of mourning for Jacob is here identified as seventy days and is remarkable in light of the fact the period of mourning for a Pharaoh was only seventy-two days. It was not until then the sons of Jacob carried the body of their father to the family tomb. After an additional seven days of mourning as a family, Jacob was buried. Those who witnessed the proceedings at the tomb concluded it was a time of very great mourning for the Egyptians.

After the death of their father (1859 B.C.), the brothers of Joseph feared his attitude toward them might change. Still they did not understand Joseph's outlook on life. "But as for you, you meant evil against me; but God meant it for good, in order to bring about as it is this day, to save many people alive" (50:20). Being surrendered to the will of God for his life, Joseph could not be bitter against his brothers.

The time came when Joseph also died in Egypt, but not before he set his great-great-grandchildren on his knees. As he looked into the eyes of a future generation, he remembered God's promise to Abraham. Israel would not always remain in Egypt. Soon they would be going home. Joseph would die in Egypt, but he too wanted to be a part of that great migration north to the land of promise. Before he died, he had a request of the people he had saved from famine. "God will surely visit you, and you shall carry up my bones from here" (v. 25). And when he died in his hundred and tenth year of life, his body was placed in a coffin in Egypt where it waited for its journey home.

PERSPECTIVE

The life of Joseph illustrates the New Testament principle probably best expressed in the statement, "And we know that all things work together for good to those who love God, to those who are the called according to His purpose" (Rom.

8:28). That does not mean all things that happened to Joseph were good. Undoubtedly, many were evil. But God used all things, even the evil ones, to accomplish His good purpose in the life of Joseph. It was that intuitive knowledge of the goodness of God in accomplishing His objectives that helped Joseph endure the hardships of his life without becoming calloused and bitter. Though the problems of our life today may differ from those of Joseph, the principle is unchanging. God is still using all things, even the evil, to accomplish His good purpose in our lives.

TWENTY-TWO

JOB:
A Man Who Was Tested

(Job 1:1–42:17)

Job was a real man who lived in the land of Uz, an area in the Sinai peninsula, though some think it is located northeast of the land of Palestine. Job was a wealthy landowner (Job 1:3, 10), his sons were homeowners in the region (v. 4). His neighbors looked up to him (29:7-25), he was a ruler in the area (v. 7), and employed a large staff (1:14, 16-18). Job, a godly man like Abram and Melchizedek, was a patriarch who offered sacrifice for his family (v. 5). He was a righteous man in God's eyes (vv. 5, 8; 2:3; Ezek. 14:14-20; James 5:11).

While many of the problems of the Book of Job are beyond conclusive resolution, the timeless character of this book allows it to communicate an important message relevant to any and every age, "Why do the righteous suffer?" After a brief historical introduction, much of the remaining book is an attempt on the part of various persons to interpret the meaning of Job's suffering. In the years since its writing, Job has been read by many who themselves can experientially identify with suffering. In the New Testament, Job is referred to as a noble example of patient endurance (James 5:11).

THE TRIALS OF JOB *(Job 1:1–2:13)*
The early chapters of the Book of Job reveal all we know for certain concerning his background and experience. He was

both "blameless and upright, and one who feared God and shunned evil" (1:1). This does not mean he was exempt from sin, but rather that he had grown to a place of mature spirituality. Nor does this mean his maturity was complete, for the account of his experience in the book which bears his name demonstrates the maturing process was still continuing. What it does mean is that Job was a good man, a man whose moral absolutes were high, and a man who had a vital relationship with God whom he knew best as *El Shaddai,* the Almighty.

Perhaps it should not be surprising that the name of God, *El Shaddai,* Almighty, occurs most often in the context of his experience of suffering. This name of God is based on the Hebrew word *shad* meaning "breast" and though translated "Almighty," it really conveys the idea of all sufficiency. A Bible teacher once noted, "Sometimes you really can't say all I want is Jesus until all you have is Jesus." Perhaps that was the experience of Job. Though he worshiped God during the times of abundance in his life, it was during his time of great loss that God became "more than enough." It is only as one has need that one recognizes how sufficient God is to meet those needs.

Job was indeed a blessed man. His seven sons and three daughters remained a close family unit even after they had left the home of their parents. His flocks and herds were enormous. Seven thousand sheep, 3,000 camels, 1,000 oxen, 500 she-asses, and a massive staff to manage the affairs of the household were the physical evidence that Job was the undisputed greatest man in the area.

But Job's immense wealth did not alter his personal piety. He regularly prayed for his children and had committed them completely to God. He was not only concerned about their sin, but he was concerned with the possibility that his good children might have sinned in their hearts. His was not a religion that was restricted to externals only. He offered the burnt offering on behalf of his children, but his desire was that the symbol of complete consecration might be realized in the heart of each child.

There have never been many men of the caliber of Job. Normally, it does not take much for Satan, the accuser of the brethren, to find some glaring inconsistency in the life of one who claims to be committed to God. Satan had access to God's presence where he brought accusations against God's people. But with Job, Satan could not find anything worth mentioning in his periodic tirades of critical accusation before God. On one such occasion, God chose to put Satan on the spot. "Have you considered My servant Job, that there is none like him on the earth, a blameless and upright man, one who fears God and shuns evil?" God asked (1:8).

But the accuser is by nature an accuser, so Satan responded by accusing God of giving "special treatment" to Job. "Does Job fear God for nothing?" (v. 9) It was obvious as far as Satan was concerned, that God had blessed Job so Job worshiped God. The accuser charged that if God should ever allow the slightest negative thing to happen to Job, Job would boldly curse God to His face.

Satan had to be silenced. His accusations against Job were completely unfounded. God would prove just how unfounded they were. When Satan left the presence of God that day, he had permission to do anything short of physically harming Job. Satan was going to take advantage of that license. But in the midst of a most unusual arrangement between God and Satan, no one thought of warning Job.

The first assault of Satan (1:13-22)
The day was special for Job; it was the birthday of his oldest son (v. 4, "his appointed day"). It was a day for celebrating and remembering. He and his wife had not joined their children in the festivities. Perhaps together they remembered the day they became parents and all of the days since then that made them such proud parents. Though Job and his wife weren't at the party, they probably celebrated just the same.

It was then that the first servant arrived looking tired and deeply disturbed. The Sabeans had attacked the men while they were plowing, killing all the other servants and stealing the entire herd of oxen and she-asses. What a thing to learn on the birthday of his son. But as he listened to the report of the servant, he noticed another servant arriving looking just as tired and more deeply disturbed.

He too was the bearer of bad tidings. "The fire of God fell from heaven and burned up the sheep and the servants, and consumed them; and I alone have escaped to tell you!" (v. 16) But there was not time to clarify this "fire of God," for as the second servant completed his report, there was a third arriving and he looked much like the first two. It was becoming obvious he too bore bad news.

"The Chaldeans formed three bands, raided the camels and took them away, yes, and killed the servants with the edge of the sword; and I alone have escaped to tell you" (v. 17). But that was not all, for there was a fourth servant arriving and his countenance betrayed he too had a message Job would prefer not to hear.

This time it was his family. A tornado had destroyed his son's house. Everyone was there at the time. No one survived the devastation except the one who was now making the report.

Twenty-four hours earlier, Job was a giant success by anybody's standards. Now he had nothing but four servants who could remind him how much he had lost. He tore his clothes and shaved his head in mourning for his children. Then he worshiped the Lord. "The Lord gave, and the Lord has taken away; blessed be the name of the Lord" (v. 21).

The final assault of Satan (2:1-13)

Job was just too godly to be overlooked in heaven. It was not long before the accuser again stood before God ready to accuse Job. But God had a question for Satan first. "Have you considered My servant Job, that there is none like him on the earth, a blameless and upright man, one who fears God and shuns evil? And still he holds fast to his integrity, although you incited Me against him, to destroy him without cause" (v. 3).

But Satan was not yet willing to admit defeat. It was Job's health. Who wouldn't serve God if their health was as good as Job's. If Job ever faced any sort of serious illness, he would curse God to His face.

Again the Lord decided to prove Satan wrong. He was free

to do anything he wanted to Job short of taking his life. Again Satan left the assembly of angels with evil intentions. Again, no one bothered to warn Job.

Satan "struck Job with painful boils from the sole of his foot to the crown of his head" (v. 7). Commentators are divided over the exact nature of the illness of Job. Some argue it was elephantiasis, a disease caused by a parasitic roundworm and transmitted to humans by the mosquito. The disease is rarely found in persons under thirty and the common symptoms are usually not manifest unless the person has been repeatedly infected over a long period of time. The complex infections which accompany the disease together with the abnormal proliferation of connective tissues result in the legs becoming abnormally large like those of an elephant.

Job's symptoms are more characteristic of another disease transmitted to humans by sandflies known as *Leishmania tropica var major. Leishmania* cases have been reported in which the victim had as many as a hundred weeping boil-like lesions. They are initially purple in appearance but later are covered with dark, crusty scales. At this stage, they itch intensely which explains why Job would scrape himself with a broken piece of pottery (v. 8). In extreme cases, scarring and mutilation may be caused by the "boils" so as to make identification of a person difficult (cf. v. 12).

As this disease progresses, the nodules generally turn to ulcers and ooze with pus. It is common for flies to lay their eggs in the sores which later hatch into maggots. Job appears also to have experienced this symptom (7:5). The use of the Hebrew word *rimman,* translated worms (7:5; 24:20), suggests these were decomposition maggots.

On seeing what had become of her husband, Job's wife advised him, "Curse God and die!" (2:9) Job refused. "Shall we indeed accept good from God, and shall we not accept adversity?" (v. 10) But still Job's trial had not ended. He was soon to be "comforted" by three of his most esteemed friends. Each was certain he knew the reason why Job had experienced such a reversal, and out of the depths of their ignorance sought to convert Job to their way of thinking.

THE COUNSEL OF ELIPHAZ *(Job 4–5; 15; 22)*

Eliphaz first offered his advice that Job was suffering because he had done something wrong. Though Eliphaz addressed Job on three occasions, he crystallized his message in his first address in the words, "Remember now, who ever perished being innocent? Or where were the upright ever cut off?" (Job 4:7) He felt that since Job was having problems, it was because there was a problem with Job.

Eliphaz was something of a mystic. His entire philosophy of life was based on a solitary experience in which he was possessed by strange feelings and, according to his own testimony, "Then a spirit passed before my face; the hair of my body stood up" (v. 15). The message he reported hearing on that occasion formed the basis of his personal theology.

THE COUNSEL OF BILDAD *(Job 8; 18; 25)*

Bildad was the second of Job's three counselors to accept the challenge of trying to convince Job of his sin. His appeal to Job was to consider the wisdom of the ages and there find his answers to life. "For inquire, please, of the former age, and consider the things discovered by their fathers" (Job 8:8). His counsel was little more than a recitation of common philosophical themes declared by the great thinkers of every age. His discourses are littered with proverbs and pious platitudes which have little or no direct relation to the real problem of Job. Like the others, he was convinced Job was being judged for his previously hidden sins.

THE COUNSEL OF ZOPHAR *(Job 11; 20)*

Zophar only addressed Job twice rather than three times as did the other two, but he too had an opinion about the trial of Job. His advice was based on what he thought he knew about God, or at least his very legalistic interpretation of God and how God should relate to people. He felt that if only Job would repent of his sin, God would withdraw His judgment. Boldly Zophar challenged Job: "For thou hast said, my doctrine is pure, and I am clean in thine eyes. But, oh, that God would speak, and open His lips against you" (Job 11:5-6).

The counselors of Job were men who had preconceived ideas they refused to abandon even when it was more than obvious they were wrong. The dogmatic attitude of his counselors had only one effect, that of making Job even more dogmatic in his defense. There was a fifth person present witnessing the conversations of Job and his three friends. As he watched and listened, Elihu became increasingly incensed. He was angry because he suspected Job was more concerned with justifying "himself rather than God" (32:2). But he was also angry with the three counselors "because they had found no answer, and yet had condemned Job" (v. 3).

THE COUNSEL OF ELIHU *(Job 32:1–37:24)*
Elihu was the youngest of those present and had hoped to hear wisdom from his aged associates. He was sadly disappointed. Yet he sensed he had an answer and he found himself eager to share it. The Spirit of God had instructed him (Job 32:7-9) and now appeared to be moving him to speak (vv. 18-20). His message was simple. Job's problem could not be resolved until Job changed his focus. Job needed not to be problem conscious, but rather God conscious. He needed to remember two things. First, God is the source of his life. "The Spirit of God has made me, and the breath of the Almighty gives me life" (33:4). Secondly, "God is greater than man" (v. 12).

Much of Elihu's speech to Job is a reminder of both the attributes and consistent actions of God. Within that topic, a number of minor themes are mentioned or referred to by the young spokesman. But perhaps the most significant result of the counsel of Elihu was that when he stopped speaking, Job was ready to hear directly from God.

THE COUNSEL OF JEHOVAH *(Job 38:1–41:34)*
How many times in the course of his reversals and his subsequent conversations with his friends had Job wondered why? No one had ever told Job about the meetings of God and Satan, and all the time he hurt, Job could only imagine God was inflicting him directly. If Job had questions for God, it is most fitting that God also had some questions for Job. In the

course of His discourse to Job, God asked Job over seventy questions calling on him to explain some of the everyday wonders one so often takes for granted. The problem was, Job didn't have any answers for these comparatively simple problems either.

How did these unanswered questions help Job? In two ways. First, if Job could not explain the simple mysteries of the universe, how could he ever hope to resolve a problem so complex as that of human suffering? Job was forced to see how unreasonable he was in questioning God. But the unanswered questions also had a second effect. Though Job himself could not answer the simple questions, he was forced to realize who alone could sort out the answers. God had the simple answers, and the hard ones also.

PERSPECTIVE: DOUBLE REWARDS *(Job 42:1-17)*
Why do the righteous suffer? If you had asked Job when it was all over, he would have probably said, "You really don't need an answer. If you have a right relationship with *El Shaddai,* the God who is Enough, you will understand His purpose for your life." To the Lord Job confessed, "I have heard of You by the hearing of the ear, but now my eye sees You. Therefore I abhor myself, and repent in dust and ashes" (Job 42:5-6).

Then there was a new problem. God was angry with the poor counsel of Job's friends which had only added to the sorrow of His servant. To escape the consequences of the wrath of God, Eliphaz was instructed, "Take for yourselves seven bulls and seven rams, go to My servant Job, and offer up for yourselves a burnt offering; and My servant Job shall pray for you" (v. 8). They were to go to their sick friend and ask him to do something they had not thought of doing for him, pray on their behalf. It seems strange that these men should speak so piously so long yet not once answer the plea of their friend to pray on his behalf.

"And the Lord restored Job's losses when he prayed for his friends" (v. 10). Before the Lord was through, Job had ten more children and his original wealth was doubled. The servant of the Lord was more than compensated for his troubles.

TWENTY-THREE

MOSES:
The Gods of Egypt
(Exodus 1:1–14:31)

During the years Israel sojourned in Egypt, the family of seventy grew into a nation of thousands. While Joseph and his memory remained alive, the nation was the beneficiary of special political and economic benefits. But after the death of Joseph, the memory of what he had done for Egypt began to fade even as a new dynasty arose in Egypt.

THE PHARAOHS OF EGYPT

From about 1675–1570 B.C., Egypt was ruled by a Semitic group of people known as the Hyksos. Racially and linguistically, these rulers were very similar to the Hebrew people. Because of this it would be easy for an Egyptian to confuse the Hebrew and Hyksos much as a non-European might confuse an Italian with a Portuguese or a non-Asian might confuse people from Korea and Japan. While this may have worked to the advantage of the Hebrews during the reign of Hyksos, it also worked to their disadavantage in the anti-Semitic reaction of the Egyptians in the eighteenth dynasty which followed.

In 1570 B.C., Ahmose I ascended the throne of the new kingdom to begin the eighteenth dynasty. He reigned till his death in 1546 B.C. and was followed by Thutmosis I (1546–1518 B.C.) and Thutmosis II (1518–1504 B.C.). Each of these Pharaohs died without a son to succeed him. This seeming lack of stability within the new kingdom would no doubt only serve to magnify the concerns of the people over both real and perceived threats to their national security. The memory of the mighty Hyksos who had ruled the nation during the previous century could only cause the Egyptian people and their leaders to view the prosperous and growing nation of Israel living in the prime agricultural region of their land with suspicion. The kind of oppression described in the opening chapters of Exodus, including the enslaving of the people and planned genocide of male children, is the kind of reaction one might typically expect of a nation like Egypt under those circumstances.

Then a remarkable thing happened in the history of Egypt. A woman named Hatshepsut became the Pharaoh and ruled from 1504–1482 B.C. Under her leadership, the eighteenth dynasty solidified its control over the land. Egyptologists today view Hatshepsut as one of the most impressive Pharaohs of Egyptian history. Conservative scholars tend to identify Hatshepsut with the daughter of Pharaoh who found the baby Moses in the Nile River.

Hatshepsut was followed by Thutmosis III, the Pharaoh of oppression (1504–1450 B.C.). Actually, he was a co-Pharaoh with Hatshepsut for much of his reign but did not have liberty to act on his own as Pharaoh until the death of Hatshepsut. Then he acted with a vengeance to destroy every memory of Hatshepsut. He defaced the buildings she had built and scratched her name off any monuments. If the conservative chronology is correct, it was this Pharaoh who sought to destroy Moses for killing an Egyptian slave master and who must have died just prior to God calling Moses back to Egypt.

Thutmosis III was followed by Amenhotep II, the Pharaoh of the Exodus (1450–1415 B.C.). Though the Egyptian chronicles record many of the athletic exploits of this Pharaoh as a young man, it is strangely silent on any great accomplishments during his reign. He apparently fathered a son, but that son never became a Pharaoh. All of the mystery surrounding Amenhotep II fits in perfectly with the events which not only marked the historic birth of the nation Israel, but also must have resulted in a traumatic social and economic crisis for the Egyptians, the Exodus (1445 B.C.).

There is a tendency among liberal scholars to date the Exodus much later in Egyptian history, during the reign of Raamses II (1280–1220 B.C.). There are several problems with this view. First, it contradicts the only biblical hints of the date of the Exodus. Galatians 3:16-17; 1 Kings 6:1; and Judges 11:26 each allude to chronological details which suggest the date 1445 B.C. Further, at least two archeological discoveries are more harmonious with an earlier rather than a later date for the Exodus. The Stele of Mernaptah dated 1218 B.C. lists Israel as one of the peoples firmly established in the land of Palestine at that time. Also, the earlier date is more consistent with the apparent time of the destruction of Jericho.

PREPARATION FOR DELIVERANCE *(Ex. 1:7–2:25)*

As Egypt was adjusting to a new era in their long and rich history, God was preparing to bring His people out of that land into the land He had promised Abraham. The preparations began over eighty years before the actual Exodus took place. First God had to find midwives who would trust Him and defy the order of the Pharaoh that all male children be killed at birth. Then He had to find a couple who would preserve the life of their son when the order to drown male children was made, and who by faith would raise that son to have the values that would help him make the right choices during the later crises of his life. Gradually, everything came together. There were midwives like Shiphrah and Puah who believed it was more important to preserve life than to destroy babies on the order of an Egyptian Pharaoh. Then one day it happened. In the home of Amram and Jochebed, a son was born.

For a while, the parents could hide their child from the authorities. It was not easy, but it was necessary. If the authorities learned a son had been born to them, that son would have been drowned in the Nile River. So, while like other parents they longed to share their joy with others, to preserve the life of their son they abstained from telling others of his birth.

Soon it became impossible to keep the secret. When the child got hungry, he became vocal. His cry for food endangered his very existence. Still, the deepest longing of his parents was that his life be spared, regardless of the cost to them personally. Soon a plan was devised and initiated by the child's mother.

First, Jochebed wove a basket out of the long green leaves of the bulrushes growing in the river. Though the weave had been tight to make it watertight, she was not going to take any chances. The basket was sealed with slime and pitch to insure it would be waterproof. Then as she placed her son in the river, she instructed her daughter Miriam as to her plan.

Though only a Hebrew slave, Jochebed must have realized how her Egyptian masters viewed the Nile River. It was more than their source of fresh water. It was numbered among their gods. It was inevitable that an Egyptian finding the baby in the river would think of it as a gift of the river god. What Jochebed may not have realized was that the child would be found by none other than Pharaoh's daughter, thought to be Hatshepsut by many conservative scholars today.

The child was not only spared but named by Hatshepsut, Pharaoh's daughter. His new name was Moses which is related to a Hebrew verb meaning "to draw out of the water" (cf. Ex. 2:10). Miriam arranged to have the child's biological mother nurse the baby on the understanding that once the child was weaned, he would enter the courts of Pharaoh to be raised as the son of Pharaoh's daughter.

For forty years Moses lived in Egypt as the son of Pharaoh's daughter. As such he was no doubt the recipient of the finest education available in that day. According to the religious convictions of the Egyptians, he would be viewed as nothing less than one of the gods of Egypt. He was being trained to someday possibly assume the throne of Egypt. But there were factors not conducive to that ambition.

First, there was the political situation in Egypt itself. For a number of years, Hatshepsut reigned as co-regent with Thutmosis III. Though they were co-regents, Hatshepsut was the dominant force during their joint reign and Thutmosis did not seem to have much influence until the powerful female Pharaoh had died. He apparently resented Hatshepsut and there is abundant evidence he defaced many of the great monuments she had erected and sought to destroy her memory in Egypt. If Hatshepsut was the "Pharaoh's daughter" of Exodus as many conservative scholars suspect, her relationship with Moses became a political liability.

The second problem was Moses himself. Though he had been raised as an Egyptian in the court of Pharaoh, he was a Hebrew by birth. Perhaps it was the death of his protector Hatshepsut that forced him to reevaluate his spiritual priorities. Whatever the cause, the result was his turning from the Egyptian hierarchy of gods to faith in the God of Israel. He determined to do what he could for his own people (Heb. 11:24-26).

But in doing so, all things came to a head. In protecting a Hebrew slave, he killed an abusive Egyptian. Soon word was out and the new Pharaoh had all the justification he needed to demand the life of Moses (Ex. 2:15). It was time to make a fundamental decision. Perhaps the decision had already been made by Moses sometime before. "By faith he forsook Egypt, not fearing the wrath of the king; for he endured as seeing Him who is invisible" (Heb. 11:27).

For forty years Moses had been a principle member in the most powerful court of the world. For the next forty years he would be a nomadic shepherd wandering about the deserts of Arabia. He married and began raising a family. And he became the keeper of the flocks of his father-in-law Jethro, the priest of Midian.

THE CALL TO MOSES *(Ex. 3:1–4:28)*
It was toward the end of that second forty-year period that Moses notes an unusual sight in the desert. While leading his father-in-law's sheep in a mountain range named Horeb, near Mount Sinai, he noted a bush burning. The unusual thing about this bush is that though it burned, that is, there was a flame, the bush itself was not consumed by the flame. Recognizing what he saw as out of the ordinary, Moses determined to get a

better look at the bush. It was then that a second unusual thing happened at the site. A voice began to speak to Moses out of the burning bush.

"And when forty years had passed, an Angel of the Lord appeared to him in a flame of fire in a bush in the wilderness of Mount Sinai" (Acts 7:30). That Angel was nothing less than a Christophany, a preincarnate appearance of Christ in the Old Testament. There at the bush, God called Moses to lead Israel out of the land of Egypt which was their land of bondage.

Moses knew enough about Egypt to know something of the immensity of the task he was being assigned. As a result, he was hesitant to accept the task. He began to object, giving God various reasons why he was not the one for the task. In the process of his objections, an interesting thing happened. As long as Moses offered God what might be considered good reasons for not accepting this call, God resolved Moses' problems. But the fifth objection of Moses had its basis only in a rebellious will, and "the anger of the Lord was kindled against Moses" (Ex. 4:14). In His anger, God agreed to make Aaron Moses' spokesman. It was apparently not part of God's original plan and for the next forty years, there would be many times Moses might have wished his brother had never been given such a degree of influence.

THE EXCUSES OF MOSES

1 "Who am I that I should go?" (I'm not fit.) *(Ex. 3:11)*
2 "What shall I say to them?" (I don't know what to say.) *(Ex. 3:13)*
3 "They will not believe me" (I will fail.) *(Ex. 4:1)*.
4 "I am slow of speech and slow of tongue" (I am not able.) *(Ex. 4:10)*.
5 "Send . . . whom ever else You may send" (Send someone in my place.) *(Ex. 4:13)*.

"Then Moses took his wife and his son and set them on a donkey, and he returned to the land of Egypt. And Moses took the rod of God in his hand" (v. 20). He had left Egypt a member of the court, but was returning as a shepherd which was an abomination in the minds of the Egyptians. He had been trained to hold the scepter of Egypt, but was returning with the rod of God in his hand. He was returning to a land in which the gods were numerous and thought to be in control of every aspect of Egyptian life. But he was returning as the spokesman for the God of the Hebrew slaves, the God who declared Himself to be the only true God. It was inevitable that the future would demand a conflict between Moses and the gods of Egypt.

THE TEN PLAGUES AND DELIVERANCE
(Ex. 7:1–13:22)

Moses did as God had commanded him. As the spokesman for Israel's God, he called on the new Pharaoh, probably Amenhotep II, to let the Hebrew slaves go that they might worship God in the wilderness. Ironically, it was Pharaoh who made the actual declaration of war which was to begin the most unusual conflict of the ages. "And Pharaoh said, 'Who is the Lord, that I should obey His voice to let Israel go? I do not know the Lord, nor will I let Israel go' " (Ex. 5:2). In the weeks to follow, Pharaoh would be introduced to the Lord in a most dramatic way. Just as Pharaoh had challenged the Lord's authority, so now the Lord would challenge the authority of Pharaoh's gods. It has been noted by many commentators that the plagues of Egypt were a phenomenon which challenged many of the principal gods of Egypt and proved them unable to resist the power of the true God.

Only after the death of the firstborn of Egypt would Pharaoh consent to let the Hebrews leave the land of Egypt. Egyptologists have discovered evidence that Amenhotep II had a son, but for some reason not explained in the Egyptian records, that son never sat on his father's throne. The reason is given in the biblical account of the origin of the Passover feast of the Jews.

On the eve of their last night in Egypt, Israel was instructed to prepare a unique sacrifice. First, they were to select a

MOSES AND THE GODS OF EGYPT (1446 B.C.)

Plague	Phenomena	Egyptian god
1	Water to blood	Osiris/Nile River
2	Frogs	Hekt
3	Lice	Seb
4	Flies	Kephera
5	Cattle	Apis and Hathor
6	Boils	Typhon
7	Hail	Shu
8	Locusts	Serapis
9	Darkness	Ra
10	Death	Ptah

yearling male out of the flocks which was without blemish. Then they were to kill the animal and save its blood. That blood was to be applied to the doorposts of the home, and the family would roast and eat the sacrifice in a meal with bitter herbs and unleavened bread. The key to the event was the applying of the blood to the doorposts of the home. God promised, "Now the blood shall be a sign for you on the houses where you are. And when I see the blood, I will pass over you, when I strike the land of Egypt" (12:13). Later that evening, the firstborn of Egypt were slain, but in the homes of the Hebrews which were under the blood, no one was harmed.

The death of the firstborn sons of Egypt had a significant impact on the Pharaoh and the Egyptians. Before dawn Pharaoh had called Moses and Aaron to order the Hebrews out of the land. The people themselves not only urged the Hebrews to leave, but gave them gold and silver and fine clothing as they left. So began the great migration of the Jews out of Egypt known as the Exodus. "And Moses took the bones of Joseph with him, for he had placed the children of Israel under solemn oath, saying, 'God will surely visit you, and you shall carry up my bones from here with you' " (13:19).

"Then it came to pass, when Pharaoh had let the people go,

that God did not lead them by way of the land of the Philistines, although that was near; for God said, 'Lest perhaps the people change their minds when they see war, and return to Egypt.' So God led the people around by way of the wilderness of the Red Sea. And the Children of Israel went up . . . out of the land of Egypt. And the Lord went before them by day in a pillar of a cloud to lead the way, and by night in a pillar of fire to give them light, so as to go by day and night. He did not take away the pillar of the cloud by day or the pillar of fire by night from before the people" (vv. 17-18, 21-22).

The Scriptures do not indicate how long it took Israel to get to the banks of the Red Sea, but when Pharaoh realized where they were, he had a change of heart. He determined to capture the slaves in the wilderness and bring them back to Egypt. It is unlikely that the Egyptian army would begin such a conquest before the period of mourning for their sons had ended. For a Pharaoh, the period of mourning was seventy-two days.

Pharaoh's army of 600 chariots chased the 600,000 Hebrew families to the banks of the Red Sea. When the people saw the dust of the chariots in the distance, they knew they were in trouble. But rather than trust God, initially they turned on Moses and blamed him for their problem. Moses responded by urging the people, "Do not be afraid. Stand still, and see the salvation of the Lord, which He will accomplish for you today. For the Egyptians whom you see today, you shall see again no more forever" (14:13). Then one of the greatest miracles of all time took place. Of all the miracles in the Old Testament, this is referred to more than any other.

"Then Moses stretched out his hand over the sea; and the Lord caused the sea to go back by a strong east wind all that night, and made the sea into dry land, and the waters were divided. So the children of Israel went into the midst of the sea on the dry ground, and the waters were a wall to them on their right hand and on their left" (vv. 21-22). "By faith they passed through the Red Sea as by dry land, whereas the Egyptians, attempting to do so, were drowned" (Heb. 11:29).

PERSPECTIVE: TWOFOLD DELIVERANCE

Israel's deliverance from Egypt was twofold, by blood and by water. Typically, their experience has application to the Christian life. Just as Israel began their national existence "under the blood," so the Christian life begins "under the blood" of Jesus who is the Lamb of God. The next step of the nation in their journey to the blessing of God is described by the Apostle Paul in the statement, "All were baptized into Moses in the cloud and in the sea" (1 Cor. 10:2). So too, the first step of the obedient Christian should be to identify with the Lord in baptism. Then as Israel traveled in the wilderness, God gave them manna to eat and water to drink. In the New Testament, Jesus is both the bread and water of life, and offers Himself to all who would desire a deeper communion with Him.

TWENTY-FOUR

AARON:
The Priesthood and Tabernacle

(Exodus 15:1–40:38; Leviticus; Psalm 90)

The victory over Egypt at the Red Sea called for a time of celebration. There was singing and dancing in the camp as they sang the song of the redeemed. Many of the women followed the lead of Miriam and played a musical instrument known as the timbrel as they sang. "I will sing to the Lord, for He has triumphed gloriously! The horse and its rider He has thrown into the sea" (Ex. 15:1, cf. v. 21). Even as they celebrated this victory over the Egyptians, they knew God would use it to shock the nations of Canaan into a depressive fear. But how soon would they forget the great and mighty things which God could and would do on their behalf. Three days later, they would again be murmuring against Moses because they believed God was failing to provide for them.

It was a three-day journey from the east bank of the Red Sea to the tiny oasis of Marah, and in those three days the people were unable to find water. When they came to Marah, they were eager to drink the water, but it was bitter and could not be drunk. The people named the oasis Marah which means "bitter" in the Hebrew language. They responded in a way which would become typical in the days to come, they complained.

When Moses prayed, God responded by directing Moses to a tree. When the tree was cast into the water, it sweetened the water so the people could drink. Though the tree is not specifically identified as to its kind in Scripture, many commentators see it as a type of the cross which in the life of the Christian removes the bitterness out of otherwise undesirable experiences (cf. Rom. 15:3-4; Gal. 3:13).

It was also at Marah where God revealed Himself to His people with a new name, *Jehovah Rapha*. This title of God is translated "The Lord who heals you" (Ex. 15:26). While the title itself seems to emphasize the healing power of God, the context in which the title is given emphasizes the preventative aspect of healing. "If you diligently heed the voice of the Lord your God and do what is right in His sight, give ear to His commandments and keep all His statutes, I will put none of these diseases on you, which I have brought on the Egyptians. For I am the Lord who heals you" (v. 26). Several writers have commented on the medical benefits of following the instructions of the Law governing various aspects of Israel's lifestyle in the wilderness.

The next stop in the wilderness journey of Israel was the oasis of Elim. At this oasis, there were twelve wells, one for each of the tribes. There were also seventy palm trees under which Israel set their camp (v. 27). In tropical regions where palm trees flourish, the people of those regions have learned they can live exclusively off the palm tree. One variety which grows in India has over 800 products which the natives of that region use. The presence of the palm trees at Elim was a demonstration of God's abundant provision for His people. The number seventy which was the number of the elders of Israel is often used in Scripture to signify the ideas of totality or completeness. Typically, Elim represents God's complete and abundant provision for His people after the bitter waters of Marah. Because of this significance, many rehabilitation-type ministries have incorporated the name Elim into their name.

But Elim was only a rest in the journey to Sinai. As they traveled out from that oasis, God provided food and water for His redeemed Israel. When Israel woke one morning, they found the ground covered with "a small round substance, as fine frost" (16:14). Not knowing what it was, they called it "manna" which is literally a transliteration of two Hebrew words meaning, "What is it?" Moses explained it was the bread God was providing for the people. "It was like coriander white seed, and the taste of it was like wafers made with honey" (v. 31). The coriander plant grows wild in the regions of Egypt and Palestine and produces small but spicy grayish-white seeds. For the next forty years, the people would eat an omer a day as God provided this bread from heaven (v. 18). An omer was a volume measurement equal to about 11.6 cups; therefore, a six-quart basket of manna would be slightly more than the daily allotment of manna for two people.

God also provided water for Israel out of a most unusual source. When the people camped at Rephidim and called to Moses to provide water, Moses was instructed by God to strike the rock in Horeb with his rod. When Moses obeyed, water came from the rock to meet Israel's need. In the New Testament, the Apostle Paul indicates the real significance of that rock in the statement, "and that Rock was Christ" (1 Cor. 10:4).

Water is a valuable natural resource in the Near East, so it is not surprising that the appearance of a river of water out of the rock should be the occasion of a military conflict between the Jews and their enemies. "Now Amalek came and fought with Israel in Rephidim" (Ex. 17:8). Amalek became the first of the many nations to attack the newborn nation of Israel.

By way of typical application, Amalek is representative of the flesh or old nature which is in constant conflict with the promptings of the Holy Spirit in the Christian life. Just as Amalek is throughout Scripture pictured as seeking to hinder the forward movement and prosperity of Israel, so "the carnal mind is enmity against God" (Rom. 8:7). When Amalek attacked Israel, the attack was from the rear hitting the weakest side of the nation (cf. Deut. 25:17-18). Similarily, the flesh seems to attack in our spiritual lives at our weakest moments. Because of the nature of Amalek, God warned there would be constant battle between Israel and Amalek from generation to generation (Ex. 17:16). Later, King Saul was commissioned "to utterly destroy" Amalek (1 Sam. 15:1-3). By way of compromise, Saul allowed Agag, the king of Amalek to remain alive. Ironically, it was an Amalekite who later claimed credit for the death of Saul in his last battle (2 Sam. 1:6-10).

It was Moses and Joshua who defeated Amalek in battle and revealed the key to winning the spiritual battle over the flesh. Though Joshua fought with great skill and energy, it was the arms of Moses lifted up in prayer that governed the outcome of the battle (Ex. 17:11). The victory was secured when Aaron and Hur held up the arms of Moses long enough for Joshua to win the war. Aaron was the priest of Israel. Moses was the prophet in Israel. Hur was the leader of the tribe of Judah, the royal tribe of Israel. Together in prayer, they are typical of the intercession of Jesus Christ, our Prophet, Priest, and King. Recognizing the true source of the military victory at Rephidim, "Moses built an altar and called its name, The Lord Is My Banner" (v. 15).

THE GIVING OF THE LAW *(Ex. 19:1–24:18)*

It took Israel three months to arrive at the first major stop in their journey to Canaan, Mount Sinai. Sinai would be the scene of great spiritual heights as Israel became the first and only nation in the history of mankind to hear the audible voice of God. But it would also be the place of great failure, the place where they would choose to worship the gods of Egypt, despite having heard the voice of God. And it would be the place where God would again establish one of His unconditional covenants and establish a new approach in His dealings with mankind in general and Israel in particular. It was at Mount Sinai that God instituted what theologians have come to call "the dispensation of Law."

At Mount Sinai, Israel saw the glory of God on the mountain in the form of a thick fog or smoke on the mountain. From the midst of the smoke, God spoke to His people in an audible voice. He reminded the people He was "the Lord your God, who brought you out of the land of Egypt, out of the house of bondage" (Ex. 20:2). On the basis of that introduction, He gave them a summary of the Law under which He required Israel to live as a redeemed nation. It was never God's intention to make the Law the means of salvation, but rather a standard of living for those who were already redeemed. In His Sermon on the Mount, Jesus made it clear that the statement of the Law in the form of the ten words or Ten Commandments as they have come to be known was more than merely a prohibition against certain isolated acts or practices. The commands applied also to the less than wholesome attitudes which when developed to full fruition result in the prohibited acts.

THE TEN COMMANDMENTS

1	"No other gods"	polytheism
2	"No graven images"	idolatry
3	"Name in vain"	profanity
4	"Sabbath"	secularism
5	"Honor parents"	rebellion
6	"Not kill"	murder
7	"No adultery"	sexual rebellion
8	"Not steal"	theft
9	"False witness"	lying
10	"Not covet"	materialism

The giving of the Law to Israel came in three forms. First, the commandments emphasized the righteous will of God in a broad summary statement. This was followed by the judgments or ordinances which governed the social life of Israel and are collected in what came to be described as the Book of the Covenant (21:1–23:33; cf. 24:7). The third expression of the Law took the form of the ordinances which governed the religious life of Israel. Most of these instructions were given to Moses in the plan of the tabernacle or in the Book of Leviticus after the tabernacle was established.

The Book of the Covenant was a practical expression of what the Law of God meant in the lifestyle of the average Hebrew man or woman. It functioned much as precedent functions in our present legal system. When a dispute had to be resolved that did not seem to be the classic textbook case, the Book of the Covenant could be consulted by the judge to discern how the matter should be resolved. It included prohibitions against occult practices and sexually deviant behavior, but it also included much more. No one would dispute it was wrong to commit an act of premeditated murder, but what if in the midst of a struggle a pregnant wife is accidentally hurt and a baby is born prematurely and dies? (Ex. 21:22-25) It was wrong to steal another man's grain, but what if while burning out an unwanted thornbush, part of the fire spread accidently and damaged your neighbor's crop? (22:6) It was agreed that mob violence was wrong, but what about the one who incites the mob, if he himself is not actually involved in the subsequent violent act? (23:2) In each of the above mentioned cases, the Book of the Covenant had specific instructions as to how the case should be decided.

The third expression of the Law, the ordinances which governed the religious practices of Israel was the Law which Jesus came to fulfill. While they were specific instructions to be followed literally by the Jews who lived under Law and may be reinstituted as part of the memorial temple and sacrifice system during the dispensation of the fullness of times or 1,000-year kingdom or Millennium as it is sometimes called; the primary meaning of this part of the Law for us today is found in its typical significance. The details of this aspect of the Law are a rich picture not only of Christ but also the Christian life. In interpreting the typical significance of the Law, a good safe general rule of thumb is to only accept types which are clearly endorsed in Scripture and never rest a belief or practice solely on your interpretation of the type. If the type is valid, it will illustrate a truth more clearly taught in another statement probably to be found in the New Testament.

THE TABERNACLE *(Ex. 25:1–40:38; Ps. 90)*
(1445 B.C.)

The fullest type in Scripture is that of the tabernacle. This was the dwelling place of God in the camp of Israel. While Moses was on Mount Sinai getting the stone tablets of the Law written by the finger of God, he also received the pattern of the tabernacle. The New Testament Epistle to the Hebrews makes it abundantly clear that the pattern of the tabernacle was a picture of spiritual truth concerning Jesus Christ. The Gospel of John also emphasizes this fact in the statement of the Incarnation: "And the Word became flesh and dwelt [literally "tabernacled"] among us" (John 1:14). The following chart lists many of the more notable aspects of the tabernacle and how they relate to Christ.

TWENTY-FOUR TYPES OF CHRIST IN THE TABERNACLE

Items in the Tabernacle	Applied to Christ
The gate *(Ex. 27:16)*	The way *(John 14:6)*
The bronze altar *(Ex. 27:1-8)*	An altar *(Heb. 13:10)*
The laver *(Ex. 30:18-20; 38:8)*	Jesus' words *(John 15:3)*
Five pillars *(Ex. 26:37)*	Five names *(Isa. 9:6)*
Gold-plated boards and bars *(Ex. 26:15-30)*	Humanity and deity of Jesus *(John 1:14)*
Blue, purple & scarlet linens *(Ex. 26:1-6)*	Heavenly origin *(John 7:29)*, Royal title *(Matt. 1:1)*, and shed blood *(Heb. 9:14)*
The door *(Ex. 26:36-37)*	The door *(John 10:7, 9)*
Table of showbread *(Ex. 25:23-30)*	Bread of God *(John 6:33-35)*
Altar of incense *(Ex. 30:1-10)*	High Priestly Prayer *(John 17)*
Golden candlestick *(Ex. 25:31-40)*	True Light *(John 1:4ff; 3:19-21; 8:12; 9:5; 12:46)*
Inner veil *(Ex. 26:31-33)*	Body of Christ *(Heb. 10:20)*
Ark of the covenant *(Ex. 25:10-22)*	Humanity and deity of Jesus *(John 1:14)*
The mercy seat *(Ex. 37:6-9)*	The propitiation *(1 John 2:2)*

The Law *(1 Kings 8:9)*	The fulfillment *(Matt. 5:17-20)*
Aaron's rod *(Heb. 9:4)*	Resurrection *(Matt. 28:6)*
Jar of manna *(Heb. 9:4)*	Hidden manna *(Rev. 2:17)*
Priest *(Ex. 28:1-2)*	High Priest *(Heb. 8:1)*
Priest's robe *(Ex. 28:31-35)*	Righteousness *(1 Cor. 1:30)*
Ephod *(Ex. 28:6-14)*	Sin bearer *(1 Peter 2:24)*
Urim & thummin *(Ex. 28:30)*	Perfection *(Heb. 4:15)*
Holy crown *(Ex. 28:36-38)*	Crowns *(Rev. 19:12)*
Breastplate *(Ex. 28:15-29)*	Righteousness *(Eph. 6:14)*
Shekinah glory *(Ex. 40:34-38)*	Glory of Christ *(James 2:1)*
Sacrifice *(Lev. 1–7)*	Lamb of God *(John 1:29, 36)*

While Moses and Joshua ascended the mountain to get the stone tablets of the Law and the pattern of the tabernacle, the camp was left in the control of Aaron and Hur. But forty days seemed a long time to the Hebrews at the base of the mountain and they began to wonder if Moses had left them or had been harmed in some way. Their reaction to the delay of Moses was to return to the ways of Egypt. They convinced Aaron to make them a golden calf and developed a new religion around their new idol (Ex. 32:1-6).

That the Israelites could apostasize just over a month from having heard the audible voice of God stirred up the wrath of God. The Lord told Moses to return to the camp adding, "Now therefore, let Me alone, that My wrath may burn hot against them and I may consume them. And I will make of you a great nation" (v. 10). This was not an idle threat, as the Scripture later affirms: "Therefore He said that He would destroy them, had not Moses His chosen one stood before Him in the breach, to turn away His wrath, lest He destroy them" (Ps. 106:23). But Moses interceded for the people and God preserved Israel from destruction.

But the sin of Israel was not without its consequences. In

his anger, Moses smashed the stone tablets of the Law written by the finger of God (Ex. 32:19). About 3,000 men who refused to identify the Lord as their God after worshiping the golden calf were killed by the Levites (vv. 27-28). Moses had to call the nation to repentance and return up the mountain himself to get a second copy of the Law before the tabernacle could be built.

The people demonstrated that their repentance was genuine by their response when called on to give gifts for the building of the tabernacle. Moses asked them to give some of the spoils they had taken from Egypt that a suitable worship center could be built for the nation. After the appeal, "then everyone came whose heart was stirred, and everyone whose spirit was willing, and they brought the Lord's offering for the work of the tabernacle of meeting, for all its service, and for the holy garments" (35:21). So great was the voluntary response of the people that Moses had to eventually ask them to stop giving (36:6). They had more than enough raw material to complete the construction of the tabernacle under the skillful leadership of Bezalel and Oholiab, two individuals called of God to specifically accomplish this task. Bezalel was the grandson of Hur and is the first man in Scripture said to be filled with the Spirit of God demonstrating the necessity of the fullness of the Holy Spirit for any work for God regardless of its nature (35:31). Oholiab was of the tribe of Dan and like his counterpart from Judah, noted for his wise heart and skill of craftsmanship (v. 35).

The tabernacle was erected according to the plan and pattern given by God. "So Moses finished the work" (40:33). Perhaps it was then that Moses prayed a prayer which has since then become a source of inspiration to all who seek to do a work for God. "Lord, You have been our dwelling place in all generations. . . . Let Your work appear to your servants, and Your glory to their children. And let the beauty of the Lord our God be upon us, and establish the work of our hands for us; yes, establish the work of our hands" (Ps. 90:1, 16-17).

It may well have been in answer to the "prayer of Moses, the man of God" that God moved into His new dwelling place in the wilderness. "Then the cloud covered the tabernacle of meeting, and the glory of the Lord filled the tabernacle" (Ex. 40:34). And there from the tabernacle, God began to speak to Moses and the Children of Israel. The various statements of God made during the next month have been preserved in the third Book of Moses called Leviticus.

THE LEVITICAL SYSTEM OF WORSHIP *(Lev.)*

Ironically, the one book of the Bible specifically said to contain more of the actual spoken words of God than any other is the book least likely to be read by a Christian today. Because so much of the Book of Leviticus is attributed to the direct statements from God, Jewish rabbis coined the phrase, "Let the pure read the pure." By this they meant children who were thought to be pure should be taught to read by reading the Book of Leviticus which came to be known as the pure Word of God. This means the first book to be read by Jesus as He grew up in Nazareth is probably the last book to be read by Christians today.

OUTLINE OF LEVITICUS

ACCESS—The Way to God *(1:1–7:38)*
ASSOCIATION—The Walk with God *(8:1–23:44)*
APOSTASY—The Warning from God *(24:1–27:34)*

There are several highlights in the Book of Leviticus which are of special significance to Christians today. The book begins with instructions concerning the five major offerings in the levitical system of worship. Most commentators agree the first of these, the whole burnt offering, is the model on which the Apostle Paul's challenge to the Romans to be "a living sacrifice" (cf. Rom. 12:1). This sacrifice involved burning the complete animal as an offering to God and came to represent the highest expression of commitment to God in the Law. There is even greater agreement that Christ offered Himself as each of these five sacrifices in His death on Calvary.

The first seven chapters of the Book of Leviticus became

the manual of sacrifice for Israel and her priests. The first part of this manual was addressed to the people and stressed their responsibility in the area of sacrifice (Lev. 1:1–6:7). The second part of this section of the book was addressed to the priests and outlined their privilege regarding the sacrifices (6:8–7:38). Only one of the five sacrifices was offered without blood, the meal offering.

THE MEANING OF THE SACRIFICES IN THE CHRISTIAN LIFE

The Whole Burnt Offering—Complete Consecration
of Life
The Meal Offering—Practical Holiness in Lifestyle
The Peace Offering—Deeper Communion or Abiding
with Christ
The Sin Offering—Restored Fellowship with Christ
The Trespass Offering—Initial Forgiveness of Sins
at Salvation

A second area of interest in the Book of Leviticus is the religious calendar of Israel as expressed in the seven feasts of the year (23:1-44). Each of these feasts has a spiritual fulfillment in the historic roots of Christianity or its future anticipations. The annual calendar of Israel was for many centuries a prophetic witness to the ministry of Christ in a new age. Much of the calendar of Israel is yet to be fulfilled.

THE FEASTS OF ISRAEL

Feast	Fulfillment
Passover	Death of Christ
Firstfruits	Resurrection
Pentecost	Holy Spirit
Trumpets	Rapture
Atonement	National conversion
Tabernacles	Messianic kingdom

The Book of Leviticus gets its name from the tribe of Levi which was the priestly tribe of Israel. Though all Levites had priestly duties, only the physical descendants of Aaron qualified to hold the office of priest. Because the office of the priest is one of the three anointed offices of Christ, the details concerning the priesthood in this book are typical of our Great High Priest.

THE PRIESTHOOD

Old Testament Priest	Christ
Earthly tabernacle	Heavenly temple
Once a year	Once for all
Beyond veil	Rent veil
Own sins	Our sins
Blood of bulls	Own blood

Leviticus 26 cites the conditions of the blessing of God on Israel as they lived under Law in the land. These included rain, an abundance in the harvest, peace, military victories, and a population increase (26:3-13). But the chapter also identifies the six evidences of the chastisement of God if the people did not obey the commandments. These chastisements included distress, drought, wild beasts, disease, famine, and ultimately a dispersion (vv. 14-39). But even in His discipline, God would not leave His people without hope. "If [literally "and" in the Hebrew] they confess their iniquity and the iniquity of their fathers, with their unfaithfulness in which they were unfaithful to Me, and that they also have walked contrary to Me. . . . Then I will remember My covenant with Jacob, and My covenant with Isaac and My covenant with Abraham I will remember; I will remember the land" (vv. 40, 42).

PERSPECTIVE

God had led Israel out of the land of bondage and was now prepared to lead them into the land of promise. Before they marched to Kadesh Barnea, He wanted them to know He would not only bless them but discipline them severely if necessary should they violate His special covenant with them. He was now ready to give them the land, the land He had promised to Abraham. Sadly, they would very soon demonstrate they were not ready to possess it. But even the rebellion of Israel could not cause God to forget His covenant, or forget the land.

Israel had experienced half a miracle but because of their failure to respond to God who had so vividly revealed Himself to them, half a miracle would be all they would experience. God had intended not only to bring that generation out of Egypt but into the Promised Land. But between the experience of deliverance and that of rest, God called His people to holiness. Their failure to respond eventually prevented their being able to experience God's rest. Believers are warned in the New Testament that the experiences of Israel in the Old Testament stand as an example to us today. Sadly, many believers today are willing to settle for half a miracle. They fail to realize God still calls those whom He has redeemed and delivered to holiness before they can enjoy the rest He has for them.

TWENTY-FIVE

MOSES:
The Murmuring Multitude

(Numbers; Deuteronomy)

As Israel left Sinai, it was time to enter the Promised Land. The Book of Numbers tells of her unbelief, how the nation refused to enter the land that God had promised to her. Because of unbelief, God required that Israel travel by way of "the wilderness, to humble you, and test you, to know what was in your heart, whether you would keep His commandments or not" (Deut. 8:2). God did not require the wilderness experience that lasted forty years. In the ideal timing of God, the period in the wilderness was nearing its conclusion and it was now time for Israel to enter into her possession.

The people of Israel rebelled against God and would not follow His leading, so for thirty-eight years they wandered about in the desert until an entire generation died off. Whereas the Book of Leviticus covers the details of only a few weeks, the Book of Numbers describes the period of an entire generation. Yet the depressing nature of that period is revealed in the Hebrew title of Numbers, *Bemidbar* meaning "in the wilderness." They were in the wilderness both geographically and spiritually. A generation which was offered a land that flowed with milk and honey, died in the wilderness because of their constant murmuring and natural tendency to rebel.

God offered to let Israel occupy Canaan, but "they could not enter in because of unbelief" (Heb. 3:19). Spiritually, there is

228 History Makers of the Old Testament

an application to the Christian life. "There remains therefore a rest for the people of God" (4:9). It is possible for a believer to miss many spiritual blessings because of the same kind of unbelief that left a generation outside of the land of promise. Negatively, the New Testament points to Israel in the wilderness as an example of what the believer should not do.

ISRAEL IN THE WILDERNESS
(1 Cor. 10:6-10)

We should not lust after evil things
Neither be ye idolaters
Neither let us commit fornication
Neither let us put Christ to the test
Neither murmur ye

THE PREPARATIONS AT SINAI *(Num. 1:1–10:10)*
As Israel prepared to march to Kadesh Barnea, God commanded Moses, "Take a census of all the congregation of the Children of Israel, by their families, by their fathers' houses, according to the number of names, every male individually, from twenty years old and above—all who are able to go to war in Israel. You and Aaron shall number them by their armies" (Num. 1:2-3). It was determined there were 603,550 men of war in the camp. Because of their rebellion, all but Joshua and Caleb would die before the nation entered the land. They would refuse to go in and fight, in part because they thought of themselves as outnumbered against the enemy, but the army that would eventually fight and win the battles would be smaller by 1,820 men (cf. 26:51). Much time was spent in counting the people and taking inventory of the tabernacle treasures before Israel began her march to Kadesh Barnea. This national census and inventory was a reminder to the people of that day and that God is an orderly God by nature.

THE WANDERING OF ISRAEL *(Num. 10:11–25:18)*
According to God's perfect timing, Israel should have been ready to march from Sinai right into the Promised Land by the

time the census was complete, but even as they left the mountain of God, the murmuring began. Three days into the journey to Kadesh Barnea, the people began complaining, raising the ire of God. God responded by sending a fire which "consumed some in the outskirts of the camp" (Num. 11:1). In their suffering, the people cried unto Moses who prayed on their behalf, and "the fire was quenched" (v. 2). Moses called the place *Taberah* meaning "a burning" to remind the people of the consequence of their sin, but rather than causing the people to increase their trust in God, the fire caused some of the people to remember the old barbeque pits they had in Egypt.

One of the problems in the camp of Israel was what the Scriptures describe as "the mixed multitude." These were non-Jews who had thought it a good idea to leave Egypt with the Israelites during the Exodus, but though they had left Egypt physically, they had never come to the place where they were prepared to give up the luxuries associated with their former life in Egypt. And one of those luxuries was meat.

God responded to the murmuring of the mixed multitude by giving them exactly what they wanted. He caused a wind to blow a flock of quail in from the sea. So large was the flock which fell by the camp of Israel, that everyone who wanted quail had plenty to eat. "He who gathered least gathered ten homers" or ten times the prescribed daily allotment of manna (v. 32). But even as the people ate the quail, "the Lord struck the people with a very great plague" (v. 33). Those who died were buried and the place was named Kibroth Hattaavah meaning "graves of lust."

Then it was Moses' own family that began to lead the murmuring. After his wife died, Moses decided to marry a black Cushite woman and was opposed in his decision by both his brother Aaron and sister Miriam. This was apparently the first case of interracial marriage in Scripture and the reaction of others to this couple's decision to marry was not too unlike the present-day opposition. But in this case, Aaron and Miriam were speaking against Moses as a prophet of God without cause.

God responded to this rebellion in leadership by calling the three siblings to the tabernacle. God apparently has a sense of humor. Because Miriam had complained about Moses marrying a black woman, God plagued Miriam with leprosy, making her "white as snow" (12:10). Even when Moses prayed for her healing, God ordered she "be shut out of the camp seven days, and after that she may be received again" (v. 14).

When the people finally arrived at Kadesh Barnea, it was clearly established that the people were in a rebellious mood. Moses selected twelve men, one from each of the tribes of Israel, to spy out the land to confirm the promise of God concerning the quality of their new homeland. And when they returned, they agreed, "We went to the land where you sent us. It truly flows with milk and honey" (13:27). But there were other inhabitants in the land including the children of Anak, a family of giants, and the present residents of the land lived in walled cities, something none of them had seen before. Ten of the twelve spies focused on the problem rather than the power of God, and could not see past the giants to the God who was bigger than all the giants of Canaan or anywhere else. Only Joshua and Caleb seemed to think God could overcome the giants.

But the people did not want to fight giants, and rather than celebrate the quality of their new homeland, they mourned the fact it could never be theirs to enjoy. When Joshua and Caleb tried to persuade the people not to rebel but to trust God and march in to claim the Promised Land, the people wanted to stone the only two faithful men among the spies. And God decided to draw the line. If Israel did not want the land, He did not want Israel. He prepared to destroy and disinherit them.

As he had on so many other occasions, Moses preserved the life of the nation by praying on their behalf. In something of a compromise solution to the situation, God agreed not to destroy them, but also not to let them into the Promised Land. They would wander in the wilderness another thirty-eight years until the rebellious generation which so often stirred up the wrath of God had completely died off. When Israel finally realized their great sin, they determined the next day to go in and fight for the land. But the open gate at Kadesh Barnea had been closed and God had withdrawn His offer to that generation.

But the rebellions of Israel in the wilderness were still not over. A conspiracy led by Korah of the tribe of Levi and Dathan and Abiram of the tribe of Reuben rose up to challenge the authority of Moses and Aaron. The movement attracted some 250 princes of Israel including many of the most popular men of that day. At its peak, Korah was able to convince most of the nation to oppose Moses at the entrance of the tabernacle.

But the size of Korah's rebellion did not cause God any undue concern. He can deal with a rebellion of a thousand as easily as a rebellion of one. Moses warned the people to separate themselves from the leaders of the rebellion, because God was going to judge who should lead Israel. "And the earth opened its mouth and swallowed them up, with their households and all the men with Korah, with all their goods. So they and all those with them went down alive into the pit; the earth closed over them, and they perished from among the congregation" (16:32-33).

The spirit of rebellion in Israel even infected Moses on one occasion. When the people again complained about the lack of water, he was instructed by God to speak to the rock and water would flow as it had on an earlier occasion when he smote the rock. But while accusing his people for their rebellious spirit, Moses himself rebelled and smote the rock a second time, thus breaking the typical significance of the rock which was Christ. Israel got their water, but because of his act, Moses himself was forbidden to lead Israel into the Promised Land.

Lack of water is a common problem in the hot arid deserts of the Near East, so it is not surprising that much of the murmuring of Israel in the wilderness was related to the lack of water. As they continued wandering about in the wilderness, they continued to complain. And God continued to judge them for their rebellious spirit. He sent "fiery serpents among the people, and they bit the people; and many of the people of Israel died" (21:6). Again the people appealed to Moses who appealed to God on their behalf. God commanded Moses to make a bronze serpent and raise it on a pole that all could see. He promised to heal anyone who when bit by the serpents would simply look to the bronze serpent. The symbol has become a symbol of the healing power of modern medicine in our day, but Jesus pointed to it as a type of the cross (John 3:14). When the plague was ended, the grateful Israelites kept it as a memorial of their preservation. Sadly, that which brought healing to Israel in the wilderness, later was used as an idol by an apostatizing nation.

There was yet one more rebellion of Israel in the wilderness. As the nation continued wandering in the plain of Moab, Balak, King of Moab, feared Israel might do to his nation what they had done to the Amorites. He hired a Gentile prophet named Balaam to curse the people of Israel. But God did not want His people cursed. Still, after some persuasion, Balaam agreed to curse Israel in return for the reward promised by Balak. But when he opened his mouth to curse the people, he could only bless them instead.

Still, Balaam was not eager to loose his reward and proposed a way in which Israel would be cursed. He knew God had forbidden Israel to marry pagan wives, and suspected Hebrew men could not resist the physical attractiveness of Midian's prettiest young women. Balaam was right. "Then Israel remained in Acacia Grove, and the people began to commit harlotry with the women of Moab" (Num. 25:1). Those who became involved with the women of Moab soon began worshiping the false god Baal Peor. So widespread was the moral lapse among the men of Israel that one man actually brought a Midianite woman to his friend in the presence of Moses at the door of the tabernacle (v. 6).

The sight of a leader in Israel involved immorally with the daughter of a Midianite chief was too much for Phinehas, the son of Eleazar and grandson of Aaron. He took a javelin and thrust it through both of them as they were involved immorally (v. 8). The problem was addressed and resolved, but not before 24,000 had "died in the plague" (v. 9), 23,000 of them in a single day (cf. 1 Cor. 10:8).

RENEWED PREPARATIONS TO ENTER THE LAND
(Num. 26:1–36:13)

In the course of time, the rebellious generation which refused to enter the Promised Land at Kadesh Barnea died and the forty-year period of wandering was coming to a close. It was time for a new generation to prepare to enter into the Promised Land. They were counted again and reminded of their responsibility to wholeheartedly follow the Lord. But this time Moses knew he would not be the one to lead his people into the land of promise. Still, he had much to tell them before they claimed the promise of God and moved into Canaan to possess their possession.

THE FINAL WORDS OF MOSES *(Deut.)*

The fifth Book of Moses known as Deuteronomy contains the final messages or sermons of Moses to his people. The name *Deuteronomy* means "second law," and the book is largely a restatement of the Law of God. It is thought of as the revival book of the Old Testament in that whenever it was prominent in the history of Israel, great spiritual blessing always followed. Immediately following the original giving of these messages by Moses, Israel possessed the Promised Land under the leadership of Joshua. Later, a revival broke out in Judah when a lost Book of the Law was found by Hilkiah, the high priest during the reign of Josiah (2 Kings 22:8). Because of the nature of this revival, many commentators believe it was the scroll of Deuteronomy that was found. It is also thought to be the scroll of Deuteronomy which Ezra taught to the returned exiles which led to the post-Captivity revival among the Jews (Neh. 8:1–10:39).

The prominent appearance of this book in later revivals in Israel's history has caused liberal scholars to conclude the book was not written until much later, perhaps during the early reign of Josiah. But a close look at the style of the book reveals it follows the pattern of the Hittite suzerainty treaties known to exist only during the time of Moses. Under the inspiration of God, Moses delivered the sermons and later wrote the manuscript following the style of his day. If the

Book of Deuteronomy were in fact written much later as the critics suppose, its style would be radically different. The Hittite treaties were unique and when that society died, they were unknown until discovered in this century by archeologists digging up the ruins of ancient Hittite settlements. A later forger would not even known this style of writing existed, much less try to copy it.

DEUTERONOMY

Preamble *(1:1-5)*
Historical prologue *(1:6–3:29)*
Stipulations: basic *(4–11)* detailed *(12–26)*
Deposition of text *(31:9; 24–26)*
Public reading *(24–26)*
Witnesses *(31:16-30; 32:1-47)*
Curses *(28:15-68)**
Blessings *(28:1-14)**

*Note reverse order of Blessings and Curses, probably due to the nature of the book.

PERSPECTIVE: RESTATEMENT OF THE LAW

Because the Book of Deuteronomy is a restatement of the Law, many Christians are tempted to overlook it and neglect it in their Bible reading and study. Yet in this book the *Shema* or first doctrinal statement of the unity of God is found, and in that context is also the command to parents to teach these truths to their children (Deut. 6:4-9). This book also gives the guidelines by which a prophet can be discerned to be true or false (chaps. 13 and 18). And for Israel, it contains a chapter which the rabbis came to understand as the prophetic history of the nation (chap. 32).

"So Moses, the servant of the Lord died there in the land of Moab, according to the word of the Lord. And He buried him in a valley in the land of Moab, opposite Beth-Peor; but no one knows his grave to this day" (34:5-6). Moses had brought his nation out of the land of bondage and led them through the wilderness for forty years. Now there was a new challenge which laid before the nation, that of possessing their possession. And for that new challenge, the people were to receive a new leader.

TWENTY-SIX

JOSHUA:
The General Who Captured the Promised Land

(Joshua 1:1–8:35)

On the death of Moses, all Israel knew a vacuum existed in leadership that would be difficult to fill. Moses had been a great man who had accomplished a great deliverance for Israel. The one who would follow Moses had to be just as great to finish the task Moses had begun. Moses had brought Israel out of the land of bondage, but now God wanted to bring Israel into the land of promise.

Some talk about born leaders, but it is rarely ever so. "Born leaders" are those who learn to lead as a result of the disciplines learned early in life. The key to becoming a successful leader is to first invest time and energy learning how to lead. That usually begins by first learning how to follow a real leader. When God had to find someone to fill the shoes of a great leader, Moses, He found that someone in the person of one who had learned how to be a great leader from Moses, Joshua.

God taught Joshua how to lead by making him the servant of Moses, a necessary part of his training. Joshua should have learned the discipline of God from his father, but there is some indication that did not happen. His father bore the name of the Egyptian god "Nun" suggesting the family had abandoned their faith in the God of Israel and become involved in the worship of Egyptian deities. God knew Joshua better than anyone knew him. He knew Joshua would someday lead His chosen people into their possession. But He also knew this leader first had to learn to lead. He put him under the discipline of Moses and taught him as a servant to obey orders. It was not until he had spent the better part of his life taking orders that he was then permitted to issue them.

Forty years prior to his crossing the Jordan River to begin his conquest of Canaan, Joshua was, like his fellow countrymen, a slave in Egypt. He was a direct ancestor of the Joseph who had helped preserve the land during a time of international famine and economic crisis, but that did not impress his Egyptian master. Nothing is known about his experiences as a slave except what might be implied from the normal experiences of others in that position. He was probably a young man who cried out to God for deliverance, a cry which was answered by God sending Moses (Ex. 3:7-10). His father had named him Hoshea which means savior or deliverer, perhaps in the hope his son might be an instrument by which that deep longing might become a reality in his experience (Num. 13:8). But it was another who would lead Israel out of the land of Egypt. Still, it would be the work of Joshua to complete the task of leading Israel into the land of promise to possess their possessions.

LEARNING TO LEAD

First there would be a time of training. For Joshua, the forty years in the wilderness was a course of study by which God prepared him for his greater work of conquest and settling the land of Canaan. It was a time of learning even when he did not want to learn. But the task was too great to leave to the ignorant and unprepared, so Joshua, the servant of Moses, who would become Joshua, the successor to Moses, was in the wilderness Joshua, the student of Moses. But if Moses was the teacher, it was the Lord Himself who prepared the curriculum.

Learning about spiritual conflict

Joshua's leadership training course began in the battle at Rephidim (Ex. 17:8-16; Deut. 3:21). It was there he first led the army of Israel against another nation. And it was there he learned that the victory on the battlefield was that which the Lord gave. While Joshua's knowledge and skill in planning and executing strategic battle plans was important, it was the up-lifted arms of Moses in prayer that determined the success of the battle against the Amalekites. There Joshua learned two important lessons. First, he discovered prayer was mightier than the sword. Second, he was reminded that God was committed to the defense of His people.

Learning about solitary convictions
The second mention of Joshua in the Pentateuch is made when he accompanied Moses at least partway up the mountain of God (Ex. 24:12-13; 32:15-18). During much of that forty-day period, Moses was alone with God receiving the Law and pattern for the tabernacle. Joshua was simply alone. The significance of this forty-day period which may have included a time of fasting is that it was a time when Joshua could engage in some self-evaluation and determine what was really important in his life. In the Scriptures, the number forty is often associated with judgment, trials, and proving.

Learning about a separated communion
The third lesson of leadership is the importance of having communion with God Himself (Ex. 33:11; Ps. 91:1). When Moses left the meeting with God in the tabernacle, Joshua remained alone with God. There is a Jewish tradition that Moses wrote not only Psalm 90, but the nine psalms which follow it. While that claim might be debated concerning some of the psalms in question, there are good reasons to believe Psalm 91 was written by Moses concerning his servant Joshua.

Learning about sectarian concerns
If Joshua was going to be a truly great leader, he was going to have to overcome what might be called "sectarian concerns." Often we limit our ability to serve God by attempting to limit God to our preconceived ideas. In his zeal for God and the

leader God had called to lead Israel, Joshua on at least one occasion came close to hindering the work of God because two men prophesied within the camp rather than outside the camp (Num. 11:28). On that occasion, Joshua learned that the moving of the Spirit of God is too important to oppose simply because of minor differences in its expression.

Learning about a sustained confidence
The single greatest factor in the lives of great men of God is their faith in God. Another experience of Joshua in the wilderness taught him the importance of a sustained confidence in God. Joshua was one of the twelve spies sent into Canaan from Kadesh Barnea, and one of the two who brought back a good report (Num. 13:16-33; 32:11-12). Joshua urged the people to trust God even though that was an unpopular position to take at the time. First, he was outnumbered in his opinion among the spies, ten to two. Second, the people themselves so opposed Joshua and Caleb they came very close to stoning them.

Learning about a strategic call
Notwithstanding the importance of all of the other lessons of leadership which Joshua learned in the wilderness, Joshua was suited to follow Moses as leader because God had clearly called him to do so (Num. 27; 34:17; Deut. 1:38; 31:7-8). Leading Israel into the Promised Land was not simply a reward for his faithfulness or recognition of his developed leadership skills. It was the result of the choice of God to call Joshua to serve Him in that task. Just as God had called Moses to lead Israel out of bondage, so He called Joshua to lead Israel into rest.

Learning about spiritual control
Ultimately, Joshua was empowered by the Holy Spirit for the task which lay before him. You cannot do the work of God without God. Joshua was one of the very few men in the Old Testament of whom it was said he was filled with the Holy Spirit (Deut. 34:9). To be filled with the Holy Spirit means to

be yielded to Him and under His control. When the Spirit of God is in control of a life, that life will accomplish what God wants it to accomplish.

PREPARING FOR TOTAL VICTORY *(Josh. 1:1–5:9)*

If the results of the career of Joshua had to be summed up in only a couple of words, those words would be "total victory." The book contains a listing of thirty-one kings which Joshua conquered, demonstrating God is mighty enough to meet any of our needs (Josh. 12:9-24). Toward the end of the book is the claim, "Not a word failed of any good thing which the Lord had spoken to the house of Israel. All came to pass" (21:45). But before Joshua and his people could claim that victory, they had to first prepare themselves. In their preparation, they illustrated several principles regarding discerning the will of God and preparing for total victory in our lives today.

Meditate on the Word of God *(1:1-8)*

The first step in preparing for total victory was that of meditating on the Word of God, which for Joshua, meant the five Books of Moses (v. 8). The Scriptures are God's self-revelation to man. Meditating on the Scriptures means to contemplate the revealed person of God and in the process internalize the Word of God. In the New Testament, meditation is described in the phrase, "Let the Word of Christ dwell in you richly" (Col. 3:16). Meditation is the God-ordained means whereby our knowledge of the Scriptures grows from little more than a trivia collection of facts to an arsenal of biblical principles by which we live the successful Christian life.

Dedicate to the work of God *(vv. 9-18)*

Second, there was an act of dedication on the part of the elders of Israel who represented the nation of Israel. When confronted with the challenge of taking the land God had promised them, Israel was eager to dedicate themselves to this unique work of God (vv. 10-18). So committed were they to doing the work of God that they voluntarily formed a "death pact" among themselves promising Joshua, "Whoever rebels

against your command and does not heed your words, in all
that you command him, shall be put to death. Only be strong
and of good courage" (v. 18).

Investigate the way of God *(2:1-24)*
The third step of preparation for total victory was an investiga-
tion of conditions in Jericho by two spies. Perhaps remembering that only two of the twelve spies at Kadesh had brought
back a good report, Joshua was careful to send out only two
men whom he could count on to bring back the information he
needed as he prepared to conquer the land. These spies were
charged with gathering information about the land, not with
making the decision as to whether they should enter the land.
That decision was already made when they dedicated themselves to the work of God.

When the spies came to Jericho, they stayed with a harlot
named Rahab. Rahab lived with her father in a home at the
wall of the city. Typically, this was usually the poorest region
of the city and the place where people who provided housing
for strangers usually lived. Rahab's father probably rented
rooms in his home to those visiting or passing through Jericho.
Tragically, it appears he also rented out his daughter to interested customers.

From Rahab, the spies learned the people of the land still
remembered how God had delivered Israel from the Egyptians
forty years earlier and feared what Israel might do to them.
When the authorities of the city came to arrest the spies,
Rahab hid them and lied about their being there. Though God
did not command Rahab to lie, nor does He condone lying, on
this occasion He allowed her lie to protect the spies.

Though Rahab was a member of a condemned race, she had
come to some degree of faith in God. Recognizing this, the
spies bound a scarlet line in the window of that home as they
left, promising she and her family would be preserved from the
destruction of the city. The color of that cord is typical of
safety through sacrifice (cf. Heb. 9:19-22). When the city was
later conquered, Rahab's life was spared. "By faith the harlot
Rahab did not perish with those who did not believe, when she

had received the spies with peace" (11:31).

The report of the spies to Joshua was enthusiastic. After telling of their experience and what they had learned, they concluded, "Truly the Lord has delivered all the land into our hands, for indeed all the inhabitants of the country are faint-hearted because of us" (Josh. 2:24).

Initiate a walk with God *(3:1–5:1)*

The next step of preparation for the people was to initiate a step of faith which is the basis of a successful walk with God. Actually, there were several steps of faith as Israel began walking with God into the land of Canaan. First, Joshua moved the camp from Acacia Grove to the banks of the Jordan (3:1). The move was significant because of what the two places involved represented to the people. Acacia Grove was the place of rebellion, the site of a great moral and spiritual decline among the people of Israel (cf. Num. 25). The Jordan River was the place of reconciliation with God. Crossing over the Jordan is typical of our death with Christ, the means whereby we are reconciled to God (Rom. 6:3-4, 6-11; Eph. 2:5-6; Col. 3:1-3). Even before Christ, John the Baptist chose several sites along the Jordan River to administer his baptism unto repentance.

The second step was setting themselves apart to God. "And Joshua said to the people, 'Sanctify yourselves, for tomorrow the Lord will do wonders among you' " (Josh. 3:5). In calling the people to sanctify themselves, Joshua was reminding them of three aspects of sanctification. First, they had a personal responsibility in the process of setting themselves apart to God. Second, sanctification was a practical preparation for the work of God. Third, it was a step of faith in anticipation of what God was soon to do among them.

The third step was perhaps the most dramatic. Israel was commanded to pass through the Jordan River on dry ground and begin marching into the water even though the river itself was still flowing and overflowing its banks. In fact, the biblical account of this miracle records God did not dry up the river until "the feet of the priests who bore the ark dipped in the edge of the water" (v. 15). God wanted His people to believe they were going to cross the river on dry ground even if they got their "socks" wet in the process.

The Jordan River was dried up as Israel crossed. Some have suggested this may have been caused naturally by a mudslide at a narrow point farther up the river near Adam. That may have been part of the means by which God accomplished this miracle, but the mudslide itself would not account for either the timing of the miracle nor the the fact that the riverbed was dry rather than soggy. By stopping the waters "in a heap" upstream, the river was effectively drained while Israel crossed to the other side.

There was also a fourth step in this renewed walk with God. After crossing the river, Joshua arranged for several men to gather stones from the riverbed which he used to build two monuments to commemorate what God had done for His people (4:1-9). One set of stones was placed on the shore where the people entered the Promised Land. The other stones were piled in the river in the place where the priests had held the ark of the covenant while Israel crossed over on dry ground. In this way, the people would have a constant reminder of what God had done for them.

As Joshua and the people demonstrated their willingness to trust Him, God acted on their behalf to do what they could not do for themselves. "On that day the Lord magnified Joshua in the sight of all Israel; and they feared him, as they had feared Moses" (v. 14). God also impressed the condemned races of Canaan with what He was prepared to do for Israel. "So it was when all the kings of the Amorites who were on the west side of the Jordan, and all the kings of the Canaanites who were by the sea, heard that the Lord had dried up the waters of the Jordan from before the Children of Israel until we had crossed over, that their heart melted; and there was no spirit in them any longer because of the Children of Israel" (5:1).

Eliminate the wrath of God *(vv. 2-9)*
There was one final act of preparation for total victory before Israel could begin their conquest of Canaan. At a place which

came to be known as Gilgal, the men of Israel circumcised themselves at the command of the Lord. This was not the way one would normally prepare for battle, but God wanted to emphasize the importance of the spiritual over the physical in winning this total victory. God would not only give them strength and victory, He would be their strength and victory.

The men of Israel needed to be circumcised because this practice had been neglected in the wilderness. Circumcision was for the Jew a confession of his faith in the covenant promises of God. After their refusal to enter the land at Kadesh Barnea, they did not circumcise their males for forty years. Now it was an act of dedication whereby the people affirmed their relationship to God and His covenant by circumcising their sons. Had it been practiced by the generation which died in the wilderness, it would only have amounted to an act of hypocrisy. God may have physically prevented Israel from commiting this hypocritical act after their denial of loyalty to Him at Kadesh Barnea.

The Scripture describes this circumcising of the army of Israel as rolling "away the reproach of Egypt from you" (5:9). The name Gilgal literally means "a rolling." Typically, Israel was rolling away any sin and evidence of sin which might invoke the wrath of God. They were eliminating the wrath of God so they could enter battle fully assured God could and would bless their efforts on His behalf.

THE CENTRAL CAMPAIGN *(Josh. 5:10–8:35)*

For the first time in thirty-eight years, Israel kept the Passover feast. In so doing, they began to eat the produce of the land God had given them and the need for manna ended. Therefore, "the manna ceased on the day after they had eaten the produce of the land; and the Children of Israel no longer had manna, but they ate the food of the land of Canaan that year" (5:12). Manna had never been given by God to satisfy Israel, only to sustain her until she could possess that which God planned to give her. With the preparation for total victory complete, it was time to claim that victory.

The conquest of Canaan by Joshua involved three major

military campaigns. The first of these was the central campaign which cut through the heart of the land. This was followed by a southern campaign against the Amorite kings and then later a northern campaign against the Canaanite kings. Over a period of about five to fifteen years, Joshua was successful in conquering each of the thirty-one kings he faced in battle. And it all began with the conquest of the alleged oldest city in the world, Jericho.

The battle of Jericho *(5:10–6:27)*

Though much of the military conquest of Canaan serves to demonstrate Joshua's brilliance as a military commander, the battle of Jericho was unique in this regard. Because it was the first city-state to be conquered, God determined to give it to Israel in such a unique way there could be no question but that the victory was His. Thus, the battle of Jericho was won miraculously when the walls of the city fell down.

Joshua's battle camp at Gilgal, though not far from Jericho, was well hidden from the view of the city. While his army was recovering from the effects of their circumcision, Joshua took the opportunity to look over the city of Jericho unobserved. At least he thought he had been unobserved. But, "it came to pass, when Joshua was by Jericho, that he lifted his eyes and looked, and behold, a Man stood opposite him with His sword drawn in His hand" (5:13).

The general who was about to conquer Canaan would not be scared off by a single soldier, so he challenged the man to identify himself, "Are you for us, or for our adversaries?" (v. 13) But rather than take one of the two sides Joshua had suggested, the man simply identified himself as the "Commander of the army of the Lord" (v. 14). Immediately recognizing the Man as his Master, Joshua humbled himself before the One he had moments before challenged and asked, "What does my Lord say to His servant?" (v. 14)

The Commander of the army of the Lord was a preincarnate appearance of Christ in the Old Testament known as a Christophany. This scene of the meeting of Joshua and Jesus has been described as a savior meeting the Saviour. Joshua was on holy ground in his meeting with Jesus and removed his shoes as instructed. Then he received God's battle plan for the conquest of Jericho.

Israel was instructed to march around the city silently and leave the site. This practice was to be repeated each day for six days. On the seventh day, they were to march around the city seven times. But on their seventh pass around the city, the priests were to blow their shophars and trumpets, and the people were to shout as loudly as they could. If the nation did as they were commanded, God promised the wall of the city would fall. This does not mean the entire wall necessarily would collapse, only that enough of the wall would fall to leave the city defenseless against the army of Israel.

The battle plan would have had a devastating effect on the people of the city psychologically just as the subsequent victory affected other city-states in the same way. They were already fearful of the Israelites even before they crossed the Jordan River. Seeing the army approach their city and silently march around the wall would have served to intensify that fear. When they saw their walls collapse on the seventh day, they would have been stunned into shock. This would make it easier for the soldiers as they actually destroyed the city.

This first city was to belong completely to God much as the firstfruits of the harvest were given to God under the legal code of Israel. As a result, looting of the city was strictly forbidden. In other cities the soldiers would be free to share in the spoils of war, but at Jericho, everything but Rahab and her family was accursed and Israel was specifically instructed to avoid contact with it. The only exception to this general rule was that the silver and gold should be collected along with any bronze and iron vessels and consecrated to the Lord and added to the treasury of the tabernacle (6:17-19).

Scholars try to explain in different ways how the walls fell. The "Break Step" explanation says the vibrations of the march cracked the masonry causing the collapse of the walls. The "Sonic Shout" explanation indicates a half million screaming Jewish soldiers, plus the ram's horn (perhaps a discord) caused the collapse. The "Earthquake Theory" suggests God used an earth tremor to collapse the walls. Finally, the "Sapping Theory" suggest the march around the city was to divert attention while soldiers dug under the walls causing them to fall outward. While God sometimes uses natural means to accomplish supernatural results, perhaps the wall fell at Jericho for no other reason than God intervening without using natural means.

God gave Israel a great victory at Jericho as part of His commitment to give them the land. Jericho was not the greatest city of that day, but as the apparent oldest it had come to represent something of the stability of the land. When Jericho fell, other kings would have known intuitively they could not resist the power of God nor the invading army of Israel.

Achan: the troubler of Israel *(7:1-26)*

But all was not well in Israel in the victory over Jericho. One man named Achan, most often described in Scripture as the troubler of Israel, took "a beautiful Babylonian garment" which should have been destroyed, and "two hundred shekels of silver, and a wedge of gold weighing fifty shekels" which should have been added to the tabernacle treasury (v. 21). According to U.S. standards of measurement, Achan had stolen about twenty ounces of gold and eighty ounces of silver from the treasury of the tabernacle in keeping the precious metals he found in Jericho. But no man sins alone. The sin of Achan became the sin of Israel. His sin affected his society.

The sin of Achan would cost Israel thirty-six lives and their only humiliation in their conquest of Canaan (v. 5). In addition to the sin of Achan, it has been suggested the initial loss at Ai was due to two other tactical errors. First, Joshua erred in sending only a few men to the small city. The name Ai means "ruin" and may have been applied to the city by the Israelites much as one might speak of a small place today as a "little dump." Joshua's actions suggest he may have begun depending on human strength rather than God. Second, there is no hint of prayer seeking the will of God concerning Ai before the initial assault. Perhaps if that prayer had been offered first, the sin of Achan would have been discovered earlier.

Achan had dedicated himself to the work of God with the rest of Israel in a death pact. By the drawing of lots, he was revealed to be the cause of Israel's problems. He gave God glory by confessing his sin (see v. 19). Because he had broken the conditions of the death pact by disobeying the clear command of Joshua, he and his family were stoned in a valley which eventually bore his name. He was buried under the heap of stones that killed him together with the garment, gold, and silver which he had stolen from Jericho.

The battle of Ai *(8:1-35)*
With the sin of Achan resolved, Israel could return to the work of conquering the Promised Land. This time Joshua involved all the army. He set a total of 35,000 men on the north and west sides of the city in two ambush parties. Then he led the rest of the army into a valley to fight the king of Ai. Joshua then feigned a defeat and retreat. When the people of Ai and the neighboring city of Bethel saw the army of Israel retreating, they left their cities unguarded and went into the valley to fight. This gave the two ambush parties an opportunity to destroy the cities. As the men of Ai and Bethel saw the city of Ai burning, they lost what enthusiasm they may have had for the battle. Knowing they had already lost, they looked for an escape, but even those who made it to the mountains were caught and killed. Some 12,000 residents of Ai were killed in battle, and the king of Ai was hung. His carcass was placed under a heap of stones at what had formerly been the gate to the now-burned city.

No mention is made in the Book of Joshua as to how Joshua defeated the king of Bethel, but it is generally assumed he was defeated in this battle. The two cities were near each other and appear to have been allied together in the battle against Joshua (v. 17). Recent archeological investigations in the region near Bethel have resulted in the discovery of ruins thought by some to be the true site of Ai. There is evidence at this sight that the city was burned about the time of Joshua's conquest of Canaan.

PERSPECTIVE

The central campaign was successful because it divided the enemy in the Promised Land. The Amorites in the south were cut off from the Canaanites in the north. Joshua concluded this part of his battle strategy by building an altar on Mount Ebal. Recent archeological research on Mount Ebal has resulted in the discovery of an altar some believe to be Joshua's altar. There he divided his army, half on Mount Gerizim, the other half on Mount Ebal, "and afterward he read all the words of the Law, the blessings and the cursings, according to all that is written in the Book of the Law" (8:34).

TWENTY-SEVEN

JOSHUA:
From Victory to Victory

(Joshua 9:1–24:33)

Joshua's name means "Jehovah saves," and his life characterized his name. He was born in the bondage of slavery in
Egypt, and Jehovah saved him physically, mentally, and emotionally, delivering him along with over 1 million Israelites.
During the forty years in the wilderness he witnessed the
continual salvation of the Lord. As "Moses' assistant" (Num.
11:28), he learned the lessons of leadership. As a spy, he
relied on God's help to faithfully bring back the accurate report
and back it with faith that God would give them the land. As a
soldier, Joshua saw the miraculous crossing of the River Jordan and capture of Jericho. As a saint, Joshua was filled with
the Spirit (Deut. 34:9), enjoyed the presence of God (Josh.
1:5; 6:27), was influenced by the Word of God (1:8), was
obedient to the will of God (Num. 32:12; Josh. 5:14) and when
he died, was deeply mourned.

But great pioneers and generals do not make great states-
men and rulers. Some only win the first battle, then fall in the
constant heat of pressure. But not Joshua. After he won the
decisive battle of Jericho and Ai, he followed his military in-
stinct and divided his enemy. He next plunged south and defeated the Amorites. Next he swept north defeating the Canaanites. In all, he defeated thirty-one city-states and so
conquered the Promised Land. Then he divided the land and

was to the end of his life, a spiritual leader to Israel.

With the initial success of Joshua in the central campaign, the kings of various city-states in the south began forming alliances in the hope that together they might defend themselves from the invading Hebrews. While most of the Amorite city-states agreed to fight together against Joshua, one of the largest and most influential of the cities opted to form a separate peace with the Hebrews.

The people of Gibeon and three neighboring cities sent a delegation to the battle camp of Israel at Gilgal. Though it was only a three-day journey from their cities to Gilgal, they began the journey in worn clothing with stale bread and old wine among their provisions. They were planning to deceive Israel into a peace pact. Their clothing and stale provisions were designed to support their story that they had come from a long distance. They appealed to Joshua to form an alliance with them, and they were successful.

The Gibeonites were successful in their deception because Israel "did not ask counsel of the Lord" (9:14). Had they prayed, they would probably have been able to avoid entering into the alliance. But three days later, when Joshua realized he had been deceived, he remained a man of his word and preserved their lives while forcing the men of Gibeon to be servants, "woodcutters and water carriers for the house of my God" (v. 23). They did this for generations.

THE SOUTHERN CAMPAIGN *(Josh. 9:1–10:43)*

It was the alliance which was formed between Gibeon and Joshua that led to the major battle of the southern campaign. When the Amorite kings realized Gibeon had made an alliance with the Hebrews, they themselves attacked Gibeon. The war alliance against Gibeon was headed by five kings of five major cities, but may have included other smaller cities. According to the archeological evidence gathered from the sites of each of the five cities identified with this alliance, they appear to have been major cities of that era. When they made their attack on the city of Gibeon, the men of Gibeon knew they needed the help of their newfound allies.

THE ALLIANCE AGAINST GIBEON

Adoni-Zedek of Jerusalem
Hoham of Hebron
Piram of Jarmuth
Japhia of Lachish
Debir of Eglon

Joshua answered the call for assistance from Gibeon by fast-marching his army by night and surprising the enemy by his sudden appearance. The surprise appearance of the army of Israel caused the merged army against Gibeon to retreat. But their retreat was hindered by a freak storm of hailstones. Because of the unique geography of the region, sudden and severe freak hailstorms with large hailstones are not uncommon. This storm actually killed more of the enemy than the Hebrew soldiers had killed (Josh. 10:11).

As the sun began to set in the west, Joshua knew he was running out of time. He asked God to extend the day so that he could continue fighting and finish the battle. At Joshua's command, "the sun stood still, and the moon stopped till the people had revenge upon their enemies . . . about a whole day" (v. 13). This most unusual miracle has been the subject of much controversy and speculation.

Some have suggested the miracle was caused by refracted light and that the earth continued its rotation and orbit but the night remained as bright as day. Others have suggested the phenomenon was the result of a comet which came too close to the earth's orbit and refracted light, or may have even struck the earth, stopping its rotation. Others suggest the rotation of the earth actually did cease for a period of about a day by the hand of God.

Though there have been persistent rumors of the discovery of Joshua's lost day by sophisticated N.A.S.A. computers, N.A.S.A. itself has not made such a claim. It is questionable if such a discovery could be made by computer technology as computers can only compute data they have been given. But there may be some evidence from the Western hemisphere that the effects of Joshua's long day were felt halfway around the world.

According to the ancient Mexican *Annals of Cuauhtitlan* also known as *Codex Chimalpopoca,* there was a time in Mexican history when "the night did not end for a very long time." This tradition was also uncovered by Bernardino de Sahagun (1499–1590), a Spaniard who collected the traditions of the aboriginal peoples of Central America. According to his published report, the people of Central America remembered a time when "the sun rose only a little way over the horizon and remained there without moving; the moon also stood still."

Joshua was successful in his efforts against the alliance against Gibeon. Though the kings escaped initially, they were captured and killed. In a series of battles following the long day, Joshua conquered Makkedah (10:28), Libnah (v. 29), Lachish (v. 31), Gezer (v. 33), Eglon (v. 34), Hebron (v. 36), and Debir (v. 38). In doing so, he secured the southern cities of Canaan for the possession of Israel and defeated the Amorites.

THE NORTHERN CAMPAIGN *(Josh. 11:1–12:24)*

The defeat of the Canaanites *(11:1-14)*
When the Canaanite kings heard what Joshua had done to the Amorites in the south, they too determined an alliance was their best defense against the unbeatable Hebrew army. An alliance was formed by many of the remaining city-states and tribal groups in the land and headed by three powerful Canaanite kings.

THE NORTHERN ALLIANCE

Jabin of Hazor
Jobab of Madon
Shimron of Achshaph

They were successful in gathering a vast army, "as many

people as the sand that is on the seashore in multitude, with very many horses and chariots" (11:4). The allied armies gathered "at the waters of Merom to fight against Israel" (v. 5).

In the face of this immense army gathered against Israel, God assured Joshua he would be the victor. Joshua led his army in a surprise ambush against the gathered armies and won a decisive victory. Perhaps because the alliance formed against them had been initiated by Jabin, king of Hazor, Joshua burned that city with fire. Archeological research at the ancient site of that city confirms both that Jabin was the dynastic title of the king of Hazor, and that the city was burned to the ground during the conquest of Joshua.

A summary of the victories of Joshua *(11:15–12:24)*
"As the Lord had commanded Moses His servant, so Moses commanded Joshua, and so Joshua did. He left nothing undone of all that the Lord had commanded Moses" (11:15). Joshua accomplished a total victory in his attempt to conquer the Promised Land. Recorded in his memoirs is a listing of the thirty-one kings he met in battle and defeated (12:9-24).

THE DISTRIBUTION OF THE LAND *(Josh. 13:1–21:45)*
Earlier in this present century, Major General O.O. Howard said of Joshua, "As regard to his genius for military leadership, he had a great natural talent for organization, for planning and the strategic conduct of a campaign; for fighting a battle and keeping the love and confidence of his soldiers, and with confidence in his own cause, never forgetting to lean on the arm of the Lord in defeat or victory." But if Joshua proved himself brilliant as a military leader, he did something few retired military leaders have accomplished with any degree of success. He also proved to be brilliant at the fine art of diplomacy when the battles were over. Joshua who conquered the Promised Land with his army, was also the Joshua who successfully divided the cities of that land to his army.

The specific territories assigned to each of the tribes was determined by the casting of lots before the tabernacle. Reuben, Gad, and the half tribe of Manasseh had already been given their possession on the east bank of the Jordan by Moses. The nine and one-half remaining tribes were assigned territory on the west bank. Joshua also designated six cities as "cities of refuge" as Moses had commanded in the wilderness. Though the Levites were given no inheritance, forty-eight cities were designated as levitical cities and included the six cities of refuge. Perhaps the best known aspect of the division of the land is the desire of eighty-five-year-old Caleb to take on the giants who had scared the ten spies into giving an evil report more than forty years earlier. Joshua honored the request and gave Caleb Hebron as his inheritance.

THE CITIES OF REFUGE

Kedesh—the sanctuary
Shechem—a shoulder
Hebron—communion
Bezer—munitions or fortress
Ramoth—the heights
Golan—their rejoicing

THE ALTAR OF WITNESS *(Josh. 22:1-34)*

With the Conquest completed, the two and a half tribes which settled on the east bank were released from their commitment to fight with Israel and permitted to return to their territory. "And when they came to the region of the Jordan which is in the land of Canaan, the children of Reuben, the children of Gad, and half tribe of Manasseh built an altar there by the Jordan—a great impressive altar" (Josh. 22:10). But when the other tribes learned of the altar, they misunderstood its significance and prepared to go to war against what they thought were apostatizing tribes. Fortunately a delegation was sent across the river to discuss the rebellion of the two and a half tribes with the suspected rebels.

In the course of their discussion, the east bank tribes were able to explain the altar was a memorial and witness of their unity with the west bank tribes rather than the center of a rival religion as suspected. To the credit of the west bank tribes, their leaders admitted they were wrong when confronted with the facts and ended their planned destruction of the territory. They learned an important spiritual principle in the process. One should be careful not to overreact to rumors, especially when they relate to suspected motives behind an otherwise harmless act.

PERSPECTIVE: JOSHUA'S FINAL MESSAGE AND DEATH *(Josh. 23:1–24:33)* (1390 B.C.)

"Now it came to pass, a long time after the Lord had given rest to Israel from all their enemies round about, that Joshua was old, advanced in age" (Josh. 23:1). He gathered together the elders of Israel to challenge them one last time before his death. The theme of his last speech to Israel was the theme of his life, the total victory that God gives.

In the course of his remarks, he warned the people to keep the Law, abstain from the worship of false gods, and refrain from intermarriage with the people outside the commonwealth of Israel. His final challenge was "fear the Lord, serve Him in sincerity and in truth . . . choose for yourselves this day whom you will serve. . . . But as for me and my house, we will serve the Lord" (24:14-15).

"Now it came to pass after these things that Joshua the son of Nun, the servant of the Lord, died, being one hundred and ten years old" (v. 29). But unlike his predecessor Moses, this leader was buried in the land promised to Abraham, the land now possessed by Israel, the land he had been responsible for conquering.

TWENTY-EIGHT

JUDGES:
Othniel, Ehud, and Deborah

(Judges 1:1–5:31)

After the death of Joshua, there was no strong leader to provide leadership for Israel in the land. But there did not appear to be a need for a strong leader for some time. The influence of Joshua was felt long after he was dead. "So the people served the Lord all the days of Joshua, and all the days of the elders who outlived Joshua, who had seen all the great works of the Lord, which He had done for Israel" (Jud. 2:7). So long as they continued to follow the Lord, the elders of the various tribes and families could and did administer the affairs of state.

Israel was not a unified nation with a capital city into which they could rally during a time of invasion (i.e., a city-state). They were a confederation of twelve tribes, comprised mostly of farmers and herdsmen. There was no central leader, only patriarchal family heads to lead their extended families.

But though they were the designated people of God in the Old Testament, they were as human as men today. It is always easier to follow the Lord when there is a cause or crisis than to maintain a walk with God after the initial crisis is past. And so in their strength, Israel became weak by failing to complete the task God had assigned them. "But the children of Benjamin did not drive out the Jebusites who inhabited Jerusalem" (1:21). "Manasseh did not drive out the inhabitants of

Beth Shean and its villages, or Taanach and its villages, or the inhabitants of Dor and its villages, or the inhabitants of Ibleam and its villages, or the inhabitants of Megiddo and its villages" (v. 27). "Nor did Ephraim drive out the Canaanites who dwelt in Gezer" (v. 29). Nor did Zebulun drive out the inhabitants of Kitron, or the inhabitants of Nahalol" (v. 30). "Nor did Asher drive out the inhabitants of Acco or the inhabitants of Sidon, or of Ahlab, Achzib, Helbah, Aphik, or Rehob" (v. 31). "Nor did Naphtali drive out the inhabitants of Beth Shemesh or the inhabitants of Beth Anath" (v. 33).

Someone has said, "The one thing man learns from history is that man does not learn from history." Sociologists, those who study trends in society, have noted societies tend to revolve in cycles. Certainly that was true in the history of Israel. In the Book of Judges, there is an obvious repetition of the social cycle which was the experience of Israel. From generation to generation the people demonstrated by repeatedly passing through the cycle of judgment and restoration that they had failed to learn anything from the experience of the previous generation.

CYCLES OF JUDGMENT AND RESTORATION

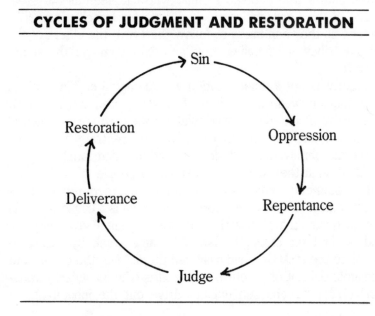

So pronounced is this pattern in the Book of Judges that it actually provides the key by which the history of events is recounted. Though there are several minor judges mentioned in the book, the history of Israel from the Conquest to the establishment of the monarchy really revolves around the conditions leading to the rise of seven major judges who were the key to the deliverance of Israel from the hands of her enemies and their subsequent ministry. Six of these judges are described in the Book of Judges. The last of the judges was Samuel the prophet and faithful priest at Shiloh.

JUDGES: SIX CYCLES OF JUDGMENT

Othniel and the Defeat of Cushan (Syrians)
Ehud and the Defeat of Eglon (Moabites)
Deborah and Barak and the Defeat of Jabin and Sisera (Canaanites)
Gideon and the Defeat of the Midianites (Arabs)
Jephthah and the Defeat of the Ammonites
Samson and the Struggle against the Philistines

But why did Israel need deliverance from an enemy which had been so soundly defeated in the total victory of Joshua? The answer to that question is hinted at very early in the book. "Then the Angel of the Lord came up from Gilgal to Bochim" (Jud. 2:1). Israel forgot that eternal vigilance is the price of liberty. Gilgal was the battle camp of Israel, the place from which Israel had marched to victory under the leadership of Joshua. The name *Bochim* means "a place of weeping." Its very name suggests discouragement and defeat.

The Angel of the Lord which was Jesus in the Old Testament had never left the battle camp, but Israel had long since stopped fighting. They formed alliances with the Canaanites who tried to move back into their former territory. At first it seemed like a good idea. They taxed the Canaanites and were able to increase their standard of living to some degree. But now they were beginning to suffer some of the side-effects of their compromise and found themselves in the place of weeping. Within a generation, things would get even worse.

"When all that generation had been gathered to their fathers, another generation arose after them who did not know the Lord nor the work which He had done for Israel. . . . And they forsook the Lord and served Baal and the Ashtoreths" (vv. 10, 13). Their apostasy led to their being subject to the wrath of God, and in His wrath, God allowed the very peoples they had preserved to become their enemies and oppress them. "Then the Lord raised up judges who delivered them out of the hand of those who plundered them" (v. 16).

A judge was not one who decided legal cases, but was usually thought of as a military leader. He was also a spiritual leader who called Israel back to God before leading them into battle. At times he became a political leader by virtue of his reputation of success on the battlefield or in spiritual realms. Many times a judge could determine the will of God for the people, hence his name. None of the judges ruled over all Israel. They usually were leaders of two or three tribes, and their sequence in the Book of Judges is not always chronological. Sometimes they overlapped.

OTHNIEL AND THE DEFEAT OF CUSHAN
(Jud. 3:7-11) (1359–1319 b.c.)

Because Israel turned from worshiping God to worshiping the idols of Baal and Ashtoreth (Jud. 2:13) and engaged in intermarriage contrary to the command of God (3:6), God raised up a Mesopotamian king named Cushan to rule over Israel for eight years. The Scripture identifies this king as "Cushan-Rishathaim," but it appears his personal name was Cushan. The expression *rishathaim* means "dirty double-crosser." That this designation appears so often in the biblical record with the name Cushan suggests Israel may have at one time formed an alliance with Cushan who then "double-crossed" them forcing them into servitude. If that were the case, this bondage was the fruit of compromise on the part of Israel.

Toward the end of the eight-year period of bondage, "the Lord raised up a deliverer for the Children of Israel, who delivered them: Othniel the son of Kenaz, Caleb's younger brother" (v. 9). Of all the men and women God chose to judge Israel, Othniel was the strongest. Throughout the course of the book, there seems to be a progressive decline in the effectiveness of the judges until Samson is unable to completely defeat his enemy, the Philistines. Also, this judge would seem like the most logical choice of a judge from a human perspective. He had won the hand of Caleb's daughter in marriage as the result of an earlier military victory and is closely identified with his father-in-law in Scripture who was certainly among the greatest men of faith in his generation.

In the case of each of the major judges in this book, the Scripture draws attention to some feature which would have been a liability in the context of their society.

THE IMPERFECTIONS OF THE JUDGES

Othniel—Nepotism
Ehud—Left-handed
Barak—Coward
Deborah—Woman
Gideon—Coward
Jephthah—Son of a harlot
Samson—Adulterer

Othniel was endued with power when "the Spirit of the Lord came upon him" (v. 10) and went to war against the Mesopotamian king. The Scriptures record nothing about the battle except that Othniel was victorious and his defeat of Cushan-Rishathaim resulted in a forty-year rest for the land. "Then Othniel the son of Kenaz died" (v. 11).

EHUD AND THE DEFEAT OF EGLON
(Jud. 3:12-31) (1301–1221 B.C.)

Again Israel turned from God, causing God to raise up an oppressor against His people. The particular nature of the sin of Israel during this period of rebellion is not revealed in Scripture, but God raised up the king of Moab who formed an alliance with the nations of Ammon and Amalek to defeat Israel and put them in bondage. For eighteen years, Eglon, king of Moab, collected tribute from Israel. That it took Israel eighteen years to turn back to God suggests something of the degree of sin they had engaged in.

In answer to the prayers of repentant Israel, God raised up a judge and deliverer in the person of a left-handed Benjamite named Ehud, the son of Gera. In ancient societies, to be left-handed was usually thought of as a liability. In extreme cases, left-handed people were burned as witches or those who were suspected of forming a league with the devil. But for Ehud, his left-handedness would be an asset.

Ehud arranged to be the one to take the tribute payment of Israel to Eglon at the latter's summer palace in Jericho. Because of its favorable climate, the region surrounding Jericho has been and is today a desirable resort center. Eglon was not the only king to build a summer palace in that region. But when Ehud took the tribute to Eglon, he hid a two-edged dagger under the right side of his garment. If there was any kind of security check of those meeting the oppressive king, it would be assumed any weapons would be hid on his left side.

Ehud convinced Eglon to meet alone with him. Eglon probably expected to receive some form of bribe in exchange for a royal favor, but Ehud drew his dagger and thrust it into the chest of the king. The murder of Eglon is described in vivid detail in Scripture. Ehud thrust it into the belly of the overweight king so hard he actually lost his grip. The blade must have penetrated the king's intestinal tract "and his entrails came out" (Jud. 3:22). Folds of fat covered the handle of Ehud's dagger leaving him without a weapon to make his escape. Nevertheless, he locked the room as he left and escaped to gather an army against the nation of Moab.

When the king's servants returned to find a locked room, they were no doubt aware of the foul odor coming from the room. They reasoned, "He is probably attending to his needs in the cool chamber" (v. 24) which means they thought he was using whatever facilities he might have had to relieve himself. Not wanting to interrupt their king while he was engaged in this activity, they continued to wait until they were embarrassed at the length of time he was taking. Finally they entered the room to discover the corpse of their king.

It is not clear the Moabites were aware of specifically what had happened, but it was clear from the death of their king that a coup was underway. Without leadership, they probably panicked and decided to get back to Moab quickly for security reasons and to have an opportunity to regroup before going after the perhaps unknown rebels. But Ehud had already anticipated this reaction and had his army stationed at the fords of the Jordan River, the most likely place to cross into Moab. "And at that time they killed about ten thousand men of Moab, all stout men of valor; not a man escaped" (v. 29). For the next eight years, Israel had rest.

But the Moabites were not the only oppressors of Israel. About this time, the Philistines began arriving in large numbers from Greece and settled on the coastal plain of Canaan. They appear to have aggressively interfered with the commerce of the region, perhaps raiding those who traveled along the main highways. As a result, "the highways were deserted, and the travelers walked along the byways" (5:6). Also, the Philistines tended to disarm those they conquered thus making any underground movement or open rebellion very difficult. But there was one very resourceful judge, though probably only a minor judge, who used an oxgoad, an eight-foot pole with one sharp end normally used to goad cattle, to slay 600 Philistines. It is not clear whether Shamgar did this in one day, or more likely the number represents a lifetime total. "And he also delivered Israel" (v. 31).

DEBORAH AND BARAK AND THE DEFEAT OF JABIN AND SISERA *(Jud. 4–5)* (1201–1161 B.C.)

"When Ehud was dead, the Children of Israel again did evil in the sight of the Lord" (Jud. 4:1). As before, their religious compromise led to moral corruption which resulted in civil catastrophe. Israel was learning experientially the truth of a proverb not yet written. "Righteousness exalts a nation, but sin is a reproach to any people" (Prov. 14:34). This time Israel was oppressed for twenty years by an alliance involving Jabin of Hazor and his general Sisera of Harosheth.

Critics of the Scripture have been quick to point out Joshua also fought a king of Hazor named Jabin and suggest this may be an evidence of the unreliability of Scripture. Acutally, archeological research at Hazor has demonstrated the amazing accuracy of the Scripture on this point. Jabin was not a personal name, but rather a dynastic title which belonged to the king of that city. Also, Jabin appears to be only a figurehead leader in his oppression of Israel. The real power of this alliance was that of Sisera. Archeologists have discovered that though Hazor was rebuilt after Joshua, the city had not returned to its former strength by this time.

On this occasion, God raised up a military leader named Barak to deliver Israel, but in his cowardice, he refused to fight unless accompanied by a prophetess named Deborah. It is not clear whether there was a female prophetic office in the Old Testament, or whether the term prophetess refers to a woman associated with a prophet, i.e., his wife. But because Barak would not fight as God commanded him without her support, Deborah told Barak he would be victorious, but that a woman would be credited with killing Sisera.

PERSPECTIVE

Deborah was perhaps the first of many women since then who have undertaken to do something for God because a man refused. The influence of dedicated women has been felt throughout history, but perhaps nowhere has it been more evident than in the field of missions. It is difficult to imagine what would be accomplished on the mission field if women had not done what men refused to do.

A battle was fought between Sisera and Barak in the valley of the river Kishon, and again God intervened to give His people the victory. "The torrent of Kishon swept them away" (Jud. 5:21). It appears the army of Sisera was caught up in a flash flooding of the river Kishon much as it did during the nineteenth century enabling Napolean to defeat the Turks, and again in the twentieth century giving the British the advantage over the same enemy.

But Sisera escaped the army of Barak. He ran to the tent of Jael, the wife of Heber, where he thought he would be safe. But while the tired and defeated general slept, "She stretched her hand to the tent peg, her right hand to the workman's hammer; she pounded Sisera, she pierced his head, she split and struck through his temple" (v. 26). "So the land had rest for forty years" (v. 31).

TWENTY-NINE

GIDEON:
The Defeat of the Midianites

(Judges 6:1–9:57)

And the Children of Israel did evil in the sight of the Lord. So the Lord delivered them into the hand of Midian for seven years" (Jud. 6:1). It was clear that Israel was not learning her lesson. As a result, an alliance of nations headed by Midian which also included the Amalekites and "the people of the East" came up against the people of Israel. This oppression was both unique and severe. The Midianites and their allies did not appear to occupy the land but rather sent in raiding parties during the prime harvest seasons to steal or savagely destroy the crops. This invasion reached into the land of Israel as far as the Philistine city of Gaza. The effect of this strategy was devastating. They would "leave no sustenance for Israel, neither sheep nor ox nor donkey" (v. 4).

God's discipline of His people was severe without question. "So Israel was greatly impoverished because of the Midianites" (v. 6). But it took this great humiliation of the people to bring them to the point where they would begin turning to God for help. But even in turning to God for help, there appears to have been some hesitancy. The people "cried out to the Lord" as was their custom when they got into serious trouble, but they apparently still worshiped Baal and refused to repent. It is significant that God responded to the prayers of His people by first raising up a prophet who reminded the people of all

God had done for the nation in delivering them from Egypt. The prophet also claimed the people had not obeyed the voice of God. The name of the prophet is not recorded in Scripture, but there is some hint that his message was widely heard and to some degree understood by the people.

When Gideon first met the Angel of the Lord, he asked the question, "And where are all His miracles, which our fathers told us about, saying, 'Did not the Lord bring us up from Egypt?' " (v. 13) It seems as though the message was heard, understood, and taught to the families of Israel, but as is so often true during times of hardship and depression, the people of Israel had difficulty believing that it had any real application to their situation.

GIDEON: THE RELUCTANT COWARD *(Jud. 6:1–7:14)* (1161 B.C.)

God selected a young coward named Gideon to be His deliverer to release Israel from the bondage of Midian. There is a tendency among some commentators to try to portray Gideon as a humble hero waiting for the call of God to take on the Midianites, but the oldest Jewish commentaries always emphasize the cowardice of Gideon. When the Angel of the Lord met Gideon at a winepress near Ophrah, Gideon was hiding in the winepress threshing wheat, fearful that the Midianites would see him. When he heard a voice call down, "The Lord is with you, you mighty man of valor" (Jud. 6:12), Gideon may well have suspected the speaker was trying to be sarcastic. That may be why he responded with such a blunt response.

Gideon's first recorded words in Scripture suggest several reasons for his initial unbelief. First, though the Lord spoke of His presence with Gideon specifically, Gideon responded, "If the Lord is with us" (v. 13), suggesting he was basing his own spiritual life on the problematic conditions he saw in others around him. Because it was clear the Lord was not with them, He could not be with Gideon, so he concluded. Further, it is significant that he referred only to the miracles in the distant past, as far back as the Exodus from Egypt. God had clearly acted on Israel's behalf in a miraculous way on several occasions since then, but Gideon had in his mind equated the involvement of God in the affairs of the life of Israel as only a bit of trivia from ancient history. Third, it is clear that his focus in this statement was on the enemy he feared. He was problem-conscious rather than power-conscious.

But Gideon's statement only confirmed God's choice of a deliverer. "Go in this might of yours, and you shall save Israel from the hand of the Midianites" (v. 14). It was clear that Gideon had everything he needed to win the decisive victory God wanted to give Israel. First, Gideon understood and would be the first to admit his own inability to win the battle. This meant God could prove Himself strong in Gideon's weakness. Second, Gideon now had a mission in life, "You shall defeat the Midianites as one man" (v. 16). But most important, Gideon's greatest resource going into battle would be the coveted presence of God Himself. "Surely I will be with you" (v. 16).

Still, Gideon was a coward and reluctant to believe these strange things that were being spoken to him by this Stranger. He wasn't the sort of person most people would think of when they thought of a deliverer. He was not only from the insignificant tribe of Manasseh, but his family was poor and he himself was at the bottom of the pecking order in his own family. The picture the Scripture portrays of Gideon is that of a scared young man with a very low self-esteem that had for years been reinforced by his circumstance in life. But in accordance with the Near Eastern standard of hospitality, Gideon urged the man to remain to enjoy a meal. It was not until the Angel of the Lord consumed the food with a fire that Gideon perceived he was speaking with God.

That realization created a new problem for Gideon. It was widely believed that if one saw God he would die, and though Gideon did not enjoy his low standing in life, his miserable existence hiding out from the Midianites was better than no life at all. God had to assure Gideon he had nothing to fear, "You shall not die" (v. 23). Only then did Gideon demonstrate the existence of a kernel of faith in his bushel of doubt. "So Gideon built an altar there to the Lord, and called it The-Lord-

Shalom" (v. 24). The name *The-Lord-Shalom* means "The Lord our peace" but in this context it also had a fuller meaning. Israel was oppressed at the time Gideon built the altar, and he had just been commissioned to engage in battle against the oppressor. In calling the altar "Peace," he was also confessing a willingness to believe the Lord would give him victory over the Midianites.

But if Gideon was going to deliver Israel from the bondage of the Midianites, he had to first get his own personal priorities in life established. Gideon's own father had an altar of Baal and associated grove of trees which appears to have been used by others in the area also. God told Gideon to destroy the altar and grove and build an altar to the Lord in its place. And God wanted Gideon to offer a burnt offering on the altar.

The whole burnt offering was an expression of complete consecration to God. That would certainly be true in this case. For seven years the Midianites and their allies had been invading the land, destroying the crops and livestock of Israel, but somehow Gideon's father had been successful in hiding and preserving the life of one bullock which had been born about the time the raids began. This highly prized bullock was the sacrifice God required Gideon to offer on the altar. It may have been the most valuable asset of the farm, but offering it to God in a burnt offering was in keeping with the true spirit of that kind of sacrifice.

Gideon, still something of a coward, waited until the sun had set before doing as he was instructed. With the help of ten servants, he destroyed the center of Baal worship while the village slept. But in the morning, his work was soon discovered and Joash, the father of Gideon, was called on to deliver up his guilty son to be punished for his action.

No one was more surprised than Joash to learn his cowardly son had undertaken such a brave act. He challenged the men of the city to let Baal fight his own battles. "If he is a god, let him plead for himself, because his altar has been torn down" (v. 31). Out of the whole experience, Gideon earned a new nickname, Jerubbaal, meaning "let him plead."

Only after Gideon had destroyed the altar of Baal was he

empowered by the Spirit of the Lord and enabled to begin gathering his army. But even as he was gathering together an army, Gideon was having second thoughts. He asked God to confirm his faith by causing a piece of fleece to be soaked with dew while the ground around it was dry. But when God did what Gideon asked, the reluctant coward was still not convinced. He asked the Lord to reverse the process as he tried it a second time. The next morning the ground was soaked, but the fleece was dry.

But if Gideon was having trouble believing God would give him the victory, it was not going to be any easier. Gideon moved his army to the well of Harod, close to the Midianite camp, but well hidden from sight. When everyone arrived for the battle, Gideon had an army of 32,000 scared men to take on the professional army of 135,000 Midianites. Though Gideon knew his army was grossly outnumbered, God told him the army of Israel was too big. Gideon was told to let anyone who was afraid of the battle to leave, and when he did so, 22,000 soldiers left him.

Still God claimed the army of 10,000 men was too big and the people were to pass through another test. The men were taken to the water to drink and separated into two companies based on the way they drank water. Most of the men got down and put their faces to the water to drink, but 300 of the soldiers lapped the water out of their hands. There are two views as to why God chose these soldiers. The first suggests God rejected those who put their face into the water to drink because they were worshiping water, one aspect of Baal worship. A second suggests the 300 who knelt and lapped water were fearful the Midianites would attack while they were not looking. God wanted 300 cowards to follow cowardly Gideon, thus showing the victory would be the Lord's. Three hundred men formed Gideon's army. The rest of the army was also dismissed.

Gideon was still hesitant to believe his 300 men could defeat the vast army of the Midianites, so God decided to build Gideon's faith in a most unique way. The same night Gideon was left with the 300 soldiers, he and his servant Purah were instructed to go down to the camp of the Midianites. The name of Gideon's servant *Purah* means "foliage" and some commentators picture the occasion of their descent to the enemy camp with Gideon hiding behind foliage with his servant. But there at the edge of the Midianite camp, Gideon overheard an unusual conversation.

One soldier recounted a dream in which "a loaf of barley bread tumbled into the camp of Midian; it came to a tent, and struck it so that it fell and overturned, and the tent collapsed" (7:13). But it was the interpretation of that dream by the second soldier that must have impressed Gideon most. He claimed, "This is nothing else but the sword of Gideon the son of Joash, a man of Israel; for into his hand God has delivered Midian and the whole camp" (v. 14).

GIDEON: THE READY CRUSADER *(Jud. 7:15-23)*
After learning about the barley bread dream, Gideon was a different man. The reluctant coward was now the ready crusader, prepared to fight the battle of the Lord. His experiments with the fleece had failed to give him the confidence he needed to serve God as a deliverer, but when he realized that even the enemy believed God was going to give Israel the victory, Gideon was ready to worship the Lord. And he was ready to fight. When he returned to his own camp that night, he roused his soldiers and began the battle.

Gideon's battle strategy involved dividing his army into three companies. Each man would have a torch, a jar, and a trumpet. They would silently surround the Midianite camp high on the hillside and keep their torches hidden in their jars. Then on a signal from their leader, they would suddenly break their jars, blow their trumpets, and shout "The sword of the Lord and of Gideon" (Jud. 7:20).

Night battles were rarely fought in those days. On the rare occasions when night battles were fought, about one man in a thousand was given the task of carrying a torch so the others could see to fight. Also, one man in a thousand was given a trumpet and blew it in battle. When Gideon's men broke their jars and blew their trumpets, the effect was stunning. Suddenly the darkness would have burst forth with bright light. The sound of the breaking jars and trumpet blasts would echo through the valley along with the shouts of Gideon's army. Sleeping soldiers were awakened from their sleep only to see what must have seemed like an ambush by an army of at least 300,000 men. They thought a thousand attackers represented each torch they saw. They may already have been afraid of such an attack even before it was launched. Quickly they grabbed their swords and began cutting at anything that moved in the shadows. Only too late would they discover they were killing their own army, "for one hundred and twenty thousand men who drew the sword had fallen" (8:10).

GIDEON: THE RENEGADE CAPTAIN *(Jud. 7:24–8:35)* (1154 B.C.)

In his victory, Gideon took an action which showed his readiness to trust not in the Lord but rather the strength of Israel. "Then Gideon sent messengers throughout all the mountains of Ephraim, saying, 'Come down against the Midianites, and seize from them the watering places as far as Beth Barah and the Jordan' " (Jud. 7:24). Many of those who answered the call to now support Gideon in the battle were among those God had told him to dismiss from the battle the day before. The fact that two Midianite leaders were captured and killed as a result of this action does not justify Gideon's apparent effort to increase the size of his fighting force when God had emphasized He wanted a small army "lest Israel claim glory for itself against Me, saying, 'My own hand has saved me' " (v. 2).

Gideon continued to chase the 15,000 Midianites who had escaped "and he took the two kings of Midian, Zebah and Zalmunna, and routed the whole army" (8:12). But he was now something of a renegade captain and on his victorious return he viciously beat the elders of Succoth with thorns and tortured the men of that city because they had not given him bread as he had driven his tired army after the Midianites (v. 16). When he got to Penuel he destroyed the city and killed the men because they too had been reluctant to give him the requested supplies.

As Gideon prepared to kill the two captured kings of Midian, he revealed his new motives for defeating the Midianites. He had been raised up by God to deliver Israel, but he was not apparently interested now in solely accomplishing the purposes of God. He reminded the two kings of a raid they had made on Tabor, and after telling them he had relatives who had died in that raid, he confessed, "As the Lord lives, if you had let them live, I would not kill you" (v. 19). Clearly Gideon was now interested in revenge.

When Gideon returned to his home in Israel, the men were ready to make him king. But after having killed the two kings of Midian, he may have realized being king was not always all it was made out to be. He did, however, have a request. He asked for all the gold earrings that had been collected as spoils of war. The men agreed, and when the earrings were weighed, Gideon had 17,000 shekels of gold, or about six pounds of gold. "Then Gideon made it into an ephod and set it up in his city, Ophrah. And all Israel played the harlot with it there. It became a snare to Gideon and to his house" (v. 27).

One of the common themes in pagan worship is that of immoral sexual practices. During the forty years of quietness which followed Gideon's victory, Gideon acquired an undisclosed number of wives, and had a concubine he kept in Shechem. But Gideon's sin was not without its consequences. "And so it was, as soon as Gideon was dead, that the Children of Israel again played the harlot with the Baals, and made Baal-Berith their god. Thus the Children of Israel did not remember the Lord their God, who had delivered them from the hands of all their enemies on every side; nor did they show kindness to the house of Jerubbaal (that is, Gideon) in accordance with the good he had done for Israel" (vv. 33-35).

PERSPECTIVE

It is interesting to note that the Scriptures begin identifying Gideon by the name Jerubbaal as soon as he made the golden ephod. The name Gideon is based on a root which means to cut down and symbolizes the great victories of his life. It was Gideon who cut down the altar of Baal and then cut down the army of Midian. But it was the name Jerubbaal which identified him with the pagan religious practices of his day. Ten times following his death, the Scriptures refer to Gideon by his pagan name Jerubbaal. Though he had accomplished such a great victory for Israel they were prepared to make him their king forty years earlier, by the time of his death, he had destroyed his reputation for God by his involvement in pagan religious practices.

The sin of Gideon was also directly responsible for the destruction of his family in the next generation. The son he had fathered by a concubine conspired to kill legitimate sons of Gideon. Only the youngest of the seventy sons of Gideon was able to escape with his life. The son of the concubine, Abimelech, convinced the men of Shechem to make him Israel's first king. The name Abimelech means "my father is king" and was actually a dynastic title of the Philistines. A part of Israel was having a king like the nations around them. But Jotham, the son of Gideon, warned of trouble ahead.

Standing near the summit of Mount Gerizim, Jotham told the parable of the trees who wanted a king. In their folly they chose the bramble bush to be their ruler, just as the men of Shechem chose Abimelech. Because of the mistreatment of the family of Gideon, Jotham declared those involved would be judged. Three years later, problems developed between the new king and his subjects. As the problems erupted into a physical conflict, Abimelech destroyed the city of Shechem and burned the stronghold of the city with the men of the city inside. Then there was another uprising in the city of Thebez. But as Abimelech tried to take the same course of action in that city, it was he who lost his life. "Thus God repaid the wickedness of Abimelech, which he had done to his father by killing his seventy sons. And all the evil of the men of Shechem God returned on their own heads, and on them came the curse of Jotham the son of Jerubbaal" (Jud. 9:56-57).

THIRTY

RUTH:
The Romance of Redemption

(Ruth 1:1–4:22)

About the time Gideon was hiding in the winepress to escape the dangers of a Midianite invasion, a small village to the south was caught up in the midst of a severe famine. This famine may have been the natural consequence of the successive invasions of the Midianites during the harvest seasons, or simply the result of a prolonged drought. Some Bible commentators suggest the combination of these two factors resulted in its severity. Like the other dozen famines recorded in Scripture, this famine also appears to have been a physical manifestation of the judgment of God.

The account of this famine is recorded in the opening verses of the Book of Ruth, originally appended to the Book of Judges. Yet unlike the Book of Judges, Ruth is an account of what was going right in Israel. It records people praying and seeing answers to their prayers without the cycle of oppression so common in the Book of Judges. Yet it is obvious from several contextual hints in the two books that these events occurred simultaneously.

Ruth begins with the expression, "Now it came to pass, in the days of." A form of this expression occurs five times in the Old Testament and always denotes impending trouble, followed by internal disorders and outward oppressions. The crisis age referred to in this context is simply described as "when the judges ruled" (Jud. 1:1). This was an era of apostasy and anarchy (cf. 2:10-13; 21:25). Though some Jewish commentators tend to identify the Boaz of this book with the otherwise unknown judge Ibzan of Bethlehem (12:8-10), the genealogy of the last chapter linking Ruth and Boaz to David suggests an earlier context; i.e., during the rule of Gideon. This would also account for the dramatic change in conditions during the decade in which the first chapter of the book is set.

But the Book of Ruth is more than a history of a family in Bethlehem. It is a love story of how a poor but virtuous widow finds her rest and fulfillment through a marriage to one of the wealthiest and most honorable men of the city. But it is also more than a love story. It is an account of faith in which a number of prayers are offered to God and without exception answered to the benefit of the one praying. But it also more than an account of faith. It is the story of how a Moabite girl, who was an alien from the commonwealth of Israel and by law under the curse of Moab, found redemption in the village of Bethlehem and was accepted into the society of the people of God. And in all this, it is a picture of every believer's relationship to God. It is the romance of redemption, a picture of what faith can and does accomplish in the life of every believer.

OUTLINE OF RUTH

1 Love's resolve
2 Love's response
3 Love's request
4 Love's reward

LOVE'S RESOLVE *(Ruth 1:1-22)*

The book begins with the record of a lot of decisions, but two stand as primary to the entire plot of the book. First there was the bad decision of Elimelech to leave Bethlehem and move to Moab. In contrast, there is the good decision of Ruth to leave Moab and move to Bethlehem. In understanding the decision-making process involved, we can learn much about how to make decisions and live with their consequences.

The setting of the beginning and much of this book is in the village of Bethlehem in Judah. Bethlehem is located on a narrow ridge about six miles south of Jerusalem. The area is surrounded by terraced slopes suitable for the cultivation of vineyards and orchards of olives and figs. In the fields beyond the terraces, wheat and barley have always been the principal crops grown. On the hillsides beyond the fields, flocks and herds were kept. Though the village was originally known as Ephrathah, it was not long before people began calling it Bethlehem which literally means "house of bread."

The first decision made in this book was a bad decision with tragic consequences. A man named Elimelech which means "my God is King" decided to leave his home in Bethlehem to travel to Moab. The Bible describes this family as "Ephrathites of Bethlehem, Judah" (Ruth 1:2) suggesting they were an old and established family in the village. By today's terminology, they were "blue bloods." Their decision to leave was probably not an easy decision to make, but that did not prevent them from making the wrong decision. There are several hints as to how Elimelech made his bad decision.

First though it was Elimelech's decision to go to Moab, it was probably made with his wife's consent. Some commentators have even suggested she may have been the driving force behind the decision (cf. vv. 20-21). If this is an accurate conclusion, the opening verses of Ruth portray a man being constantly nagged by his wife to take a course of action he knows to be wrong.

But the fault in making this bad decision was not exclusively that of Naomi. As Elimelech considered the situation, he soon began developing his own little compromises by which he could justify his decision to go to Moab. First, he would only go "to sojourn" (v. 1). The Hebrew word *gur* refers to a status as resident aliens. In his original decision to move to Moab, it was never his determination to remain.

Second, he would only go to "the country of Moab" (v. 1) literally "the fields of Moab." The Hebrew word used in this context seeks to draw a distinction between the fields belonging to the nation Moab and the actual land of Moab which would have included the cities. Perhaps he thought he could avoid the contamination of Moab by avoiding the cities. It was the same kind of erroneous logic Lot, the father of Moab, had once used to justify moving toward Sodom.

But if Elimelech was going to leave Bethlehem, why would he choose to go to Moab? The Moabites were descendants of an incestuous relationship between Lot and his oldest daughter (Gen. 19:29-38). As a people, they had often opposed Israel by refusing them water and bread during their Exodus from Egypt and hiring Balaam to curse the nation (cf. Deut. 23:3-7). As a result, there were ingrained religious and cultural reasons that kept Israel from even wanting to have relations with the neighboring nation. And at the time Elimelech left, Moab was at war with Israel.

Perhaps Elimelech really didn't have a choice once he had decided to run from the discipline of God. The Midianites and their allies had invaded Israel as far as Gaza which was a Philistine stronghold. Some commentators believe those who tried to escape to Egypt were attacked on the road to Egypt. There were few other refuges left for one committed to leaving Israel.

Beyond this, there was also the visibility factor. He could actually see Moab. The green pastures of Moab, though forty to sixty miles away, would have been visible to Elimelech from his home high in the village of Bethlehem. And as his wife continued to remind him of all the problems in Bethlehem, he could look out his window and see the lush green pastures of Moab in the distance.

Eventually the decision was made and the family moved. But once they arrived in Moab, conditions were even better than they imagined. The decision was made to remain there (Ruth 1:2). The change in the Hebrew verb suggests a change of heart in Elimelech once in Moab. "Then Elimelech, Noami's husband, died" (v. 3). Though not expressly stated as such, the context almost certainly implies the necessity of interpreting this death as a judgment of God.

But the death of Elimelech seems to have had little effect on the spiritual state of the family. "They dwelt there about ten years" (v. 4). Again the verb change demonstrates a change of heart in Moab. They had come to the place where they were prepared to settle down and live in Moab as home. Naomi's sons married wives chosen from the women of Moab and there is no indication anyone gave any thought to returning home to Bethlehem. Eventually the sons also died leaving behind three widows to fend for themselves. Only then did Naomi decide it was time to go home to Bethlehem. But it was not an evidence of spiritual renewal in her life. On the way home she succeeded in convincing one of her daughters-in-law to stay in Moab where she could worship the false gods of that land rather than following Naomi to Bethlehem (v. 15). This was not a spiritual suggestion by Naomi. But only one was convinced not to migrate to Bethlehem.

Even in this first chapter, the faith of Ruth is contrasted with the apostasy of Israel. Despite the persuasive arguments of her mother-in-law, Ruth could not be persuaded to abandon her faith in God and commitment to Naomi. "And Ruth said, 'Entreat me not to leave you, or to turn back from following after you; for wherever you go, I will go; and wherever you lodge, I will lodge; your people shall be my people, and your God, my God' " (v. 16). Only when Naomi realized Ruth was "determined to go with her" did she cease trying to convince her to return to Moab (v. 18).

Still, Ruth's commitment had little immediate impact on Naomi's disposition. On their return to Bethlehem, Naomi was recognized by the women of the village who remembered her. But she urged them to no longer call her Naomi which means "pleasant" but rather Mara meaning "bitter," "for the Almighty has dealt very bitterly with me. I went out full, and the Lord has brought me home again empty. Why do you call me Naomi, since the Lord has testified against me, and the Almighty has afflicted me?" (vv. 20-21)

What a contrast in the words of this very bitter lady. Naomi took the name of God which is characteristically involved in comforting those in sorrow *(Shaddai,* cf. Job), and used it to accuse God of mistreating her. This statement reflects an inner attitude and suggests she had come to the place where she recognized the wrongness of her prior decisions and actions, but had not yet come to the place where she was ready to repent of that sin. But for the sake of an ignored, perhaps even despised young widow from Moab, Naomi would have no part in the blessing of God.

LOVE'S RESPONSE *(Ruth 2:1-23)*

Ruth and Naomi returned to Bethlehem in the late spring about the time of the barley harvest (Ruth 1:22). As they settled into their new home, it was only natural that Ruth should recognize the opportunity to work in the harvest. Under the Law, God had made provision for the poor by allowing them to glean grain from the fields after the harvesters had finished their work. As a result, the poor often gathered in the fields a distance behind the harvesters to gather up that which remained. Ruth's first sight of Bethlehem may have included seeing a group of gleaners following the harvesters in the fields. As there was little else a virtuous widow could do in that culture to provide for her needs, it was obvious she would soon be spending much of the harvest season in the fields.

But even though the gleaners were insured a means to provide for themselves under the Law, they were not always welcomed by the landowners. Sometimes they were abused emotionally and physically by the reapers who considered them easy prey. This would be especially true in the case of a young and attractive widow from Moab. As she set out that morning to glean in the fields, Ruth suspected she might have to try several fields before finding one in which she could be safe. As it worked out, the field she chose first would be the only field she would have to work.

"She happened to come to the part of the field belonging to Boaz, who was of the family of Elimelech" (2:3), but the events that followed suggest God was the guiding hand behind this apparent coincidence. When Boaz visited his reapers in the field, it did not take long for him to notice Ruth. It was love at first sight. He urged her to glean only in his fields and to feel free to glean among those who were doing the actual reaping. He offered her the food and water he had provided for his own reapers. He warned the men who worked in the fields not to abuse Ruth but to even leave extra grain in the field for her to glean.

While Boaz was attracted to Ruth by her physical beauty (cf. 3:10), he was also impressed by her character. He had heard people talking about Ruth and had formed a positive impression based on what he knew. As he explained to Ruth in the field, "It has been fully reported to me, all that you have done for your mother-in-law since the death of your husband, and how you have left your father and your mother and the land of your birth, and have come to a people whom you did not know before" (2:11). At the same time, Boaz offered a prayer for Ruth. "The Lord repay your work, and a full reward be given you by the Lord God of Israel, under whose wings you have come for refuge" (v. 12). Little did he know at the time the role he would later play in that "full reward."

By the end of the day, Ruth had reaped of the generosity of her newfound friend Boaz. After beating out the grain, she had "about an ephah of barley" (v. 17). An ephah is equivalent to about three pecks and five quarts. The significance of the amount of grain Ruth was able to glean is evident when it is realized this is about ten times the daily allotment of manna which God provided for Israel in the wilderness (cf. Ex. 16:16). It is no wonder her mother-in-law wanted to know all the details as to how the day had gone. And when Naomi heard Ruth mention the name of Boaz, she began to see more than grain growing in the fields of Bethlehem.

LOVE'S REQUEST *(Ruth 3:1-18)*

Naomi knew Boaz was "kinsman" and as such could marry Ruth as a kinsman redeemer. She urged Ruth to glean only in the fields of Boaz, and Ruth complied with that request. And during the months of the barley harvest and wheat harvest, the relationship between Ruth and Boaz began to grow.

Toward the end of the harvest season, it was customary for the landowner and his workers to "camp out" on the threshing floor. It had not been that long since the invading Midianite raiders had confiscated the annual harvest by waiting till it had been threshed, then attacking. Knowing this, most farmers were reluctant to leave their crops unguarded on the threshing floor. For however long it took to complete the harvest, everyone associated with the harvest lived on the threshing floor of the farm.

Naomi saw this as an opportunity for Ruth to appeal to Boaz to marry her as a kinsman redeemer. She instructed Ruth to wash, anoint herself with perfumes, and dress in new clothes. Then she told Ruth to wait till Boaz had eaten and was asleep before approaching him. Only then was she to uncover his feet and wait for him to wake. By uncovering his feet, the draft would cause him to wake from his sleep as his feet got cold. Ruth did as she had been instructed and at midnight, Boaz woke from his sleep.

It was then Ruth requested that Boaz act as her redeemer. "Take your maidservant under your wing, for you are a near kinsman" (Ruth 3:9). Boaz was favorable to the suggestion, but realized there was one who had a prior claim to Ruth should he choose to take it. He told Ruth he would insure that one of the two would act as her kinsman and he would settle the details of the matter in the morning. Probably because he realized it would be unsafe for Ruth to wander home at midnight, he urged her to remain with him and the others on the threshing floor till morning. But even before the others awakened, Ruth was on her way home to her mother-in-law with six measures of barley.

LOVE'S REWARD *(Ruth 4:1-22)*
Naomi had been around long enough to know what love did to a man. She urged Ruth to sit and wait knowing the matter would be settled before the day ended. So while Naomi and Ruth waited in their home, Boaz made his way to the city gate.

According to the legal customs of the day, Boaz called the other kinsman aside in the gate and gathered ten elders of the city to witness the transaction. He told the other kinsman that Naomi planned to sell a piece of property. Under the Law, a family could not sell their land outside of their own family. This meant Boaz and the other kinsman were the only qualified purchasers. The other kinsman agreed to purchase the land until he learned he must also at the same time marry Ruth the Moabitess. "And the near kinsman said, 'I cannot redeem it for myself, lest I ruin my own inheritance. You redeem my right of redemption yourself, for I cannot redeem it' " (Ruth 4:6). Ironically, the kinsman who refused to exercise his right to redeem Ruth fearing it would ruin his inheritance is unknown by name today whereas the descendants of Boaz sat on the throne of David.

To seal the agreement, the other kinsman "took off his sandal" (v. 8). This ancient custom signified he was giving Boaz the right to trample over his rights as a kinsman redeemer. Then before the elders of the city, Boaz declared his intention to marry Ruth the Moabitess.

The two were married and in the process of time, a son was born to Ruth. There was the usual celebration surrounding the birth of a son, but for Naomi, this son was very special. It was the cause of her and the other women of the village worshiping the Lord as they remembered how God had provided the means whereby a family could be redeemed. Naomi, who had become Mara, was Naomi again. Perhaps because of all the worship of God surrounding the birth of the son, the child was named Obed which means "worshiped."

PERSPECTIVE

The story of Ruth is a demonstration of grace. The problem of a famine turned into abundance on the threshing floor. An outcast Moabite girl is taken into the commonwealth of Israel. And then there is the child. Even Naomi and the others in their enthusiasm could not have realized just how special this child really was. "Obed begot Jesse, and Jesse begot David" (Ruth 4:22). And from David came Jesus Christ.

THIRTY-ONE

JEPHTHAH:
The Defeat of the Ammonites

(Judges 10:1–12:15)

Though there were some individuals like Ruth who in the midst of turmoil maintained a strong faith in God, it was far more common in those days to find people straying from their commitment to God. At least six times during the course of history covered in the Book of Judges, the people passed through the complete cycle of sin, judgment, and restoration. Each time they were delivered, they forgot the Lord and what He had done for them. Very soon after the death of the particular judge who had delivered the people, the people resorted to their old ways of idol worship. They were the people of God in a unique covenant relationship with the Lord, but they preferred to worship the gods of the Canaanites.

The reason for this continual backsliding in Israel is attributed to the lack of central authority. "In those days there was no king in Israel; everyone did what was right in his own eyes" (Jud. 21:25). Unlike the glory years of Joshua, the people did as they wanted rather than dedicating themselves to the work of God. When they abandoned the work of driving out the Canaanites, they began making alliances with them. Soon they were worshiping Canaanite gods, and before long, the Canaanites whom they had preserved to collect tribute payments became their oppressors. While Ruth the Moabitess found her rest by trusting in the Lord God of Israel, the people of Israel themselves turned to the gods of the Canaanites to find only turmoil, confusion, and eventually oppression.

THE GODS OF THE CANAANITES

Much of the idol worship of this era centered around the idols Baal and Ashtoreth. Baal was the chief god among the Canaanites. His name means "lord" and includes the idea of possession. Originally, the idol's full name was Baal-Shemaim which means "lord of heaven." He was the sun god and was worshiped because he was thought to bring light and warmth to his worshipers. Because of the importance of the sun in producing a harvest, Baal was also thought to produce the harvest. Prolonged droughts which destroyed the crops were thought to be evidences of the displeasure of this god. To appease this god during this time, the people would offer human sacrifices to Baal. This usually involved offering the worshiper's firstborn who was burnt alive. This practice is described in Scripture as "passing through the fire" (cf. 2 Kings 16:3; 21:6).

Because the worship of Baal tended to be localized, the expressions of worship varied from village to village. Sometimes he took on the name of the city, i.e., Baal Hermon or Baal of Hermon (cf. Jud. 3:3). At times there were temples built to him. Such temples built in Samaria and Jerusalem are referred to in Scripture (1 Kings 16:32; 2 Kings 11:18). The ordinary offering made to Baal seems to have consisted of burning incense (Jer. 7:9), though on occasion it also included human sacrifices (19:5). From the record of the confrontation between Elijah and the priests of Baal, it is apparent the worship of this god could also include slashing one's own body with knives.

During those times Israel returned to the worship of Baalim (Jud. 8:33), a plural form of the name of Baal, which probably means several of the Baal gods were being worshiped in the land at the same time. The Baal gods identified in Scripture include Baal-Berith (Baal of the Covenant—v. 33), Baal Gad (Baal of Good Luck—Isa. 65:11), Baal Hamon (Baal of the Multitude—Song 8:11), Baal Hermon (Jud. 3:3), Baal Peor (Num. 25:3), and Baal-Zebub (Baal of the Flies—2 Kings 1:2-

3, 16). In the New Testament, this last expression of Baal is one of the titles of the devil (Beelzebub).

Ashtoreth was the chief goddess of the Canaanites and the female counterpart to Baal. She probably began as the Babylonian god Istar which was tied to the worship of the morning and evening stars. However, in Canaan, she was viewed as the moon goddess just as Baal was the sun god. As Ashtoreth came to be recognized as something of a fertility goddess, her worship involved immoral sexual practices by groups of men and women. Prostitution was widely practiced in her name. Just as the name Baalim is the plural of Baal, so the name Ashtaroth is the plural of Ashtoreth. There were many Baalim, so there also came to be many Ashtaroth.

But Baal and Ashtoreth were not the only false gods Israel worshiped during their days of declension. "Then the Children of Israel . . . served the Baals, and the Ashtoreths, the gods of Syria, the gods of Sidon, the gods of Moab, the gods of the people of Ammon, and the gods of the Philistines; and they forsook the Lord and did not serve Him" (Jud. 10:6). It was almost as though Israel was prepared to adopt any god it could find to fill the void left when they abandoned their worship of the Lord. That they followed after so many false gods of the Canaanites and others suggests the gods were unable to meet their needs. All they could offer was bondage and oppression.

THE MINOR JUDGES OF ISRAEL
(Jud. 10:1-5; 12:8-15) (1154–1110 b.c.)

While the Book of Judges records the ministry of six major judges who led Israel out of bondage back to God, there are also several judges of a minor character who are identified briefly in this book. They are called minor judges not in the sense that they were inferior to the other judges, but rather in the same sense that we refer to the Minor Prophets. While they also delivered Israel, very little is recorded of them and their ministries making it difficult to determine if they were successful in leading Israel through a complete cycle of repentance from sin and restoration to God. In addition to Shamgar (Jud. 3:31), the following judges may be considered in this way.

MINOR JUDGES OF ISRAEL

Tola (Issachar)—*10:1*
Jair (Gad)—*10:3*
Ibzan (Bethlehem)—*12:8*
Elon (Zebulun)—*12:11*
Abdon (Pirathonite)—*12:13*

Tola, the son of Puah belonged to the tribe of Issachar and lived in Shamir, in Mount Ephraim. The assigned territory of this tribe included this region southwest of the Sea of Galilee. His ministry as a judge lasted twenty-three years and ended with his death. Though it is said he delivered Israel, no mention is given of the enemy he overcame. As many of Israel's judges tended to have only a regional ministry, it is doubtful if Tola was widely known outside his tribe.

Tola was followed by Jair, a Gileadite who judged Israel for twenty-two years. Again, very little is known about this judge. There is no indication he was involved in any military struggle during his reign as judge. It is known that he had thirty sons which may imply Jair had several wives, but there is no record to confirm this. That these sons rode ass colts and had their own cities suggests the family was something of a financial dynasty.

Ibzan of Bethlehem is sometimes identified with Boaz by Jewish commentators but it is a highly unlikely association. Boaz appears to have been an older man when he married Ruth and there is no hint that he was polygamous. Ibzan on the other hand fathered sixty children, thirty sons and thirty daughters, which strongly suggests he had several wives. Ibzan served as judge a total of seven years.

Elon, a member of the tribe of Zebulun, judged Israel for ten years after Ibzan. Whereas Ibzan was from the south, Elon lived in that part of Galilee belonging to the tribe of Zebulun. On his death, he was buried in Aijalon.

The last of the minor judges of this period was Abdon, the son of Hillel, also described as a Pirathonite. This latter designation probably refers to his hometown. Pirathon was a town located about six miles west of Shechem. Though he only served as judge eight years, he had forty sons and thirty grandsons who rode ass colts which were a symbol of financial success and prosperity. This means Abdon must have been an older man when he began his ministry as a judge

JEPHTHAH THE GILEADITE *(Jud. 10:6–12:7)*
(1110–1104 B.C.)

Perhaps the most controversial of all of the judges was the illegitimate son of Gilead named Jephthah. He was born as the result of his father's involvement with a prostitute and was apparently adopted into the home of his biological father shortly after his birth. But later other children were born to Gilead by his wife and those sons began treating Jephthah as an outcast. As the legitimate sons aged, they eventually formally cast Jephthah out of the home so as to insure he would have no part in the inheritance of their father.

The tragic picture of family life as portrayed in the home of Gilead may not have been too unusual in those days. Israel had again wandered from God and was pursuing a wide assortment of pagan gods including Baals and Ashtoreths (Jud. 10:6). The widespread immorality which tended to characterize these pagan rituals no doubt resulted in the births of many unexpected children. Because these practices included group orgies, the question of paternity could not always be established with any degree of certainty. In this respect, Jephthah may have been one of the fortunate ones in that his father was identified.

Such regression to idolatry on the part of Israel again stirred the anger of the Lord. The result this time was an eighteen-year oppression of the land by both the Philistines and the Ammonites. But toward the end of this period, Israel finally began to realize the error of their ways, and repented. "So they put away the foreign gods from among them and served the Lord. And His soul could no longer endure the misery of Israel" (v. 16). After they had dealt with the foreign gods, they were ready to deal with their foreign oppressors. Very soon their opportunity to do so would come.

The Ammonites gathered their army together and set up a

military camp in the city of Gilead. The people and leaders of
that city fled their homes and gathered together in Mizpah.
This left plenty of room between the two armies as Israel
attempted to resolve an important problem. "And the people,
the leaders of Gilead, said one to another, 'Who is this man
who will begin the fight against the people of Ammon? He shall
be head over all the inhabitants of Gilead' " (v. 18).

For some time the problem remained unresolved. There
may have been men in the city who would have liked to become the tribal head, there were none prepared to take the
risk required in going to war against the army of Ammon. But
events beyond their control were forcing the elders of the city
to take a course of action they might only think of under
desperate circumstances. "Now it came to pass after a time
that the people of Ammon made war against Israel" (11:4).

The invasion of the Ammonites created a crisis which could
only be met by decisive action. What had been something of a
topic of discussion now became an absolute necessity. They
needed a leader to wage war against the aggressor. They
needed a leader who knew something about battle strategy
and had some experience on the battlefield. They needed
someone who had proven himself valiant in conflict, someone
they could follow confidently into battle. In all the time they
discussed the problem of a leader, there was only one man
who seemed to qualify, as much as they disliked the thought of
him being their leader. But something had to be done, and
done quickly. "And so it was, when the people of Ammon
made war against Israel, that the elders of Gilead went to get
Jephthah from the land of Tob" (v. 5).

When Jephthah had been run out of town by his half-brothers, he had gone to the town of Tob not far away from Ramoth
Gilead. He became engaged in several military conflicts and
earned the coveted title "mighty man of valor" (v. 1). A number of men of low character began following Jephthah as their
leader and seem to have formed something of a standing army.
Now that the Ammonites were invading Israel, those same
half-brothers, now the elders of the city, were coming to him
for help.

Jephthah did not let the elders forget their former treatment of him. But the men of the city had changed their minds about Jephthah. In their distress, they needed him more than they disliked him. They affirmed they would make Jephthah head of Gilead if he would defeat the Ammonites. When Jephthah had confirmed their promise to make him head of Gilead, he returned with the elders to Mizpah.

In his initial dealings with the Ammonites over the conflict, Jephthah attempted the diplomatic approach. He sent messengers to the king of Ammon to discern the reason for the sudden conflict. The battle was claimed to be the result of a boundary dispute. According to the king of Ammon, "Israel took away my land when they came up out of Egypt, from the Arnon as far as the Jabbok, and to the Jordan. Now, therefore, restore those lands peaceably" (v. 13). The Ammonites were disputing the right of Israel to hold land they had taken 300 years earlier as a result of a military conflict.

Jephthah realized he could not make the suggested concession to such an outlandish request. He reminded the king of Ammon of the true historical background of the conflict to which he referred (vv. 15-23). He further reminded the king of Ammon's own policy of keeping that territory conquered in battle (v. 24). He went on to note Israel had settled the land and been living there for 300 years, and none of the Ammonite kings seemed to believe the land was their land or made any effort to reclaim the land (vv. 25-26).

With the breakdown of diplomatic talks over their differences, a military solution to the problem was inevitable. "Then the Spirit of the Lord came upon Jephthah, and he passed through Gilead and Manasseh, and passed through Mizpah of Gilead; and from Mizpah of Gilead he advanced toward the people of Ammon" (v. 29). As he went out to battle against the Ammonites, Jephthah knew it would take more than his own expertise and that of his army on the battlefield to insure a victory over the enemy. The victory that could be his would only happen if it was given to him by the Lord. Therefore, Jephthah made a vow to the Lord as an expression of his commitment to God. "And Jephthah made a vow to the Lord, and said, 'If You will indeed deliver the people of Ammon into my hands, then it will be that whatever comes out of the doors of my house to meet me, when I return in peace from the people of Ammon, shall surely be the Lord's, and [or] I will offer it up as a burnt offering' " (vv. 30-31).

The battle against Ammon was violent and resulted in "a very great slaughter" (v. 33), but Jephthah and the army of Israel were the victors. But as he returned home the victor, his only daughter ran out to meet her victorious father. What should have been a happy reunion was suddenly turned into a sorrowful occasion as Jephthah remembered his vow. It was his daughter who was to be offered to the Lord.

Conservative scholars are divided in their opinion as to Jephthah's actions concerning his daughter. Some argue he offered her as a human sacrifice to God much as Israel might have offered their children to Baal at other times. Of course, God never endorsed the principle of human sacrifice but rather opposed it throughout the Law (cf. Lev. 18:21; 20:2-5; Deut. 12:31; 18:10). Still, that in itself does not mean Jephthah did not burn his daughter on an altar to God. Even years later in the history of Israel, human sacrifice was not entirely unknown (cf. 2 Kings 3:27; 16:3; 17:17; 2 Chron. 33:6; Jer. 7:31; 19:5; 32:35).

Others believe Jephthah did not sacrifice his daughter but rather dedicated her to God as a virgin for life. There is no question that Jephthah "carried out his vow with her which he had vowed" (Jud. 11:39), but there may be some question as to what that vow was. The Hebrew text which records the vow suggests Jephthah said, "Then it shall be, that whatever comes forth of the doors of my house to meet me, when I return in peace from the children of Ammon, shall surely be the Lord's, *or* I will offer it up for a burnt offering" (v. 31, literal translation). This being the case, Jephthah could have kept his vow to the Lord and preserved the life of his daughter by dedicating her to the Lord as a virgin for life. The Hebrew word translated "lament" (v. 40) could also be legitimately translated "celebrate." The decision of the translator in translating this word depends on whether he believes Jephthah's daughter was sacrificed and mourned or dedicated and pre-served. In the latter case, the daughters of Israel celebrated either the fact her life had been preserved by her father or that she was celebrated for her faithfulness in fulfilling her father's vow.

TWO VIEWS OF JEPHTHAH'S VOW ("LAMENT"—CELEBRATED)

1 She was killed and sacrificed.
2 She was dedicated as a virgin for life.

Jephthah's problems were not over with the victory over the Ammonites. When the Ephraimites learned of Jephthah's victory over the Ammonites, they were offended they had not been invited to fight and share in the victory. They gathered a substantial army and marched to Gilead to fight against Jephthah.

The Ephraimite action left Jephthah understandably upset. He reminded them there had been an earlier appeal for help that had been ignored by the Ephraimites. In the heat of their verbal conflict, the Ephraimites stooped to name-calling and called the Gileadites "fugitives of Ephraim among the Ephraimites and among the Manassites" (12:4). The men of Gilead retaliated not with words but swords. Suddenly they found themselves in the midst of another battle.

One of the keys to winning a military struggle is to control the enemy's escape route. Jephthah and his men very quickly secured control of the fords of the Jordan River and established a sort of border crossing. They specifically asked all those trying to cross the river if they were Ephraimites. Of course, knowing the state of conflict that existed at the time, the wise thing for an outnumbered Ephraimite soldier to do was say no. But there was a second test that had to be passed before safe passage across the river would be permitted.

Jephthah's men asked the one planning to cross the river to say the word "Shibboleth" which means stream. Though the two armies spoke the same language, there appear to have been minor differences in the dialect they spoke. One of these was a tendency of the Ephraimites to pronounce the phonetic sound "sh" as "s." As a result, as the Ephraimites uttered the special password to cross the river, they betrayed their true identity by pronouncing it "Sibboleth." The plan effectively identified the Ephraimites to the soldiers, and 42,000 were killed in this conflict.

For six years, Jephthah judged Israel. It appears his ministry was limited only to the northeastern part of the nation. He lived in the cities of Gilead as the head of the clan, and when he died, "was buried in one of the cities of Gilead" (v. 7).

PERSPECTIVE: SPEECH BETRAYS CHARACTER

Just as the Ephraimites were betrayed by their speech, so today many people betray their inner character or lack of character by their speech. Jesus taught His disciples mankind was defiled from within and such things as evil speaking proceed from an evil heart. It is possible to look like a Christian and act like a Christian, but sooner or later the speech of a pretender will betray him. Only when there is an inner change can the tongue be controlled. Even then, it will still reflect what is within.

THIRTY-TWO

SAMSON:
The Struggle against the Philistines

(Judges 13:1–16:31)

And the Children of Israel did evil in the sight of the Lord, and the Lord delivered them into the hand of the Philistines for forty years" (Jud. 13:1). Among the enemies of Israel in the Old Testament, the Philistines were certainly among the most powerful. When God raised up a judge to deal with the oppression of the Philistines, he was commissioned only to "begin to deliver Israel out of the hand of the Philistines" (v. 5). It would not be until much later that David would finish what Samson had begun.

Though there were Philistines in Palestine as early as Abraham, they dramatically increased in number and influence during the period between the Exodus and the establishment of the monarchy in Israel. This was due largely to a mass migration of central Europeans into the Aegean area. This forced the Greek "Sea Peoples" to find another homeland. It appears one of their original intentions was to occupy Egypt. Both Raamses III (1168–1137) and his successor Merneptah are recorded as successfully defending that nation from an invasion of the sea peoples.

As the Philistines settled in Palestine toward the end of the Bronze Age, their knowledge of smelting iron gave them a decided advantage not only in trade but also in military power. It was their custom to disarm the people they conquered and this together with their own superior weapons and chariots insured any attempted rebellion would indeed be short-lived. It is therefore significant that Israel's champions against the Philistines each used unconventional weapons.

The Philistines maintained much of their Aegean culture as they settled in their new homeland. Like the other tribal nations of that time, they tended to credit all their military victories to their gods which included Baal-Zebub, Ashtoreth, and Dagon. But unlike many of their contemporary nations, the Philistines did not necessarily believe the power of their gods had to be demonstrated by the total army being engaged in battle. There is some evidence the Philistines practiced the Aegean idea of battle by "championship" where a single champion from each side would fight to prove the power of the gods of each nation. The champion who won was considered to have demonstrated which god was stronger and which army would win if a physical battle were fought (cf. Goliath). It is therefore ironic that God would raise up his own champion who singlehandedly could take on and kill a thousand Philistines without a sword. It is also significant that God should raise up this strong man from the weakest of the tribes of Israel.

Dan was the first tribe to lose its territory to another people. By the time the Angel of the Lord first appeared to the wife of Manoah, much of the tribe had already migrated south and settled in a kind of refugee camp situated between Zorah and Eshtaol (13:25). The tribe which was not strong enough to defend its own territory was not the likely place to look for a champion to deliver Israel, "but God has chosen the foolish things of the world to put to shame the wise; and God has chosen the weak things of the world to put to shame the things which are mighty" (1 Cor. 1:27).

THE WIFE OF MANOAH *(Jud. 13:1-25)*
(1123 B.C.)

The life of Samson can be outlined in relationship to the four women who dominated his life to some degree. The first of these was his mother who is never named in Scripture but described only as the wife of Manoah. This woman of the tribe of Dan was barren. In the culture of the Near East, this condition was generally viewed as an evidence of the displeasure of God, yet her barrenness was soon to come to an end. "And the Angel of the Lord appeared to the woman and said to her, 'Indeed now, you are barren and have borne no children, but you shall conceive and bear a son' " (Jud. 13:3).

At that first meeting of the Angel of the Lord and the wife of Manoah, the woman was instructed to abstain from wine, strong drink, and foods classified as unclean in the Law. The reason for this action on her part was that the son was to be "a Nazarite to God from the womb" (v. 5). Under the Law, there was a provision made for the man who was led to dedicate himself to a particular work for God. As a Nazarite, he was to demonstrate his commitment to God and the work he was doing for God by observing three conditions which were symbols of his dedication. Normally, this vow would be taken for a limited period of time, but on at least three occasions in Scripture, an unborn child was designated as a Nazarite from the womb (cf. also 1 Sam. 1:11; Luke 1:15).

CONDITIONS OF THE NAZARITE VOW

1 Not eat or touch the unclean
2 Not drink wine or strong drink
3 No razor to cut his hair

The wife of Manoah was impressed with the message from the Angel of the Lord, but failed to recognize this as a Christophany or preincarnate appearance of Christ. Still, she was aware of the fact that the man who spoke with her was unusual. When relating the conversation to her husband, she described the man as "a man of God" which was a usual designation for a prophet but noted also "His countenance was like the countenance of the angel of God, very awesome" (Jud. 13:6). She related fully the instructions she had received concerning the prenatal care of their son and his destiny as "a Nazarite to God from the womb to the day of his death" (v. 7).

Manoah demonstrated his deep faith in God by praying to

the Lord and requesting a second visitation of this "Man of God." His purpose in making this request was that the supposed prophet would "teach us what we shall do for the child who will be born" (v. 8). He realized the great responsibility that would be his as the father of this very special son and sought further instruction that he might be everything a father should be to his son. "And God listened to the voice of Manoah" (v. 9).

The second time the Angel of the Lord appeared to the wife of Manoah, she was sitting alone in a field. Knowing her husband wanted to meet this prophet, she quickly ran out to get him. When Manoah arrived, the Angel of the Lord confirmed He was the One who had appeared to Manoah's wife earlier. The earlier message was repeated and emphasized. When Manoah realized he was talking with the Angel of the Lord, he offered to prepare a kid and serve it to his guest as a meal. The Angel said he would not eat the food but rather encouraged Manoah to offer it as a burnt offering unto the Lord. When Manoah asked the Angel His name, he was told it was Secret or Wonderful, one of the distinct titles of Christ in the Scriptures (cf. Isa. 9:6).

When Manoah prepared his burnt offering and a meal offering and placed it on a rock, the Angel performed a miracle. As the flame ascended from the sacrifice, "the Angel of the Lord ascended in the flame of the altar" (Jud. 13:20). The understanding of this couple was further enlightened. They now knew the One they had thought was a Prophet, and then later realized was an Angel, was in reality God. While Manoah felt certain he would die, having seen God, his wife pointed out that the acceptance of the sacrifice by the Lord suggested their lives would be preserved.

"So the woman bore a son and called his name Samson" (v. 24). The name Samson or *shimshon* as it is in Hebrew means "sunny." The nearby city of Beth Shemesh (the house of the sun) may have suggested the name Samson to the parents. This child was to be the one God planned to use to begin delivering Israel from the oppression of the Philistines. He was the recipient of the blessing of the Lord and was endued with great strength by the Spirit of the Lord. Yet this strong man of Israel had a glaring weakness in his character which would eventually destroy him. He failed to learn to discipline himself in controlling his own desires, and "Whoever has no rule over his own spirit is like a city broken down, without walls" (Prov. 25:28).

THE WOMAN OF TIMNAH *(Jud. 14:1–15:20)*
(1104 B.C.)

This lack of self-discipline first became evident in Samson's choice of a bride from among the Philistines. Under the Law, Israel had been specifically instructed not to intermarry with those of other nations who worshiped other gods. This in itself should have prevented Samson from selecting a Philistine bride. Also, Samson must have known by this time he had been raised up by God to begin delivering Israel from the Philistines. Having a Philistine wife would certainly compromise his ability to do what he knew God wanted him to do.

When Samson told his parents he wanted to take the Philistine as his bride, they naturally objected, suggesting that he find a wife from among his own people. But Samson was insistent and his father finally consented to make the necessary arrangements. What Samson failed to tell his parents was that he also had an alternative motive in marrying the Philistine woman. "He was seeking an occasion against the Philistines" (Jud. 14:4).

As Samson made his way to Timnah to meet with his bride-to-be, he was attacked by a young lion in the vineyards of Timnah. As a Nazarite, Samson was not to eat or drink of the fruit of the vine. That being the case, one is left wondering what Samson was doing in the vineyard. The most probable explanation of his actions was that Samson was on the verge of violating one of the conditions of his Nazarite vow. If this was the case, the attack of the lion may have been an interruption sent by God to prevent him from falling into sin. But in his willingness to take what he wanted, Samson would eventually violate every aspect of his vow. Samson who could conquer armies, could not control himself.

VIOLATIONS OF THE NAZARITE VOW

1 Touched dead lion/ate unclean honey
2 Attended a drinking feast
3 Cut his hair

When Samson returned to the Philistine city to take the woman to be his wife, "he turned aside to see the carcass of the lion" (v. 8). There he discovered a swarm of bees were using the decaying carcass of the lion as a hive and it was filled with honey. He took some of the unclean honey and ate it. Though he shared it with his parents, he was careful not to tell them where he had found it, just as he had avoided telling them he had killed the lion in the vineyard originally. Samson must have known his parents would object to his compromise of his Nazarite vow had they known the truth.

It was customary to conduct a seven-day drinking feast as part of a marriage, and for the next week, Samson was the host of such a feast. The couple was married early in the week-long celebration, but the marriage was not consummated until the groom took his bride home on the last night of the feast. Samson used the occasion of the feast to make a wager with the thirty Philistine men who gathered at the feast as his companions. If they could solve a riddle, he would give each of them a new garment. But if they failed, it was they who were to give him the new garments. The riddle was expressed by Samson in the words, "Out of the eater came something to eat, and out of the strong came something sweet" (v. 14). Despite their efforts, the Philistines were unable to resolve the riddle during the next three days.

When the Philistines realized they could not solve the riddle, they threatened Samson's wife calling on her to tell them the riddle or be burned alive with her father in her father's house. Rather than telling her husband of the threat and letting him defend her, she chose to manipulate him into revealing the secret of the riddle. In taking this course of action, she was exposing herself to grave danger and cutting herself off from any defense she would have against those threatening her. As it turned out, even though she did as they requested, they still burned her and her father (15:6).

Samson's wife "wept on him the seven days while the feast lasted" (14:17). She accused Samson of not loving her and keeping secrets from her. Finally, as the result of her constant nagging, he told her the secret of the riddle, "then she explained the riddle to the sons of her people" (v. 17). The men were able to win the wager, but Samson was not deceived as to how they had learned the answer. He paid off his debt by making a quick trip to Ashkelon and killing thirty Philistines. The garments of his victims were then given to the men of the city. In his anger, Samson returned to his father's house forgetting his bride. To save the forsaken bride any undue embarrassment, she was given in marriage to the "best man" as was the custom of those days.

Sometime later, Samson cooled off enough to realize he had forgotten to bring his bride home. He returned to Timnah to collect her only to learn her father had married her off to the best man. The father offered the girl's younger sister as a substitute wife for Samson, arguing she was prettier than the daughter Samson had intended to marry, but Samson refused. As he left the city, he caught 300 foxes and tied them together in pairs. He then attached torches to their tails and sent them running wild through the fields, vineyards, and orchards of the city. The crops, vineyards, and olive groves were all destroyed by the ensuing fire. When the men of the city learned Samson was the cause of this catastrophe, they burned his wife and father-in-law. Samson engaged in physical conflict with a number of Philistines on that occasion "he attacked them hip and thigh with a great slaughter" (15:8).

Understandably, the Philistines were upset with Samson's actions. When they learned Samson was living at the top of the rock of Etam, they came against Judah in battle. Eager to avoid a military conflict with the Philistines, the men of Judah sought to negotiate a peace with the Philistines. The terms to which they agreed involved turning Samson over to the Philistines bound. Samson agreed to let the men of Judah bind him

and turn him over to the Philistines provided they agreed not
to fall on him themselves. They bound him in two new cords
and took him to a hill.

The Philistines were overjoyed when they saw their enemy
bound and offered to them, but they did not realize how strong
Samson could be when endued with the power of the Holy
Spirit. As they shouted "against him," Samson broke the cords
and began fighting against the Philistines. Not having a weapon, "he found a fresh jawbone of a donkey, reached out his
hand and took it, and killed a thousand men with it" (v. 15).
The victory Samson won on that occasion resulted in the re-
naming of the place *Ramath Lehi* meaning "the hill of the
jawbone." "And he judged Israel twenty years in the days of
the Philistines" (v. 20).

THE HARLOT OF GAZA *(Jud. 16:1-3)*

For twenty years, Samson judged Israel and apparently controlled his own desires to some extent, but toward the end of
that period, he was again attracted physically by a Philistine
woman. He made a trip to Gaza and spent a night with a
prostitute in that city. When the men of the city learned he
was there, they set an ambush intending to kill him as he left
the city the next morning.

About midnight, Samson got up and left the harlot. Some
writers have suggested Samson may have begun to realize the
error of his way and decided to leave before he compromised
himself any further. It was customary for cities to lock their
gates at night as part of the defense of the city. When Samson
came to the locked gate, he lifted them and carried them
thirty-eight miles toward the city of Hebron. The men who sat
in ambush waiting for Samson were undoubtedly stunned as
they saw this man lift approximately 4,000 pounds (two tons)
and carry them off. It is no wonder that none of them apparently made any effort to attack Samson as he left the city.

Those who believe Samson's hike to Hebron that night represented something of a spiritual renewal in his life point to the
significance of the two places involved in the thirty-eight-mile
pilgrimage. Gaza was one of the five principal cities of the

Philistines which are consistently portrayed in Scripture as outside the covenant blessings of God. The city of Hebron in contrast is the place of fellowship with God and is often portrayed in Scripture with that emphasis. If Samson's escape from Gaza was a step back toward fellowship with God, it was a step that would very soon be retraced by the strong man as he again fell victim to another woman.

DELILAH OF SOREK *(Jud. 16:4-31)*
(1084 B.C.)

The fourth woman to exert an influence over Samson was Delilah of Sorek. Sorek was a valley near Gaza and though Delilah herself is never identified as a Philistine, she was certainly in league with the leaders of that nation. When the five lords of the Philistines learned of Samson's interest in Delilah, they approached her and offered to each pay her 11,000 pieces of silver if she could uncover the secret of his strength. Even by contemporary standards, that amounts to a small fortune. The immensity of this reward is perhaps best illustrated when it is realized Judas Iscariot betrayed Jesus for only 30 pieces of silver. Delilah agreed to try to learn the secret of his strength in exchange for the reward.

DEADLY LOVER'S GAME

1 Bind with bow strings
2 Bind with new ropes
3 Weave my hair
4 Cut my hair

Delilah sought to learn the secret of Samson's strength by playing a "deadly lover's game." After she had set Samson at ease, she appealed to him to reveal the secret of his strength. Samson played along with the game giving her false answers. But each time he did so, he was getting closer to revealing the true source of his strength. What he did not realize was that Delilah had men waiting and watching to take him as soon as the true secret of his strength was revealed. Only when Delilah was convinced she knew the source of his strength, did she call the lords of the Philistines to collect her reward.

When Delilah knew the strength of Samson could be destroyed if his hair was cut, she caused him to sleep on her lap. While he slept, she had a man cut the seven braids of Samson's hair and then began to beat him to wake him up. As he awoke to the by now familiar words, "The Philistines are upon you, Samson" (Jud. 16:9, 12, 14, 20), he assumed he could shake them off and fight them as he had done at other times. Tragically the Scripture records, "but he did not know that the Lord had departed from him" (v. 20). The strong man of Israel was without his strength, and he was about to suffer the consequences of his sin. He was bound and blinded by the enemy he had sought to destroy and taken to the prison where he would do the work of a woman grinding out Dagon's grain. In a sudden reversal of circumstances, the former victories of Samson now came back to haunt him in his greatest defeat.

THE CONSEQUENCE OF SIN *(16:21)*

Blinding
Binding
Grinding

PERSPECTIVE: NEVER BEYOND HOPE

Samson was not destined to end his life in the service of the Philistine god Dagon but rather in the service of the Lord God of Israel. After Samson became a prisoner, his hair began to grow again. He would have one more opportunity to use his God-given strength in accordance with the purpose God had established for his life.

The Philistines were eager to celebrate their great victory over Samson and attribute it to their god Dagon. They gathered their people to the temple of Dagon and offered sacrifices to their god and feasted together. As the celebration continued, a decision was made to bring Samson to the temple as a form of entertainment. He was taken from the prison and brought into the temple where everyone could see him.

The temple of Dagon was a massive two-tiered structure which rested on a series of pillars for support. While there were a number of pillars between the two floors of the temple, the weight of the second floor was supported primarily by the corner pillars. Samson had a boy who was acting as his guide take him to these support pillars in preparation for his final battle with the Philistines. Resting against those pillars, Samson prayed one last time. "O Lord God, remember me, I pray! Strengthen me, I pray, just this once, O God, that I may with one blow take vengeance on the Philistines for my two eyes!" (Jud. 16:28) Realizing this final battle would cost him his life, he added, "Let me die with the Philistines!" (v. 30)

With one last demonstration of the immense strength God had given him, Samson moved the support pillars from their place causing the roof of the building to collapse and killing those who were in the temple of Dagon. While there is no record of the total number of people killed in the destruction of the temple of Dagon, there were about 3,000 men and women on the roof alone at the time of the collapse. "So the dead that he killed at his death were more than he had killed in his life" (v. 30).

THIRTY-THREE

ELI:
The End of an Era

(Judges 17:1–21:25; 1 Samuel 1:1–4:22)

As the era of the Judges drew to a close, the history of Israel seemed to be progressing toward increasing darkness. Each judge seemed weaker than his predecessor and each oppressor more powerful. The twelve tribes each operated separately and God's people were a loose confederation. Their only center of authority was the tabernacle at Shiloh. And in the end, a weak man, Eli the high priest, was not able to hold his family together, much less the nation. Both a judge (1 Sam. 4:18) and priest, he watched his life unravel before his eyes. Eli was described as fat and each time he appears in Scripture, he is sitting or sleeping. He seems to be sincere and gentle, but entirely lacking firmness to correct his sons or protect the priesthood.

While the Book of Judges recorded a limited degree of success in winning a degree of liberty for the people, they rarely followed after the Lord beyond the life span of the judge. Increasingly men were abandoning the authority of God as established in the Law and doing that which seemed right in their own opinion (Jud. 17:6; 21:25). As the era drew to a close a series of chaotic events served to demonstrate just how fragile the social fabric of Israelite society had become.

Several of the events recorded in the final chapters of the Book of Judges occurred during the historic narrative of the book but were collected at the end to demonstrate the character of the nation during the final days of that era. Despite

---

CHAOS AT THE END OF AN ERA

---

1 Priest for hire *(Jud. 17)*
2 Danite migration *(Jud. 18)*
3 Levite's concubine *(Jud. 19)*
4 Civil war *(Jud. 20)*
5 Kidnapped wives *(Jud. 21)*
6 Eli can't recognize a praying woman *(1 Sam. 1)*
7 Hophni and Phinehas *(1 Sam. 2)*
8 God calls the boy Samuel *(1 Sam. 3)*
9 Departed glory *(1 Sam. 4:3-22)*

---

the prohibition of the Law regarding the making of graven images for worship (idolatry), at least one mother in Israel took silver and had a silversmith make an idol (17:4). Her son Micah became the owner of a number of gods and established his son as a priest even though they were not Levites (v. 5). Later, he was able to hire a Levite to be his personal priest in his syncretistic religion for the sum of ten shekels of silver and a new suit annually. The arrangement, however, proved only to be temporary. When the Levite was given money to be a priest to the migrating tribe of Dan, he gladly sold his services for the more prestigious position.

With the compromising Levite and Micah's gods, the Danites themselves settled in northern Palestine. They attacked and destroyed the isolated community of Laish and rebuilt the city, calling it Dan. The Levite and false gods were established as part of the worship at the tabernacle which remained in Shiloh.

Another Levite also strayed from his calling and took to himself a concubine. But the concubine became involved with other men and eventually left the Levite to return to her father's house in Bethlehem in Judah. It was four months before the Levite made the trip to Bethlehem to reclaim his concubine (19:2).

As the Levite traveled home with his concubine, he found himself unable to find housing in the city of Gibeah. He decided to spend the night in the streets, but met an old man from his home region who was at the time living in Gibeah and offered to house the Levite and his concubine for the night. Later that evening, certain men of the city came to the house intending to engage in homosexual acts with the Levite. In an effort to discourage the men from their intended actions, the host offered to let the men abuse his daughter and the Levite's concubine. "So the man took his concubine and brought her out to them. And they knew her and abused her all the night until morning; and when the day began to break, they let her go" (v. 25).

As the Levite prepared to continue his journey home the next day, he found his abused concubine lying dead on the doorstep. He placed her body on his donkey and returned home. There he severed her body into twelve pieces and sent the pieces to the different regions of Israel. The severed body of the abused concubine angered the nation, "and the congregation gathered together as one man before the Lord at Mizpah" (20:1). From there they attacked the tribe of Benjamin. The battle virtually devastated the tribe with some 25,000 Benjaminites dying in that day. The 600 men of the tribe who escaped hid out at the rock of Rimmon for four months.

Later, the men of Israel realized the civil war had virtually resulted in the extinction of one of the tribes of Israel, but not before they had made a vow not to give their daughters to the men of that tribe in marriage. When they repented of their actions against the tribe of Benjamin, they proposed two plans by which the men who had survived the battle and escaped would secure wives. First, because the men of Jabesh Gilead had failed to join Israel in the battle, they were attacked and destroyed. The only residents of the city who were preserved were some 400 young virgins who were then offered to the men of Benjamin as wives. That action only provided wives for every two out of three men who had survived the battle. To secure another 200 wives, the men of Benjamin were encouraged and permitted to kidnap "the daughters of Shiloh" that left the city during a certain feast of the Lord which was held annually in Shiloh. This second plan provided the rest of the needed wives for the tribe of Benjamin.

The degenerate lifestyles and actions of the Levites in the Age of the Judges reached their utter depths of degradation in the persons of Hophni and Phinehas, the sons of Eli and the priests of the Lord in Shiloh. Their father may have had great ambitions for his sons when he named them as they were born, but they failed in every way to live up to expectations. The name *Hophni* means "strong," and Phinehas was probably named after the third high priest of Israel, who was a personification of righteousness. But the sons of Eli were weak and wicked, so much so they earned the reputation of being "sons of Belial" (1 Sam. 2:12). Though God had made provision for the priests to remove a portion of some offerings for themselves as it boiled, the sons of Eli bullied worshipers into giving them raw meat they could later roast rather than the boiled beef (vv. 13-17). This was a practice apparently learned from their father by the lesson of example. In addition to their abuse of the offering, they were also involved immorally "with the women who assembled at the door of the tabernacle of meeting" (v. 22).

An unnamed prophet warned Eli that he kicked "at My sacrifice and My offering which I have commanded in My habitation, and honor your sons more than Me, to make yourselves fat with the best of all the offerings of Israel My people" (v. 29). Apparently, Eli complained about burning up good meat in sacrifice to God. He kept it as did his sons, and God made reference to their overweight condition. Then God announced Eli's life would be cut off and his sons killed in their youth. The sin of Hophni and Phinehas was rebuked by their father and an unnamed prophet of God, but still there was no repentance on their part. "They did not know the Lord" (v. 12) and brought disgrace on the holy things of God. It was this attitude on their part that led to the loss of the very glory of God from Israel and resulted in their own deaths on the battlefield.

They must have felt God would give them a victory over their enemies no matter how they profaned His holy name.

They did not realize the judgment of God on the people of Israel and the family of Eli. "And when they joined battle, Israel was defeated by the Philistines, who killed about four thousand men of the army in the field" (4:2).

The military defeat against the Philistines caused people to begin asking an important question. "Why has the Lord defeated us today before the Philistines?" (v. 3) It was obvious to all observers that the loss was an evidence of the displeasure of God. It was an important question that needed to be asked, but they were asking the wrong people. It was widely known that Samuel was the one God was communicating with, but it was Hophni and Phinehas who still held the office of the priesthood and the elders of the nation who wielded the political clout. Between them they were able to ask the right question, but could only arrive at the wrong answer. "Let us bring the ark of the covenant of the Lord from Shiloh to us, that when it comes among us it may save us from the hand of our enemies" (v. 3).

It was customary in those days when a nation went into battle to take their gods into battle with them. Perhaps as they had fought the Philistines, some of the Israelites had gotten close enough to the camp to see the Philistine god Dagon in a prominent place. Israel did not have an idol it could carry into battle, but the ark of the covenant was perhaps the most sacred portable article that was prominent in their worship of God. And so rather than trusting God for victory over the Philistines, they chose to place their confidence in a box they could see and carry from Shiloh to the battle.

Though Eli himself was concerned with the decision to remove the ark from the tabernacle, Hophni and Phinehas could see no problem with the plan. Eli's indecision and passive nature again allowed his sons to make a tragic mistake. Their religion had become little more than ritual and a convenient setting for their other less noble interests. Still, they knew the religion of Israel had some meaning to many people in the land. Carrying the ark to the battlefront would raise the spirits of the people and help them fight with greater zeal. As far as these two priests were concerned, it was simply a matter of conducting a mammoth pep rally before the next battle and then returning home later that night.

With the arrival of the two priests bearing the ark of the covenant, the people became excited. The defeated army took heart as they saw the box that they were convinced would win them the battle. Their pitiful moans of failure were transformed into a jubilant shout of victory. The echo of the celebration echoed from mountain to mountain. It did not take long for the Philistines to discern what must be happening in the Israelite battle camp.

"God is come into the camp," they concluded. "Woe to us! For such a thing has never happened before. Woe to us! Who will deliver us from the hand of these mighty gods? These are the gods who struck the Egyptians with all the plagues in the wilderness" (vv. 7-8). The situation was serious for the Philistines. Twice they had unsuccessfully attempted an invasion of Egypt and twice they were repelled and defeated. Now they were engaging in battle against what they perceived to be the gods that had so humiliatingly defeated the Egyptians during the Exodus. It was almost certain they could not stand against so powerful a set of gods. But they really had no choice in the matter. If there ever was a time they must do their best, it was now. It was either fight or forever be enslaved to the Israelites.

But the Philistines had it all wrong. God was not in the camp. The people's excitement was not over God, but over a gold-plated wooden box containing a number of unique objects important to the worship of God. And Israel had it all wrong too. There is a world of difference between a wooden box covered in gold and the presence of God. But as it was, the two confused and deceived armies marched into battle again to fight. "There was a very great slaughter, and there fell of Israel thirty thousand foot soldiers. Also the ark of God was captured; and the two sons of Eli, Hophni and Phinehas, died" (vv. 10-11).

Tension was everywhere present in Shiloh as the people eagerly awaited news from the battlefront. Eli, now blind in his old age, could not see the torn clothes and dirty face of the downcast soldier as he ran into the city and shared the awful news with the people. But he could still hear well enough to discern the mournful cry of the people as they first heard the news Eli didn't want to, but knew he had to, hear. "Israel has fled before the Philistines, and there has been a great slaughter among the people," the soldier explained. Then he added, "Also your two sons, Hophni and Phinehas, are dead, and the ark of God has been taken" (v. 17).

PERSPECTIVE: THE HOPELESSNESS OF LIFE WITHOUT GOD

It was more than Eli could take. In his shock at the news of the ark being taken in the battle, he fell back off his seat into a gate. The combination of Eli's weight and age made his fall into the gate fatal. He broke his neck and died.

Eli was not the only one in the family to be shocked with the news. His daughter-in-law, the wife of Phinehas, was pregnant and very close to the end of her term. When she heard the news from the battle and was told of the death of her father-in-law, she went into a premature labor. As the midwives assisted in the birth, they tried to encourage the young mother and widow, but she had her mind on other things. When told she had given birth to a son, all she could do was name him Ichabod. The ark was gone. The glory was departed from Israel. Life was not really worth living without the glory. The child was born, but the mother did not survive.

The ark of the covenant would be returned by the Philistines within seven months, but the newborn baby Ichabod would be old enough to fight for his nation before the glory would return. For more than twenty years, Israel would lament the departed glory of God.

THIRTY-FOUR

SAMUEL:
From Judges to Kings

(1 Samuel 1:1–8:22)

During the bleak and depressing time of the end of the Judges, there was a new ray of sunshine coming over the horizon. The last judge, Samuel, was the best, in that he prepared Israel for the united kingdom and greatness. He was born before the death of Eli. Perhaps the weak Eli made a contribution to Samuel he couldn't make in his own sons.

THE BIRTH OF SAMUEL *(1 Sam. 1:1–2:21)*

In the city of Ramathaim Zophim, a man named Elkanah married a woman he deeply loved named Hannah. The marriage was a picture of everything a marriage should be. The name *Elkanah* means "God is possessing," and his wife's name *Hannah* means "grace." In many respects it was a home in which God was honored as possessor and His grace experienced. Annually the couple made their way to the tabernacle at Shiloh to worship *Jehovah Sabaoth,* the Lord of hosts. But it was not a marriage without its problems, and the biggest was a physical problem with Hannah. "The Lord had closed her womb" (1 Sam. 1:5-6).

As much as Elkanah loved his wife Hannah, it was important to him to have an heir. He could trace his descendants back several generations, to Abraham, the father of the nation itself. His own family had settled in Ephraim for four generations and was well established in the community. So because Hannah could not provide the needed heir, Elkanah married a second wife, one named Peninnah, who became the mother of his children. While it resolved one problem for Elkanah, it introduced a host of new ones in his family. As a wise man would later advise a sultan, "First learn to live with two tigresses, and then expect to live happily with two wives."

If a second wife caused problems for Elkanah, it only served to intensify the suffering of Hannah. Barrenness was considered a sign of the displeasure of God in the Near East. This means it was only natural for Hannah's best friends to suspect she was being judged by God for some hidden sin in her life. The new wife became a constant source of irritation and "provoked her severely, to make her miserable" (v. 6). Even her own husband didn't understand and tried to minimize the problem when they talked (v. 8). Increasingly, Hannah found herself weeping uncontrollably. She didn't feel like eating and couldn't enjoy the feasts in Shiloh as she once had. Inside she was deeply hurt, but there was no one to turn to for help. To even discuss the problem with the spiritual leaders at Shiloh, Hophni and Phinehas, was probably to invite their physical abuse of her. Ultimately, Hannah had only one hope, so she turned to the Lord in prayer.

"Then she made a vow and said, 'O Lord of hosts, if You will indeed look on the affliction of Your maidservant, and remember me, and not forget Your maidservant, but will give Your maidservant a male child, then I will give him to the Lord all the days of his life, and no razor shall come upon his head' " (v. 11). She continued in prayer, pouring out her soul to the Lord. Her prayer was intense, coming out of the deep sorrow and bitterness of her soul, but it was also a quiet prayer offered to God at a lonely spot in the tabernacle. She moved her lips, uttering her prayer to God; but so great was her sorrow that the sound never left her mouth. If one listened carefully, he would hear few words between her sobs; but it was a prayer that was heard in heaven.

Even Eli the priest, who was sitting nearby at a post in the tabernacle, failed to realize Hannah was praying. For various reasons, he lacked spiritual insight. From all appearances, she looked like a woman who had had too much to drink and had staggered into the tabernacle stone drunk. He had seen many women in that state before, yet had never come to the place where he could tolerate the destructive and intoxicating influence of wine and strong drink. But as he began his standard speech, he was surprised to learn that the one he was addressing was not a common drunk but an uncommon woman of faith. What else could he do but recognize the faith of this woman and grant her a blessing. "Go in peace," he answered, "and the God of Israel grant your petition which you have asked of Him" (v. 17).

The blessing of Eli gave Hannah the deep-seated assurance that God was going to answer her prayer and give her a son. She was no more pregnant when she left the tabernacle than she was when she had arrived earlier that day, but down deep inside she knew that condition would soon change. She had prayed and gotten her answer from heaven. For the first time in a long while, she felt as though she could really enjoy a meal; so she ate. It was even beginning to show on her face. "Her face was no longer sad" (v. 18).

Within weeks of returning home to Ramah, everyone but Hannah was surprised to first hear the rumors and then hear them confirmed. Barren Hannah was pregnant. In the course of time, the child was born. It was a son, and Hannah insisted on naming him Samuel. The name Samuel means "asked of God," and Hannah wanted everyone to know her son was God's answer to her prayer. She remembered her vow; yet at the same time realized her responsibility as a mother. She would wean the child before returning to Shiloh; and when the child was weaned, he would be given back to the Lord in the service of the tabernacle.

To give up a son is difficult for any mother, but to give up an only son after years of barrenness must have been a particular challenge to Hannah. Still, there was no hesitation on her part. As soon as the child was weaned, Hannah took him to the tabernacle. She found the old priest Eli and reminded him of the day he had found her alone and praying. "For this child I prayed," she confessed, "and the Lord has granted me my petition which I asked of Him. Therefore I also have lent him to the Lord; as long as he lives he shall be lent to the Lord" (vv. 27-28).

Far from being a time of sorrow, this visit to the tabernacle was a time of rejoicing. This time Hannah's prayer to the Lord had a totally different character. "My heart rejoices in the Lord; my horn is exalted in the Lord; I smile at my enemies, because I rejoice in Your salvation" (2:1). Hannah's praise to the Lord on this occasion became the basis later of Mary's Magnificat, her expression of praise as she realized the honor of bearing the Son of God (cf. Luke 1:46-55). And when Elkanah and his wife Hannah returned home to Ramah, "the child ministered to the Lord before Eli the priest" (1 Sam. 2:11).

Each year the couple returned to worship the Lord at Shiloh, as their custom had been before the birth of Samuel; but now there was an added attraction attached to their pilgrimage. Far from feeling sorry for herself that God would take away her son, Hannah looked forward to seeing Samuel each year. As they prepared for their trip, Hannah would add the final touches to the coat she had been making for her son. When they arrived in Shiloh with the family sacrifice, she had a gift of her own for the one she had already given to the Lord.

The consistent faith of Elkanah and Hannah did not escape the notice of Eli. "And Eli would bless Elkanah and his wife, and say, 'The Lord give you descendants from this woman for the loan that was lent to the Lord' " (v. 20). And that is exactly what the Lord did. Barren Hannah later became the mother of an additional three sons and two daughters. "Meanwhile the child Samuel grew before the Lord" (v. 21).

THE CALL TO SAMUEL *(1 Sam. 3:1–4:1)*

In the spiritual darkness that seemed to envelop Israel during those days, Samuel was a brilliant, shining light. Not only did he mature physically and spiritually, but he soon became popular among the many visitors to the tabernacle. Though much of what occurred in and about the tabernacle was dishonorable to

God, Samuel faithfully "ministered to the Lord before Eli" (1 Sam. 2:11, 18; 3:1). It was particularly difficult to excite people to serve God in a day when faith was declining even among the priests of the Lord. It had been a long time since a priest or prophet had spoken with authority on behalf of God; and on the few occasions when that did happen, it was so rare as to be something of a novelty. People had come to the place where they no longer were concerned over the silence from heaven. The dark days of the Judges had acclimatized generation after generation to spiritual lethargy.

Then one night it happened! Samuel was just bedding down for the night when he thought he heard someone calling. The voice was not familiar, but at that late hour it had to be Eli. Quickly he got out of bed and ran to Eli. But when Samuel announced his presence, Eli denied he had called him and sent him back to bed. Obediently, Samuel returned to the place he was accustomed to sleeping. But as he tried to sleep while the lamp flickered in the tabernacle, he heard the voice again. As he had done earlier, he ran to Eli and announced his presence. But again Eli denied he had called him and sent him back to bed.

Samuel heard his name called a third time. As before, he got up and ran to Eli. Perhaps his voice had a little more conviction this time as he arrived and declared he had heard Eli call him. Eli's eyesight had been failing for some time, but as Samuel waited for his instructions, he saw a very distant look in Eli's eyes he had not seen before. They almost seemed to get glassy and fill with tears as Eli thought about something out of the distant past.

Could it really be? Eli wondered as he listened to Samuel for the third time since originally sending him to bed that night. *Could it really be after so long?* he pondered. Silently he began thinking and remembering. *Perhaps it is. And if it is, it would only be right that this boy would hear it,* he rationalized. He had known for years that most of the nation, indeed most of his own family, was deaf to the voice of God. He was perhaps more concerned about the spiritual state of the nation than most, but in his introspective honesty he had to admit that even he was not all he should have been. But Samuel was different. This little servant was faithful. *Yes it must be,* Eli concluded silently. "Then Eli perceived that the Lord had called the boy" (v. 8).

This time there was something Eli wanted young Samuel to do. Initially, the required course of action was as before. Samuel was to return to bed and try to get to sleep. But if heard the voice again, he was to remain where he was and respond with the words, "Speak, Lord, for Your servant hears" (v. 9). It seemed like an unusual response, but Samuel was in the habit of obeying Eli. He made his way back to bed. Again, the voice called out, but this time Samuel responded as Eli had instructed him. "And the Lord said to Samuel, 'Behold, I will do something in Israel at which both ears of everyone who hears it will tingle' " (v. 11).

As the Lord revealed His plan of action to Samuel, the sleepy boy became increasingly wider awake. By the time the Lord had concluded His message, Samuel was wider awake than he had ever been before at that hour of the night. It was not the kind of message he wanted to relate to Eli, yet somehow he knew Eli was going to ask. How could he tell the old priest who had raised him as a son that God was going to destroy the family of Eli? He knew Eli himself was concerned about the growing evil of his sons Hophni and Phinehas, but the time to settle accounts had come, according to God. In a single day, the line of the priesthood of Eli would come to an end. He was really afraid to tell Eli.

As the sun rose the next morning, Samuel ran to open the doors of the tabernacle as was his usual custom. There was only one course of action to follow. Samuel would do his best to avoid Eli all day. That way, Eli would not ask about the message and Samuel would not have to be the bearer of bad tidings. But that plan of action was doomed to failure before it had even been implemented. No sooner had Samuel opened the doors when he head the familiar voice of Eli calling him.

"Perhaps Eli will forget about the confusion of last night and not ask," Samuel hoped as he responded to Eli's call. Eli remembered and asked. There was nothing Samuel could do but tell Eli the message—the whole message. As much as he wanted to spare Eli the pain of knowing God was going to judge his family so severely, Samuel knew he would be less than faithful if he hid anything.

As he told Eli the news, Eli seemed to understand. The old priest was not angry with Samuel. It was almost as though he had anticipated the message before he heard it from Samuel. Eli and his family had drifted a long way from where they should have been spiritually, but he knew he deserved all he was hearing and more. "It is the Lord," he concluded passively. "Let Him do what seems good to Him" (v. 18).

That would not be the last time young Samuel would hear from God. Very soon Samuel's reputation as a budding prophet spread throughout the land from Dan to Beersheba. Whenever Samuel related a message from the Lord, things happened exactly as he said they would. There had not been anything like it in the land for a long time. Samuel was gathering a national following. "Then the Lord appeared again in Shiloh. For the Lord revealed Himself to Samuel in Shiloh by the word of the Lord. And the word of Samuel came to all Israel" (3:21–4:1).

THE ARK TAKEN BY THE PHILISTINES
(1 Sam. 4:2–6:21)

After Eli's death, Samuel became the spiritual leader of the nation. He had a tent at Shiloh and he could offer sacrifices for the nation, but the ark of the covenant was in enemy hands. How could the presence of God dwell in a heathen nation?

After defeating Israel, the Philistines had Israel's ark of God and carried it proudly back to Ashdod. It was more than just a gold-plated box to them. It was proof they were the mightiest army on the face of the earth. They were mighty enough to capture the mightiest of gods among the nations. It was the physical evidence that proved their god Dagon was stronger than even the mysterious gods of the Israelites.

The Philistines would not hold these erroneous conclusions for long, however. As was their custom following a military victory, they brought the gods of their defeated enemy and laid them at the feet of their god Dagon. Symbolically, the action expressed the belief that the god of the enemy was now subservient to the Philistine god. While God was tolerant in allowing Israel to abuse and misrepresent the ark in the battle, He would not stand for allowing the Philistines to perpetuate their myth at the expense of His reputation. When the men of Ashdod came to view their idol Dagon the next morning, they found the idol had fallen forward on its face before the ark, as though it were paying homage to the defeated god.

The problem was quickly corrected by the Philistines as they raised Dagon back to his more prominent position. But the next morning the idol had fallen forward again. This time, Dagon's head and hands had been cut off and the stump of the idol lay prostrate before the ark. Because of what happened, the priests and worshipers of Dagon in that city began the custom of stepping over the threshold of Dagon, avoiding the "sacred spot" where the idol had fallen.

But the problems were not over for the Philistines. A mysterious outbreak of tumors affected the city. The description of the infliction and the response of the Philistines to the conditions suggests the disease may have been the bubonic plague. This disease is usually transmitted by the bite of a flea from small rodents, such as rats, squirrels, or mice (cf. 1 Sam. 6:5). It is characterized by chills, fever, nausea, and the formation of mounds or "bubos" in the regions of the lymph nodes, armpits, and groins. If uncontrolled, the plague can have a devastating effect on the infected area. More than a fourth of the world's population died as a result of this plague during the Middle Ages. As recently as 1910, over 60,000 deaths were attributed to this disease during an epidemic in China.

While the men of Ashdod may not have been able to diagnose and treat the disease, they realized it was related to their possession of the ark of God. They insisted they no longer wanted to house the sacred treasure of Israel. At a meeting of the lords of the Philistines, it was decided to move the ark to Gath. But the plague then affected the men of that city and they insisted the ark be moved again. And so it was moved to Ekron, but again the plague affected the men of the city. As tumors continued to appear in the "secret parts" of their bodies and they continued burying those who died as a result of the plague, the consensus of the people was to send the ark back to Israel.

It had taken the Philistines seven months to come to the place where they were willing to send the ark back to Israel, yet even then they were reluctant to do so unless it was absolutely necessary. The Philistine priests and diviners agreed to send the ark back with appropriate gifts, but only to do so in such a way that it was most likely the ark would not get to Israel unless this supposed god really had the power to find its own way home. "Now, therefore, make a new cart, and take two milk cows which have never been yoked, and hitch the cows to the cart; and take their calves home, away from them" (v. 7).

The two milk cows who had never borne a yoke were the most unlikely beasts one could choose to bear the ark (or any load, for that matter) on a cart or wagon. As soon as their calves were taken back to the barn, the cows should have naturally gone back to the barn after them. The last thing that could be expected was that the cows would find their way along a road they had never traveled and take the ark directly to the Israelites. The people who had suffered through the plague were convinced they had been cursed by the mysterious ark, but the priests of Dagon, Baal, and Ashtoreth had too much at stake to give up that easily. So they increased the odds against the ark getting safely back to Israel and reasoned, "If it goes up the road to its own territory, to Beth Shemesh, then He has done us this great evil. But if not, then we shall know that it is not His hand that struck us; it was by chance that it happened to us" (v. 9).

But there was no question in the minds of the lords of the Philistines as to the cause of the plague by the time the sun set that evening. The cows pulled their wagon and cargo directly to the city of Beth Shemesh, never going off course the least. The men of the city were in the fields harvesting wheat when they saw the ark appear on the horizon. Seven months earlier, the ark had been lost in battle. Now it was returned.

Though it was important to get the harvest in, it was more important to thank God for the return of the ark. The cows carried the ark right to a large rock in the field of a man from Beth Shemesh named Joshua. Then they stopped as though they knew what was to follow. Wood was split and the cows themselves became "a burnt offering unto the Lord" (v. 14).

The men of Beth Shemesh could not help noticing the ark as it arrived uncovered in their city, but they should have known better than to place it on public display or inspect its interior. Because they "looked into the ark," God judged the men of the city, "and the people lamented, because the Lord had struck the people with a great slaughter" (v. 19). As a result of the deaths of so many of their people, the men of Beth Shemesh appealed to the inhabitants of Kirjath Jearim to come and get the ark. They agreed, and the ark was moved to the house of Abinadab where it remained for the next twenty years.

THE REVIVAL AT MIZPAH *(1 Sam. 7:1-17)*
Though God had demonstrated His power to the Philistines in a most unusual way, it was two decades later that Israel saw that power effective against the Philistines in battle. But Samuel the prophet, the last of the judges, understood the glory of God would never return to Israel, nor would Israel experience the power of God in its warfare against the enemy until the nation repented and came back to God. And so it was that Samuel traveled through the land, calling on Israel to repent and demonstrate that repentance by putting away the foreign gods that had become a part of their religious experience. His message was simple. "If you return to the Lord with all your hearts, then put away the foreign gods and the Ashtaroth from among you, and prepare your hearts for the Lord, and serve Him only; and He will deliver you from the hand of the Philistines" (1 Sam. 7:3).

The message was consistent with what Samuel had always believed and taught, but this time it was different. After two decades of drifting from the Lord, Israel was now ready to hear what God wanted them to do. "So the Children of Israel put away Baals and the Ashtaroth, and served the Lord only" (v. 4). It was a time of revival in Israel, and Samuel recognized it was the right time to call for a national assembly to seal the revival and prepare for the anticipated victories from God. He called the nation to meet with him at Mizpah, and the nation responded. Several things happened at Mizpah which illustrated the unusual character of this Old Testament revival.

The first of these was the unusual custom of pouring out water to the Lord (v. 6). This is the only occurrence of this ritual in Scripture. The ancient Targum paraphrases this statement, claiming "they poured out their hearts in repentance." This was probably the spiritual significance of this symbolic act of pouring out water. Second, there was a national day of fasting at Mizpah. This was accompanied by a third feature of the revival, the confession of sin. Fourth, "Samuel judged the Children of Israel in Mizpah," no doubt settling and resolving many long-standing disputes which existed among the people. Fifth, the assembly at Mizpah was characterized by an emphasis on prevailing prayer (v. 8). Sixth, the revival was a time of total consecration to God as demonstrated by the offering of a burnt offering (v. 9). Finally, it was a time when the people were eager to give God glory for what He had done on their behalf (v. 12).

This revival had a significant effect on the life of Israel, not only at that time but also for generations to come. The most immediate result was the defeat of the Philistines (v. 13). Not only were they defeated at Ebenezer (the stone of help), but "they did not come anymore into the territory of Israel. And the hand of the Lord was against the Philistines all the days of Samuel." A secondary result was the establishment of peace between Israel and the Amorites (v. 14). But many commentators also believe the revival at Mizpah marked the beginning of "the school of the prophets," which later produced men like Elijah and Elisha. Some writers have even suggested this school of the prophets may have been the means by which David was instructed in the Word of God and drawn into his deep commitment to God.

Unlike the short-lived effects of many revivals today, this

revival changed the character of the nation for a lifetime. "So Samuel judged Israel all the days of his life" (v. 15). Some writers have suggested Samuel's four-city annual tour of ministry hints at four fundamental principles for enjoying the continuing effects of a revival. These include maintaining a constant fellowship with God, taking time to periodically judge sin in your own life, watching or taking heed to yourself and your doctrine, and recognizing your privileges as a believer who is seated in the heavenlies with Christ Jesus.

CIRCUIT OF SAMUEL

Bethel—fellowship with God
Gilgal—self-judgment
Mizpah—watchfulness
Ramah—in the heavenlies

PERSPECTIVE: AT THE END OF THE AGE OF THE JUDGES *(1 Sam. 8:1-22)*

"Now it came to pass when Samuel was old that he made his sons judges over Israel" (1 Sam. 8:1). But the age of the judges was coming to a close. Like the sons of Eli, Samuel's own sons did not share their father's commitment to the Lord. They were influenced by money and would make decisions based on which party offered the most attractive bribe. The people did not mind being judged by Samuel, but they did not want to be abused by his sons. They took their protest directly to the faithful old prophet. "Look, you are old, and your sons do not walk in your ways. Now make for us a king to judge us like all the nations" (v. 5).

The popular request was upsetting to Samuel who interpreted it as a personal attack against all he had done for the nation as a judge. But as he prayed about the matter, the Lord made it clear the people had not rejected Samuel but rather the Lord Himself. God had not given Israel a king, though provision for a king had been made in the Law, because He wanted to rule Israel directly. He told Samuel He was now going to give

Israel what they requested, but wanted them to know exactly what they were asking for first.

Samuel reviewed before the people some of the characteristics of kings that he was certain they had overlooked. To have a king meant having sons drafted into his army and daughters drafted into his service. It meant losing the best vineyards and olive groves, and something new in the experience of Israel—taxes. He warned the people the day would come when they would cry out to God because of the king they longed for, but that would happen too late. But as much as he tried, Samuel could not dissuade the people from their decision. "No, but we will have a king over us," they insisted, "that we also may be like all the nations" (vv. 19-20).

God was prepared to meet the people halfway. He would give them a king, but Israel would never "be like all the nations." They were unique in that He had formed an eternal covenant with the nation and its father, Abraham. "Then the Lord said to Samuel, 'Heed their voice, and make them a king.' And Samuel said to the men of Israel, 'Every man go to his city' " (v. 22).

THIRTY-FIVE

SAUL:
The Beginning of the Monarchy
(1 Samuel 9:1–16:23)

Israel's demand for a king so that it might be like the other nations brought the nation into a new era of its history. Initially, God had governed the nation through the patriarchs or heads of families. With the Exodus out of Egypt (which became the historic birthday of the nation), God began using judges to govern the nation. Moses was the first man to hold the office of a judge; Samuel was the last. Now Israel was moving into an era in which God would lead the nation through a king.

While some commentators argue Israel should never have had a king and, therefore, claim the age of the judges should never have ended, the teaching of Scripture suggests otherwise. It was always in the plan of God to someday govern the nation with a king, but as is often the case even today, the people ran ahead of God's plan and demanded a king before God was ready to give one to them. The people demanded a king ten years before David, God's chosen king, had been born.

In blessing his sons, the patriarch Jacob had identified Judah as the tribe which would produce the king. "The scepter shall not depart from Judah, nor a lawgiver from between his feet, until Shiloh comes; and to Him shall be the obedience of the people" (Gen. 49:10). Certain events which had occurred may have delayed the birth of God's chosen king. The first of these was the incestuous relationship Judah engaged in with his daughter-in-law Tamar. Under the Law, this disqualified any descendant from becoming king until the tenth generation. The fact that Ruth was a Moabitess explains the importance of "the generations of Perez" (Ruth 4:18-22). According to this reckoning, David was not only the tenth generation following Judah and Tamar, it was also at least ten generations from Lot's incestuous relationship with his daughter that Ruth was given access into Israel. David was the first one in the line which God could make king and not compromise His own high standard for that high office.

That David was the intended first king of Israel in the mind of God is emphasized by the royal genealogy of Jesus Christ (Matt. 1:1-17). Though several men identified in that genealogy held the office of the king, only one is so identified—David the king (v. 2). Those who recognize a special significance in biblical numerology argue that the very order of the genealogy in Matthew, dividing the list into three groups of fourteen, also serves to emphasize the importance of David as the king. The Hebrew script for the number fourteen is also the Hebrew spelling of the name David. If this was the intent of Matthew in recording the genealogy in this way, verse 17 of the passage alone stresses the relationship between Christ and David.

But ten years before the birth of David, Israel was insistent on receiving from God what He had intended to give them as a blessing. This was at least the third time Israel had demanded a king before God was ready to give them a good king. The people had asked Gideon to be their king, but Gideon refused and intruded into the office of the priesthood, reintroducing the practice of idolatry into the national life of the nation. Later, at least part of the nation made Abimelech, one of the sons of Gideon, their king; but his three-year reign ended violently with the destruction of Shechem and Thebez, and the death of Abimelech at the hands of a woman. Now this was the third time they demanded a king, and what God had intended to give the nation as a blessing was about to become a curse.

Everything was wrong in their demanding and receiving a

king in the person of Saul, the son of Kish. Saul was from the wrong tribe, Benjamin rather than Judah. He was followed by the people for the wrong reason: his physical appearance rather than his spiritual relationship with God. The criterion which led to his choice in the first place was wrong, that the nation should become like other nations rather than remain unique in their covenant relationship with God. The timing of his selection was wrong—a generation too early. And because everything rises or falls on leadership, everything went wrong under his leadership.

Israel would have three kings before a civil war would result in the division of the kingdom. Ironically, each of these kings would complete a reign of forty years. The number forty often appears in Scripture representative of a period of judgment or evaluation. What are considered the forty-year reigns of the first three kings of Israel are described fully enough in Scripture to indicate God's evaluation of each king and his accomplishments.

THE KINGS OF THE UNITED MONARCHY

Saul (1051–1011 B.C.)
David (1011–971 B.C.)
Solomon (971–931 B.C.)

THE SELECTION OF SAUL AS KING OF ISRAEL
(1 Sam. 9:1–12:25)

From all appearances, Saul was the ideal choice of the people for king. The Scripture's first description of him states he was "a choice and handsome young man. There was not a more handsome person than he among the Children of Israel. From his shoulders upward he was taller than any of the people" (1 Sam. 9:2). He first met Samuel the prophet while searching for the lost asses of his father. Commenting on this, F.B. Meyer suggested, "He was called while seeking his father's straying asses. . . and there was a good deal of the wild-ass nature about Saul." Later, God would warn Samuel about making character judgments based solely on one's outward or physical appearance. Saul was a textbook example of one who was physically attractive and could make a good first impression, but in character where it really counts, he lacked a deep and meaningful relationship with God.

As Saul and one of his servants looked for the lost asses, they traveled throughout much of central Palestine. About the time their supplies had run out, they came into the vicinity of Samuel's home. As they discussed their situation, Saul proposed going home and giving up on finding the lost asses; however, his servant proposed visiting the prophet of the city to seek help. The response of Saul in this situation suggests a lack of deep spiritual commitment on his part.

This appears to have been the first time there was any interest in turning to God for a solution to their problem, and that was only after they had exhausted their own resources unsuccessfully. Also, Saul objected initially to seeking out the man of God, arguing, "If we go, what shall we bring the man? For the bread in our vessels is gone, and there is no present to bring to the man of God" (v. 7). Like many carnal Christians and unsaved people today, Saul had apparently concluded the prophet would only help them if they gave him a substantial gift. Only when the servant promised to come up with the fourth part of a shekel of silver (v. 8) did Saul agree to go to the prophet for help. A shekel of silver was the basic coin in the economy of Israel in the Old Testament. As Jesus later observed, "For where your treasure is, there your heart will be also" (Matt. 6:21). The insignificant value of Saul's "offering" is emphasized when compared to David's willingness to spend fifty shekels of silver to offer burnt and peace offerings to the Lord (cf. 2 Sam. 24:24-25). Their lack of spiritual commitment is further emphasized by the fact that they were unaware of the significant religious celebration about to take place in the city and had to be instructed by a group of girls on their way to draw water at the community well (1 Sam. 9:11-13).

What Saul did not realize at the time was that God had already talked to Samuel about him the day before. As Saul and his servant approached the aging prophet, the Lord said to Samuel, "There he is, the man of whom I spoke to you. This one shall reign over My people" (v. 17).

Despite the fact that Samuel was and had been for a generation a well-known and loved prophet, Saul was unable to recognize him when he met him face-to-face. He actually stopped Samuel to ask him for directions to the seer's house (v. 18). Samuel responded by identifying himself, telling Saul the asses had been found, and inviting him to be his guest. Saul, who had gone to find Samuel with his fourth of a shekel of silver as an offering, suddenly found himself the guest of honor in the prophet's residence in that city. He was given a seat of honor at a banquet of about thirty persons and given a prime cut of meat for a meal. That night, Samuel gave both Saul and his servant lodging before sending them home the next day. Interestingly enough, Saul apparently forgot to give his gift to Samuel when he became the recipient of the gifts of honor, food, and housing.

As Samuel escorted Saul and his servant out of the city the next day, Samuel requested a private audience with Saul. The servant was sent on ahead to wait for Saul as he heard "the word of God" (v. 27). "Then Samuel took a flask of oil and poured it on his head, and kissed him and said: 'Is it not because the Lord hath anointed you commander over His inheritance?' " (10:1) Samuel then gave Saul instructions as to where he should go from their meeting. The route Samuel gave to Saul involved the mention of four places which represented four disciplines of the spiritual life Saul needed if he would be a good king over Israel.

The first place mentioned was Zelzah, which was the location of the tomb of Rachel (v. 2). There he would be told the asses had been found and that his father was sorrowing for his son. The implication of the father's sorrow suggests he may have feared his son had run into foul play and was dead. This and the emphasis on Zelzah as the place of Rachel's tomb suggest the meaning of this place as death. Saul was a man consumed with pride which would destroy him if he did not come to the place of death to self. Sadly, there appears to have been no effort on Saul's part to deal with his pride.

The second place mentioned in Samuel's instructions to Saul was the terebinth tree of Tabor (v. 3). The name *Tabor* means "purity" and stresses another area in the life of Saul which needed to be dealt with. His actions surrounding the initial meeting with the prophet demonstrated he did not have a pure walk with God. Like Christians today, Saul needed this practical holiness to maximize his service for God. At the terebinth of Tabor, Saul would meet three men with three kids, three loaves of bread, and a skin of wine. Some commentators believe these items are representative of the sin offering and the body and blood of Christ which is the means by which the Christian attains holiness.

The third place Saul was sent was to Bethel, also called the hill of God (v. 5). At Bethel, the Spirit of the Lord would come on Saul and he would prophesy with the prophets gathered there (v. 6). Saul's unique relationship with the Holy Spirit at this place, together with the meaning of the name Bethel and its historic role as a place of fellowship with God, suggest the need for a deeper communion and fellowship with God for the man who would be king. Again, this also is a need for any and all who would serve God in any capacity.

Finally, Samuel urged Saul to go to Gilgal where he would meet once again with the aging prophet. There burnt offerings and peace offerings were to be offered on Saul's behalf. Gilgal is the place of self-judgment in the Old Testament and stresses the importance of "taking heed" to oneself. The burnt offerings and peace offerings to be offered during the course of the week stress the place of commitment to and fellowship with God in the life of the believer. It is a constant necessity in the Christian life to watch particularly these two areas of our relationship with God because it is so easy to wane in our commitment and to wander from the place of fellowship. Seven is often a number signifying completeness in Scripture; so some writers suggest that spreading the sacrifices over seven days was a warning to Saul to continually judge his commitment and fellowship throughout his reign as king.

Saul began following the Prophet Samuel's instructions but

did not apparently understand the spiritual realities implied. When the Spirit of God came upon him and he prophesied with the prophets, those who knew him questioned the apparent change in Saul asking, "Is Saul also among the prophets?" (vv. 11-12) The saying became a widely repeated proverb of the time, a kind of national joke that someone like Saul might be considered among the prophets of the land. Saul did not apparently go from Bethel to Gilgal as instructed.

Samuel called the nation back to Mizpah, the place of the great revival at the beginning of his ministry where God gave Israel a great victory over the Philistines. There he again stressed to the people how wrong they were in demanding a king and rejecting the rule of God in the process. Using the means of casting lots, the prophet began what may have seemed like the process of choosing a king. Eventually the lot fell on Saul, but he was nowhere to be found. After inquiring of the Lord, the people were directed to the baggage where they found their new king hiding. Some commentators suggest this demonstrates the great humility of Saul at the beginning of his reign (cf. 15:17). Others suggest Saul was embarrassed and that his pride had been offended, noting that the criticism surrounding his prophesying had turned him from his appointed journey to Gilgal. Because of "false humility," which is really pride, Saul was then unwilling to tell even others in his family of the prophecy of Samuel concerning his reign as king (10:16). Still, because of Saul's physical attractiveness, most of the people were excited about having him rule over them as king. Not everyone, however, was convinced Saul was capable of saving Israel (v. 27).

Soon after Saul had been anointed as king over Israel, he was called on to lead Israel into his first battle. Nahash the Ammonite camped against the city of Jabesh Gilead. In order to avert a battle and the ensuing loss of life, the men of Jabesh appealed to Nahash for a peaceful solution to the brewing conflict. Sadistically, Nahash agreed to make a peace treaty with the city on the condition that he would then gouge out the right eyes of the people. The unacceptable terms of Nahash's offer then led the elders of the city to turn to Israel for help.

When the messengers told the people of Gibeah the situation, they began wailing and weeping. Hearing the reaction of the crowd, Saul inquired as to the cause. As he learned of the situation at Jabesh, Saul was incensed with anger. He took a pair of oxen and cut them into pieces. The pieces were then sent throughout all Israel with a warning to the people they too would be cut apart if they did not follow Saul and Samuel into battle against Nahash. The severe message from their king had the desired effect on the people, "and they came out with one consent" (11:7). After gathering an army of 330,000 men, Saul sent a message of support to the elders of the city of Jabesh. By early afternoon the next day, Saul had divided his army into three companies, successfully attacked the Ammonites, slaughtered and scattered the enemy, and won a decisive victory in his first battle as king.

The victory over Nahash caused the people to increase in their admiration for their king. Some of the people wanted to gather up and kill those who had earlier questioned Saul's ability to lead as king. But basking in the glory of his victory, Saul objected to the propostion. "Then said Samuel to the people, 'Come, let us go to Gilgal and renew the kingdom there' " (v. 14). Samuel had tried to get Saul to Gilgal earlier, but Saul failed to go there on his own. Now the prophet seized the opportunity to take the entire nation to Gilgal, knowing the king would join them there to be publicly honored.

At Gilgal, Samuel took the opportunity to deliver what would be his last message to the nation. First, he challenged the people to identify any abuse he had performed in serving in the office of prophet, priest, and judge. The people responded by affirming, "You have not defrauded us or oppressed us, nor have you taken anything of any man's hand" (12:4). Though the people had earlier objected to the corruption of Samuel's sons, their response to the prophet on this occasion suggests that, unlike Eli, Samuel had dealt with his sons—either leading them to repentance of their corruption or eliminating them from the office they had abused.

Then Samuel reviewed the history of Israel, stressing how God had demonstrated His concern for Israel and how the nation had forgotten God and rejected Him. Again he emphasized how wrong the people had been in demanding a king from God, and sought to prove the point through a miraculous demonstration of the power of God. On Samuel's request, the Lord sent a heavy thunderstorm which destroyed much of the wheat harvest which had just ripened. The people responded to this miracle by acknowledging their sin and asking the prophet to pray for them (v. 19). Samuel then comforted the people, acknowledging their sin had not yet involved turning from God completely. Before dismissing the people that day, he stressed God would bless them only as they feared the Lord and served him wholeheartedly (v. 24). Describing his own role as a spiritual leader in the land, Samuel declared, "Moreover, as for me, far be it from me that I should sin against the Lord in ceasing to pray for you; but I will teach you the good and the right way" (v. 23).

THE REJECTION OF SAUL AS KING OF ISRAEL
(1 Sam. 13:1–16:23)

Within two years, Saul was beginning to experience difficulty in leading the nation as king. He had formed a standing army of 3,000 men and sent the others home intending to call on them only when they were needed. His standing army had been divided into two companies: a thousand men under the leadership of his son Jonathan, and the rest under his own leadership. Despite the fact that Saul had the larger number of soldiers under his leadership, he did not seem to be winning any decisive battles. It was Jonathan, with a smaller army, who defeated the Philistine garrison in Geba, but still Saul took credit for the significant military victory. But that victory was advertised not only in Israel but also among the Philistines. The Philistines responded by sending a massive invasion force into Israelite territory which included 30,000 chariots and 6,000 horsemen in addition to an unspecified number of foot soldiers.

The invasion of the Philistines had a devasting effect on the morale of Israel. Many Israelites took refuge in mountain caves hoping to hide from the invading army. Others crossed the Jordan taking refuge in Gilead and Gad. Those who were willing to follow Saul into battle met him at Gilgal, but even then "all the people followed him trembling" (1 Sam. 13:7).

Saul waited at Gilgal for Samuel who was to offer the traditional sacrifice before the nation went into battle. He waited a week but Samuel did not come when the king had expected. As he saw his army beginning to scatter, he called for the sacrifices to be brought to him. It was customary for the priest to offer both a burnt offering and peace offerings before a battle, but Saul was getting desperate. His standing army of 3,000 had dwindled to a mere 600 as the Philistines invaded. Saul took the burnt offering and intruded into the office of the priesthood by offering on the altar himself.

"Now it happened, as soon as he had finished offering the burnt offering, that Samuel came; and Saul went out to meet him, that he might greet him" (v. 10). Samuel immediately challenged Saul for his actions in offering the sacrifice. Saul began making excuses for his action. First, he blamed the people, noting they had begun scattering (v. 11). Second, he accused Samuel of being late in coming to offer the sacrifice. Furthermore, he noted the Philistines were already gathered against Israel at Michmash. His fourth excuse identified his fear that he would soon be attacked by the Philistines and had "not made supplication to the Lord" (v. 12). This statement almost suggests Saul viewed the sacrifices as a sort of good luck charm rather than an act of consecration. Finally, Saul claimed he had to force himself even then into taking the course of action which he had taken.

The excuses impressed neither Samuel nor God. Samuel warned Saul, "But now your kingdom shall not continue. The Lord has sought for Himself a man after His own heart, and the Lord has commanded him to be commander over His people, because you have not kept what the Lord commanded you" (v. 14). Within two years of becoming king, Saul had lost his popularity with the people and influence with God. Though he would continue to hold on to his throne for the next thirty-eight years, he knew God had rejected both him and his descendants from the throne. This was the first of three occasions when Saul rebelled against the clearly revealed word of the Lord.

CONSEQUENCES OF THE REBELLION OF SAUL

His heirs lost the heritage they could have had
  (13:13-14)
His own ministry was hindered and suffered *(15:28)*
His physical life was shortened *(28:19)*

When Samuel left, Saul numbered his army, but did not apparently engage in any conflict with the Philistines. As the Philistine army attacked the cities of Israel and subjected the people, Saul and his army remained in Gibeah. In keeping with their long-established policy, the Philistines disarmed the nation so much so that the only known weapons in the land apparently belonged to Saul and Jonathan.

While the Philistines continued to conquer Israel, Saul apparently took no action against the invading army. He moved into a defensive position and "was sitting in the outskirts of Gibeah under a pomegranate tree which is in Migron" (14:2). The name *Migron* means "fear" and describes not only the place Saul was hiding but also the emotional state of both Saul and his army. His son Jonathan, however, felt the best defense was a bold and daring offense. Without first consulting with his father, Jonathan and his armorbearer scaled the steep ridge between Michmash and Gibeah and attacked the first Philistine garrison they encountered.

In that initial struggle, the two Israelites killed about twenty men over an area of about half an acre. Though the victory was insignificant in light of the size of the invading army of the Philistines, it shook the confidence of the Philistines which was further disrupted by an earthquake occurring about the same time. "And there was trembling in the camp, in the field, and among all the people. The garrison and the raiders also trembled; and the earth quaked, so that it was a very great trembling" (v. 15).

When Saul heard of the confusion within the Philistine camp

and realized Jonathan and his armorbearer were missing, he organized his small army and attacked. They were assisted in fighting the Philistines by a number of Israelites who had formerly supported the Philistine army. As word of the defection of these Hebrews spread quickly through the Philistine army, the Philistines began suspecting each other and began fighting among themselves. "So the Lord saved Israel that day; and the battle shifted to Beth Aven" (v. 23).

In the heat of the battle, Saul forbade his army to eat until the sun set. So severe was the order that even though the men of the army saw honey dripping from honeycombs in the forest, no one even paused to sample it. Jonathan, however, had not heard the order and helped himself to the honey when he was hungry. At the end of the battle that evening, Saul finally allowed his men to eat. In the midst of enjoying his victory over the Philistines, Saul moved closer to God. "Then Saul built an altar to the Lord. This was the first altar that he built to the Lord" (v. 35).

Saul realized he had the advantage in the battle and might lose his momentum if the battle was delayed. He decided the best course of action for Israel was to surprise the disorganized Philistines with a night attack. But when he sought counsel from God, God was silent. Saul perceived the silence of God was due to a violation of his earlier prohibition against eating during the battle. By use of casting lots, Jonathan was exposed as the guilty party. When Jonathan confessed to his action, a self-willed and stubborn Saul sentenced his son to death. Only when the people intervened on Jonathan's behalf was he spared.

The whole incident revealed the weak character of the king and led to constant struggles for the nation. Saul's willingness to kill his son was not the sign of a leader but rather a dictator. Though some Christian leaders fail to remember it, there is a difference between a leader and a dictator. A leader is someone you want to follow. A dictator is someone you must follow. Because of his personal insecurity, Saul could not bear having his orders broken even when the guilty party was ignorant of the order at the time and was primarily responsible for the victory. Only when faced with what seemed a greater act of rebellion on the part of the army was Saul then willing to spare the life of his son.

Before the controversy over Jonathan erupted, Saul was inclined to lead a night attack against the Philistine army before they had time to reorganize and recover from the battle of the day. But by the time Jonathan's life had been spared, Saul had lost interest in fighting the Philistines. Probably his confidence had been shaken by the people's refusal to let Jonathan die. Regardless of the reason, Saul not only abandoned what was probably a wise strategy, (i.e., the night ambush), but also "returned from following the Philistines" (v. 46). But the limited victory over the Philistines did not mean the end of his struggles. Throughout his reign, Saul was engaged in constant warfare defending his borders on several fronts. "And there was fierce war with the Philistines all the days of Saul. And when Saul saw any strong man or any valiant man, he took him for himself " (v. 52).

For several generations, Israel had been engaged in conflicts with the Amalekites. They were the first nation to attack the Israelites, and did so shortly after the nation had crossed the Red Sea out of Egypt (Ex. 17:8-16). Finally the time had come when God determined to destroy the Amalekites once and for all. Samuel went to Saul and told him the message from God challenging Saul to "go and attack Amalek, and utterly destroy all that they have, and do not spare them. But kill both man and woman, infant and nursing child, ox and sheep, camel and donkey" (1 Sam. 15:3). God intended to wipe Amalek and everything associated with the rebellious nation from the face of the earth.

Saul and his army went out to fight against the Amalekites and won a decisive victory. "But Saul and the people spared Agag and the best of the sheep, the oxen, the fatlings, the lambs, and all that was good, and were unwilling to utterly destroy them. But everything that was despised and worthless, that they utterly destroyed" (v. 9). The incomplete act of obedience was the second major act of rebellion in the reign of Saul and would result in yet another rebuke from Samuel.

Saul must have known what Samuel's response to their compromise would have been, and Saul appears to have gone to great lengths to avoid any conflict with the prophet. The route of his return journey home led him to make a wide circle around Ramah, the home of Samuel, rather than the more direct route one would normally have taken. But Saul would not so easily escape the judgment of God. God told Samuel what the rebellious king had done and where Saul could be found. Once again, Samuel confronted Saul with his sin, and once again, Saul began making excuses for his rebellion.

SAUL'S EXCUSES

1 Profess innocence *(v. 20)*
2 Blame people *(vv. 21, 24)*
3 Make concession *(v. 24)*
4 Play tough *(vv. 25, 27)*
5 Restate with admission *(v. 30)*
6 Show false repentance *(v. 31)*

Samuel's message of judgment on Saul was clear. "For rebellion is as the sin of witchcraft, and stubbornness is as iniquity and idolatry. Because you have rejected the word of the Lord, He also has rejected you from being king" (v. 23). When Saul later accidentally tore the mantle of the prophet, Samuel added, "The Lord has torn the kingdom of Israel from you today, and has given it to a neighbor of yours, who is better than you" (v. 28). Saul could have no question in his mind that God was displeased with his failure to utterly destroy the Amalekites as He had commanded. Though Saul seemed to repent on this occasion, his actions suggest his repentance was not genuine. It was Samuel who finally had to kill Agag, not Saul. Ironically, when Saul later died in battle against the Philistines, it was an Amalekite who came to David claiming responsibility for killing Saul (cf. 2 Sam. 1:1-16).

Even though Samuel had delivered the message of judgment to the rebellious king, Samuel himself had grown to like Saul and mourned on the king's behalf. The prophet continued to mourn until God intervened and sent him to Bethlehem with a new task. He was to go to the house of Jesse and find among his sons the one who would sit on the throne in the place of Saul. Knowing how Saul would react if he learned Samuel had anointed another man as king, Samuel took a heifer with him and planned to offer it as a sacrifice to distract attention from his real purpose.

When he came to the house of Jesse, he asked Jesse to present his sons. One by one, the sons of Jesse passed before the aging prophet. When Samuel was introduced to Eliab, the oldest son of Jesse, he was certain that was the one God wanted to be king. Eliab "looked" like a king. It was the same mistake the people had made twenty-six years earlier in choosing Saul as king. God warned Samuel, "Do not look at his appearance or at the height of his stature, because I have refused him. For the Lord does not see as man sees; for man looks at the outward appearance, but the Lord looks at the heart" (1 Sam. 16:7). On this basis, each of the seven sons of Jesse presented to Samuel was rejected.

Finally, the youngest son of Jesse was called for and brought to Samuel. Immediately the Lord made it clear that David was the one. "Then Samuel took the horn of oil and anointed him in the midst of his brothers; and the Spirit of the Lord came upon David from that day onward" (v. 13).

PERSPECTIVE: THE MINISTRY OF MUSIC AFFECTS THE TOTAL PERSON

As David was anointed with oil and the Holy Spirit, Saul was plagued by an evil spirit. In an effort to resolve this situation, David was selected to come to the palace and play for the king. "And so it was, whenever the spirit from God was upon Saul, that David would take a harp and play it with his hand. Then Saul would become refreshed and well, and the distressing spirit would depart from him" (1 Sam. 16:23). The royal counselors realized the tremendous power that skillfully played music could have on their king emotionally, physically, and spiritually.

THIRTY-SIX

SAUL:
His Pursuit of David

(1 Samuel 17:1–31:13; various Psalms)

David remained in the palace as a type of court minstrel until a major invasion of the Philistines forced Saul to return to the battlefield. Though his three oldest brothers joined the army of Saul, David returned to his father's home to care for the flocks of his father. It is estimated David was seventeen years old at this time and, therefore, exempt from military duty. Also, with three of his sons fighting in the army of Saul, Jesse no doubt needed his youngest son to help take up the slack on the farm. It seemed like another battle would be fought that David would not be allowed to participate in.

Because David is earlier described as "a mighty man of valor, a man of war" (1 Sam. 16:18), many commentators believe he may have been involved in a few minor skirmishes with the Philistines near his home in Bethlehem even though he was still three years too young to be numbered among "the men of war." Every indication of David's early actions suggests he was eager to do his part in defending his nation from its enemies. This would be especially true in that he was one of the few people who knew who the next king of Israel would be.

But as much as David wanted to be in the battle, the man after God's own heart was prepared to accept the direction God set for him in life. He returned to his father's house and remained under his authority after his brief residence in the palace in the service of Saul. For almost six weeks David led the flocks of his father over the hills of Bethlehem.

DAVID AND GOLIATH *(1 Sam. 17:1-54)*
While David watched the flocks of his father, his three older brothers and those fighting with them engaged in a prolonged stalemate of daily skirmishes with the Philistines which failed to decide a clear victor. In such cases, it was customary among the Greek armies to propose the battle be decided by a championship contest. The Greeks had a democratic view of heaven in which they believed the various gods voted in support of each other as their subjects went to war. The god who got the largest vote was the one who was assured of winning the battle. Fatalistically, the Greeks therefore concluded the battle could be determined if a representative champion from each army met in a fight to the death. They reasoned this would determine how the gods had voted in heaven and also result in saving lives which might otherwise be lost in the battle.

Among the Philistines was a man of Gath named Goliath. He stood nine feet three inches tall and would have probably weighed 500–600 pounds. Some writers believe Goliath's mammoth size may have been due to a tumor of the pituitary gland, a known cause of giantism today. One of the frequent complications of this condition is "tunnel vision," caused by the enlarged tumor interfering with the inner fibers of the optic nerves (cf. 1 Sam. 17:42). Though this may have made Goliath a little clumsy on his feet, he was nevertheless well able to handle himself in military conflict. He was "a man of war from his youth" (v. 33) and had earned such a reputation as to be the appointed champion of the Philistines (v. 4).

For forty consecutive days, the giant of Gath challenged the army of Israel to a championship battle every morning and evening. The army was probably still engaged in hand-to-hand conflict during this period, and the lack of military progress against the Philistines together with the constant defiance of Goliath discouraged and scared the Israelite army. The nation

Israel was fighting for its national existence, and each day it was becoming increasingly less convinced it could or would win.

As the battle continued into its second month, Jesse became increasingly concerned over the fate of his sons and the army of Israel. Because there was not the extensive communications media which exists today, Jesse had probably not heard any reliable news about the battle since his sons left to fight with Saul. He called his youngest son David in to travel to the front and take supplies to his older brothers. Jesse also asked David to return with news of the progress of the battle.

David left very early the next morning and lost no time getting to the battlefield. He arrived just as the army of Israel was launching its morning offensive and, in his youthful enthusiasm, he joined in. He shouted, cheering on his national army and, after leaving the supplies he had brought with the keeper, ran into the army to join with the fighting unarmed. Quickly he found his brothers and they began exchanging greetings. Then, for the eighty-first time since the battle had begun forty-one days earlier, the booming voice of Goliath echoed again across the valley of Elah. "I defy the armies of Israel this day; give me a man, that we may fight together" (v. 10).

As David waited to see who would go out to defeat Goliath, he soon realized there was a real problem on the battlefield. The men who moments before had enthusiastically jumped up and run down toward the battlefield were now fearful and visibly shaken at the appearance of Goliath. As David began to ask questions, he learned the king had offered riches, the hand of his daughter in marriage, and a tax-free status to the man who successfully defeated Goliath. He also learned that none of the men in the army were giving serious thought to collecting the reward.

As his older brother Eliab overheard David's conversations with the other men, he became angry and accusingly misjudged David's motives for being at the front. Eliab's pride had been challenged since his kid brother (whom Eliab was supposed to be fighting to protect) seemed to think Goliath could be beaten. Probably Eliab was expecting David to begin putting pressure on his big brother to take on Goliath. Because Eliab was, like the rest of Saul's army, not trusting in God for the victory, the very size of Goliath was enough to discourage him from fighting. Typical of the actions of some carnal Christians today, Eliab responded to the presence of a spiritual person by falsely accusing that person of having less than honorable motives.

In frustration, David responded to Eliab's unwarranted accusations with an expression which has often been repeated in a wide variety of circumstances, "What have I done now?" (v. 29) This question was followed by a second which was really more of a statement. "Is there not a cause?" So convicting was the affirmation of David that Eliab was unable to respond. In fact, every time David spoke with confidence that day, he effectively silenced his critics.

The backslidden army of Israel refused to defend the name of its God which had for forty days been blasphemed by the Philistine giant. But David was totally surrendered to the purpose of God and, therefore, willing to fight the necessary battle. As word began spreading through the camp of David's willingness to accept Goliath's challenge, it was not long before David was summoned to appear before King Saul in his tent.

Initially, Saul tried to discourage David from engaging himself in the battle. David claimed he would be victorious over Goliath because he had been victorious over a bear and lion which had tried to take one of his father's sheep. David attributed his victory over the bear and lion as well as his anticipated victory over Goliath to the Lord. His confident expectation of victory was based on his past experiences of trusting God in a crisis experience. Trusting God in a crisis situation always leads to a greater confidence in God.

When Saul saw he could not dissuade David from fighting Goliath, he agreed but urged him to at least wear his armor. The teenage David stood there as his tall king placed armor on his body. Naturally, the armor designed for the king did not fit the teenager, and David found himself refusing armor for the battle. All he carried into battle that day was his shepherd staff and a sling. While a sling was not the usual sort of weapon one would use in battle, an accurate thrower could throw a stone eighty yards and hit an object as small as a man's head. As David walked down the hill into the valley of Eliah that day, he was going to serve God with what was in his hand, separating himself from the unfaithful army of Israel, and standing alone for God against the enemy of God.

PRINCIPLES OF SPIRITUAL VICTORY

1 Total surrender to the purpose of God
2 Future expectations based on past experiences
3 Serve God with what is in your hand
4 Separate from unfaithful
5 Stand alone

As David passed by the brook, he stooped down and picked up five smooth stones. To this day, the spring floodwaters still deposit thousands of small, round stones in the bed of the brook each year. The question has been asked why David chose five stones if he was trusting God in the battle. Some commentators suggest he chose one for Goliath and one for each of his four brothers. Others argue he choose one stone for each of the five cities of the Philistines. More likely, David simply gathered several stones so as not to be presumptuous as he went out to meet Goliath.

When Goliath realized his challenge was being met by a teenage boy, he began ridiculing David and cursing him. David responded by affirming his confidence that the Lord would give him victory. He appears to have been the only Israelite on the battlefield that still believed "the battle is the Lord's" (v. 47). As David ran toward the Philistine giant, he reached his hand into his bag and took out a stone. Quickly he placed it in his sling and slung it toward Goliath. The stone hit its mark, sinking into the forehead of Goliath. Normally, a man hit by a stone would fall backward, but Goliath fell on his face, indicating he was totally unconscious as a result of the blow. Because David himself did not have a sword, he took the sword of Goliath and used it to sever the giant's head from his body.

With all of the enthusiasm of youth, he then grabbed the head of the giant and carried it to Jerusalem. Some writers believe David had, even at this early age, planned to someday take Jerusalem and make it his capital, and that he carried the head of Goliath to that city as a kind of warning gesture, i.e., Jerusalem's days were numbered.

DAVID: THE CHAMPION OF ISRAEL
(1 Sam. 17:55–19:17; Ps. 59)

So zealous was David for his first battle trophy that when he appeared before Saul later that day, he was still holding the head of Goliath in his hands. David was not unlike other adolescent youths who wear letter sweaters or other tokens of victory to show off. He was reintroduced to the king, this time not as a minstrel or overly zealous kid, but as a respected and experienced soldier. Even though David was still young, too young to be a man of war, Saul made him a leader in the army and began sending him out to lead soldiers into battle.

When Saul and David were finished talking, the young champion of Israel met another member of the royal family, Jonathan. A deep bond of friendship immediately developed between these two young men which lasted for the rest of Jonathan's life. "The soul of Jonathan was knit with the soul of David, and Jonathan loved him as his own soul" (1 Sam. 18:1). In the years to come, David's enduring friendship with Jonathan would be one of the ways God would preserve David's life and encourage the anointed one when he got discouraged.

As David led his men of war into battle as instructed by King Saul, he won a number of military victories over the enemy. He became increasingly more accepted and liked by the people of the land as well as those with whom he worked in the palace. But in his insecurity, Saul began to view David as a personal threat. His fear grew into paranoia and resulted in him hating David.

The breakdown in the relationship between David and Saul began when Saul overheard the singing of the women of the city as David returned from a battle with the Philistines. Celebrating the success of the Israelites over their enemies, the women of the city took to the streets with dancing and various musical instruments and joyfully began singing their chorus, "Saul has slain his thousands, and David his ten thousands" (v. 7).

As is true with much poetry, the actual claim was probably not meant to be taken literally, but Saul became upset when he heard it. He complained the people were ascribing more military victories to David than to him. Inasmuch as Saul had been in constant armed struggle during his entire reign and David had only recently begun fighting, it is most probably that Saul had in fact personally killed more of Israel's enemies than had David. Yet one might suppose that if the chorus had been altered accordingly, Saul would then have been upset that David's name had come first in the refrain. In his insecurity, Saul could not share the limelight with anyone. "So Saul eyed David from that day forward" (v. 9).

Saul had promised to give the one who conquered Goliath his own daughter as part of the reward, but Saul made no move to honor that promise. His concern was not to bless but rather destroy David. The day after the women danced in the street singing their refrain about the victories of David, Saul was again being tormented by the evil spirit. David was brought to Saul to comfort him with music, but as David played, Saul saw his opportunity to kill him. Quickly the king seized his javelin and threw it at the unsuspecting minstrel. When Saul realized his aim was off, he grabbed the javelin again and was able to get a second shot before David escaped.

The thing Saul feared most about David was not his popularity with the people but his fellowship with God. "Now Saul was afraid of David, because the Lord was with him, but had departed from Saul" (v. 12). Realizing he had failed to kill David himself, Saul adopted a different strategy to destroy his rival. He promoted David to the rank of captain over a thousand, anticipating David would soon find an enemy he could not defeat and lose his life trying. To insure David's involvement in the battle, Saul again offered his daughter to David in marriage if he would fight valiantly.

Saul's plot failed. David was not killed by the enemy but

continued to grow in popularity with the people and grow in fellowship with God. When it came time for Merab, Saul's daughter, to be married, she was given to Adriel, the Meholathite rather than David. For a second time Saul refused to honor his word and fulfill his promise to David (v. 19).

After the marriage of Merab to Adriel, Saul learned his daughter Michal was among the many women who were finding David attractive and growing in their admiration for him. Saul saw this as yet another chance by which he could destroy David. Saul made sure David heard of a third offer of a wife. David was told Saul was prepared to let David marry his daughter if he could provide proof of killing a hundred Philistines by an appointed time. The proof of their deaths, therefore, would be delivering the foreskins of the victims to the king (vv. 20-29).

The Scripture does not state how long David was given to accomplish his mission against the Philistines; however, it is implied the time must have been so short as to involve an unnecessary risk on the part of David to perform it. Saul was confident David would be killed in attempting to defeat the Philistines. But well within the limit set by Saul, David and his men were able to deliver twice what had been requested. This time Saul did follow through on his promise, and Michal became the first of several wives in the harem of David. The multiple wives of David and other men such as Jacob is descriptive of their behavior, not normative experience for others to follow. Monogamy is commended by the Creator God (Gen. 2:24) and Jesus (Matt. 19:6) and is the norm for today.

Saul's hatred for David continued to grow until he finally called his servants in and ordered the assassination of David (1 Sam. 19:1). Among those present on that occasion was Jonathan, Saul's son and friend of David. Jonathan warned his friend of the immediate danger and urged David to hide. Then he went to his father and talked with him on David's behalf. As he defended David's loyalty to Saul, Jonathan was successful in convincing Saul to rescind his order to kill David, and the two were at least temporarily reconciled.

David continued to serve his king faithfully, fighting against the enemies of Israel. In the course of doing so, David led an attack against the Philistines which resulted in a great slaughter of the Philistines and significant victory for Israel. But at a time when Saul should have been celebrating the national victory, he was again possessed with the evil spirit. Once again David sat before him with his harp, trying to help the king. And once again Saul tried unsuccessfully to kill David. Quickly David escaped from the king and went to his own home.

Saul was intent on killing David this time and sent men to guard David's house that night and kill him in the morning. David soon became aware of the presence of these messengers of death and suspected their true purpose. He responded to their presence by pouring his heart out to God in prayer. "Deliver me from my enemies, O my God; defend me from those who rise up against me. Deliver me from the workers of iniquity, and save me from bloodthirsty men. For lo, they lie in wait for my life; the mighty gather against me, not for my transgression nor for my sin, O Lord" (Ps. 59:1-3).

Michal realized she was trapped between her love for her husband and her father. She warned David to escape with his life. She felt confident her father would not allow her to be harmed and remained behind to delay any search which might be made for her husband. She let him out through a window, probably holding one end of a rope or sheet while David climbed down the wall. After David had escaped, she took one of the idols she apparently possessed and placed it in David's bed so that it looked like the body of a man. Where the head belonged, she placed a goatskin pillow to look like the back of a man's head poking up through the covers.

When the messengers of Saul came in the next morning to kill David, Michal showed them the bed and claimed her husband was sick and could not be moved. The messengers failed to inspect the bed before reporting back to the king. Only when they were sent back to get David, bed and all, did they realize they had been tricked. When Saul asked Michal why she had allowed David to escape, she defended herself by falsely claiming David had threatened her life if she did not do so.

DAVID THE FUGITIVE
(1 Sam. 19:18–27:12;
Pss. 13; 34; 52; 54; 56–57; 63; 142)

David the shepherd, who had become David the champion, was now David the fugitive. "So David fled and escaped, and went to Samuel at Ramah, and told him all that Saul had done to him" (1 Sam. 19:18). Soon word leaked back to the king that David was in Ramah with Samuel. Saul immediately sent men to Ramah to take David. But when the men arrived at Ramah and saw Samuel and a group of prophets prophesying, they too were overcome by the Spirit of God and began to prophesy. When Saul learned what had happened, he sent a second group to accomplish the mission, but they too began to prophesy as they came to the city. The second group was followed by a third group which had the same thing happen to them. Finally, Saul himself went to Ramah to find David, and as he came near the place where David and Samuel were staying, he too began prophesying. Once again an earlier proverb from the life of Saul became a popular joke among the people, "Is Saul also among the prophets?" (v. 24)

Perhaps remembering how Jonathan had earlier convinced Saul to preserve David's life, the fugitive left Ramah and appealed to Jonathan for help. Initially, Jonathan did not believe his father was involved in a plot against David's life, but agreed to protect David until the charge was proven. It was two days later that Saul realized his son Jonathan had helped David escape. The king's wrath was then directed toward his son. "Then Saul cast a spear at him to kill him, by which Jonathan knew that it was determined by his father to kill David" (20:33).

His father's attempt on his life left Jonathan in deep emotional turmoil. In anger, he stormed out of the room and refused to eat that day. That anger later turned to grief as he thought of his friend David who was the primary target of Saul's wrath. These emotions were mixed with a sense of shame, not only because he had been publicly humiliated by his father, but because his father had also humiliated him by his angry outburst. Also, Jonathan was torn apart emotionally, knowing he would have to separate himself from his dear friend in order to better protect him from his father.

The next day, David and Jonathan met according to their prearranged plan. In their moving moments together, two of the closest friend that have ever been, parted company. So emotionally charged was the atmosphere of that meeting that David wept uncontrollably for some time. As they parted, they renewed their promise of mutual friendship, not only for their lifetime on earth, but for eternity. For the rest of his life, Saul would spend much of his time hunting for David to kill him. And for the rest of his life, Jonathan would be loved more by David than by any other person on earth.

DAVID THE FUGITIVE

1 Priest at Nob *(21:1)*
2 Achish at Gath *(21:10)*
3 Cave of Adullam *(22:1)*
4 Parents to Moab *(22:3)*
5 Abiathar escapes *(22:20)*
6 Keilah saved *(23:1)*
7 Wilderness of Ziph and Maon *(23:15)*
8 En Gedi cave *(24:1)*
9 Wilderness of Ziph *(26:2)*
10 Achish at Gath *(27:2)*

While David's years wandering as a fugitive from Saul were trying times for the man who would be king, this was also an era in his life when many of the psalms were written. While many of the psalms were difficult to place in a definite historical context with absolute certainty, there are several in which contextual titles or details within the psalms themselves suggest the historic background of their composition.

Just as on at least two occasions David escaped direct attempts on his life because Saul hurled a javelin at him, so David had at least two occasions in which there could be no question that David could have killed Saul had that been his desire (24:4; 26:7-12). On both occasions, David's close advi-

THE PSALMS OF THE FLEEING YEARS

Psalm	Text	Historic Context
56	21:10-11	When David first came to Gath and the Philistines realized they had the champion of Israel in their control.
34	21:12-15	When David appeared before Abimelech and feigned madness.
142	22:1-2	When David fled to the cave of Adullam and was joined by about 400 men.
63	22:5	While David was in the wilderness of Judah.
52	22:9-22	When Doeg the Edomite reported to Saul that David had been to the house of Ahimelech.
13	23:15	Probably just prior to David's receiving encouragement from Jonathan, i.e., at David's most discouraging moment.
54	23:19	When the Ziphites came to Saul offering to help deliver David to the king.
57	24:3-4	When David escaped from Saul in the cave in En Gedi.

sors urged David to kill Saul, arguing the act would have been in harmony with God's promise to give David the throne. But on both occasions, David refused to lay his hand against the one God had anointed as king of Israel. Ironically, it was in a battle with the Philistines, the very enemy of Israel which Saul had hoped would kill David, that King Saul and his son Jonathan would both die. Saul's constant pursuit of David over a period of more than a decade had actually driven David into Philistine territory for protection.

THE END OF SAUL *(1 Sam. 28:1–31:13)*

"Now it happened in those days that the Philistines gathered their armies together for war, to fight with Israel" (1 Sam. 28:1). For some time David and his men had lived with the Philistines and fought against their common enemies. When the Philistines attacked Israel, a genuine conflict of interest arose. The problem arose of David compromising himself by fighting in a battle against Israel. Or David could betray an ally and fight against the Philistines. But at this time the Amalekites had invaded his city of Ziklag and burned it with fire. Therefore, David was occupied in rescuing the families of his men from the Amalekites. He was not in the battle between Israel and Philistia when Saul was killed.

As the Philistine army gathered, Saul became increasingly fearful of what might take place. "And when Saul inquired of the Lord, the Lord did not answer him, either by dreams or by Urim or by the prophets" (v. 6). In the latter years of his reign, Saul had driven away everyone that could have helped him at his moment of need. David, who had never lost a battle against the Philistines, was in exile in Philistia. The priests whom he would normally consult for spiritual counsel had been killed by Doeg the Edomite on the king's command. Samuel the prophet was dead. Every legitimate means of discerning the will of God was unavailable to Saul because he had refused them.

In his desperation, Saul turned to the illegitimate practice of divination. Earlier in his reign, Saul himself had launched an all-out campaign against occult practices and killed many of those who practiced as mediums. But some mediums had escaped his purge, and now he turned to one of them for help. When he asked for a medium, his advisors directed him to a woman of En Dor who practiced witchcraft. Disguising himself, he and his servants left under the cover of darkness for a meeting with the witch.

Initially, the witch of En Dor was cautious, fearful the stranger and his friends who had knocked on her door might have come to set a trap for her. Once assured her guest was sincere in his expressed desire to communicate with the dead, she agreed to call up Samuel the prophet as requested.

Suddenly the woman shrieked with terror as she saw what she had not expected to see. Conservative theologians are divided in their interpretation of what exactly happened at that moment. Some claim she had expected a demon or familiar spirit and was shocked when God sent Samuel instead. Others argue the woman was a hoax who had planned to con her distraught customer but was terrified when a demon appeared impersonating the deceased Prophet Samuel. Almost immediately, she realized who her guest was and, in her fear, identified him as Saul.

Saul tried to calm the woman and asked her what she had seen. She described her vision as that of an old man covered with a mantle (symbol of a prophet). With the mention of the mantle, Saul began to remember. At his last meeting with Samuel he had torn that mantle and been told that God would tear away the kingdom from him. Just prior to that act almost forty years earlier, Samuel had uttered those words which now seemed significantly prophetic: "For rebellion is as the sin of witchcraft" (15:23). Now Saul had gone from rebellion against the Lord to witchcraft. "And Saul perceived that it was Samuel, and he stooped with his face to the ground and bowed down" (28:14).

The message Saul received that night was not encouraging. God was about to give the kingdom to David. Israel was about to lose its battle against the Philistines. And within twenty-four hours, Saul himself would be dead.

"Then immediately Saul fell full length on the ground, and was dreadfully afraid because of the words of Samuel. And there was no strength in him, for he had eaten no food all day or all night" (v. 20). Saul's response to the severe message of judgment is similar to reported cases of extreme conviction coming on those who are deeply involved in sin during times of great revival power. So convicted of his sin was Saul that he was unable to move and had no appetite for food. Similar cases have been reported where a person lies prostrate for up to three days before repenting of his sin and being aware of a restoration to fellowship with God. Some commentators believe this was Saul's final call to repentance.

If that is so, it is particularly significant that it was the witch of En Dor that first spoke to Saul, offering him food and urging him to get up. When he refused initially, his friends, who knew where to find the forbidden witch and how to set up a meeting with her, also urged him to get up and eat. They tried to deal with the symptoms of his guilt feelings by giving him a meal and getting him rested rather than allow him to deal with the spiritual cause of his problem and resolve it by repenting of his sin.

The witch and Saul's false friends were ultimately successful in convincing Saul to rise from the floor and eat. In doing so, they broke the spell of conviction that had possessed Saul. Saul ate and rested that night. The next day he went out into battle to his death and into eternity having failed to respond to God's final call to him to repent.

The battle against the Philistines was fierce and scattered the army of Israel. Many of the men fighting for Israel lost their lives that day. In the heat of the battle, Saul himself was fatally wounded by the archers of Philistia. Realizing the severity of his wounds, Saul killed himself by falling on his sword. When his armorbearer thought his king was dead, he followed Saul's example and took his own life. Three of Saul's sons also died in that battle.

As the Philistines stripped and looted the slain Israelites, the bodies of Saul and his sons were discovered. In accordance with a common military practice of that day, the bodies of the royal family were beheaded and their heads circulated throughout the cities of the Philistines as trophies of their victory over Israel. Saul's armor was placed in the treasury of the goddess Ashtaroth and his naked body was hung on the wall of the city of Beth Shan with those of his sons.

But Saul had not died without friends. The men of Jabesh Gilead remembered how Saul had led Israel into battle forty years earlier and preserved their city. A group of the bravest men of that city raided the wall of Beth Shan by night and returned to their city with the four decapitated corpses. There they burned the bodies and buried their bones under a tree.

The city fasted seven days in mourning for their slain king.

PERSPECTIVE: SPIRITUAL REALITY IN THE LIFE OF SAUL

The life and death of Saul pose a very difficult question relevant to the spiritual state of Israel's first king. Sometimes this question is expressed, "Was King Saul saved or lost?" While no one seems willing to suggest Saul was a model of spirituality, there is a legitimate difference of opinion among conservative scholars as to the exact nature of Saul's relationship with God. Part of the difficulty encountered in deciding this issue is due to the difficulty of applying a New Testament standard to an Old Testament experience. Those who believe Saul was saved admit he was at best carnal; but such biblical statements as "You will . . . be turned into another man" (1 Sam. 10:6) and the few occasions where Saul built altars (14:35), sought the counsel of the Lord in his decision-making process (v. 37; 28:6), and ordered the destruction of the witches (v. 9) suggest some evidence of the existence of a spiritual relationship with God.

Others argue Saul was lost spiritually and usually point to his clearly wrong actions in trying to kill David and Jonathan, his bad attitudes of hatred, jealousy, and anger, his murder of the priests at Nob, and consultation with the witch of En Dor as evidence of his unsaved state. Perhaps the real reason it is so difficult to be sure about the spiritual state of Saul is that the life of sin yields the same fruit whether the sinner is one who is unsaved or simply a carnal Christian who fails to live by faith.

THIRTY-SEVEN

DAVID:
The King

(2 Samuel 1:1–10:19; Psalms 30; 60)

On the death of Saul, David was the king designated by God. But as is often the case, there was a period of confusion in Israel following the death of Saul. David was living in the country which had defeated Israel and killed Saul. Therefore, he was not immediately accepted as king. One of the sons of Saul, Ishbosheth, was able to secure enough support to establish a rival reign as king over the northern tribes of Israel for seven and a half years.

David had only been back in Ziklag a few days when he heard of the deaths of Saul and his dear friend Jonathan. David was approached by a young man with torn clothes and dust on his head. When the man saw David, he fell on his face before him and "prostrated himself" (2 Sam. 1:2). When asked where he had come from, the man responded, "I have escaped from the camp of Israel" (v. 3).

Even though David was living in the land of the enemy and under their protection, he still had a deep love for his people Israel and realized he would someday rule over them. But his own problems with the Amalekites had kept him occupied during the most recent Israel-Philistia conflict and he had not yet heard from his usual sources how the battle had gone. It was, therefore, only natural that he should ask this young soldier how the battle had gone.

As David listened to the young messenger, he heard how Israel had fled in the midst of the battle, resulting in the loss of many lives including both Saul and Jonathan. He was not prepared to accept the deaths of his king and his friend on the basis of one man's unsubstantiated testimony; so he began to probe further, asking the messenger how he could be certain the king and his son Jonathan were in fact dead.

The messenger told David an "eyewitness" account of the death of Saul and presented the crown and bracelet of Saul as proof of the king's death. In the process of telling the story, the messenger made several claims. First, he identified himself as an Amalekite, a surviving member of the tribe Saul had been commanded by God to destroy fourteen years earlier. Second, he claimed Saul had unsuccessfully tried to take his own life by leaning on his spear. He further claimed Saul had asked him for help, requesting the Amalekite kill him. Finally, he admitted to killing Saul and removing the king's crown and bracelet to bring them to David.

The testimony of the Amalekite appears to conflict with another account of the death of Saul, and this has created problems for some interpreters of Scripture. The two accounts can be harmonized in either one of two ways. First, some scholars argue Saul did try to commit suicide but failed. His armorbearer did not realize Saul had failed and responded by successfully taking his own life. Later, as Saul groaned in pain dying from both the fatal wounds of the archers and his own attempted suicide, he saw the Amalekite and had him finish the job. A second view of some scholars argues the Amalekite found the body of Saul after the battle and took the crown and bracelet to David. The story about killing Saul was created by the Amalekite in hopes of impressing David and receiving a reward. Those who hold this second view note it is highly unlikely an Amalekite would be fighting in the army of Israel, especially in light of the fact they were engaged in their own battle against Ziklag at the time.

David and his men responded in mourning for the loss of Israel. "And they mourned, and wept and fasted until evening for Saul and for Jonathan his son, for the people of the Lord, and for the house of Israel, because they had fallen by the sword" (v. 12). Then David responded to the Amalekite's own claim of responsibility by sentencing and executing the man for destroying the Lord's anointed. David himself had had opportunity to take the life of Saul, but had refused because God had anointed Saul king of Israel. It is interesting to note David's observation, "Your blood is on your own head, for your own mouth has testified against thee, saying, 'I have killed the Lord's anointed' " (v. 16). This does not mean the Amalekite was necessarily guilty, only that he had made a claim that caused him to appear guilty.

DAVID'S REIGN IN HEBRON
(2 Sam. 2:1–5:12; Ps. 30)

When David learned of the deaths of Saul and Jonathan, he "inquired of the Lord, saying, 'Shall I go up to any of the cities of Judah?' " (2 Sam. 2:1) He knew Samuel had anointed him as king and successor to Saul, but there had always been a question of timing in David's mind. He had assumed God would remove Saul from the throne when the time was right, but before returning to Judah, David wanted to be certain. God assured David he was to return to Hebron with his men. When David settled in Hebron, "the men of Judah came, and there they anointed David king over the house of Judah" (v. 4).

As David became king of Judah, he learned it was the men of Jabesh Gilead who had buried the bodies of Saul and his sons who had been slain in battle. David sent a messenger to the men of that city expressing his own appreciation to them for what they had done and encouraged them as the newly anointed king of Judah. But it would be seven and a half years before that city and others of the north would become a part of David's kingdom.

Abner, Saul's former captain of the host, remained loyal to the dynasty of Saul and established a surviving son of Saul, Ishbosheth, on the throne of Israel as king. With the single exception of the tribe of Judah (which had anointed David as its king), Israel recognized Ishbosheth as their new king and followed him.

The names of the sons of Saul illustrate how far this king had wandered from his recognition of the true God of Israel. His oldest son Jonathan was named in recognition that Jehovah answers prayer. His second son was named Ishuai (Ishvi) probably because of some physical resemblance to his father. He is also called Abinadab (1 Chron. 8:33), which expressed Saul's willingness to serve the Lord. But by the birth of his third son, Saul had turned from the Lord to himself as the source of the nation's salvation. Ultimately, he was naming his sons after the idols which so often caused Israel to wander from God. When Saul died in battle, his oldest sons died with him, representing his testimony concerning God and himself. All that remained was his shame.

SONS OF SAUL

Jonathan—Jehovah has given
Ishuai (Abinadab)—Resembling (willingness)
Malchishua—The king is salvation
Esh-Baal (Ishbosheth)—Man of Baal (shame)

Having two kings in Israel was bound to create problems, so it is not surprising that much of David's reign in Hebron involved him in a civil war. The war began at a meeting of the two armies by the pool of Gibeon. It appears the meeting was intended to be a peaceful meeting of the two sides until Joab, David's general, and his men took twelve of Abner's men and killed them with their own swords. "And there was a very fierce battle that day, and Abner and the men of Israel were beaten before the servants of David" (2 Sam. 2:17). At the end of the battle, Judah had recorded 19 casualties. Abner's men had lost 360.

So severe was the battle that day that the men of Israel were soon scattered and fleeing the battle. Among those on the run was Abner himself. As he escaped the battlefield, he was pursued by Asahel, the brother of Joab. Even at this point in the battle, Abner apparently believed Joab could be trusted. He pled with Asahel to stop pursuing him, claiming he did not want to kill him in self-defense as it would hinder relations between Joab and himself. But Asahel did not listen and finally Abner was forced to defend himself. Taking the butt end of his spear, Abner hit Asahel, probably intending to wind him so that he could escape. But the spear penetrated Asahel's chest cavity and Joab's brother died.

Despite the severe defeat Israel had that day, it marked the beginning rather than the end of the long war between the two kings. During that period, there was a gradual strengthening of David's men and weakening of Abner's men. At times it seemed as though the war would continue without end. Then something happened between Ishbosheth and Abner that resulted in events which led to a quick end to the conflict.

Ishbosheth accused Abner of being involved with Rizpah, one of the concubines of Saul. In the context of those times, the charge amounted to that of treason and sedition. When a rebel wanted to usurp a throne, he would most often engage in relations with the wives and concubines of the king to demonstrate his authority over the throne. Abner had become increasingly stronger in the kingdom, and Ishbosheth, like his faher before him, was becoming suspicious of a potential rival to the throne. There is no indication that there was any foundation for the charge against Abner.

Abner was understandably upset with Ishbosheth's accusation. He reminded the king of his loyalty to the dynasty of Saul and pointed out that he had not betrayed Ishbosheth to David despite apparent opportunities to do so. In his rage, Abner declared God would transfer the kingdom to David from Saul. Ishbosheth was stunned and scared into silence, "because he feared him" (3:11).

For over seven years, Abner had been loyal to Ishbosheth, not only establishing him on the throne but also fighting on his king's behalf and defending him from Joab. But the false charge of Ishbosheth against him turned his loyalty from the dynasty of Saul to a new dynasty of David. Abner sent a message to David requesting a treaty of peace be made between them. David agreed on the condition that his first wife, Michal, the daughter of Saul, be brought to him.

Though David was a man after God's own heart and followed the commandments of the Lord in most areas of his life, his greatest failures in life related to his family relations. This was in part due to his failure to apply biblical principles to this area of his life. Rather than adopt the biblical pattern of monogamy, David acquired at least eight wives and eleven concubines during his lifetime. In requesting here to be reunited with his first wife, he was also violating a biblical principle. Under the law, if a wife acquired another husband after a period of separation from her husband, it was viewed as an "abomination before the Lord" if she went back to the first husband (Deut. 24:4). Later, Michal would become a source of irritation to David.

David made his league with Abner, in effect uniting the kingdom under his leadership. After establishing a peace with Abner, David sent him away to gather Israel in peace. But not everyone was happy with David's actions. Joab was still bitter over the fact that Abner had killed his brother Asahel. Joab went into a tirade over David's decision to make peace with Abner. After expressing his opinion to David, Joab left the king's presence to take matters into his own hands. Without consulting David, "he sent messengers after Abner, who brought him back from the well of Sirah" (2 Sam. 3:26).

When Abner returned to Hebron, Joab was there to meet him. "Joab took him aside in the gate to speak with him privately, and there stabbed him in the stomach, so that he died for the blood of Asahel his brother" (v. 27). When David later learned of the death of Abner at the hand of Joab, he strangely lamented, "Should Abner die as a fool dies?" (v. 33) Despite the strange words, David's fasting and mourning of that day convinced the people he was sincere in his sense of loss for his friend and that the plot to kill Abner had not been initiated by the king.

David's comment concerning Abner's dying as a fool dies should be understood in the context of the cities of refuge in Israel. If a man took the life of another by accident, he was safe from relatives of the deceased who might seek vengeance only so long as he remained in a city of refuge. Hebron was one of the six cities of refuge. Joab could not take the life of Abner until he "took him aside in the gate" (v. 27). At the time of his death, Abner was literally steps away from safety. Some commentators see Abner in his death as a picture of the unsaved man in conviction who "comes to the gate" but never takes the step of saving faith and trusts Christ to save him.

The death of Abner left Ishbosheth and his people in a state of confusion, disarray, and fear. Two of Ishbosheth's own captains plotted a coup and killed their king as he slept in bed during the heat of the day. Traveling by night, they took the head of Ishbosheth to David in Hebron, probably expecting to be rewarded for their efforts. But David was not at all impressed with the murder of "a righteous person in his own house on his bed" (4:11). Baanah and Rechab, the men who had killed Ishbosheth, were executed by David for the murder of their king. David took the head of Ishbosheth and "buried it in the tomb of Abner" (v. 12).

The death of Ishbosheth left Israel without a king. The elders of Israel had already discussed the possibility of making David their king when Abner had defected, and now took that course of action. The kingdom was again reunited and David was anointed king over all Israel. This was the third time David had been anointed as a king.

With the civil war resolved, David turned his attention to the city of Jerusalem. The Jebusites thought they were secure in their city, so much so that they claimed even the blind and the lame could defend it. But David took the city by coming through the water shaft, a tunnel under the wall by which water was brought into the city. He then made that city his capital for the remaining years of his reign. Even to this day, Jersualem is sometimes called "the city of David." He lived in the fort of the city until carpenters and masons from his ally Hiram, king of Tyre, finished building his palace. "So David knew that the Lord had established him as king over Israel, and that He had exalted his kingdom for His people Israel's sake" (5:12). At the dedication of his palace, David wrote a psalm of thanksgiving and praise for what God had done for him (Ps. 30).

DAVID'S REIGN IN JERUSALEM
(2 Sam. 5:13–10:19; Ps. 60)

Jerusalem was already important in Israel's history even before it was conquered by David. Melchizedek, to whom Abraham had paid tithes, was king of (Jeru)Salem (Gen. 14:18). In conquering this city, David acquried this dynastic title "a priest forever according to the order of Melchizedek" which later was ascribed to Jesus (cf. Ps. 110:4). Also, Jerusalem was the place where Abraham nearly offered his son Isaac to God in a burnt offering. Being built on a hill, the city was visible from Bethlehem, and David may have dreamed of conquering it even as a boy in Bethlehem.

After establishing his throne in Jerusalem, David fought and defeated the enemy of Israel which Saul had neglected while pursuing David. He finished the task begun by Samson "and drove back the Philistines from Geba [Gibeon] as far as Gezer" (2 Sam. 5:25).

As Moses had prepared Israel to conquer the land, he told the people God would establish a central place of worship once they had settled the land (cf. Deut. 12). God would not confirm that place until the dedication of Solomon's temple, but David realized it was time to bring the ark of the covenant to Jerusalem. Perhaps his defeat of the Philistines caused him to remember how they had transported the ark back to Israel on a cart (1 Sam. 6:7-8). David, therefore, chose that method to carry the ark to Jerusalem despite the fact God had already instructed how the ark should be carried (cf. Num. 4:5-15).

Though David's intentions were honorable, he tried to do a right thing in a wrong way, and the result led to the death of a man named Uzzah. As the cart shifted, Uzzah reached for the ark to prevent it from falling, but God killed him as he touched the side of the ark. Fearful and angry over the death of Uzzah, David stopped the journey of the ark and had it removed from the cart and carried it into the home of Obed-Edom the Gittite. The ark remained there for three months before David resumed the project of taking it to Jersualem.

This time the ark was carried by men, and the spirit of the occasion was once again festive. Those who bore the ark had only begun the journey when David began offering his sacrifices. In his enthusiasm at the time, "David danced before the Lord with all his might; and David was wearing a linen ephod" (2 Sam. 6:14).

When Michal, Saul's daughter and David's first wife, saw David dancing in the clothes of a commoner before God, she was offended at her husband's willingness to set aside his regal robes on such an occasion. Sarcastically, she met her husband with the words, "How glorious was the king of Israel today, uncovering himself today in the eyes of the maids of his servants, as one of the base fellows shamelessly uncovers himself!" (v. 20) The uncalled-for remark marked a breach in David's relations with his wife. He made it clear he would humble himself before God willingly, even if he appeared contemptible to the queen. "Therefore, Michal the daughter of Saul had no children to the day of her death" (v. 23).

With the ark in Jerusalem and David spending more time in his palace, not having to fight enemies, it began to bother him that he should live in such comfortable surroundings but the ark should remain in a tent. He discussed the matter with Nathan the prophet, and was encouraged to build the temple he desired to build. But later that night, Nathan received a message directly from the Lord concerning that particular matter.

God wanted the prophet to deliver a message to the king. He was to remind David, "Thus says the Lord of hosts: 'I took you from the sheepfold, from following the sheep, to be ruler over My people, over Israel' " (7:8). God blessed David, giving him rest from his enemies, but God did not want David building His temple. God established a covenant with David that will be the foundation of the government of the thousand-year reign of Christ. It would be the son and heir of David, a son not even born yet, who would be the builder of the temple. As much as David may have wanted to undertake this project, he would not be allowed by God to build the temple.

Rather than become frustrated over God's refusal to allow him to build a temple, David responded to Nathan's message from God with a prayer of humble thanksgiving to God for what He had already done for him and praise for who God is. If he could not build the temple, he would do what he could. By the end of David's life, he had designed the temple and gathered most of the materials needed for its building. In the interim, David continued his battles against the enemies of Israel. Even on the battlefield, David took time to worship God. Some of his psalms were written in the context of these military struggles (cf. 8:13; Ps. 60).

David spent much of his time as king fighting the enemies Saul had neglected during his rule. As David went out to battle after battle, he must have been reminded often of the years Saul had pursued him and tried to destroy him. But David was not bitter. On the contrary, David began making inquiries concerning possible descendants of Saul to whom he could demonstrate "kindness for Jonathan's sake" (2 Sam. 9:1). When he learned of a lame son of Jonathan named Mephibosheth living in Lo Debar, David invited him to Jerusalem to eat at the king's table as one of his sons. Some commentators see David's actions toward Mephibosheth as a picture of salvation by grace. The grace of David was extended to helpless Mephibosheth, brought him into a position of blessedness, and sustained and kept him.

David's desire to honor others was not always appreciated. When Nahash, the king of Ammon, died, David sent a delegation to honor his son Hanun as he took the throne of his father. David had appreciated the kindness shown him by Nahash and sought to extend the same to Hanun. But the princes of Ammon were suspicious of David's motives and assumed the delegation had come as spies. "Therefore Hanun took David's servants, and shaved off one half of their beards, and cut off their garments in the middle, at their buttocks, and sent them away" (10:4).

The actions of Hanun not only humiliated the men sent to honor the new king, but insulted David and the nation of Israel. David responded by going to war against Ammon. When the Ammonites realized they had provoked the wrath of David and were unable to defend themselves, they hired 33,000 Syrian mercenaries to fight with them. But David so soundly defeated the Syrians that they sought to make peace with Israel at any cost. "So the Syrians were afraid to help the people of Ammon anymore" (v. 19).

PERSPECTIVE: THE VULNERABILITY OF IMMINENT VICTORY

With the defeat of the Syrians, the cities of Ammon should have fallen with little or no struggle. But the war raged on between Israel and Ammon not only weeks but years. It would be three years before David would take the royal city of Rabbah (today's city of Amman, Jordan) and add the crown jewels of that city to his own treasury. But during that time, he would also enter his darkest hour in an otherwise bright relationship with God.

THIRTY-EIGHT

DAVID:
The Latter Days

(2 Samuel 11:1–24:25; 1 Kings 1:1–2:11; Psalms 3; 7; 18; 72)

God elevated David from the humble task of caring for sheep to the majesty of ruling Israel during a time of great national success and prosperity. But the prosperity of Israel during his reign was not just a chance happening. It was the blessing of God on "the man after God's own heart." David and his kingdom were honored by God because they honored God in all they did. Generations later it would be affirmed, "David did what was right in the eyes of the Lord, and had not turned aside from anything that He commanded him all the days of his life, except in the matter of Uriah the Hittite" (1 Kings 15:5).

The darkest hour of David's life began one sleepless night in Jerusalem. Israel was again at war, and again Israel was winning. They were defeating the Ammonites and had laid siege to the city of Rabbah. It was largely a waiting game now, and David had decided to wait it out in his own bed in Jerusalem rather than to go to the battlefield with his men. In fact, he had suspected Ammon would not be much of an enemy to defeat, so he had sent his men to fight under Joab while he himself remained in his palace. But he just couldn't get to sleep one night no matter how hard he tried. Maybe some fresh air would help, so he went to the roof of his house to walk about.

BATHSHEBA: THE WIFE OF URIAH THE HITTITE
(2 Sam. 11:1-27)

It was while he was standing on the roof that he first saw Bathsheba. She was bathing at the time and the absence of clothing only served to accentuate her physical beauty. As David continued watching, he began asking questions. He learned her name was Bathsheba, the wife of one of the thirty-seven elite military commanders identified as "David's mighty men." He knew her husband Uriah well. Uriah had proved himself a soldier of excellence on the battlefield where it counted. And he knew where Uriah was at the time—camped out in Ammon waiting for the city of Rabbah to fall.

No longer was David interested in trying to get to sleep. It was Bathsheba who now captivated his mind. Watching her bathe at a distance, he decided to bring her closer. It would be less conspicuous if she were to come to the palace than if he were to go to her home, so he sent a messenger to summon her to his presence. There in the ornate palace and in the presence of her respected and beloved king, she succumbed to his improper advances. They found themselves sharing a common bed betraying an honorable husband and faithful friend. By morning Bathsheba had returned home, and no one had to know what had taken place. But Bathsheba had conceived, and very soon thereafter both she and her king realized they had a problem to resolve.

The advantage of being king is that there are times you can pull strings and do things no one else could do. David was sure he had a plan that was guaranteed to work. It was about time he got another report from the battle and he would call Uriah to return with the report. He would return to Jerusalem, spend a few nights with his wife, then return to the battle where he was needed. How could Uriah resist the charms of his lovely wife! When she later gave birth to her child, Uriah would remember the weekend he had come home from the battle and simply assume he had fathered the child.

But Uriah was a disciplined soldier who would not allow himself to enjoy the simple pleasures of life when there was a battle to be won. Though his home was in the city, Uriah insisted on sleeping at the door of his king's palace. "The ark and Israel and Judah are dwelling in tents," he explained, "and my lord Joab and the servants of my lord are encamped in the open fields. Shall I then go to my house to eat and to drink, and to lie with my wife? As you live, and as your soul lives, I will not do this thing" (2 Sam. 11:11). Uriah's statement amounted to an oath sworn on the life of his king.

David did not have much time to act. He knew Bathsheba would begin to show evidences of her condition soon and he did not want to find himself in the midst of a moral scandal. He decided to try again. He invited Uriah to be his guest at a banquet the next night and made sure Uriah was drunk before he left. But even in his drunken state, he did not return home to his wife but remained at the palace. It was time for David to initiate his alternative approach to resolving the problem.

The next morning, David sent Uriah back to the battle with sealed orders for Joab. Uriah was to be sent on a suicide mission which would attempt to storm the walls of Rabbah. David made it clear to Joab he wanted to receive the report of Uriahs' death. Though Uriah had held the life of his king in high regard, David counted the life of Uriah as expendable in covering his sin. The storming of the walls was a disaster for Israel, but a success for David. Several soldiers lost their lives in the battle, including one named Uriah, the Hittite. When Bathsheba learned of the death of her husband, she mourned as was expected. "And when her mourning was over, David sent and brought her to his house, and she became his wife and bore him a son. But the thing that David had done displeased the Lord" (v. 27).

David had covered his tracks, but he was unable to shake the guilt of his sin. Throughout the whole ordeal of trying to cover his sin, there was a recurring fear that what he had done might be discovered and exposed. The growing guilt and fear combined to age him physically and cause him much discomfort. Later David himself confessed, "When I kept silent, my bones grew old through my groaning all the day long. For day and night Your hand was heavy upon me; my vitality is turned into the drought of summer" (Ps. 32:3-4). But the inner conviction of sin in David's heart failed to bring this king to repentance. Now it was time for God to initiate His alternative approach to resolving the problem.

NATHAN: THE PROPHET OF COURAGE AND CREATIVITY *(2 Sam. 12:1-31; Ps. 51)*

"Then the Lord sent Nathan to David" (2 Sam. 12:1). Nathan had the difficult task of calling a popular yet unrepentant king to repentance. Much had already been done to hide the sin that had been committed and Nathan had been informed by God that David had arranged the death of Uriah. If the king was willing to kill one of his most trusted soldiers and able to cover his sin, certainly he would not stop at killing a prophet also. Even before Nathan arrived at the palace that day, he knew he was taking a course of action that could endanger his life. He also knew if he was going to be successful at turning his king back to God, he would have to be creative in his approach to the king.

God had brought David out from the sheepfold to lead Israel as king, but he had never taken the shepherd out of David. Therein was Nathan's hope of success. As he appeared before the king, he asked for the king's opinion concerning the matter of a stolen sheep. David listened intently as Nathan explained how a poor man had only one sheep and had cared for it as best he could. Then he heard how a rich man with a large flock of sheep and herd of cattle stole the poor man's sheep to feed a guest he was entertaining rather than have to give up one of his own sheep. David's blood began to boil as he heard of the mercenary actions of the rich man. The man deserved to die, the king concluded, but not before he restored the stolen lamb fourfold.

Emphatically, Nathan seized the moment. "You are the man," he declared (v. 7). With piercing eyes Nathan looked at the fearful king and declared the accusation of the Lord. God had given David much and had been willing to give David much more if he wanted it, but David had stepped over the line in the matter of Uriah, the Hittite. He was guilty of murder and guilty of adultery, and there would be a severe price to pay for his sin. Briefly Nathan reviewed what David's sin would cost the fallen king. There would be no hiding this time, "for you did it secretly, but I will do this thing before all Israel, before the sun" (v. 12).

PROPHETIC WOE

1 Sword will never depart your home
2 Evil will rise from within
3 Your wives will be taken
4 Enemies will blaspheme you

David himself had called for the stolen sheep to be repaid fourfold, and that was the price David would have to pay. In the months and years to come, David would see his own children victimized and suffer as a consequence of his night with Bathsheba and subsequent covering of his sin. A baby would die. A daughter would be raped by her own brother who would then be killed by another son. As David lost the moral leadership of the land, one of his own sons would lead a coup strong enough to send David running from his own palace. The consequence of this sin would run its course until the fourfold punishment was paid in full. The mighty King David was powerless to control these circumstances. There was nothing he could do but watch the events unfold in the years to come, and contemplate the serious consequences and severe penalty of sin. Before his account was stamped "paid in full," there would be tears and anger, sadness and fear. Not even the king was above the Law of God.

FOURFOLD PAYMENT

1 Death of infant son
2 Rape of daughter Tamar
3 Murder of Amnon
4 Death of Absalom

It was time for David to stop trying to hide his sin and begin dealing with it. As he turned back to God in repentance, he prayed what has since become one of the most beloved of all of the psalms. "Have mercy upon me, O God, according to Your loving-kindness; according to the multitude of Your tender merices, blot out my transgressions" (Ps. 51:1). In the course of his prayer, David traveled the seven successive steps back to the place of full communion with and service for God. When David repented, Nathan reported a second message from heaven. "The Lord also has put away your sin; you shall not die" (2 Sam. 12:13).

Though God forgave David, there were still problems. "However, because by this deed you have given great occasion to the enemies of the Lord to blaspheme, the child also that is born to you shall surely die" (v. 14). Nathan left the palace, but before long David received word his youngest son was extremely sick. For a week he prayed and fasted to the Lord for the child, but the child's condition only got worse.

SEVEN STEPS BACK TO COMMUNION WITH GOD

1 Sin thoroughly judged before God *(Ps. 51:1-6)*
2 Forgiveness through the blood *(v. 7)*
3 Cleansing *(vv. 7-10)*
4 Spirit-filled for joy and power *(vv. 11-12)*
5 Service *(v. 13)*
6 Worship *(vv. 14-17)*
7 The restored believer in fellowship with God

Night after night he went without sleep as he watched and prayed, but these were prayers that would be refused. So intense was his prayer for his sick child that his own servants feared to tell him when the child died. But when David realized the child was dead, he broke his fast and returned to a more normal lifestyle. He knew there was nothing he could do to bring the child back to life, and rested in the hope they would someday be reunited beyond the grave (2 Sam. 12:23).

The loss of a child was especially sorrowful to its mother.

"Then David comforted Bathsheba his wife, and went in to her and lay with her. So she bore a son, and he called his name Solomon. And the Lord loved him" (v. 24). On the birth of Solomon to David and Bathsheba, Nathan returned with a different message than that which he had brought the previous year. He called Solomon, the newborn child, "Jedidiah," which means "beloved of the Lord." The birth of Solomon was a confirmation from God that the sin the couple had been involved in about two years previous was indeed forgiven by God.

But Israel was still fighting the battle at Rabbah. It was there David had sent Uriah on a suicide mission as he tried to cover his sin. Now that his sin had been forgiven and that forgiveness had been confirmed to him in the birth of Solomon, it was time to finally deal with the problem at Rabbah. Joab had finally cut off the water supply to the city and knew the end of the siege was very near. David gathered together his army and led them once more into battle. When they won the battle, David had a new crown of gold and gemstones along with other spoils of war added to his royal treasures. The Ammonites who survived the battle were enlisted by David as manual laborers for his continuing construction projects. "Then David and all the people returned to Jerusalem" (v. 31).

Though they would still experience complications in their lives stemming indirectly from the sin in which they had engaged, both David and Bathsheba realized a ministry in the lives of others born out of suffering they had experienced during that time and later. David's confession of sin became a favorite psalm among those familiar with the book, and Bathsheba trained her son to learn from his father's mistake. It is not surprising that her son would years later remember three particular lessons taught him by his mother during his formative years. First, he was not to give his "strength unto women, nor thy ways to that which destroyeth kings" (Prov. 31:3). Second, he was to avoid the use of wine or strong drink (vv. 4-7). Third, he should be quick to speak on behalf of and defend the cause of the poor and needy (vv. 8-9). The rest of his life might have been different if David had remembered these principles in his dealings with Uriah the Hittite.

AMNON: THE RAPE OF TAMAR *(2 Sam. 13–14)*
Because David compromised himself morally in the matter of
Uriah the Hittite, he lost the moral authority and leadership he
had possessed in his own home. Sometime after the victory at
Rabbah, a favorite son of David named Amnon also decided to
yield to an uncontrolled physical desire and in the process
raped his own sister. Though the actions of his son angered
David, he did not apparently take effective action to resolve
the problem.

Tamar was the daughter of David by his wife Maacah and,
therefore, only a half sister to Amnon whose mother was
Ahinoam of Jezreel, one of the two wives he married during
his years as a fugitive from Saul. As often happens in situations
where children of different families are brought together into a
new home, Amnon was attracted physically to Tamar. His
initial feelings toward her grew until he became frustrated in
his desire for her and became lovesick for her. When his
cousin Jonadab probed Amnon to find out what was wrong with
him, Amnon confessed his secret love for Tamar. Jonadab
proposed to Amnon that he should fake a sickness to convince
David to let Tamar care for him.

The plan worked, and soon Tamar was baking bread for her
brother. Amnon arranged things so he had Tamar alone in his
bedroom and then seized his unsuspecting sister and attempted to seduce her. She resisted his advances and pleaded with
him not to abuse her. "However, he would not heed her voice;
and being stronger than she, he forced her and lay with her"
(2 Sam. 13:14).

After raping his sister, his deep love for her turned into an
even deeper hatred. He sent her out of his presence. She
appealed to him to resolve the situation he had created which
would have probably involved going to his father, confessing
his act, and taking Tamar to be his wife. But Amnon refused to
listen to his sister. When he could not convince her to leave,
he called for a servant to remove her physically. Being sent
from Amnon's room after being abused, she tore the garment

she was wearing, a garment worn by the virgins of the king's household, placed ashes on her head, and began crying. When her brother Absalom realized what had happened, he brought his sister into his own home. "And Absalom spoke to his brother Amnon neither good nor bad. For he had forced his sister Tamar" (v. 22).

It was two full years later that Absalom took revenge on Amnon for what he had done to his sister Tamar. Absalom invited the princes of the kingdom to a banquet celebrating the shearing of the sheep. The true purpose of Absalom in gathering his brothers together was to insure the presence of Amnon whom he sought to kill. Absalom instructed his servants to kill Amnon when Amnon's "heart [was] merry" (v. 28). "So the servants of Absalom did to Amnon as Absalom had commanded" (v. 29).

The initial response of the sons of David was to run in fear. They apparently believed Amnon was the first to fall victim of a mass slaughter planned by Absalom. Indeed, the initial report of the event that reached David stated all the men had been killed by Absalom. Later, one of his nephews correctly reported that only Amnon had been killed by Absalom.

Amnon was widely mourned within the royal family and among their servants. Absalom must have realized his actions would at best alienate him from his brothers. As he saw his brothers running in terror from Baal Hazor toward Jerusalem, he fled to Geshur. For three years he remained in exile from his family and friends in Jerusalem. "And King David longed to go to Absalom. For he was comforted concerning Amnon, seeing he was dead" (v. 39).

As much as he longed for his son Absalom, it was more than five years from the murder of Amnon before David welcomed his son into his presence. Absalom was allowed to return to Jerusalem after his three-year exile only after a wise woman who had been coached by Joab convinced David he was wrong in not bringing Absalom back to Jerusalem. Even then, David refused to meet with Absalom for two years despite efforts on the part of Absalom to gain admittance. Only after Absalom arranged for the ripe field of Joab to be burned did he attract enough attention in the palace to gain admittance to the presence of David. "And when he had called for Absalom, he came to the king and bowed himself on his face to the ground before the king. And the king kissed Absalom" (v. 33).

ABSALOM: THE HEIR WHO COULDN'T WAIT
(2 Sam. 15:1–19:40; Ps. 3)

Absalom's handsomeness attracted the notice of the people even when David refused to see him. "Now in all Israel there was no one who was praised as much as Absalom for his good looks. From the sole of his foot even to the crown of his head there was no blemish in him" (2 Sam. 14:25). But Absalom worked hard to build on that popularity. He would go to the gate of the city to meet those who had grievances they wanted to present to the king. After inquiring as to the nature of the problem, Absalom agreed with the man that he had a good point and would win his cause if the matter came to be judged. But Absalom would lament: the king had failed to appoint a judge to hear his case and so the man was out of luck. Then he would sigh, "Oh, that I were made judge in the land, everyone who has any suit or cause would come to me; then I would do him justice" (15:4). Day after day Absalom met with disgruntled citizens and led them through the same scenario. "So Absalom stole the hearts of the men of Israel" (v. 6).

It did not take long for Absalom to gain widespread public support for his cause using this method. Soon he was ready to make his move. Absalom secured permission to leave Jerusalem and travel to Hebron on the guise of paying a vow to the Lord. But Absalom sent spies throughout the land as he prepared to lead a strong conspiracy against his father David. Among those who followed Absalom was one of David's wisest political counselors, Ahithophel.

When David learned the details of the conspiracy led by Absalom, he realized he could not defend himself adequately if Absalom attacked him immediately in Jerusalem. Thus the decision was made by the king that he and his loyal supporters should flee the city before Absalom attacked. Yet as they left, David noticed one man who could do more for him in Jerusalem than on the run. He turned to Hushai, and asked him to risk his life by pretending to defect to Absalom. David knew Absalom would get wise counsel from Ahithophel and needed his own wise counselor on the inside of Absalom's cabinet to insure the rebel prince would not accept it.

As David began his flight into the wilderness, Hushai awaited the arrival of Absalom in Jerusalem. He did not have to wait long. He met with Absalom and convinced him he would serve the new king as he had served the old king. Absalom apparently decided to accept the advice of both counselors and make his own decisions if and when the two men could not agree.

The first thing Ahithophel suggested to Absalom was that he enter into relations with his father's concubines who had been left in Jerusalem to keep the palace. This was a common gesture on the part of a rebel to demonstrate his authority over the preceding reign. Absalom agreed to follow Ahithophel's advice in this matter and "went in to his father's concubines in the sight of all Israel" (16:22).

Second, Ahithophel wisely advised Absalom to take a select group of his present army and pursue David immediately while he had an advantage. It was here that Hushai was able to help in the defense of David. He convinced Absalom a better plan would be to wait until he was in a stronger position before pursuing his father. He argued that though David's resources were small, the men who followed him were experienced soldiers and could win an initial skirmish if attacked by a small band of soldiers. Hushai argued this would demoralize the troops of Absalom and discourage the fringe element among those following the new king. Then Hushai secretly sent a warning to David informing him of the state of affairs. "Now when Ahithophel saw that his counsel was not followed, he saddled his donkey, and arose and went home to his house, to his city. Then he put his household in order, and hanged himself, and died; and he was buried in his father's tomb" (17:23).

By the time Absalom finally began pursuing his father, David's men had had time to organize. David divided the men who were with him into three companies, each under the leadership of one of his mighty men of valor. He himself planned to fight with the men in the struggle but the people objected. He was their king, and even if half the soldiers died on the battle-fields against Absalom, the other half would still need their king. David agreed to stay behind but urged his men to "deal gently" with Absalom.

The battle went well for David's men that day and 20,000 of Absalom's men fell in battle. Absalom himself was a casualty of the battle. While riding through the forest, Absalom got tan-gled in a tree. When his hair was tangled in the branches, his mule rode on, leaving him suspended and helpless. One of David's men found him and reported to Joab. Disregarding David's instructions, Joab killed Absalom and buried him under a heap of stones in the forest. When David later learned of the death of his son, he mourned his loss. Out of this whole situa-tion was born yet another psalm (Ps. 3).

The death of Absalom marked the end of the most serious threat to the kingdom David had experienced to that point in his life. Joab reminded David it was a time of rejoicing that the coup had failed, rather than a time of mourning. David re-turned to Jerusalem and sat in the gate to judge the nation. Word was sent throughout the land that David was again in control to encourage the people and settle the strife that had developed when he had fled Absalom. It was a time of recon-ciliation and rejoicing. Every effort was made to reunite the kingdom under its king.

SHEBA: THE REVOLT OF ISRAEL
(2 Sam. 19:41–20:22; Ps. 7)

But there were still dissatisfactions with David as king. Some of the men of Israel objected that David seemed more inter-ested in the regional concerns of Judah than in the other tribes. The men of Judah argued that would only be natural because David was one of them. Israel replied that they repre-sented ten tribes to the one tribe of Judah. There did not appear to be a resolution to this war of words between the tribes of Israel and Judah. The circumstances of this period in the life of David may have been the context of several psalms, including Psalm 7.

Seizing the opportunity of the moment and hoping to capitalize on the dissatisfaction and confusion that existed in the land, a Benjamite named Sheba, the son of Bichri, presented himself as a leader of another movement against the right of David to reign. With the exception of the tribe of Judah, all Israel began following Sheba. David saw this threat as even greater than the coup led by Absalom and ordered an immediate pursuit of the rebel forces before they could get established in the fortified cities. Because Amasa delayed in gathering his army, David sent Abishai and Joab in his place. When Amasa joined the army as they pursued Sheba, Joab took advantage of the opportunity and killed Amasa.

Joab led the army until they trapped Sheba and his men in Abel of Beth Maachah. There they laid siege to the city and began to destroy it. As the people saw a mound being built and heard the battering rams of Joab's men pound against their wall, they realized their fate was sealed. A woman of the city called for Joab and attempted to negotiate a peaceful solution to the conflict. Joab agreed to spare the city if they delivered Sheba to him. The woman agreed to send the head of Sheba over the wall. She was successful in convincing the people of the city to agree to the terms she had negotiated, and Sheba was beheaded. When Joab received the head, he led his army back to Jerusalem.

THE CORONATION OF SOLOMON
(1 Kings 1:1–2:11; Ps. 72)

As David approached the end of his life, he weakened physically and spent much of his time in bed. While in this state, yet another attempt to seize his throne was launched by one of his sons. Adonijah conferred with Joab and Abiathar the priest and, with their support, presented himself as heir to his dying father's throne.

David had earlier promised Bathsheba their son Solomon would be the heir. When she learned of Adonijah's actions, she and Nathan approached David with the problem. David responded by ordering an immediate coronation of his son Solomon. Zadok the priest took oil from the tabernacle and anointed Solomon as king. The action on the part of David led to widespread rejoicing as the people celebrated their new king. As part of the coronation celebration, David wrote what would be his final psalm (Ps. 72).

Soon Adonijah and his followers heard the noise of the coronation and learned what it meant. "And all the guests who were with Adonijah were afraid, and arose, and each one went his way" (1 Kings 1:49). Solomon chose not to mar the celebration of that day by killing his adversaries but rather decided to give them a second chance to prove themselves.

As David came to the end of his life, he called his son Solomon aside one last time. He charged Solomon to be faithful to the Lord and His commandments, stressing this as a key to the blessing of God on the kingdom. He warned him of individuals he thought might be a threat to the security of the throne and should not, therefore, be trusted. He also advised his son of individuals who should be honored and rewarded by the new king because of the way they had treated David. It was the last opportunity David would have to advise his wise son. "So David rested with his fathers, and was buried in the City of David" (2:10).

PERSPECTIVE

Even the man after God's own heart was not exempt from falling to human passion and becoming involved in immorality. His initial response to a guilty conscience was not too unlike those who today attempt to hide and cover their sin. God finally had to expose David publicly to bring him to repentance and the place of blessing again.

But even when David finally did repent, there were still consequences of that sin to be faced in the remaining days of his life. His family and children paid part of the price associated with those consequences. Even today, David's affair with Bathsheba is among the best known events in the life of David.

But God forgives sin thoroughly. While others might remember David for his failings, the New Testament commentary on David is summed up in the words, "David . . . served his own generation by the will of God" (Acts 13:36).

THIRTY-NINE

SOLOMON:
The Greatness of the Kingdom

(1 Kings 2:12–11:43; Proverbs; Ecclesiastes; Song of Solomon)

David built a great kingdom during his forty-year reign as king, and then at the end of his life turned it over to his son Solomon. The reign of Solomon was unique in the history of Israel in that it was characterized by an extended period in which the nation was at peace with other nations and had no serious internal threat of a rebellion or coup. Two reasons for this period of rest from war are suggested in Scripture. First, David had done his job well and destroyed the enemies of Israel during his reign. Second, Solomon was the wisest man to ever live and used that wisdom at least initially to resolve minor problems before they became major crises.

Solomon, the son of David and Bathsheba, was born about two years after David's sin involving Bathsheba and Uriah. Soon after his birth, Nathan the prophet told the proud parents of the boy that God had named him Jedidiah, meaning "beloved of the Lord." In this sense, the birth of Solomon was a further evidence of the grace and forgiveness of God extended toward David after his repentance.

THE WISDOM OF SOLOMON *(1 Kings 2:12–4:34)*

Soon after the death of his father David, Solomon faced his first test as the new king of Israel. His brother Adonijah who had been unsuccessful in declaring himself heir to David's throne, approached Bathsheba to ask her to intercede on his behalf. He reminded Solomon's mother he had been declared king before Solomon came to the throne, but suggested all he wanted was one request granted. He asked that Solomon give him in marriage Abishag, the last concubine of David.

Bathsheba viewed the request as reasonable and agreed to plead his cause before the new king. But when Solomon heard the request, he discerned the request was yet another threat to his throne by Adonijah. He realized Adonijah was older than he and, therefore, would normally be considered heir to the throne. Also, it was customary for a rebel king to enter into relations with the wives and concubines of the former king to demonstrate his authority to take the throne. Adonijah's request was, therefore, a veiled coup and Solomon responded with firm and direct action. He began a purge of the leaders of the attempted coup and removed his enemies from their positions of authority.

ADVERSARIES OF SOLOMON

1 Adonijah
2 Abiathar
3 Joab
4 Shimei

The first of his adversaries to be dealt with was Adonijah himself. Had he succeeded in his coup, he would have ended the life of Solomon. As the wise king observed, "Adonijah has . . . spoken this word against his own life!" (1 Kings 2:23) Solomon found himself forced into a position where he was faced with no other option. "So King Solomon sent by the hand of Benaiah the son of Jehoiada; and he struck him down, and he died" (v. 25).

Abiathar the priest was another that had been involved in Adonijah's attempted coup. This was the priest who had originally joined with Joab in helping Adonijah take the throne while David was on his deathbed. In his office as a priest, Abiathar wielded a strong influence over the people even beyond the religious concerns of the tabernacle. It is probable he would have been the priest to officiate at the official coronation of Adonijah had the coup been successful. "So Solomon removed Abiathar from being priest to the Lord, that he might fulfill the word of the Lord which He spoke concerning the house of Eli in Shiloh" (v. 27).

Joab had lived long enough to realize his life also was in danger. Though Joab had not joined in other rebel causes, he did ally himself with Adonijah. He would probably have retained his position as a military advisor and leader in the new government had they succeeded in defeating Solomon. Because of his influence over the army and his potential for leading an armed revolt against Solomon at a later date, Joab was destined to die. Also, before his death David had charged Solomon to see that justice was done regarding Joab's taking of innocent blood.

Joab responded to the threat on his life by pleading sanctuary. In his first attempt to take the throne, Adonijah had been successful in preserving his life by taking hold of the horns of the altar (1:50). Joab took that course of action on this occasion but without success (2:28-34). Ironically, one of the reasons Joab was killed was because of his refusal to recognize the sanctuary which Abner had attained by fleeing to a city of refuge.

There was a fourth man Solomon may have suspected as being involved in the coup. Shimei had cursed David as he fled during Absalom's revolt, and though David had preserved the life of Shimei, the dying king had also warned his heir to beware of the man (vv. 8-9). Perhaps because he was not clearly implicated in the coup attempt, Solomon did not take his life but rather placed him under house arrest. The suspicion was too great against Shimei to leave him free to travel throughout Israel perhaps to reorganize rebel forces. Shimei was ordered to live in Jerusalem and promised his life would be preserved only so long as he remained within the city limits.

Though Shimei agreed to the terms of Solomon and moved to Jerusalem, he left the city limits three years later to retrieve two runaway servants. In violating the terms of his agreement with Solomon, Shimei had sentenced himself to death. Solomon reminded Shimei of his earlier agreement and of his abuse of David during the Absalom revolt. "So the king commanded Benaiah the son of Jehoiada; and he went out and struck him down and he died. And the kingdom was established in the hand of Solomon" (v. 46).

Even before his accession to the throne, Solomon was recognized for his wisdom (v. 9). After wisely dealing with internal threats to his authority, he turned his attention to potential international threats. "Now Solomon made a treaty with Pharaoh king of Egypt, and married Pharaoh's daughter; then he brought her to the City of David" (3:1). Thus allied with Egypt, Solomon had established a powerful allied force that would prevent potential enemies from attacking.

As Solomon began his reign, he was deeply committed to the Lord. As part of his worship of God, he offered a thousand burnt offerings to the Lord in Gibeon. In response to that expression of commitment, God appeared to Solomon in a dream, offering to give him whatever the king requested. In recognition of his own perceived inability to wisely rule over Israel in his youth, Solomon responded, "Therefore give to Your servant an understanding heart to judge Your people, that I may discern between good and evil" (v. 9).

That Solomon had asked God for wisdom rather than wealth or an improved quality of life so impressed God that He gave Solomon a promise of not only wisdom, but also wealth and a long and peaceful reign. When Solomon awoke from his sleep, he went to the ark of the covenant in Jerusalem and offered additional burnt offerings and peace offerings. Shortly thereafter, Solomon was confronted with a problem which demonstrated the new dimension of wisdom which he had received from God.

Two prostitutes appeared before Solomon with a dispute they wanted settled. Both women were new mothers, but one mother had accidently taken the life of her child while she slept with it. Both mothers were now claiming the living child was her own and refused to claim the dead child.

After hearing the complaint of the two women, Solomon decided the case by ordering the living child to be severed and each mother would be given half. Though one of the women agreed with the settlement, the other objected, offering to withdraw her claim on the child if the child's life were preserved. Solomon discerned the maternal instincts of the true mother and decided the case in her favor. "And all Israel heard of the judgment which the king had rendered; and they feared the king, for they saw that the wisdom of God was in him to administer justice" (v. 28).

Whereas David appeared to rule as a benevolent dictator making most of the decisions and being at the center of all action, Solomon appeared to be a better manager and delegated authority to others. David did not seem to have the efficient organization. But Solomon organized and implemented a large organization to administer the affairs of the nation during his reign. This had several positive effects. First, this helped insure an increased standard of living for the people of the land (4:20). Second, it helped insure the security of the kingdom throughout the reign of Solomon (v. 21). Third, it further established Solomon's reputation for wisdom (v. 30). Finally, it freed up the king so he could devote time to other interests, including the collecting of proverbs and writing of songs (v. 32).

THE YOUNG LOVE OF SUCCESS

The third of the wisdom books traditionally attributed to Solomon is entitled "The Song of Solomon." Like his father before him, Solomon had a deep love for music which resulted in his writing a thousand and five songs during his life (1 Kings 4:32). The Song of Solomon is related to Solomon in its introductory verse (Song 1:1) and refers to him by name in the song itself (3:11; 8:11-12). Traditionally, the Song was thought to be a love song written by Solomon when he was a young shepherd in the fields of Bethlehem who was in love with a Shulamite girl. She did not believe or know he was the heir to the throne until he returned to marry her. Therefore, it is a book of pure love. Because the song makes specific reference to themes relating to human sexuality, traditions say the rabbis allowed only males over the age of thirty to read the book. Others say the book was written to all, making human sexuality a part of life.

Some historic commentators interpreted the Song of Solomon as an allegory of God's love for Israel and/or the church. Among the best known devotional commentaries based on this view is J. Hudson Taylor's volume entitled *Union and Communion.* Recently, some conservative commentators have suggested the book was not one of Solomon's love songs but rather the love song of a shepherd and his Shulamite spouse who remained faithful to the one she loved despite the advances made to her by Solomon. Those holding this latter view point to Solomon's reputation for immoral behavior (3:9-10) and confession of sexual frustration (Ecc. 7:25-29) to suggest it highly unlikely Solomon would express love to the Shulamite in the way the shepherd seems to do in this book. Some holding this second view also see an allegorical interpretation of the book and application to the spiritual relationship between Christ and the believer. The primary application of the book according to all recent commentators is to teach four essential principles which tend to build the relationship between a husband and his wife in marriage.

However, the Song of Solomon probably suggests the beauty of love, both physical and emotional. This elevation of love is violated by Solomon in his later life. Evidence shows that he wrote the book early; it was probably among his first writings. The key verse is Song of Solomon 2:7, "Do not stir up nor awaken love until it pleases." This suggests a young person should not stir up sexual passion until a person is ready for marriage fulfillment. The story is simple in its beauty. Solomon and the Shulamite girl fall in love as they work in the field. (Solomon didn't expect to be king because he was not the firstborn and his mother was not a Hebrew.) Solomon leaves for Jerusalem, and the anguish of separated love is expressed and anticipated. He returns for her and they visit her home. There she is finally vindicated for all the rebukes she received while growing up.

RELATIONSHIP PRINCIPLES IN THE SONG OF SOLOMON

The Principle of Commitment *(8:6)*
The Principle of Companionship *(5:16)*
The Principle of Control *(2:7; 3:5; 8:4)*
The Principle of Communication *(2:1-3)*

THE WORSHIP OF SOLOMON *(1 Kings 5:1–9:9)*

One of the chief concerns of Solomon early in his reign was the building of the temple his father David had desired to build. The plans had been drawn and much of the supplies for building the temple had been collected by his father David, but God had not allowed David to build the house of God.

No expense was spared by Solomon in erecting the temple his father had wanted to build. The finest craftsmen and materials were imported at great expense. Solomon introduced conscription to raise the number of laborers which would be needed for the job. Stones were mined and cut before shipping to reduce the need for on-site cutting of stones. Though Solomon invested huge resources into the building of the temple, it still took seven years to complete the task.

Solomon's temple was one of the marvels and wonders of the ancient world. It was twice the size of the tabernacle and completely overlaid in gold. In later years when the remnant would return to the land after a seventy-year absence the glory of Solomon's temple would still be remembered.

On the completion of this temple, Solomon organized what may well have been the most spectacular dedication service of any religious structure in the history of mankind. Thousands of musicians and singers were a part of the planned music for the occasion. The number of sacrifices offered on this occasion was so great that no attempt was made to count them. But the most spectacular feature of the service was unplanned. God Himself attended the celebration and filled the temple with His Shekinah glory cloud. The people and priests could do nothing but recognize and enjoy the presence of the glory of the Lord.

Clearly, that day was among the most spectacular in the long history of God and His people.

At a moment like that, it is hard to believe there would ever be a time when Israel might not be enthusiastic in its zeal to worship, serve, and follow God. But God knew that many times would come when His people would rebel against Him. That evening, God appeared to Solomon to warn of a time when Israel might be subject to the judgment of God, and to propose a strategy that would bring spiritual renewal to replace the wrath of God with the blessing of God. Throughout history, the principles revealed by God that evening have been recognized as the key to experiencing revival blessing.

---

2 CHRONICLES 7:14—THE KEY TO REVIVAL

---

1 Humbling of self
2 Prayer
3 Seeking the face of God
4 Repentance from known sin

THE WEALTH OF SOLOMON *(1 Kings 9:10–10:29)*
Solomon was so incredibly wealthy as a king in the Near East that other monarchs found it difficult to believe how prosperous Solomon and his nation were before they witnessed it for themselves. Much of this wealth was acquired as a result of Solomon's organization of international trade. In essence he bought raw materials at wholesale prices and sold the finished products at retail prices. So large were Solomon's stables and storehouses in contrast to those of other kings that archeologists today have no difficulty in identifying the ruins they have discovered in his various principal cities.

The wealth of Solomon is seen in part in some of the gifts he exchanged with other kings. To celebrate his twentieth anniversary as king, Solomon gave Hiram king of Tyre twenty cities in appreciation for his help in building the temple and royal palace. This meant Solomon turned over the tax money from them to Hiram. The King of Tyre responded by sending a gift of 120 talents of gold valued then at well over $3.5 billion. His annual income was estimated to be well in excess of $20 billion (1 Kings 10:14-15). He sat on an ivory throne that was overlaid with the finest gold, and every drinking vessel in the palace was pure gold.

But his wealth was the result of his wisdom in dealing with economic matters. When the Queen of Sheba met with Solomon, she concluded, "It was a true report which I heard in my own land about your words and your wisdom. However, I did not believe the words until I came and saw it with my own eyes; and indeed the half was not told me. Your wisdom and prosperity exceed the fame of which I heard" (vv. 6-7).

THE WEAKNESS OF SOLOMON *(1 Kings 11:1-43)*

But there are times when wisdom is not enough. Solomon yielded to his moral weakness and married 300 wives and had more than 1,000 concubines. His sexual misconduct became widely known throughout the land as people spoke of the king's chariot being "paved with love by the daughters of Jerusalem" (Song 3:10). Solomon's moral lapse had consequences which stretched far beyond his own tarnished reputation and sexual frustration.

Solomon married foreign wives who brought their foreign gods into the palace. Solomon himself may not have worshiped the gods but in allowing his wives to do so, he unwittingly encouraged the practice of idolatry in Israel. As Israel turned from God to idols, the people were removing themselves from the place of blessing (1 Kings 11:3-8).

Also, Solomon began to get materialistic in his attitude toward his wealth. Rather than view his riches as an evidence of the blessing and favor of God, Solomon began to desire wealth for its own sake, which led him to wander even further from God. God had promised David his son would reign, but the blessing of God on the nation thereafter would be dependent on its relationship to the Lord. As Solomon began wandering from God, God gave Solomon something he had never experienced before as king—adversaries (v. 9).

Three men in particular became sources of irritation to Solomon in his latter years. The first was Hadad, an Edomite living in Egypt who decided to return to Edom and reestablish his kingdom. There was and would continue to be a long history of conflict between Israel and Edom. The second source of irritation was Rezon, who ruled over Syria. He had a small army in Damascus and "abhorred Israel" throughout the reign of Solomon. The third person God raised up against Solomon was one of his own men, Jeroboam, who would eventually be the first king of the Northern Kingdom after the split in the nation. The Prophet Ahijah told Jeroboam the kingdom would be divided and he would reign over ten tribes. When Solomon learned this, he tried to kill Jeroboam. But Jeroboam escaped and took refuge in Egypt until Solomon was dead.

THE WRITINGS OF SOLOMON

Traditionally, three wisdom books of Scripture have been attributed to Solomon. These books are so designated because they attempt to deal with problems of life both in the philosophical and more practical realms. When properly understood and applied to life, these books and other wisdom books and psalms contain a wealth of principles on which the life of faith can rest. Recognizing this, many Christian leaders have adopted the practice of reading some portion from the wisdom literature of Solomon each day (usually a chapter of Proverbs). Even today, the information contained in these wisdom books demonstrates that Solomon was indeed the wisest man to have ever lived.

THREE BOOKS OF WISDOM

1 Proverbs
2 Ecclesiastes
3 Song of Solomon

The Book of Proverbs

There is a sense in which the Book of Ecclesiastes, which follows the book of Proverbs, is really an introduction to the other. The frustrating experiences of the preacher led him to "set in order many proverbs" (Ecc. 12:9). As H.A. Ironside noted in his commentary on the Proverbs, "The last seven verses of Ecclesiastes form a fitting introduction to the book which in our Bibles immediately precedes it. . . . In these words we have the divine reason for the Book of Proverbs. God would save all who heed what is there recorded from the heart-breaking experiences and aimless wanderings of the man who was chosen to write them."

The Book of Proverbs represents the finest wisdom literature of Solomon. A proverb is a principle of life reduced to one statement. This book represents the principles by which Solomon ruled his kingdom and gained his influence. After a brief introduction including a statement of purpose, the proverbs of Solomon are arranged in five distinct groupings within the book. Probably the Book of Proverbs should be viewed as a collection of five books written separately and then brought together at a later date, i.e., during the reign of Hezekiah. With the exception of "the words of Agur the son of Jakeh" (Prov. 30:1-33), all of the proverbs were written by or for Solomon who is credited in Scripture as having uttered 3,000 proverbs during his life (1 Kings 4:32). Some proverbs were not added to the book until long after Solomon died (Prov. 25:1). Also, at least some proverbs were learned by Solomon from others (cf. 31:1).

Though most of the book contains an apparently random selection of short, pithy sayings or principles, the first part of the book, entitled "The Words of the Wise" (1:6b–9:18), appears to have a more exact order and sequence of thought in its declarations. Some conservative Bible teachers explain this difference claiming this part of the book is the instructions prepared by rabbis (teaching priests) appointed by David to teach the law of God to his son and heir to the throne. Those who hold this view point to the often-repeated phrase "my son" in this section of the book (which is typical of rabbinical teaching) and to the numerous apparent parallels between the teaching of this part of the book and the Book of Deuteronomy.

THE PROVERBS OF SOLOMON

Introduction *(1:1-6a)*
The Words of the Wise *(1:6b–9:18)*
The Proverbs of Solomon *(10:1–24:34)*
Proverbs of Solomon copied by Hezekiah *(25:1–29:27)*
The Words of Agur ben Jakeh *(30:1-33)*
The Words of King Lemuel *(31:1-31)*

The Book of Ecclesiastes

The Book of Ecclesiastes identifies its author by the title "the Preacher." Though Solomon is not specifically named in the book, the Preacher is identified as both the Son of David and king in Jerusalem (Ecc. 1:1). The only person the Preacher could be on this basis is Solomon. In this book, perhaps written toward the end of his life, Solomon recounts the vanity of his various life experiences, concluding that the futility and emptiness of life demonstrates rather than negates the need for sound knowledge and wisdom. The author's purpose in writing the book is stated in the last chapter: "And moreover, because the Preacher was wise, he still taught the people knowledge; yes, he pondered and sought out and set in order many proverbs" (12:9).

Over the years since its writing, many interpreters of the Scripture have encountered problems in this book of the Bible. At times it seems that the author is teaching something contrary to the clear teaching of another part of Scripture. Indeed, various historic and contemporary cults have appealed to obscure passages in the Book of Ecclesiastes to prove their variant doctrinal themes are taught in the Bible. But the problems associated with Ecclesiastes are not problems with the book but rather reflect the interpreters' failure to recognize the two distinct kinds of knowledge taught in this book. As the author himself declares, *"the words of the wise* are like *goads,* and *the words of the scholars [collected sayings]* are like well-driven *nails,* given by one Shepherd" (v. 11, italics added). In interpreting this book, one must distinguish between the ten "goad" passages (1:2-11, 12-18; 2:1-11, 12-23; 4:1-3, 4-12, 13-16; 5:1-7, 8-17; 6:1-12) and the seven "nail" passages (3:1-11, 12-13, 14-21; 7:1-29; 8:1–9:18; 10:1-20; 11:1–12:7). As

AN ANALYSIS OF THE TWO KINDS OF KNOWLEDGE IN ECCLESIASTES

Kind	Symbol	Source	Effect	Purpose	Result
The words of the wise	Goads	Reflections of man	Demonstration of the vanity of life	To convince one of his inability to find true fulfillment in living	Memories Concerns Guilt Fears Failure Frustration
The collected sayings	Nails	Revelation of God	Demonstration of the value of life	To provide one a source of stability and security in life	Stability Inner peace

noted on the chart above, each of these two kinds of knowledge has a different source, effect, purpose, and life result.

In the Book of Ecclesiastes, Solomon recounts a summary of his spiritual struggles in life which he encountered in his pursuit of happiness. Out of that experience, he arrives at two fundamental conclusions about life. First, contentment and real fulfillment in life is found in the gifts and heritage of God (cf. Ecc. 2:24-26; 3:22; 5:18-20). Second, the fundamental duty of man is to express his reverential trust in God by observing the principles of Scripture in the practice of his lifestyle (12:13). Ecclesiastes is the spiritual autobiography of a wise man who failed to apply much of his wisdom in life.

PERSPECTIVE

Solomon's reign was powerful, but his life ended in tragedy. He was brilliant, yet he lived contrary to the wisdom God gave him. He began with the dedication of the temple and sought the wisdom of God, but became selfish, greedy, and inhuman. Whereas Saul was only a military king who represented the twelve tribes as he led them in guerilla attacks, David united the kingdom and did what Saul omitted. David centralized his rule in a palace, in a city, and with a centralized place of worship. But Solomon extended the border of the kingdom beyond David's conquest and obtained peace. He effected international trade with a fleet of ships; became a patron of the arts with books, literature, and poetry; built cities, warehouses, a copper industry, and fortification. Whereas David ran the kingdom out of his courtroom, Solomon delegated and administered a bureaucracy that was well organized and well managed. He had a court of servants, a harem, managers, and slaves to work his fields and build his cities. He was a benevolent despot. He had immense tax burdens on the people. His foreign wives influenced him to worship false gods and dabble in pagan theology (1 Kings 11:1-8). Before his death the kingdom began to rot and after his death it divided.

When God makes a person great, he should not abandon the principles that God used to make him great. The wisdom that made Solomon great was discarded and he lost the blessing of God.

FORTY

JEROBOAM AND REHOBOAM:
The Division of the Kingdom

(1 Kings 12:1–15:8; 2 Chronicles 10:1–13:22)

Too often it is at a man's strongest point that he falls the farthest and suffers the greatest consequences. Certainly that was true in the life of Solomon. His wisdom established the kingdom and resulted in his great power and international reputation. But the folly of his later years gave birth to the seeds of dissension in the kingdom which resulted in civil strife and brought an end to the unity of the kingdom. Ironically, one of Solomon's enemies was raised up to be king over the rebel tribes of the north. They had rejected the leadership of Solomon's son, Rehoboam.

Jeroboam was an industrious young man who quickly earned a reputation for himself during the reign of Solomon. Recognizing the positive character evident in Jeroboam and his leadership potential, Solomon placed him in authority over two of the twelve tribes, Ephraim and Manasseh. It was while Jeroboam was serving his king faithfully in that capacity that he had an unusual meeting with the Prophet Ahijah. The prophet had a message from God for him.

Jeroboam was wearing a new garment when Ahijah found him alone in a field. The prophet took the robe off Jeroboam and tore it into twelve pieces. Then he asked Jeroboam to take ten of the pieces of the robe. In doing so, the prophet explained how God would divide the kingdom in the next generation and give ten tribes to him. When Solomon later learned of this meeting, Jeroboam became a wanted man. To escape the wrath of his king, Jeroboam escaped to Egypt and remained there for the remainder of Solomon's reign.

THE DIVISION OF THE KINGDOM
(1 Kings 12:1-24; 2 Chron. 10:1–11:4)

After the death of Solomon, the heir apparent to the kingdom was his son Rehoboam. This son of Solomon would sit on the throne of his father for eighteen years. Shechem was the city selected for the great coronation of the new king. All Israel gathered in anticipation. With the change in leadership, many of the people hoped for some changes in the civil policies under which they were governed. Solomon had amassed great wealth and had enjoyed a luxurious lifestyle during his reign, and much of that was at the expense of the people. Many hoped his son Rehoboam might be persuaded to cut the costs of governing the nation and, in that way, reduce the burden of taxation.

As the time to crown the new king approached, Israel sought for a spokesman who would plead their case before the new king. Jeroboam was the one who seemed like the logical choice. He had been an honored official in the government of Solomon at one time and understood how things worked in the royal court. Jeroboam was persuaded to leave his self-imposed exile in Egypt to be the spokesman for Israel at the coronation of the new king.

A meeting between the soon-to-be-crowned king and representatives of Israel, including Jeroboam, was arranged; a proposal from the people to the king was made. If the new king Rehoboam would reduce the burden of taxation, the people would be his willing servants. It was unusual that the people of a nation should attempt democratic reforms by making such proposals to a king, and Rehoboam was careful not to make a hasty decision. The people had been taxed for forty years under the reign of his father, and he knew three more days of the same would not upset those who had brought their concern to him. He announced he would respond to their proposal in three days and arranged for the people to meet with him again at that time. In the interim, King Rehoboam consulted with a number of political advisors.

But the counsel of his advisors was by no means uniform. When he consulted with the older men who had advised his father, they suggested the proposal of the people be considered and adopted as policy. "If you will be a servant to these people today, and serve them, and answer them, and speak good words to them, then they will be your servants forever," they advised (1 Kings 12:7). But Rehoboam was not sure he liked that advice and sought the opinion of his peers. They suggested the young king needed to demonstrate his strength as king and let the people know who was governing whom. They proposed the king respond to the request by increasing the tax burden and teaching them a lesson. This course of action would bring increased revenue into the royal court and would not require the new king to sacrifice any of the luxuries he had grown accustomed to as the son of Solomon.

When the representatives met with the king at their appointed time, the king spoke harshly to them and made it clear he would not consider their proposal. The leaders left the meeting disillusioned. The ten northern tribes of Israel felt alienated and abused by the southern rulers. This time they had had enough. They announced their intention to reject the leadership of King Rehoboam and returned to their homes in the north.

Apparently, Rehoboam did not take the announcement of the northern leaders seriously. Perhaps he felt they were simply hot under the collar and, given time, would cool off and fall back into line. Some time later, King Rehoboam had a project he wanted accomplished and needed workers. He sent Adoram, his officer in charge of forced labor, into a northern city to get recruits, but the people stoned the man to death. Though Rehoboam was safely away from the skirmish, he saw enough to realize the people were steadfast in their decision to reject his leadership. If they would stone such a prominent officer of his court as Adoram, the king rationalized his life was also in danger. Quickly, he sped back to Jerusalem in his chariot to avoid a conflict for which he was not prepared.

When Rehoboam returned to Jerusalem, he began to assemble his army to attack the north and bring the rebels into line. Though only Judah was loyal to its king and strong enough to contribute to the army, King Rehoboam was still able to gather 180,000 experienced soldiers. Word of the mobilization of an army in Judah must have leaked out to the northern tribes. Any exuberance the rebels may have enjoyed over the stoning of Adoram and their symbolic victory over the court of Rehoboam must have faded as they realized the consequence of their action. To this point in the rebellion, the northern tribes had been content not to have a king, probably relying on the elders of each city to administer social justice. But the threat of invasion changed the situation. Again, the name Jeroboam came to mind as the people sought a king under whom they could rally. Jeroboam was offered the throne and became the first king of the new alliance of the ten northern tribes. Israel became the name for the north, and Judah the south, after the tribe by that name. Later the tribe of Benjamin joined with Judah. Jeroboam of the north reigned about twenty-two years from 931 to 910 B.C.

All that had taken place appeared from a human perspective to be the result of a bad decision on the part of Rehoboam. If Rehoboam could break the rebellious spirit of the northern tribes through a military conquest, he felt sure he could regain control and unite the kingdom. But what he had failed to realize was that these events were consistent with God's prophecy of some years earlier. God had allowed men to play out their natural roles to accomplish what He had years earlier said would happen. Rehoboam's military invasion of the north may have had a chance of succeeding, and now it was time for God to once again intervene more directly in the life of His people. The Prophet Shemaiah carried the message of God to Rehoboam and the loyal tribes of Judah and Benjamin. "Thus says the Lord: 'You shall not go up nor fight against your brethren the Children of Israel. Let every man return to his house, for this thing is from Me' " (1 Kings 13:24). Though Judah was not all it should have been in its relationship with

God, on this occasion they obeyed the message delivered by Shemaiah and returned to their homes.

THE APOSTACY OF JEROBOAM
(1 Kings 12:25–14:20; 2 Chron. 11:5-17)

After the threat of attack from the south was removed, Jeroboam was confronted with the task of administering a new nation as its first king. He was faced with a problem unique to his nation. Most of the nations of the Near East had a national god or series of gods which they worshiped and which served as a major unifying force in the nation. The new nation of Israel was unique in that it worshiped Jehovah but that worship required of the people regular pilgrimages to Jerusalem, the capital of the Southern Kingdom of Judah. As Jeroboam considered this situation, he saw several problems.

The first of these problems was the realization that the worship of Jehovah by both Israel and Judah could eventually lead to a reunification of the nations which was contrary to Jeroboam's personal ambition. Second, as the worship of Jehovah required the paying of tithes and offerings in Jerusalem, 20 to 30 percent of the gross national product was going into the treasury of another nation. Then there was a third problem. The nation of Israel had come into being in part because of another king's refusal to consider tax reform. This meant Jeroboam had to be careful not to overtax his people if he wanted to retain his throne. The fourth problem with this system was a consequence of the previous two. Because Jeroboam was limited in his ability to tax, he was limited in his ability to provide services to his people. However, Rehoboam in the south was limited in the number of services he needed to provide his people and had no restrictions as to how much money he raised. As a result, Rehoboam was able to fortify at least fifteen cities during his reign (2 Chron. 11:5-12) at a time when Jeroboam was forced to practice financial restraint. As his people traveled to the south to worship Jehovah, they would see the improvements in Judah and contrast it with the poverty and neglected fortifications in the north. As a result, they would want to reunite the two kingdoms.

For the northern king, the solution to the problem was simple. If Israel had its own national god, all of the money going to the treasury in Jerusalem would remain in Israel. There would be no reason for the people to travel into Judah and they would, therefore, not realize how well off the south was at a time when the north was hurting. Also, a unique god for Israel reduced the likelihood the people would want to see a reunification of the two nations.

Northern King Jeroboam worked with others to develop a national religion. Two golden calves were erected at either end of the nation so the people would not have to travel to Jerusalem. He established the fifteenth day of the eighth month as the national feast ·day. Priests were recruited throughout the land who were sympathetic to this new approach to religion. Jeroboam himself participated in the new religion, offering gifts on the altar in Bethel as an example to his people.

Rather than having a unifying effect on his nation initially, Jeroboam's actions actually caused him some losses of support. Within the nation, there were many who had a genuine faith in God, whole pilgrimages to Jerusalem were more than a religious ceremony. When Jeroboam expelled the Levites from the priesthood in the north and set his own priest in their place, the Levites abandoned their possessions and migrated to the south where they would be free to serve God according to the dictates of their own conscience. "And after the Levites left, those from all the tribes of Israel, such as set their heart to seek the Lord God of Israel, came to Jerusalem to sacrifice to the Lord God of their fathers. So they strengthened the kingdom of Judah, and made Rehoboam the son of Solomon strong for three years, because they walked in the way of David and Solomon for three years" (vv. 16-17).

God did not allow Jeroboam to lead the nation of Israel into idolatry without a severe warning. God commissioned a prophet to travel to Bethel on a day when Jeroboam was offering a sacrifice to deliver a stern warning to the new king. The prophet was directed by God to travel north to deliver the message and return home the same day, refusing to even eat or drink in the apostate Northern Kingdom. As Jeroboam stood by the altar at Bethel to offer incense, the prophet appeared to deliver his message. The prophet warned of a time the ministers of the altar would be burned on the altar during the reign of the yet-to-be-born Josiah. The prophet insisted the altar would be torn down and the ashes on it would be poured out as a sign that his prophecy would come to pass.

In anger, Jeroboam turned from the altar and pointed to the prophet who dared to bring a prophetic warning to the king and nation. He ordered his men to seize the prophet, but even as he spoke the words, the arm he had raised against the man of God withered. "The altar also was split apart, and the ashes poured out from the altar, according to the sign which the man of God had given by the word of the Lord" (1 Kings 13:5).

Jeroboam at once realized the prophet and his withered arm were sent by God. He pleaded with the man of God to pray on his behalf that the arm would be restored. The prophet agreed and Jeroboam's arm was healed. Then Jeroboam offered the prophet his hospitality and a reward, but the prophet rejected both offers, citing his commission from God. The prophet obeyed God, left the city of the altar, and started for his home in the south.

Word of the strange confrontation between Jeroboam and the prophet from the south quickly swept through the city of Bethel. Among those who heard of the event was an old prophet still living in Bethel who longed to have fellowship with those who shared his faith in Jehovah. When he heard the prophet had just left town, he had his sons saddle an ass, and the old prophet rode out to find the man of God. Eventually he found the man resting under a tree. When he invited the southern prophet to his home, the prophet refused, again citing his commission from the Lord. Then the old prophet of Bethel responded, "I too am a prophet as you are, and an angel spoke to me by the word of the Lord, saying, 'Bring him back with you to your house, that he may eat bread and drink water' " (v. 18). The old prophet's lie was enough to cause the hungry and tired southern prophet to return to Bethel in violation of the Lord's commission.

As the two prophets sat at the table eating and drinking together the old prophet of Bethel did receive a revelation from God. God's message to the disobedient southern prophet was as stern as had been His message to Jeroboam. "Because you have disobeyed the word of the Lord, and have not kept the commandment which the Lord your God commanded you . . . your corpse shall not come to the tomb of your fathers" (vv. 21-22).

After the meal, the southern prophet began to make his way home. But when he had gone a little way, he was attacked by a lion and killed. Though a lion will normally eat what it kills, the lion remained at the site and neither ate the prophet nor killed the donkey. When the prophet in Bethel learned what had happened, he recovered the body and buried it in his own tomb. The severity of God's judgment on the southern prophet convinced the Bethel prophet the prophecy against the altar would come to pass; but Jeroboam continued to lead his nation into deeper sin.

It took the serious illness of his son and heir to convince Jeroboam of his need for God. Only then did he remember the uniqueness of the religion of Judah and the worship of Jehovah over that which he had created. When Jeroboam needed to hear from God, he sought out the prophet of the Lord, Ahijah, who had years earlier told him he would someday be king. Jeroboam gave his wife directions to disguise herself and search for Ahijah to learn what would become of the sickness of their son.

The disguise was really unnecessary so far as Ahijah was concerned, for he had lost his sight as he had grown old. But even the disguise did not fool the blind prophet, who identified the wife of Jeroboam even as she approached him. God had forewarned the prophet to expect her coming in disguise and had given the prophet a message for the wavering king of the north.

"And so it was, when Ahijah heard the sound of her footsteps as she came through the door, he said, 'Come in, wife of Jeroboam. Why do you pretend to be another person? For I have been sent to you with bad news' " (14:6). The prophet went on to explain how God would judge the wavering king for his evil practices, including that of idolatry. God would "bring disaster on the house of Jeroboam, and . . . take away the remnant of the house of Jeroboam, as one takes away refuse until it is all gone" (v. 10). The queen had come to learn the fate of her seriously ill son, and the prophet responded to her concern even before she had opportunity to ask. Her son would die the moment she stepped inside the gate of her city. "And all Israel shall mourn for him and bury him, for he is the only one of Jeroboam who shall come to the grave, because in him there is found something good toward the Lord God of Israel in the house of Jeroboam" (v. 13).

All that the prophet promised happened just as he had said. Jeroboam's wife returned to Tirzah to arrive home just as her son died. He was buried and the people mourned just as she had been told. The vivid fulfillment of the prophecy concerning the death of her son was a demonstration of the certainty with which the rest of the prophecy would be fulfilled in future generations. Jeroboam continued to reign until his death, a total of twenty-two years, when he was succeeded by his son Nadab; but he did so with the knowledge that he and his family would be judged by God for his sin.

THE APOSTACY OF REHOBOAM
(1 Kings 14:21-31; 2 Chron. 11:18–12:16)

The division of the kingdom resulted in an initial period of prosperity in southern Judah. This was due largely to the influence of the Levites and righteous remnant which left the north and came to Jerusalem. But Rehoboam counteracted any positive influence made by the Levites and settlers from the north. Contrary to the biblical guidelines for the domestic life of the king, Rehoboam began to build a harem until he had eighteen wives and sixty concubines. In his later years, Rehoboam encouraged his twenty-eight sons to follow his example by searching out many wives for them.

But the problems in Judah reached beyond the palace walls. Judah also became involved in the pagan worship of their neighbors, worshiping pillars scattered throughout the land on high hills and under trees. As Judah practiced these pagan rites, a class of people known as the *gedeshim* came into being (1 Kings 14:24). The Hebrew word *gedeshim* refers to men who practiced sodomy and prostitution as a part of their religious rituals. These men were becoming in practice the new priests of Judah.

God could not allow His people to continue in sin unchallenged. In Egypt, He found the instrument He could use to accomplish His purpose in the life of Judah. A number of years earlier, a Libyan had taken the throne of Egypt with dreams of conquering Asia. Archeologists are not certain if Shishak, or Sheshenq I (as he is known to contemporary Egyptologists), began the Twenty-second Dynasty by conquering the preceding dynasty, or if he acquired the throne by marriage to an Egyptian princess. Shishak was the Pharaoh under which Jeroboam found protection in the latter years of Solomon's reign and appears to have formed some kind of alliance with the Northern Kingdom according to the engraved record of his reign on the south wall of the Temple of Amon at Karnak. In Shishak's mind, an invasion of Judah would not only further his ambition to control Asia, but may have been a demonstration of Egypt's solidarity with Jeroboam's Northern Kingdom.

Judah was overwhelmed as they witnessed the invasion of Shishak and his alliance army of 1,200 chariots, 60,000 horsemen, and a vast number of additional foot soldiers. The cities Rehoboam had fortified were seized, and the army was close to taking all Judah. As the army approached Jerusalem, Shemaiah the prophet approached Rehoboam with a message from God. The prophet explained to the king that this invasion of Judah was the hand of God against Judah for her sin. The simple message resulted in an expression of some degree of repentance by the king. His acknowledgement of the righteousness of God in this invasion probably resulted in the sparing of his life. God determined to give Judah a degree of deliverance from Egypt. But Rehoboam's repentance came so late that Shishak still plundered much of the wealth of Judah, the palace, and temple, including the gold shields of Solomon.

Rehoboam continued to reign in Jerusalem another twelve

years after the Egyptian invasion but soon returned to his old ways. "And he did evil, because he did not prepare his heart to seek the Lord" (2 Chron. 12:14). His reign lasted a total of seventeen years (931–913 B.C.) and was characterized by constant battles with Jeroboam. When he died, his son Abijah inherited the throne of David.

PERSPECTIVE

With the privilege of leadership comes the responsibility of leading wisely. As Solomon's reign came to an end, Israel was divided into two kingdoms because of the lack of wisdom demonstrated on the throne. In the remaining years of both the Northern and Southern Kingdoms, wisdom was often lacking on the throne. They failed to respond to the directive of the proverbs, a directive which helps people today exert a positive influence in their sphere of influence. "Wisdom is the principle thing; therefore get wisdom. And in all your getting, get understanding" (Prov. 4:7).

FORTY-ONE

KING ASA AND THE KINGS OF THE NORTH:
Judah's Stability and Israel's Wandering

(1 Kings 15:9–16:28; 2 Chronicles 14:2–16:14)

Asa was a godly king who took the throne of Judah and strengthened the southern tribes. Israel in the north had a series of ungodly kings who continued to wander from God. In fact, during the reign of Asa in Judah, no fewer than six men served as king over the Northern Kingdom of Israel. The political turmoil in the north during this era of stability in Judah had a marked effect on the people of God in both kingdoms. God's dealings with His people during these years were consistent with His unchanging nature. As Judah experienced revival and drew closer to God, He blessed that kingdom. But as apostate Israel followed its wandering kings and continued to stray from God, they moved closer to the inevitable judgment of the Lord for their sin.

THE WANDERING KINGS OF ISRAEL

Nadab *(1 Kings 15:25-28)* (910–909 B.C.)
Nadab, the second king in the north, did not assume the throne until the second year of Asa's reign in Jerusalem. When he did become king, his reign lasted only two years. They were years marked by his evil character. "And he did evil in the sight of the Lord, and walked in the way of his father, and in his sin by which he made Israel sin" (1 Kings 15:26). So

great was the sin of Jeroboam and his son Nadab that they succeeded in provoking "the Lord God of Israel to anger" (v. 30). In light of the consistent teaching of Scripture concerning the long-suffering nature of God, the provocation of God by the house of Jeroboam suggests something of the severity of its evil behavior.

That being the case, it is not surprising that Nadab had enemies even within his own nation. Neither is it surprising that those who opposed this second king of the northern tribes did so violently. While Nadab and his army were laying siege to the Philistine city of Gibbethon, a soldier from the tribe of Issachar named Baasha saw and seized an opportunity to rid Israel of an evil king and insure for himself a position in the nation. "Baasha killed him in the third year of Asa king of Judah, and reigned in his place" (v. 28). Though there is no suggestion in the biblical text that Baasha acted in this coup at the specific directive of God, the action was the means by which an earlier promise of judgment on the house of Jeroboam was fulfilled. But a precedent was set. Many of the northern kings would be assassinated and each family reign would be short-lived. In the south, the bloodline of David would continue on the throne and the nation generally respected the monarchy.

Baasha *(15:28–16:7)* (909–886 B.C.)

If northern Israel was relieved to escape the oppressive rule of evil King Nadab, their sense of relief was short-lived. As is often the case in political revolutions, the cure proved worse than the disease. The character of Baasha, new king of Israel, was consistent with that of the previous two. "He did evil in the sight of the Lord, and walked in the way of Jeroboam, and in his sin by which he had made Israel sin" (15:34). It was not long before God would again intervene in the affairs of the Northern Kingdom and send His prophet with a message for the one who sat on the throne.

"Then the word of the Lord came to Jehu the son of Hanani" (16:1). When God needed a prophet He could trust to faithfully communicate His word to Baasha, the Prophet Jehu (not to be confused with the later King Jehu) was the man He chose. The message was severe. Baasha had been the instrument of judgment on the house of Jeroboam, but was himself guilty of the same sins. As the prophet spoke the message of the Lord in his hearing, Baasha learned his family was to be placed under the same curse as the former dynasty. "Surely I will take away the posterity of Baasha and the posterity of his house, and I will make your house like the house of Jeroboam the son of Nebat" (v. 3). Baasha reigned as king in Israel for twenty-four years, but they were years in which Israel continued to drift farther from God. On the death of Baasha, his son Elah assumed the throne of Israel.

Elah *(vv. 10-20)* (886–885 B.C.)
The fourth king of Israel proved to be the last monarch of Israel's second dynasty in less than fifty years. Elah reigned only two years as king before he was assassinated in a coup led by one of his own military leaders, Zimri. Zimri was the commander over half of the chariots in Israel's army. While the rest of the army was engaged in a military conflict at the Philistine city of Gibbethon, Zimri took the throne. Elah had drunk heavily at a party hosted by his steward Arza. Zimri found the drunk king and killed him in the home of Arza; then systematically killed the other descendants of Baasha. So thorough was Zimri in his purge that "he did not leave him one male, neither of his kinsmen nor of his friends" (v. 11). Again a prophecy delivered by one of God's prophets had been fulfilled in the political life of Israel, and Israel had a new king.

Zimri *(vv. 10-20)* (885 B.C.)
But the new king had what amounts to one of the shortest reigns in history—one week. When word reached the people fighting at Gibbethon of Zimri's coup, they appointed their own king, Omri, who led the army to Tirzah and laid that city under siege. As Zimri recognized he was king of a people in revolt against their king, he chose not to fight. "And it happened, when Zimri saw that the city was taken, that he went into the citadel of the king's house and burned the king's house down

upon himself with fire, and died" (v. 18). Now the apostate nation Israel witnessed the suicide of its leader.

Tibni *(vv. 21-22)* (885–880 B.C.)

Though the nation was agreed they did not want Zimri reigning over them, they were not as agreed when it came to the question of who should be king in his place. Confusion reigned. Many of the people were willing to follow Omri, who had led the army into battle against Zimri, but a significant portion of the nation chose rather to follow Tibni, the son of Ginath, and made him their king. As a result, the northern tribes found themselves with two kings, each with his own following among the tribes.

Little is known about Tibni, contender for the throne. His name means "intelligent," and this may suggest something concerning his character. It appears that Omri had a clear majority support both among the army and people at large; yet a comparison of the few verses referring to this period in the history of Israel suggests the civil war between Tibni and Omri lasted about four years. That Tibni could have survived as a contender that long against one as popular as Omri suggests Tibni may have been a brilliant military strategist. "But the people who followed Omri prevailed over the people who followed Tibni the son of Ginath. So Tibni died and Omri reigned" (v. 22).

Omri *(vv. 21-22)* (885–874 B.C.)

In the thirty-first year of the reign of Asa in the south, Israel's sixth king of that period took the throne of the reunited nation of ten tribes in the north. With the accession of Omri to the throne of Israel, the third dynasty of the Northern Kingdom began. For a period of time, Israel in the north was to experience a period of political stability, but the general character of that dynasty meant Israel, in her period of political stability, was still wandering spiritually from her God. This apostate dynasty would lead Israel into one of her darkest hours spiritually, but brightest hours politically.

When Omri took the throne of Israel, the capital was still in

Tirzah. The palace was to some extent restored after the fire at the defeat of Zimri; and Omri reigned from that city for six years. During that period, Omri was involved in two significant actions. The first was the four-year civil war with Tibni which is discussed earlier. The second was the beginning of an alliance with the Phoenicians. As was customary in that day, the alliance was achieved in part by a marriage involving the royal families of the two nations involved. As a result of this alliance, Ahab, the son of Omri and heir to the throne of Israel, married the daughter of Ethbaal, a Phoenician king. The Phoenician wife of Ahab was named Jezebel. Though her name simply means "unmarried," because of the recorded actions of this Jezebel, the name has become synonymous with the idea of the incarnation of wickedness, especially in a woman. Jezebel's zeal for the worship of Baal was such that she earned the distinction of becoming the first woman in biblical history to assume the role of a religious persecutor. When Omri formed this alliance with Phoenicia, sealing it with the marriage of his easily influenced son to the strong-willed Jezebel, he set the stage for what amounted to a foreign ruler assuming the throne of Israel in the next generation.

It was during the reign of Omri that the capital of Israel was moved from Tirzah to Samaria. Omri bought the hill of Samaria, located about forty-two miles north of Jerusalem, from a man named Shemer for two talents of silver, worth about $4,000. Part of the purchase contract established between these two men appears to have included the naming of Omri's city after the former owner. Though the two names are different in English, in Hebrew both are spelled the same (v. 24).

Omri's choice of Samaria for a capital demonstrated his military insights in that the selection was of one of the most defendable sites in Israel at that time. Though the hill of Samaria is surrounded by higher mountains on three sides, those mountains were located beyond the range of weapons of that day. Further, the slope of the hill is so steep as to discourage an invading army from even attempting what would amount to a suicide assault. Perhaps the ease with which Omri had taken the former capital of Tirzah alerted him to the vulnerability of that city. In moving the capital to Samaria, Omri overcame that problem and gave himself a more defendable capital. Historically, the only successful battle strategy against this new capital was the final siege.

Though Omri provided the political and military leadership Israel needed after a period of confusion and disorder, he failed in his spiritual responsibilities as a king. Like so many others before him, he led Israel in various idolatrous practices which kept the people from a vital relationship with their God. If Omri excelled his predecessors in his political astuteness and military wisdom, he also excelled them in his reprobate character. "Omri did evil in the eyes of the Lord, and did worse than all who were before him. For he walked in all the ways of Jeroboam the son of Nebat, and in his sin by which he had made Israel sin, provoking the Lord God of Israel to anger with their idols" (1 Kings 16:25-26). The death of Omri in 874 B.C. marked the beginning of the reign of his son Ahab.

THE REIGN OF GOOD KING ASA IN THE SOUTH
(1 Kings 15:9-24; 2 Chronicles 14:2–16:14)
(911–870 B.C.)

During the years Israel was ruled by the six wandering monarchs, the Southern Kingdom of Judah had the advantage of political stability and was ruled by a single monarch, Asa. This godly king proved to be a great builder of the nation. He experienced military success in conflicts with those who threatened the independence of his nation. The forty-one-year reign of Asa can be characterized by religious reform or revival, an ambitious policy of rebuilding the national defense, and the successful defense of his nation from invading armies. Though Asa himself had his shortcomings, he shone as a light for the southern nation of Judah as Israel continued wandering in darkness.

Asa was probably in his early twenties when he assumed the throne of his father Abijah. He was probably the oldest of his father's twenty-two sons and may have been born prior to his father's polygamous marriages. Though he came from a less-than-spiritually ideal background, Asa had a heart for God.

"Asa's heart was loyal to the Lord all his days" (1 Kings 15:14; 2 Chron. 15:17). Because of his desire to obey the Lord, Asa led his nation through two major periods of spiritual renewal. Because the king made obedience to the known will of God a personal priority, the Lord responded by giving Judah periods of rest from war.

During his first decade on the throne, Asa called on his people to seek the Lord. His civil policy at this time included repentance evidenced in the removal of altars, high places, pillars, and images devoted to the worship of pagan deities. He also urged the people "to observe the Law and the commandment" (14:4). This may suggest Asa had the ability to read the Scriptures for himself. One of the responsibilities of the king under the age of the Law was that of making his own copy of the Law, i.e., the first five books of the Old Testament. As the king copied the Law, he learned the standard which God expected of the nation. When this standard was contrasted with the reality of the national state, the king then would normally lead his people in religious reforms. Some have suggested one of the reasons the Northern Kingdom continued to fall into apostasy was related to the apparent inability of their kings to read and write. This would have prevented them from writing their own copies of the Law. As a result, the beginnings of their reigns were not characterized by spiritual revival which was necessary to bring the people back into a closer relationship with God. Judah, on the other hand, had several kings with the ability to read and write who led the nation back to God in periodic revivals.

During this decade, Asa also invested in the refortification of the cities of Judah. Asa recognized the Lord had given the nation a period of rest because the nation had turned to God and wisely determined to fortify while they had that opportunity. Walls, towers, gates, and bars (i.e., over windows in the wall or gate) were added to existing cities. During this period, an army was gathered, trained, and given arms to defend the nation. Of the 580,000 men in this army, 240,000 were archers.

Though the nation had taken steps to defend itself, the first major threat to Judah's security was an invading army of a million men led by a king named Zerah. Little is known about this Zerah apart from what is recorded about him in the biblical account of this conflict. This is largely due to the fact that so little is recorded in any of the extra-biblical records of this period. Some Egyptologists identify Zerah with the Egyptian pharaoh Usarkon I, while most contemporary scholars believe he is better identified with Usarkon II. The names Zerah and Usarkon are very closely related in Semitic languages. The biblical text identifies Zerah as an Ethiopian, which has been explained in several ways by competent scholars. Some believe there was an otherwise unknown king of Ethiopia named Zerah who may have ruled for a time over the Nile valley. A second possibility is that Usarkon II is here called an Ethiopian in an anticipatory sense as the next dynasty of Egyptian rulers was Ethiopian kings (i.e., Twenty-third Dynasty of Egypt).

When Asa met Zerah for battle outnumbered more than two to one, he did so in dependence on God. He recognized that God was so related to His people that an attack on the people of God was in reality an attack on God Himself. Asa reminded God of the nation's unique relationship with God as he prayed, "Lord, it is nothing for You to help, whether with many or with those who have no power; help us, O Lord our God, for we rest on You, and in Your name we go against this multitude. O Lord, You are our God; do not let man prevail against You!" (v. 11)

The Lord responded to the prayer of Asa and gave Israel a significant and decisive military victory that day. "So the Ethiopians were overthrown, and they could not recover, for they were broken before the Lord and His army" (v. 13). As a result of the battle, the army returned to Jerusalem victorious, bearing the booty they had claimed from the enemy camp. Also, they "carried off sheep and camels in abundance" (v. 15). It was a time of great rejoicing as they returned to their capital.

Often in the history of God and His people, God has blessed them when they called on Him in their helplessness, only to have them turn from Him in their time of abundance. Perhaps it was to warn Judah not to fall into this common trap that the Spirit of God came on the Prophet Azariah and prompted him to take a message to the victorious king and his army. The message was simple: "The Lord is with you while you are with Him. If you seek Him, He will be found by you; but if you forsake Him, He will forsake you" (15:2). The prophet reminded the king that the nation had come through a period of spiritual darkness and ignorance, a period in which they were "without the true God, without a teaching priest, and without Law" (v. 3). The prophet not only commended the king for the beginnings of a national return to God but also reminded him there was much work still to be done.

Asa was encouraged by this message from God to engage in further reforms. During this phase of reform the practice of sodomy was opposed and the altar was restored. As people in the Northern Kingdom recognized the blessing of God on Judah, many chose to migrate south. About the same time as the Feast of Pentecost, Asa gathered the nation together at Jerusalem for a national religious assembly. During that time, the people celebrated in the worship of God and "entered into a covenant to seek the Lord God of their fathers with all their heart and with all their soul; and whoever would not seek the Lord God of Israel was to be put to death, whether small or great, whether man or woman" (vv. 12-13). So sincere were the people in their commitment to this voluntary covenant that Asa removed his own grandmother "from being queen mother, because she had made an obscene image of Asherah" (1 Kings 15:13). Asa tore down the Canaanite goddess and burned the image to ashes. Though a few high places remained in the land where some of the people may have worshiped false gods, the Scriptures make it clear that Asa's heart was right with the Lord.

As Baasha witnessed the migration of his people to Judah, he began to fortify the city of Ramah located near the boundary which separated the two nations. Baasha may have been taking the action primarily to keep his own people from migrating south, but Asa viewed it as a threat to the defense of Judah. Recalling that his father had formed an alliance with

Damascus, Asa sent a gift of some of the temple wealth to Ben-Hadad, king of Syria, with a request that Syria attack Israel's northern boundary. Ben-Hadad agreed and did so, distracting Baasha from his work at Ramah. When Baasha left Ramah to do battle with Ben-Hadad, Asa invaded Ramah and took away the building materials which had been brought there. With them, Judah rebuilt parts of her own forts of Geba and Mizpah.

While Asa's plan made sense from a military perspective and was successful in accomplishing the immediate goal, it also demonstrated a wavering in the king's faith. When faced with an apparent threat from Israel, Asa was more willing to depend on the king of Syria than on the Lord. Again the Lord sent a prophet, this time Hanani, to meet with the king. However, this time the message from God was not one of encouragement but rather one of rebuke. Asa's response to the message was also different. Rather than move into a deeper relationship with the Lord, he got angry with the prophet and imprisoned him. Because of his pent-up anger, Asa also began to be oppressive to others about him. God had promised to bless Asa as long as he sought after the Lord, but as he wandered in his relationship with God, God began to withdraw His hand of blessing. King Asa, who had enjoyed long periods of peace during his reign, was now to be engaged in a constant struggle with King Baasha. Within three years, Asa found himself with a gout-like disease in his feet that would eventually take his life. Yet in all this, Asa did not return to the Lord.

The final biblical commentary on Asa observes, "And his malady was very severe; yet in his disease he did not seek the Lord, but the physicians" (2 Chron. 16:12). This is the only reference to physicians in the Old Testament and some writers have taken this verse to suggest it is wrong to seek medical help for a physical problem. Such a conclusion overlooks three very important contextual considerations. First, the physicians referred to here are not trained doctors as we might use the term today but rather very primitive "medicine men" who might have believed in mystical or magical powers of herbal and other "homemade" remedies. Their prescriptions would more often call for warts of toads and eyes of bats than proven medical remedies to treat properly diagnosed diseases. Second, it has been suggested that the meaning of the name Asa could be translated "physician." The biblical author may be pointing out Asa was more prepared to trust Asa than the Lord. Third, Asa had earlier entered into the national covenant that called for a death penalty for one who failed to seek the Lord. Yet in his final illness, Asa refused to honor his own word. His death was not a judgment of God on the king for seeking medical help but rather the consequence of Asa's own refusal to honor an earlier commitment.

PERSPECTIVE

Despite his wavering during the final years of his life, Asa was essentially a good king. But even the best of kings has his flaws. Still, Asa was a source of blessing for Judah because he led his nation back to God. As Israel wandered far from God through a succession of kings, Asa brought Judah into a deeper relationship with God. Upon the death of Asa, his son Jehoshaphat ascended to the throne. Jehoshaphat was only five years old when his father had called on God for help in the battle against Zerah, yet the event seems to have made a profound impression on the young boy. When Jehoshaphat ruled in Judah, he too sought to follow the Lord wholeheartedly. In northern Israel, however, King Ahab was earning the reputation of being one of the most reprobate men to sit on the apostate throne.

FORTY-TWO

ELIJAH:
The Man of Like Passion and Power
(1 Kings 16:29–22:53; 2 Kings 1:1–2:15)

In a day in which so many speak of striving for excellence, it is to some degree difficult to comprehend the disastrous trend among the kings of Israel. It appears that each succeeding northern king excelled the other only in doing greater evil. The biblical commentary on each king is that he was more evil than all that came before. But perhaps the most diabolical of these evil men was none other than Ahab, the son and successor of Omri. The Scriptures vividly describe the character of this king on at least two occasions. "Now Ahab the son of Omri did evil in the sight of the Lord, more than all who were before him" (1 Kings 16:30). Just in case the reader missed the significance of this comment, the same writer later elaborated, noting, "But there was no one like Ahab, who sold himself to do wickedness in the sight of the Lord, because Jezebel his wife stirred him up. And he behaved very abominably in following idols, according to all that the Amorites had done, whom the Lord had cast out before the Children of Israel" (21:25-26).

It is not surprising, therefore, that the people of Israel, like their evil kings, came to have a low regard for the worship of Jehovah. Vast numbers of their host were eagerly willing to engage in the worship of Jezebel's Tyrian Baal. Perhaps the degree to which Israel had sunk is best illustrated in the experience of one Hiel of the city of Bethel. For over 500 years the ruins of Jericho had been left undisturbed, according to the command of God. The people understood the prophecy of Joshua that the city would only be rebuilt at the cost of the rebuilder's own family. But during this dark hour of Israel's history, Hiel chose to build what would become the beautiful resort city of Jericho, in total disregard of Joshua's warning. Even as his firstborn died as the foundations of the city were laid, he continued building until the gate was complete and his youngest son had joined his older brother in the grave.

But it is in the darkest night that the stars also shine brightest. Out of the Palestinian wilderness, God raised up a prophet who, though he never sat on a throne, was in many respects the leader of his era. In the New Testament, Elijah the Tishbite is described as "a man with a nature like ours" (James 5:17). But the record of his life is that of a man possessing power with God. His was the life yielded to the service of God which, in that yielded state, was effective in changing the apparent course of human history.

ELIJAH AND THE FAMINE *(1 Kings 17–18)*

Little is known about the life of this mysterious prophet of God before his abrupt appearance one day before the king of Israel. There is no knowledge of a town called Tish. Perhaps "Tishbite" does not describe his hometown, but his character. The word comes from a derivative of "stranger." Elijah was a loner when it came to getting things done. The nation had wandered far enough, and God sent His prophet with a message of judgment in hopes of turning wicked King Ahab and His people from the worship of Baal to the worship of Jehovah. Baal was the god of the elements, and the God of Israel was about to declare war on this pagan deity, meeting him on his own turf. "As the Lord God of Israel lives, before whom I stand, there shall not be dew nor rain these years, except at my word" (1 Kings 17:1). And after Elijah made his announcement to King Ahab, the prophet left as abruptly as he had entered.

The next morning, an amazing "coincidence" would take

place in the land. There would be no morning dew and the sky would be cloudless. For a while the king might enjoy this "break in the weather," but before long the absence of rain and dew would be more than a coincidence, even in the mind of the wicked King Ahab. Soon the warm summer days would be viewed as blistering-hot days of drought. Those who enjoyed the absence of rain would soon plead with their anemic gods for clouds and torrents of rain. As the king came to the realization that the absence of rain was indeed related to the prophecy of Elijah, the life of Elijah was in danger. But God's purpose in the life of Elijah was not to simply parch the Palestinian soil. It was important to God that the life of His prophet be preserved. As soon as Elijah had delivered his message to the king, God directed Elijah into the wilderness out of the view of the king, who would eventually come looking for the prophet. He was alone, as his name suggests.

The prophet's sanctuary was near a mountain stream (wadi) named Cherith, a tributary of the Jordan River. Very soon both food and water would be at a premium in Israel. Elijah would drink water from this brook until it too dried up from the heat of the drought. God would provide the prophet with food by means of ravens who had been commanded to bring him bread and meat. Twice daily the ravens brought their meals to the prophet until the mountain stream became a muddy creek and then a dry riverbed. Only then did God suggest a different source of provision for his faithful prophet.

God directed His prophet to the city of Zarephath (meaning crucible or place of testing), a city ruled by Jezebel's own father. At Zarephath, God provided for Elijah through the agency of a poor, starving widow. Elijah first met the widow as the was gathering sticks for her final meal with her son. The famine had taken its toll on her meager resources, and in her mind the situation was then hopeless. She had determined to make one last meal to share with her son and then await the inevitable. That was the woman to whom Elijah said, "Do not fear; go and do as you have said, but make me a small cake from it first, and bring it to me; and afterward make some for yourself and your son" (v. 13).

The request of the prophet was not without a promise of blessing. If the woman would give first of her resources to the prophet of God, God would insure that the resources left would not run out before the end of the famine. As absurd as the request must have seemed in the context in which it was made, it offered a glimmer of hope in an otherwise hopeless situation. And it was to that hope that the widow would grasp. "So she went away and did according to the word of Elijah; and she and he and her household ate for many days" (v. 15).

Elijah became a resident of the home of the widow and her son during much of the remaining days of the drought. As the land burned with the sun, the anger of Ahab and Jezebel continued to burn against the prophet who had claimed responsibility for the drought. Days turned into weeks, and weeks into months. Forty-two months would pass before a cloud would again appear in the sky and the earth would drink up the rain that would fall. As conditions became more severe in the land, the search for Elijah intensified. Jezebel herself thought she could eliminate the judgment of God by eliminating God's prophets. She began to systematically eliminate the prophets of Jehovah from the land. Those who were not killed escaped into hiding. But in her search for the prophets of Jehovah, there was only one prophet the evil king and queen really wanted to find.

The widow must have certainly been aware that the former princess of her city was looking for the one who slept in her house. It must have been difficult for her emotionally to understand how the prophet accused of bringing drought to the land was also the one who had brought food to her house. But when she awoke one morning to find the corpse of her son lying lifeless in his bed, she was certain she was somehow being judged for harboring a wanted man named Elijah. "What have I to do with you, O man of God? Have you come to me to bring my sin to remembrance, and to kill my son?" she demanded (v. 18).

Elijah took the body of the young man to his own room and stretched himself out over the corpse. He began to intercede to God on behalf of the woman and her son. Three times he prayed that God would restore life to the son. "Then the Lord heard the voice of Elijah; and the soul of the child came back to him, and he revived" (v. 22). When confronted with her son alive again, the widow was able to resolve the questions about Elijah which had been plaguing her mind. "Now by this I know that you are a man of God, and that the word of the Lord in your mouth is the truth" (v. 24).

"Now it came to pass after many days that the word of the Lord came to Elijah, in the third year, saying, 'Go, present yourself to Ahab, and I will send rain on the earth' " (18:1). Even as God sent Elijah out looking for Ahab, Ahab himself was engaged in a search of his own. After three and a half years without rain, the land had become so parched that pasturelands on which cattle and other animals could graze were at a premium. Even Ahab and his trusted servant Obadiah were engaged in the search for suitable pasture for the king's horses and mules. The two had gone in different directions, hoping to find the treasured field. Elijah chose to find Ahab by finding Obadiah and sending him after the king.

Obadiah was a man caught in the crunch between two worlds. His name means "the servant of the Lord," and there was a sense in which that appears to have been true of his character. At a time when Jezebel was committed to killing the prophets of the Lord, Obadiah had provided sanctuary and provisions for 100 of them. Yet, on the other hand, Obadiah was also the servant of Ahab, the most evil king in the history of Israel to that date. He served a royal house that introduced the worship of the Tyrian Baal to the land of Israel. As one as knowledgeable about the true religion of Israel as Obadiah, he must have recognized the conflict of interest which that created. The conflict of two worlds was most evident as the royal servant met the fugitive prophet. Though Obadiah was willing to recognize Elijah as his master, Elijah reminded Obadiah he also had a royal master, Ahab. Elijah may have known of the work of Obadiah in preserving the lives of 100 prophets, but like Jezebel, Obadiah had at the same time silenced their voices and eliminated their effectiveness. Even at his meeting with Elijah, Obadiah was reluctant to commit himself in obedience to the known will of God. Finally he yielded and bore the message to his king: Elijah was found and wanted to meet with Ahab.

During the years of the drought, Ahab had not only searched his own land for the prophet but also enlisted the aid of other nations in his attempt to find and exterminate the one he viewed as the "troubler of Israel." He did not have to be told twice of the presence of Elijah. Immediately, he ran to meet and accuse the Prophet Elijah of being a "troubler of Israel." But Elijah was ready for the king. It was Ahab who had troubled Israel with his worship of Baal and flagrant disregard for the Law of God. Elijah would bring an end to the drought but not before he first met with the prophets of Baal and Asherah. It would be a final battle between the gods of Tyre and the God of Israel. The battle was to be staged on Mount Carmel near the coast; and on Elijah's directions, the king called his nation to witness the event.

At the mountain, Elijah called the people of God to cease from their wavering between two gods and determine to worship only the God who could prove Himself real. The people stood silent as the prophet continued explaining his plan. Two altars would be built, one to Baal and one to Jehovah. On each, a sacrifice would be laid, but neither would be lit with fire. The challenge was that the God who was real should demonstrate himself real by providing the flame.

The challenge seemed reasonable to the people assembled that day. It was certainly not threatening to the worshipers of Baal. They felt he was the god of the elements and if any god could send fire down from heaven, it was certainly Baal. Even if for some reason he had failed to provide rain on the earth, they still believed he could cause the fire to fall. And so they began to call: " 'O Baal, hear us!' But there was no voice; no one answered" (v. 26).

The situation was just too much for Elijah to observe without making his own sarcastic comments. When Baal had failed to answer initially, the prophets became more intense in their pleading. Elijah encouraged them to continue making fools of themselves, mocking them. "Cry aloud, for he is a god; either he is meditating, or he is busy, or he is on a journey, or perhaps he is sleeping and must be awakened" (v. 27). Throughout the afternoon they continued to abuse themselves and call on the name of their false god, but still "there was no voice; no one answered, no one paid attention" (v. 29).

As the sun began to set in the west, Elijah called the people to himself. The prophets of Baal had had enough time to bring down fire and they had failed. Now it was Elijah's turn. He repaired the broken-down altar of the Lord and dug a trench around it. Then he had men fill four water pots with water and pour it out over the sacrifice. When they completed that task, Elijah had them do it again and again until a dozen water pots of water had soaked the sacrifice and the altar and filled the trench surrounding the altar. Then Elijah began praying. "Lord God of Abraham, Isaac, and Israel, let it be known this day that You are God in Israel, and that I am Your servant, and that I have done all these things at Your word. Hear me, O Lord, hear me, that this people may know that You are the Lord God, and that You have turned their hearts back to You again" (vv. 36-37).

"Then the fire of the Lord fell and consumed the burnt sacrifice, and the wood and the stones and the dust, and it licked up the water that was in the trench" (v. 38). The miracle was decisive and there could be no question which god had answered by fire. The people were ecstatic and began to chant, "The Lord He is God!" But the repentance which Elijah sought on the part of the people had to go beyond mere words. He ordered the seizure and execution of the false prophets and it was done. Then, turning to Ahab, he delivered his second message about the weather, the opposite of what he predicted three and a half years earlier. "Go up, eat and drink; for there is the sound of abundance of rain" (v. 41).

Elijah's message to Ahab was as much a statement of faith as had his initial message been three and a half years earlier. There was no distant thunder nor were there any clouds in the sky. But Elijah had a calm assurance from the Lord that it would soon begin to rain and so announced to the unbelieving king the certainty of what was about to happen. Then Elijah made his way to the top of Mount Carmel and began to pray for the promised rain. He prayed seven times before his servant saw a small cloud begin to rise out of the sea. Very soon thereafter, "the sky became black with clouds and wind, and there was a heavy rain" (v. 45).

ELIJAH AND HIS FLIGHT TO SINAI *(1 Kings 19)*

Ahab could not help but be impressed after what he had seen that day at Mount Carmel. When he returned to Jezreel, he excitedly told his wife Jezebel all that had transpired on the mountain. But Jezebel was not as enthusiastic as her husband when she learned her prophets had been killed. She sent a personal message to Elijah that adequately expressed her feelings. "So let the gods do to me, and more also, if I do not make your life as the life of one of them by tomorrow about this time" (1 Kings 19:2). When Elijah heard the message, he demonstrated the truth of the New Testament claim that he was just like us—and he ran.

He ran from Israel to Judah (the protection of another kingdom) and went as far south in Judah as he could go. Then, leaving his servant in Judah, he continued to run south into the wilderness until he dropped exhausted under a tree. He prayed that God would take his life and let him die, and then he fell asleep. He was awakened from his sleep by an angel who fed him bread and water. Elijah ate the meal and then fell asleep again. A second time the angel awakened him and fed him. This time the angel told him he had a long journey ahead of him. Elijah did not know it at the time, but it would be forty days before he would again taste food.

Elijah continued his journey south until he came to one of the most sacred spots in the history of God and His dealings with His people—the mountain of God, Sinai. There he hid himself in a cave until he heard from God. When God spoke, He asked his prophet a question. "What are you doing here, Elijah?" (v. 9)

Elijah answered the question but failed to identify the real reason he was in the cave. He claimed to be the sole surviving faithful believer in Israel. God told him there were at least

7,000 in Israel who had not been involved in the worship of Baal. The real reason Elijah was there hiding in the cave was due to his depression. Jezebel's threat against his life had sent him into a cycle of self-pity. To break this depression, Elijah needed a change of focus and a change of attitude. God directed the prophet to stand on the mountain peak.

As Elijah stood on the pinnacle, the Lord passed by him. First, there was a mighty wind that tore into the mountain, setting loose large boulders from the crevice of the hillside. That was followed by a massive earthquake which shook the very mountain on which he stood. After the earthquake there was fire. Yet in all these phenomena of raw power, the Lord was absent. Only then did the Lord make His presence known in a still small voice asking again that haunting question, "What are you doing here, Elijah?" (v. 13)

God had things for Elijah to do and could not afford to have a discouraged prophet standing on a mountain feeling sorry for himself. God commanded him to anoint Hazael king over Syria and anoint Jehu king of Israel. God told Elijah He would replace him with another, and Elijah was to anoint Elisha to serve in this role.

Departing from the mountain, Elijah found Elisha plowing in the field with twelve yoke of oxen. When young Elisha realized he was being called to follow Elijah, he first asked to return home to say good-bye to his parents. But that was not characteristic of the kind of commitment required of a prophet of the Lord. Realizing this, Elisha took a yoke of oxen and offered it as a sacrifice to Jehovah. In this symbolic act, the would-be successor to Elijah was burning his bridges behind him and wholeheartedly embarking on a life of service to a single master.

AHAB AND SYRIA (1 Kings 20)

Elijah was not the only problem Ahab had to face as ruler of Israel. During the reign of Ahab, Ben-Hadad of Damascus invaded the Northern Kingdom of Israel on more than one occasion. On his first invasion of Israel, Ben-Hadad led an alliance of thirty-two kings against Ahab. The massive army laid siege to the city of Samaria and awaited the inevitable surrender of Ahab. In his arrogance, Ben-Hadad sent a message to the king of Israel, laying claim to all of the assets of the nation. "Your silver and your gold are mine; your loveliest wives and children are mine" (1 Kings 20:3). Recognizing the hopelessness of his situation, Ahab readily agreed to the terms of surrender.

But the victory had come too easily for Ben-Hadad. He sent the messenger back to Ahab with further instructions. Not only would Ben-Hadad accept what he had earlier demanded, but his servants would run an inspection of the homes in the city and take whatever appealed to them. When the king learned this condition of the terms of surrender, he called together the elders of the city for consultation. Together they decided they must resist the invading army.

The kings of Syria were already well into their victory celebration when they received the news the city would resist. The drunk Ben-Hadad ordered his men to prepare for battle as he continued drinking with his fellow kings. But in the city of Samaria, Ahab received some unexpected encouragement. A prophet of the Lord informed Ahab the young princes of the province would aid the king in defeating the Syrian army. Encouraged with this promise of God, Ahab gathered the 232 princes and an army of 7,000 Israelites and went out to do battle with the Syrians. "And each one killed his man; so the Syrians fled, and Israel pursued them; and Ben-Hadad the king of Syria escaped on a horse with the cavalry" (v. 20).

Though Israel had a great victory over the Syrians, it was not to be the last time that nation would invade the land during Ahab's reign. The prophet warned the king they would return the next year, and the king needed to begin now to prepare for the inevitable battle. The Syrians themselves evaluated what had happened in the battle and came to their own conclusions. To their way of thinking, the gods of a nation had different realms of influence and the best gods could only win where they were strongest. They judged Israel's god to be a god of the mountains and their own to be the god of the plains. This meant the reason they had lost was because the battle had been staged in the mountains. They concluded they could defeat Israel if they could lure them into a battle on the plains. A year after their defeat, a massive Syrian army marched into Israel to fight in the plains.

Again, God sent a prophet to His people to encourage them. The prophet explained the Syrian battle strategy was based on a defective view of the God of Israel and assured them of the Lord's intention to give Israel a second decisive victory over the Syrians. A week later the two armies engaged in conflict with disastrous results for the Syrians. A hundred thousand Syrians were killed in a single day of conflict. Ben-Hadad and the rest of his army escaped into the security of the city of Aphek. But even there the invading army was not safe. A portion of the city wall caved in, killing 27,000 men.

Trapped inside the city, Ben-Hadad could only rely on the mercy of Ahab to escape with his life. He offered to return the cities his father had taken from Omri and allow Ahab free access to Damascus. Rather than kill the invading king as was customary, Ahab chose rather to agree and make a covenant with Ben-Hadad. The king of Damascus escaped with his life, but Ahab again found himself having offended the God of Israel. The Lord sent a prophet with a message for the king. "Because you have let slip out of your hand a man whom I appointed to utter destruction, therefore your life shall go for his life, and your people for his people" (v. 42).

NABOTH'S VINEYARD *(1 Kings 21)*
For three years, Israel was not engaged in war with Syria, and Ahab's treaty with Ben-Hadad seemed to be working. There was peace in the Northern Kingdom. But no longer distracted with having to fight an enemy, Ahab began noticing things closer to home which he had previously overlooked. Next to Ahab's palace in Jezreel was a vineyard owned by a man named Naboth. It was a good vineyard and Ahab decided he wanted to purchase it and turn it into a vegetable garden. But the property was Naboth's inheritance and he was reluctant to sell it at any price. Upset with his failure to purchase the land, Ahab returned to the palace and fell into depression. He sepa-

rated himself from others socially and refused to eat. It was not long before Jezebel became concerned about her husband and went to discern what was wrong.

When she learned Ahab wanted Naboth's vineyard and had been refused it, she assured him she would get it for him. Immediately she set in motion her plan. Naboth was falsely accused of having cursed God and the king and was stoned outside the city in accordance with the penalty in the Law for such action. When it was confirmed that Naboth was dead, Jezebel then urged her husband to go down and claim the vineyard for himself. "So it was, when Ahab heard that Naboth was dead, that Ahab got up and went down to take possession of the vineyard of Naboth the Jezreelite" (1 Kings 21:16).

As Ahab walked through his new vineyard, he was met by Elijah with a message from God. God was aware of all Ahab and Jezebel had done. Elijah predicted they would pay with their lives, the house of Ahab would come to a violent end and be totally destroyed, and that the wild dogs and birds common to that region would eat the carcasses of his sons and wife when they died. The sin of Ahab would not go unrewarded.

On hearing this message from Elijah, Ahab did something he had never done before. He acknowledged his own responsibility and sin. "So it was, when Ahab heard those words, that he tore his clothes and put sackcloth on his body, and fasted and lay in sackcloth, and went about mourning" (v. 27). His actions were those common to one repenting of sin in the Old Testament. And just as his sin had not gone unnoticed by God, neither did his repentance escape the all-seeing eye of the Lord. "And the word of the Lord came to Elijah the Tishbite, saying, 'See how Ahab has humbled himself before Me? Because he has humbled himself before Me, I will not bring the calamity in his days; but in the days of his son I will bring the calamity on his house' " (vv. 28-29).

AN ILL-FATED BATTLE
(1 Kings 22:1-40, 51-53; 2 Kings 1)

The alliance between Jehoshaphat, king of the south, and Ahab, king of the north, involved only one major military endeavor—that of Ahab's third campaign against Syria. As godly Jehoshaphat was visiting Ahab on something of a state visit, Ahab raised the question of Judah's involvement in Israel's conflict with Syria. Three years earlier, Ahab had preserved the life of Ben-Hadad in exchange for a promise that all the cities of Israel would be returned. Still, the city of Ramoth Gilead remained under Syrian control. Ahab determined to take the city, but was hesitant to do so without the support of Judah.

Jehoshaphat agreed to unite his forces with those of Ahab, but there was a catch. The godly king of Judah was accustomed to consulting with the prophets of the Lord before engaging in major commitments, such as a battle. Ahab agreed to this condition and gathered 400 prophets of the Lord together to put the question to them. "Shall I go against Ramoth Gilead to fight, or shall I refrain?" (1 Kings 22:6)

Led by the evil Prophet Zedekiah ben Chenaanah, the prophets unanimously agreed Ahab should go to war and would return victorious. But something about the prophecy did not sit well with the visiting king of Judah. "Is there not still a prophet of the Lord here, that we may inquire of Him?" he asked (v. 7).

Ahab acknowledged there was one prophet who had not been invited to appear before the king. In the past, Micaiah had nothing positive to say about the king, and Ahab viewed it as something of a personal vendetta against him. Because Jehoshaphat wanted to hear from him, Ahab sent for him, but made it clear to his guest that he expected only the worst from Micaiah.

A trusted messenger was sent to the prophet requesting he appear before the king. Loyal to his king, the messenger attempted to prompt the prophet concerning the nature of his message. He urged the prophet to be favorable to the king on this one occasion and agree with the verdict of the other prophets. But all Micaiah would commit himself to was to speak only the message of the Lord.

When asked by the king what he should do, Micaiah urged him to go into battle. But when the king pressed him, Micaiah prophesied a message different from the others and offered an unusual explanation as to why his message differed. He claimed Ahab would lose his life in this battle and that the other prophets were speaking under the influence of a lying spirit. He argued God wanted to deceive Ahab into going to war and an angel of heaven had offered to do so by being a lying spirit to the king. This claim upset Zedekiah, who sincerely believed he had spoken under the influence of the Spirit of God. Ahab ordered the Prophet Micaiah to be imprisoned "until I come in peace" (v. 27). But even under the threat of imprisonment, Micaiah insisted his message was from the Lord.

Ahab disguised himself for the battle and rode his chariot to war, disregarding the warning of Micaiah. During the course of the battle, an archer fired a random arrow with his bow over the battle lines, wounding Ahab the king of Israel. By sundown, the wound had proved fatal. The body of the king was returned to Samaria. Ahab had bled profusely in his chariot as a result of the wound, so someone went to the city pool to clean the chariot. As he did, the dogs of the city came out to lap up the blood of Ahab, just as Elijah had prophesied.

The reign of Ahaziah, son of Ahab, over Israel was to be a short one. Shortly after assuming the throne, he fell through the lattice of his upper room and was seriously injured. In his despair, he sent his messengers to the priests of Baal-Zebub in Ekron to learn if he would survive. Elijah met the servants on their way to Ekron to give them the answer to their question. The king should have recognized the reality of the God of Israel rather than run after the foreign god of Baal. Elijah assured the messengers the king would not survive his fall.

Ahaziah was surprised when his servants returned so soon after they left for Ekron. When he asked them why they were back so soon, they told him of their meeting with Elijah. When the king heard the men describe the prophet, he immediately knew who the prophet was. He responded by sending a captain with fifty men to arrest Elijah and bring him before the king.

When the captain arrived at the home of Elijah and called on him to surrender, God sent down fire to destroy the captain and his men. A second group was sent to arrest Elijah, and they met the same fate. A third group was sent, but this time the captain used a different approach. Rather than call for the surrender of the prophet, he pleaded with Elijah to preserve his life and his men. Elijah agreed to go with the captain and appeared before the dying king to deliver the same message. In accordance with the prophecy, Ahaziah died. Because he had no heir, his younger brother Jehoram assumed the throne (2 Kings 2:1-15).

THE TRANSLATION OF ELIJAH *(2 Kings 2:1-15)*

But despite the major world events of that era involving the various kings and kingdoms of the world, the man who changed history was the prophet of God, Elijah. But even when the prophet was no longer needed in his own generation, God was not through with him. Centuries later Elijah would appear with Moses and Christ on the Mount of Transfiguration. Still centuries later, he will preach in the streets of Jerusalem during the Tribulation where he will finally face death. When the time came to remove the mighty prophet from the world, God chose a way more spectacular than the fire of Mount Carmel or the display of God's power on Mount Sinai.

As the day of Elijah's departure drew near, other prophets were acutely aware what was about to happen. It was the sort of thing everybody knew but no one wanted to discuss with the prophet himself. As Elijah and Elisha passed from city to city, those in the school of the prophets (ministerial students) knew the day had come, but only young Elisha followed the aging prophet, despite Elijah's apparent willingness to let him remain behind. When they came to the Jordan River, there would be one more miracle to be performed by the prophet of power. Taking his mantle, he struck the water and the two passed over on dry ground.

Young Elisha was to be rewarded for his faithfulness. As he had requested, he would receive "a double portion" of the spirit of Elijah, i.e. the right of prophetic succession, but only if he were there when Elijah departed. "Then it happened, as they continued on and talked, that suddenly a chariot of fire appeared with horses of fire, and separated the two of them; and Elijah went up by a whirlwind into heaven" (2 Kings 2:11). All that remained of Elijah on earth was his mantle, which had fallen to the ground. Since the mantle was symbolic of the office, young Elisha picked it up.

Elisha made his way back to the river, bearing the prophet's mantle. As he came to the riverbank, "he took the mantle of Elijah that had fallen from him, and struck the water, and said, 'Where is the Lord God of Elijah?' " (v. 14) For the second time that day, a path was cleared in the river, allowing the prophet to pass over. Those in the school of the prophets who witnessed this miracle had no difficulty discerning its meaning. "The spirit of Elijah rests on Elisha" (v. 15).

PERSPECTIVE

Many Christians today would be enamored of the appearance of a spokesman for God with the power of God so evident in his life, as was the case of the Prophet Elijah. Some would even secretly long for that spiritual reality in their own Christian life. Such a longing is not beyond the realm of possibility. The New Testament describes this mighty prophet of power as "a man with a nature like ours" (James 5:17). But through prayer and personal yielding to God, Elijah attained power with God and was able to pray the prayer of faith. Years ago, young Dwight L. Moody heard another preacher claim, "The world has yet to see what God can do through a young man wholly committed to Christ." Though Moody accomplished much for God during his life and ministry, toward the end of his life he suggested the world had still not seen what God could do through such a dedicated life.

FORTY-THREE

ELISHA:
The Prophet of Twice the Power

(2 Kings 2:15–13:25; 2 Chronicles 20:31–24:27)

When Elisha returned alone, some of the sons of the prophets wanted to go out and recover the body of Elijah. Though Elisha knew such a search would be futile, he finally consented to allow fifty men to go. After three days, they returned, having failed to find the body of Elijah. Elijah reminded them he had opposed the plan initially, thus asserting his new authority as the God-ordained leader of the prophets.

Elisha, the successor of Elijah, was a part of the same prophetic tradition but in many respects was more different from his predecessor than he was similar to him. The contrast of these two prophets, both ordained of God for a particular ministry during their time, is a reminder that God may often use those radically different from others to accomplish His purpose. One should not assume that because he is not like someone else being greatly used of God he is somehow not an important part of what God wants to do. God used two men who could not have been more different than Elijah and his successor Elisha.

THE POPULAR MINISTRY OF ELISHA
(2 Kings 2:19-25)

Some commentators interpret the expression "a double portion of your spirit" (2 Kings 2:9) as the intensity of the power

433

of God resting on the prophet. While that may or may not be implied, it is probably better understood in terms of the Hebrew custom to divide an inheritance equally among all survivors but to designate one son, usually the firstborn, an official heir by giving him a double portion of the inheritance. It is interesting to note, however, that for every recorded miracle in the life of Elijah, two such miracles are attributed to Elisha in the biblical record.

Even as the sons of the prophets returned, having failed to find the body of Elijah, Elisha began his ministry of miracles. The men of Jericho came to him with a problem. Something had gone wrong with their water supply. Elisha salted the water at its source and assured the men it would no longer be polluted. As he left the city to go to Bethel, Elisha was mocked by a large group of young adults. Elisha responded by pronouncing a curse on them in the name of the Lord. "And two female bears came out of the woods and mauled forty-two of the youths" (v. 24). God was confirming with miracles that Elisha was the prophet of the hour.

Many of the miracles of Elisha were designed to help those in need. On one occasion he was approached by a distressed widow because creditors came to take her sons as slaves after her husband died. She pleaded with Elisha for help as she had no resources of her own to pay the debt. Young Elisha responded by having her borrow as many vessels as she could and pour out her oil into the vessels. As old Elijah had earlier done, the oil was multiplied and the widow was able to sell it and pay her family's debts. She even had enough left over to meet the needs of her family.

On another occasion, Elisha raised the son of a Shunammite woman in whose home he had often been a guest. Again, many have noted the similarity between this and another of Elijah's miracles. But Elisha also had miracles unique to his own ministry. When the prophets had accidentally poisoned a stew they were making, Elisha neutralized the poison by adding flour to the pot. On another occasion, the prophet fed 100 hungry men with twenty loaves of barley and a grain offering. Not only was the hunger of the men satisfied, but there were leftovers as well. On yet another occasion, Elisha recovered a borrowed ax head that had been lost in the Jordan River by causing it to float. These and other miracles characteristic of the ministry of Elisha have caused some Bible teachers to argue Elisha was typical of Christ in his ministry just as Elijah's ministry was more typical of that of John the Baptist.

THE FINAL DAYS OF JEHOSHAPHAT
AND JEHORAM OF JUDAH
(2 Kings 3:1-27; 2 Chron. 20:31–21:20)

As Elisha was becoming established in his new role as head of the school of the prophets, the king of Israel planned an expedition to deal with the rebels in Moab. Perhaps because Jehoshaphat had allied himself with the two previous kings of Israel, and the co-regent of Judah by this time was related by marriage, Judah was invited to join in this battle. The king of Edom was also invited to be a part of this campaign and the march began through Judah and Edom toward Moab.

The alliance of kings marched around the southern tip of the Dead Sea, traveling a full week without finding a supply of fresh water. Again it was Jehoshaphat who called on the king of Israel to seek the counsel of a prophet. Elisha was a part of the number and was called on for help. Elisha made it clear that God would help only because of the presence of the godly King Jehoshaphat. He commanded the people to dig trenches in the soil. When the people did so, fresh water began slowly seeping into the trenches. By morning, the trenches were full of fresh water. This technique is still used by shepherds of that region to provide fresh water for their flocks (2 Kings 3:4-20).

When the men of Moab looked out over their city wall the next morning, they saw the trenches of water around the camp of the allied armies but misinterpreted its meaning. Because of the color of the soil in that region, the water looked like blood in the morning light. The men who had been prepared for battle assumed the armies of Israel, Judah, and Edom had begun fighting among themselves the night before and had succeeded in destroying each other. Quickly they made their way to the camp, intending to plunder it, unprepared for the ensuing battle.

By the time the men of Moab realized their mistake, it was too late. The battle raged against Moab, driving those who were not killed back into their cities. City after city fell under the attack until even the king of Moab realized the situation was hopeless. He gathered around him 700 skilled soldiers in a final desperate attempt to break through to the king of Edom, but the attempt was unsuccessful. Moab was given over to a form of idol worship which included human sacrifice. The king of Moab may have been appealing to his gods, or simply surrendering to the invading army as he mounted the city wall for his final act. "Then he took his eldest son who would have reigned in his place, and offered him as a burnt offering upon the wall" (2 Kings 3:27).

Jehoshaphat died not long after the victor over Moab, leaving his son Jehoram the sole king of Judah. And with the death of Jehoshaphat died also a person who had been distinguished among the recent kings of Judah. Jehoram his son chose to abandon his godly heritage and follow after the false gods of the other nations. "And he walked in the way of the kings of Israel, just as the house of Ahab had done, for the daughter of Ahab was his wife; and he did evil in the sight of the Lord" (8:18; 2 Chron. 21:6). In order to secure his place on the throne, Jehoram killed his obvious competition, his six brothers.

Because the king of Judah departed from following the Lord, the Lord withdrew His hand of blessing from the nation. Suddenly Jehoram found himself facing various insurrections which he could not adequately handle. First, there was a revolt in Edom. Though he responded promptly with a night raid and won the battle, he failed to stop the revolt. Then Libnah revolted from the domination of Judah also. Some commentators believe the revolt of Libnah is the same as the invasion of the Philistines and Arabians (vv. 16-17). During that invasion Jehoram lost everything except the youngest of his sons. In the midst of these problems, Jehoram was the object of the prophecy of Elijah. True to that promise, Jehoram was plagued with an incurable disease in his intestines. "It happened in the course of time, after the end of two years, that his intestines came out because of his sickness; so he died in severe pain" (v. 19). Though his body was buried in Jerusalem, no one mourned his death and he was not buried with the other kings. On his death, his son Ahaziah assumed the throne for a year. Beginning with this king, the next several rulers over Judah are not acknowledged in Matthew's genealogy of Christ.

ELISHA AND THE SYRIANS *(2 Kings 6:24–7:20)*

While godly Judah of the south was entering a dark hour in her history, ungodly Israel seemed to be getting a break in her problems. The king of Syria planned a secret raid against Israel, but God informed Elisha of the plan who in turn warned the king. When the plans of Syria had been frustrated several times in this way, the king of Syria began suspecting that one of his trusted advisors was a spy for the king of Israel. By this time, some of the advisors had learned what had been happening and informed their king that Elisha was predicting their attack.

The miracle-working ability of Elisha was well known in the kingdom of Syria. A respected leader in the Syrian army had contracted leprosy some time previously. Unable to find help in Syria, Naaman had taken the advice of an Israelite maid and sought out Elisha. Eventually Naaman was convinced to follow Elisha's advice to bathe seven times in the Jordan River. When he had done so, he was completely healed. The miracle of Elisha had been so dramatic that Naaman himself voluntarily abandoned the worship of his gods to worship Jehovah (2 Kings 5:1-19). Because Naaman was close to the king, it is reasonable to assume word of the power of this prophet spread widely in the court of Damascus.

The king of Syria decided to capture Elisha before attacking Israel and "sent horses and chariots and a great army there, and they came by night and surrounded the city" (6:14). When the servant of Elisha saw the vast army the next morning, he expressed his concern to the prophet. But Elisha was confident of the Lord's protection. He prayed for his servant until the servant was able to see a host of angels present to defend the prophet. On Elisha's request, the Lord blinded the army of Syria, enabling Elisha to lead the army into the presence of the king of Israel.

When Elisha had marched the army of Syria to Samaria, he then prayed again that the army might receive its sight. No one was more surprised to see the captured army of Syria than the king of Israel. Unsure how to respond, Jehoram turned to the prophet for advice. Elisha advised the king not to kill his prisoners but rather to feed them and send them home to Syria. The king did so, and for a time there were no more Syrian raids into Israel.

"And it all happened after this that Ben-Hadad king of Syria gathered all his army, and went up and besieged Samaria" (v. 24). Because of the physical features of the region where the city had been built, a siege of the city was the only military strategy that had any hope of success against Samaria. As the army of Syria cut off supplies entering the city, the resulting food shortage drove up prices on even such undesirable items as the head of a donkey and the droppings of doves. Things got so bad that mothers agreed to kill their children and eat their carcasses to survive. As conditions worsened in the city, the king began blaming Elisha for the invasion and subsequent problems. But when the prophet was confronted by the king and his officers, Elisha simply responded that there would be an overabundance of food in the city the next day. One of the king's officers found that claim too incredible and rebuked Elisha. Elisha assured him that he would see it come to pass but not eat any of the food.

What no one in the city realized was that God had done something unusual in the camp of the Syrians. The Syrians had been caused to hear the noise of invading chariots and had fled the camp in haste, fearing Israel's allies had arrived to fight on their behalf. The empty camp of the Syrians was not discovered until four lepers who had depended on the charity of Samaria came up with their own survival plan (7:6-7).

When the famine hit Samaria, there was a food shortage in the city, which meant the lepers outside the city were unable to get their usual scraps. Four such lepers concluded they might be able to get food from the Syrian camp and determined to try their luck. They reasoned the worst that could happen was they would be killed by the Syrians, which was much better than dying the slow death of starvation that appeared inevitable. But when they came to the camp, they found it abandoned. After partaking of the provisions themselves for some time, they determined to tell those in the city what they had found. They returned to the city walls that same night and told the gatekeepers what they had discovered (vv. 8-10).

When the retreat of the Syrians had been confirmed the next morning, the people stampeded to plunder the Syrian camp. Though there was an attempt to keep things orderly, the starving people of the city panicked and raced through the city gate to the food supply. The king's officer who had found the prophecy of Elisha too incredible the day before was trampled to death in the process (v. 17).

The siege of Samaria would not be the last of Elisha's dealings with the Syrians. Some time later, Elisha himself made a trip to Damascus. Ben-Hadad was sick at the time and when he heard Elisha was in town, he sent his servant Hazael to inquire of the prophet concerning the sickness and to find out if he would recover. When Hazael asked Elisha, he received two answers. "And Elisha said to him, 'Go, say to him, "You shall certainly recover." However the Lord has shown me that he will really die' " (8:10). Then the prophet stared at Hazael and began weeping.

When Hazael asked Elisha why he was weeping, the prophet answered that the Lord had made him aware of the terrible acts of violence that Hazael would inflict on Israel when he became king of Syria. Hazael objected to the prophecy, claiming he would never engage in such gross activities. But the next day Hazael murdered Ben-Hadad. Elisha simply left the city, his work there completed. "But it happened on the next day that he took a thick cloth and dipped it in water, and spread it over his face so that he died; and Hazael reigned in his place" (v. 15).

THE REIGNS OF AHAZIAH (841 B.C.) AND ATHALIAH *(2 Kings 8:25-29; 9:27-29; 11:1-3, 13-20; 2 Chron. 22:1-12)* (841–835 B.C.)

The death of Jehoram in Jerusalem did not bring to an end the wickedness that characterized his reign. His son Ahaziah assumed the throne "and he walked in the way of the house of Ahab, and did evil in the sight of the Lord, as the house of Ahab had done, for he was the son-in-law of the house of Ahab" (2 Kings 8:27). The only significant accomplishment of his brief reign was an alliance in battle with his uncle, the king of Israel, against Hazael king of Syria. In the course of the battle, the king of Israel was wounded and returned to Jezreel to recover from his wound. Rather than return to Judah, Ahaziah decided to visit his sick uncle.

Elisha also sent one of the sons of the prophets to the battle at Ramoth Gilead with a mission of his own. The prophet was to find one Jehu ben Jehoshaphat and privately anoint him king over Israel. When the mission had been accomplished, the prophet was to open the door and flee without delay. The young prophet did as he was commissioned and Jehu was recognized as king of Israel. Jehu became an efficient and successful king after the Machiavellian order, for he murdered many dozens of people (9:1-10).

The first act of Jehu was to kill the previous king. He ordered the leaders loyal to his cause to prevent anyone from going back to Jehoram to warn him. When Jehu was spotted with his company, a messenger was sent out from the king to determine the nature of the visit. Twice messengers were sent out who did not return to the city. Eventually, the watchman concluded the troops were being led by Jehu, who had a reputation for being a reckless chariot driver. It was not until Jehu was in Jehoram's room that the king recognized the plot. As Jehoram tried to escape, Jehu drew his bow and shot him. He then ordered the body to be cast in Naboth's vineyard in accordance with the prophecy of Elijah (vv. 11-26).

Ahaziah was with his uncle at the time of Jehu's attack, but managed to escape temporarily. Jehu pursued him to Megiddo where the king of Judah died. Because he was a descendant of

David, his body was carried back to Jerusalem for burial. But in the process of tracking down Ahaziah, Jehu also found forty-two nephews of the king of Judah, whom he also murdered because they were descendants of Ahab (10:1-12).

The next victim of Jehu was Jezebel. When Jehu came to the city gate, Jezebel greeted him from a window in an upper room of her house. Jehu called out, asking who in that room was loyal to him. The two or three eunuchs who responded were then ordered to throw Jezebel out. She died in the fall, and when men came back to get her body for burial, all they could find were the palms of her hands and feet and remains of her skull. The rest had been eaten by dogs just as Elijah had prophesied (9:30-37).

Ahab had appointed his seventy sons kings over the cities of Israel. These also were murdered in Jehu's purge. The elders of the cities beheaded these sons and sent their heads to Jehu. Though the new king offered to let the cities elect new kings to replace the descendants of Ahab, they chose rather to be under the rule of a single king, Jehu.

There was also rampant bloodshed in the Southern Kingdom of Judah. "Now when Athaliah the mother of Ahaziah saw that her son was dead, she arose and destroyed all the royal heirs of the house of Judah" (2 Chron. 22:10). Only the baby Joash escaped this plot against the royal house of Judah. The child and his nurse were hid in a closet from those doing the killing, and he was eventually moved to the temple where he remained the next six years. During that time, Athaliah ruled over the kingdom of Judah.

In a strange chain of events, while Athaliah reigned in Judah, Israel was reigned by a king devoted to some degree to the worship of Jehovah. Jehu led a reform of the land abolishing the worship of Baal. He did this by gathering all of the worshipers of Baal to offer a sacrifice. After he had confirmed that all those present were worshipers of Baal, he had his men execute those in the temple of Baal. The idols and temple were then destroyed and burned. "Thus Jehu destroyed Baal from Israel" (2 Kings 10:28).

Jehu's recognition of the Lord resulted in the promise of

God that his descendants would sit on the throne for the next four generations. However, Jehu recognized Jehovah in the way that some might join a church but not experience salvation. Like Jehu, many men get ahead in business because following godly principles will prosper a man, even when he doesn't know the God of the principles. None of the kings of northern Israel experienced Old Testament salvation, including Jehu; even though he had an outward reformation Jehu still permitted the worship of golden calves in both Dan and Bethel. Nevertheless, Jehu was as righteous as the kings of Israel seem to have gotten.

THE REIGN OF JOASH *(2 Kings 11:4-12; 12:1-21; 2 Chron. 23:1-11; 24:1-27)* (835–796 B.C.)

Though evil Athaliah had successfully usurped the throne of David in the south, she did not appear to have ever enjoyed the popular support of her people during her six-year reign. Finally the time came when Jehoiada the priest decided the nation would be better off ruled by a seven-year-old heir than the evil queen. With both widespread military and religious support, the priest made arrangements to crown Joash king of Judah.

The careful planning of Jehoiada led to a successful coronation of the young king. It was not until the service in the temple concluded that the people began to clap and chant, "Long live the king!" Then Athaliah was aware of what had happened. "When she looked, there was the king, standing by a pillar according to custom; and the leaders and trumpeters were by the king. All the people of the land were rejoicing and blowing trumpets" (2 Kings 11:14).

Athaliah must have realized her own end was near. She viewed the coronation as an act of treason against her. She was taken from the temple and killed at the stable entrance to the palace. Thus the descendants of Ahab ceased to have an influence in both kingdoms.

Joash was a good king while he was under the influence of Jehoiada the priest. Under his influence, the people entered into a covenant with the Lord and destroyed the idols. Priests involved in the worship of Baal were replaced. Temple worship was again restored on a regular basis. During the early years of Joash's reign, money was collected for the repair of the temple in a box called the "Joash Chest."

While Judah again experienced a time of revival, the beginning of the end was taking place in the Northern Kingdom of Israel. Hazael began attacking the border towns of Israel as Jehu came to the end of his reign. On his death, his son Jehoahaz assumed the throne. Like most of the other kings of Israel, the new king led his people into the sins that had previously become commonplace in the nation. As a result, Israel was under the displeasure of God and was constantly oppressed by Syria throughout the seventeen-year reign of Jehoahaz.

At the same time, spiritual life was improving in the Southern Kingdom of Judah. The repairs of the temple continued throughout the lifetime of Jehoiada the priest. By the time of his death, the temple economy had been restored and burnt offerings were being offered continually. But on the death of the priest, Joash was influenced by the princes of the land and began worshiping false gods and idols. Even as Joash was falling into the sin of idolatry, Jehoahaz in Israel was beginning to realize the high cost of his idolatrous practices on his nation. "So Jehoahaz pleaded with the Lord, and the Lord listened to him; for He saw the oppression of Israel, because the king of Syria oppressed them" (13:4).

As He had done so many times before, God raised up a deliverer for His people. As a result, Israel escaped temporarily from the oppression of Syria. But after the crisis passed, Israel did not change its lifestyle which had originally brought about the problems with Syria in the first place. The idols remained in Samaria and the people continued living in sin. Though they were free from their struggle with Syria, the national defense consisted of "only fifty horsemen, ten chariots, and ten thousand foot soldiers; for the king of Syria had destroyed them and made them like the dust at threshing" (v. 7). On the death of Jehoahaz, his son Jehoash began his sixteen-year reign over what was left of Israel.

As Jehoash began his reign over Israel, Elisha became ill with a sickness which would prove fatal. Out of respect for the aging prophet, the king of Israel made his way to Elisha's deathbed. There Elisha told him to take his bow and shoot an arrow out the window. Elisha then told Jehoash the arrow was symbolic of the victory Israel would have over Syria. Then the king was told to hit the arrows against the ground. Three times Jehoash hit the ground with his arrows. Elisha became angry and explained if the king had hit the ground five or six times, Israel would have defeated Syria. As a result of Jehoash's actions, however, Israel would have only three more victories over their Syrian oppressors.

One of the reasons from a human perspective that Israel was no longer engaged in a struggle with Syria was that Syria was fighting a new enemy—Judah. God tried to warn His people that Joash's new direction was wrong, but without success. "Yet He sent prophets to them, to bring them back to the Lord; and they testified against them, but they would not listen" (2 Chron. 24:19). When the son of Jehoiada the priest, Zechariah, rebuked the people, they conspired under the king's direct command to stone him in the court of the temple. "So it happened in the spring of the year that the army of Syria came up against him; and they came to Judah and Jerusalem, and destroyed all the leaders of the people from among the people, and sent all their spoil to the king of Damascus" (v. 23). During the conflict, Joash was wounded. After the army of Syria had plundered the land and returned to Damascus, one of his own servants killed the king in retaliation for the murder of Zechariah. Joash was buried in Jerusalem but not with the kings. His son Amaziah was then raised to the throne.

"Then Elisha died, and they buried him" (2 Kings 13:20). But even in death, Elisha would perform a miracle. "So it was, as they were burying a man, that suddenly they spied a band of raiders; and they put the man in the tomb of Elisha; and when the man was let down and touched the bones of Elisha, he revived and stood on his feet" (v. 21).

PERSPECTIVE

Christians today sometimes confuse ministry strategies or expressions of personality with the degree of spiritual reality characterizing a ministry. Certainly the examples of Israel's two great prophets Elijah and Elisha should call that approach to evaluating a ministry into question. Elijah was a controversial, confrontational prophet of God who spent much of his time isolated from social engagements. His handpicked successor built his ministry on a more relational approach to the ministry. Each man proved to be God's spokesman for that hour. While Christians may identify with a biblical model of ministry as reflected in the life and ministry of a particular prophet or apostle, they should be careful not to condemn other believers who elect a different pattern of ministry in serving the same Lord. "Now there are diversities of gifts, but the same Spirit. There are differences of ministries, but the same Lord. And there are diversities of activities, but it is the same God who works all in all" (1 Cor. 12:4-6).

FORTY-FOUR

ISAIAH:
On the Hinge of the Kingdom's History

(1 Kings 14:1-22; 15:1-12, 17-38; 16:1-20; 2 Chronicles 25:1-28; 26:1-23; 27:1-9; 28:1-27; Isaiah 1–7)

Isaiah's name means "Jehovah has saved," and in his lifetime he saw the Northern Kingdom collapse and go into captivity and the Southern Kingdom came to the edge of national disaster, but "Jehovah has saved" them. He is famous for the book that bears his name and he is characterized as the "St. Paul of the Old Testament."

Isaiah was born into a family of rank, with easy access to the king (Isa. 7:3), intimacy with priests (8:2), and he became the court preacher. Whereas some of the prophets spoke primarily to the people, Isaiah's influence was primarily with the nation's leadership; during his life the Southern Kingdom experienced revival.

Tradition claims he was a cousin to King Uzziah, but there is no support to it. He lived in Jerusalem, was married, and had two sons. Isaiah was a great orator whose choice of words reflect education and refinement. He was a poet whose literary structure has been defined as "beauty and strength." He is powerful in denunciation but rhythmatic in expression.

Isaiah had a vision of the "thrice-holy" God in the death-year of Uzziah, 740 B.C. Since he was still preaching when Sennacherib attacked Jerusalem in 721 B.C., he had forty years of fruitful ministry. The vision that Isaiah had was the only one recorded, and this probably included his call to prophetic ministry. Uzziah had been an effective king in military strategy, business advances, and religious enthusiasm. Perhaps Isaiah had too much loyalty for Uzziah. As a court advisor, Isaiah probably saw his dreams shattered when Uzziah intruded into the priesthood and was stricken with leprosy. It was then Isaiah saw the Lord, high and lifted up. His view of a majestic Sovereign changed his life. After this deepening experience, his horizons were practically unbounded.

But to see the contribution of Isaiah, we need to examine the half century before he came on the scene. Amaziah assumed the throne of Judah (796–767 B.C.) and, like his father before him, began his reign as a righteous king. Though he did not eliminate the high places his father had allowed, he did execute those involved in the plot against his father Joash as soon as the kingdom was in his control. Further, he reorganized the army of Israel and found 300,000 men he could depend on in battle. As Elisha had prophesied, Israel was three times victorious over Ben-Hadad, king of Syria. Perhaps this was why Amaziah determined to hire an additional 100,000 mercenaries out of Israel. But no sooner had he set aside about $250,000 in silver to pay their wages when the king was warned by a prophet, "The Lord is not with Israel—not with any of the children of Ephraim" (2 Chron. 25:7). Heeding the warning from God, Amaziah dismissed the mercenaries from his army and sent them home. They returned to the Northern Kingdom with great anger directed toward Judah. As they returned, they plundered the cities of Judah in their path.

Amaziah took his troops and marched against Edom to capture the city of Seir. In the battle and subsequent events surrounding the conquest of Seir, 20,000 Edomites were killed. But in returning to Judah, the king brought back the gods of the Edomites. He was again confronted by a prophet. This time it was not a message of encouragement but one of rebuke. When the king refused to accept the prophet's advice, the prophet responded, "I know that God has determined to destroy you, because you have done this and have not heeded my counsel" (v. 16).

On his return to Jerusalem, Amaziah learned of the activities of the Israelite mercenaries and declared war against Israel. The two armies met to fight at Beth Shemesh in Judah. Though the Lord was not with Israel, neither was He with Judah, as they had abandoned Him for the gods of the Edomites. As a result, Israel prevailed in the battle and destroyed part of the wall of Jerusalem. As the army of Israel returned north, they did so bearing the vast wealth of the temple and royal palace, along with the hostages that had been captured in the battle against Edom.

On the death of Amaziah, his sixteen-year-old son Uzziah became king of Judah. "And he did what was right in the sight of the Lord, according to all that his father Amaziah had done. He sought God in the days of Zechariah, who had understanding in the visions of God; and as long as he sought the Lord, God made him to prosper" (26:4-5).

The era of Uzziah (792–740 B.C.) was one of great prosperity for Judah. The king earned a reputation as a great builder and warrior. Isaiah witnessed the rapid growth of his nation. Judah built the city of Elath and erected defensive towers at the gate of Jerusalem. Uzziah had inventors develop new weapons capable of firing large stones and arrows at invading armies and had them installed in the towers. Because of Uzziah's personal interest in husbandry, he had vineyards planted throughout the nation. His large herds were scattered throughout the land and defensive towers similar to those in Jerusalem were erected for their protection. He gained military victories over the Philistines, Arabians, and Meunites. Also, he began receiving tribute from the Ammonites. He opened a port on the Red Sea. "His fame spread as far as the entrance of Egypt, for he strengthened himself exceedingly" (v. 8). Under Uzziah the nation had a degree of prosperity that it had not enjoyed since King Solomon.

Uzziah's great success must have gotten to him. He began to think more highly of himself than was proper and took on responsibilities that were not his. He intruded into the priesthood. When confronted by priests in the temple for burning incense, a ministry reserved for the priests, Uzziah got angry that anyone should challenge his authority. Even as he stood in his rage with the incense in his hand, "the Lord struck the king, so that he was a leper until the day of his death" (2 Kings 15:5). Uzziah lived another ten years, dwelling in a "separated" house for lepers. He could not sit on the throne as a leper. His son Jotham began reigning as king at that time (750–732 B.C.).

Jotham "prepared his ways before the Lord his God" (2 Chron. 27:6). He built parts of the temple, cities in the Judean countryside, and castles and towers in the forest. He also defeated the Ammonites and began exacting tribute from them. But even as Israel fell to the Assyrians, Jotham found himself engaged in battle with both Israel and Syria.

As the Southern Kingdom prospered, the Northern Kingdom was eroding. On the death of Menahem in Israel, his son Pekahiah assumed the throne. His brief two-year reign came to a violent end when his captain, Pekah ben Remaliah, killed him in the castle and took the throne for himself. Pekah reigned twenty years in the final days of Israel (752–732 B.C.), but his lifestyle was as evil as the kings who had sat on that throne before him. It was during his reign that Israel's captivity really began. The tribes of Reuben and Gad and the half-tribe of Manasseh became increasingly involved in the pagan practices God had banned from His people. "So the God of Israel stirred up the spirit of Pul king of Assyria, that is, Tiglath-Pileser king of Assyria. He carried the Reubenites, the Gadites, and the half-tribe of Manasseh into captivity" (1 Chron. 5:26).

Ahaz the son of Jotham began to reign as king of Judah in the south (735–716 B.C.). This Judean king was so evil as to engage in human sacrifice and even offered his own son in a sacrifice. Early in his reign he was confronted with the struggle with the allied forces of northern Israel and Syria. Since it looked like the Southern Kingdom would lose, the people began to wonder if they could survive the battle. It was in this context God sent Isaiah to the Judean king.

Isaiah assured the king Judah would survive the conflict with Israel and Syria. Isaiah offered a sign from God by way of verification. But Ahaz was not interested in what the prophet had to say and refused the sign. Probably God had intended the sign as a means of strengthening the faith of the people, but Ahaz had refused the sign in unbelief. As a result, Isaiah spoke of a sign God would give, but it would be a sign performed long after Ahaz had died. "Behold the virgin shall conceive and bear a Son, and shall call His name Immanuel" (Isa. 7:14).

The south was not defeated, but the Northern Kingdom was lost. The captivity of Israel had begun.

The defeat of Israel posed a serious threat to the security of Judah. For years the prophets of God had warned of Israel's fate. Some of the same prophets had also warned Judah of its own coming day of judgment. Ahaz realized Syria now posed a military threat to the security of Judah. Something had to be done about it and Ahaz was prepared to act.

But gone were the days when those who sat on the throne of David shared David's commitment to his God. In the valley of Elah, young David had been willing to take on Goliath because the Philistine giant had blasphemed the name of Israel's God. Now Ahaz, a descendant of David, would go to meet another enemy of Judah and Judah's God, but his would be a different response. "Now in the time of his distress King Ahaz became increasingly unfaithful to the Lord. This is that King Ahaz. For he sacrificed to the gods of Damascus which had defeated him, saying, 'because the gods of the kings of Syria help them, I will sacrifice to them that they may help me.' But they were the ruin of him and of all Israel" (2 Chron. 28:22-23).

In his abandoning of the God who had brought Israel out of Egypt, he engaged in a systematic removal of the religion of Jehovah from Judah. In the process he destroyed the instruments used in the worship of God in the temple and sealed the doors of that magnificent edifice built by Solomon for the worship of Israel's God. Then, throughout his capital, he established pagan centers of worship, idols devoted to the gods of other lands. "And in every single city of Judah he made high places to burn incense to other gods, and provoke to anger the Lord God of his fathers" (v. 25).

Hoshea, the last king of the northern tribes, like so many kings of Israel before him, "did evil in the sight of the Lord" (2 Kings 17:2). But the evil of Hoshea was not as severe or extreme as that of previous kings. When Shalmaneser IV, king of Assyria, who had succeeded Tiglath-Pileser came up against him, Hoshea agreed to pay tribute to the Assyrians and continued to serve in his office as king. But Hoshea did not intend to pay that tribute. Secretly he began making an alliance with Egypt whom he hoped would deliver his nation from the yoke of the Assyrians. But before anything could be finalized, word leaked out and the king of Assyria learned of Hoshea's secret discussions with the king of Egypt. When the tribute from Israel failed to arrive, Shalmaneser IV appeared quickly before the gates of Samaria. For three weary years (v. 5) the city was under siege before it finally surrendered to Sargon II who had succeeded Shalmaneser. The land was depopulated and Hoshea spent the remaining days of his life in an Assyrian prison.

When the Assyrians defeated their enemies, it was their policy to remove them from their homeland and establish settlements in the newly conquered territory. According to Assyrian records, exactly 27,292 were taken captive. "Then the king of Assyria brought people from Babylon, Cuthah, Ava, Hamath, and from Sepharvaim, and placed them in the cities of Samaria instead of the Children of Israel; and they took possession of Samaria and dwelt in its cities" (v. 24).

As a result, the Northern Kingdom disappeared. In accordance with the superstitions of that day, the new settlers established a religion loosely based on the worship of the God of Israel. But the faith of the Samaritans as they were later called was a hybrid faith. A priest of the Lord who had been captured by Assyria was returned to Bethel to teach the new inhabitants of that land how they should worship God; but the result was a merging of the practices of the true religion of Israel and the pagan worship to which the people were accustomed. "They feared the Lord, yet served their own gods—according to the rituals of the nations from among whom they were carried away" (v. 33).

PERSPECTIVE

Though Isaiah ministered in the south as a prophetic seer, he could not miss seeing Jehovah's message of judgment in the north. He constantly warned Judah that she would fall. Perhaps the influence of Isaiah was best felt on the next king of the south, Hezekiah. As so often happened, an ungodly king had a godly son.

FORTY-FIVE

ISAIAH:
The Revival Years

(2 Kings 18:1–23:30; 2 Chronicles 29–35; Isaiah 36:1–39:8)

Isaiah had two sons who symbolized his message. The first was named Shear-Jashub which means, "a remnant shall return." Isaiah predicted the south would go into Captivity, but a remnant would return to the Holy Land. His second son was named Maher-Shalal-Hash-Baz meaning "hasten to the spoil, hurry to the prey," the message of imminent judgment.

The Book of Isaiah is divided into three distinct parts. Chapters 1–35 deal with messages of judgment and the key word is Assyria. When young Isaiah began to preach, the north was not concerned with Assyria, whose capital was Nineveh, but with another nation with a similar name—Syria, whose capital was Damascus. The second portion of the book, chapters 36–39 is a historical section that describes the invasion of Assyria and the reaction of Hezekiah. The final section deals with the promise of a coming deliverer (the Messiah) and the restoration of the kingdom. The key word is Babylon, which would conquer the Southern Kingdom. When Isaiah wrote, Babylon was not yet a world power.

Hezekiah began his reign at age twenty-five (716 B.C.). Hezekiah was a revival king, and one of the factors in that revival was the ministry of Isaiah that called the nation to repentance. Even before the Northern Kingdom fell, the influence of Isaiah and Hezekiah was being felt.

HEZEKIAH *(2 Kings 18–20; 2 Chron. 29–32)*
(716–697 B.C.)

On the death of wicked King Ahaz, his son Hezekiah assumed the throne of Judah. He was only twenty-five years old at the time, but in his youth he possessed a zeal for the Lord which his father had not known. "He trusted in the Lord God of Israel, so that after him was none like him among all the kings of Judah, nor any who were before him. For he held fast to the Lord; he did not depart from following Him, but kept His commandments, which the Lord had commanded Moses" (2 Kings 18:5-6).

Another reason for the revival was that Hezekiah was a reading king. Possessing this ability made it possible for him to read the Law of God and make a personal copy as required in the Law of Moses. Perhaps it was while he was doing this at the beginning of his reign that he realized how far Judah had drifted from the expectations of God. He responded by instituting a series of reforms designed to remove the idolatry his father had introduced and restore the worship of Jehovah in the temple. A significant portion of the Book of Proverbs is attributed to the collecting and copying work done by King Hezekiah (Prov. 25:1–29:27).

Hezekiah began by first gathering the priests and Levites together and calling them to a renewed consecration to God. The king determined to reopen the temple. After being challenged by the king, the priests and Levites began the work of making temple repairs and preparing the temple for worship. Sixteen days later they reported to the king that all had been done.

Hezekiah did not waste any time in restoring the worship of the Lord to the nation. "Then King Hezekiah rose early, gathered the rulers of the city, and went up to the house of the Lord" (2 Chron. 29:20). The first day of renewed activity at the temple, seven bulls, seven rams, seven lambs, and seven goats were offered as an offering of consecration on the part of the leadership of Jerusalem. Then the people themselves brought their offerings. So many animals were brought to the altar that the few priests present had to enlist the aid of the

Levites to help in the preparation of the sacrifices. Together the king and people rejoiced in the sudden return to the worship of God. It was evident to all that God had prepared the hearts of the people for this moment of revival.

But for Hezekiah, this moment of revival was not enough. He issued a call not only to Judah but to all Israel before she was conquered by Assyria, calling on them to come to Jerusalem to observe the Passover. Such a call for united worship had not been issued to the whole people of God since the reign of Solomon. But the time had come when such a call was possible. Politically, the northern nation of Israel was very weak. A succession of evil kings had led the nation into the deep bondage of sin. Very soon that spiritual bondage would be manifest in the final captivity of the nation. Though Hoshea sat on the throne of Israel, Hezekiah could appeal directly to the people of Israel without fearing a military response from Hoshea. Even as Israel went to Jerusalem to worship, Hoshea was secretly engaged in discussions with the king of Egypt, hoping to form an alliance that would enable him to get out from under the oppression of Assyria. In just three years, the Assyrian king would set the final siege around the city of Samaria. Perhaps the invitation by the revival king Hezekiah was God's final appeal to the north before she was defeated and taken captive. The people of the north responded, but not the leadership (30:1-22).

The gathering of the nation together in Jerusalem resulted in a turning again to God among the people of both nations. When the week-long celebration of the Passover had ended, the people did not want to leave. For another week they continued in the city, worshiping the Lord in sacrifices and singing. Not since the time of Solomon had such rejoicing been known in the streets of Jerusalem. But this revival was more than an emotional high. The renewed commitment of the people of God resulted in a removal of idols, not only in Jerusalem and Judah, but in the tribes of Israel also. Among the idols destroyed during this revival was one called Nehushtan. This was perhaps the most unusual idol of Israel as it was one God Himself had commanded to be built. He had instructed Moses to erect a brass serpent in the wilderness to bring healing to those bitten by poisonous snakes, but years later this brass serpent, intended for Israel as a picture of what God would eventually do not only for them but the whole world as He raised His own Son on a cross, had become the subject of worship itself (30:23–31:1).

Following this revival, both the kings of Israel and Judah refused to pay tribute to the Assyrian king. Even though their actions were similar, they were not the same and had different results. When the northern king Hoshea stopped sending tribute to Assyria, he trusted in Egypt to help him in his subsequent struggle. Assyria attacked Samaria, and three years later the king of Israel was taken to an Assyrian prison. But when southern king Hezekiah determined to throw off the yoke of the Assyrians, his trust was in God. Though he later wavered in his faith, the Assyrians did not capture Jerusalem.

It was not until fourteen years into his reign that Sennacherib turned his attention to Judah and began an invasion into that land. But when the Assyrian army began taking the outer cities of Judah, King Hezekiah of Judah quickly made an agreement to pay tribute to them in exchange for an end to their invasion. It would cost the king 300 talents of silver and 30 talents of gold to save his nation from war. Without hesitation, Hezekiah sent the tribute. The gold included in that initial payment included gold cut from the doors and pillars of the temple (2 Kings 18:13-16).

Physically, things did not go well for Hezekiah. He became sick with a serious illness that threatened his life. The recorder of this illness used the Hebrew word *shechim* to describe the condition. This word may refer to either boils or furuncles. Both of these conditions are caused by the bacterium *Staphylococcus aureus*. Some of the more virulent strains of this bacteria may be fatal. This is especially true if the victim's resistance is low or if boils appear near the nose or lips. Though Hezekiah's illness could have been one of several diseases, the use of a fig poultice to treat the illness suggests the presence of boils. Even today, green figs are used in this way as a home remedy to draw out the infection of boils. In the case of Hez-

ekiah, this sickness came at a particularly low time in his life
and threatened it (Isa. 38:1).

God sent Hezekiah the Prophet Isaiah to warn him of the
seriousness of his condition and urge him to prepare to die.
There is no indication in Scripture that this illness was the
result of sin being judged in Hezekiah's life, nor was the message of Isaiah necessarily intended as a rebuke for anything
wrong in the life of the king. God simply informed the godly
king the time had come that he would die, and gave him time
to prepare his estate. Hezekiah responded to the news with
prayer and weeping. He was seriously concerned for the
future of the Davidic dynasty. It was an act of faith that prayed
for extra years so he could have a son to carry on the line (vv.
2-8).

The Lord responded to the prayer of Hezekiah in an unusual
way. He commanded Isaiah, "Return and tell Hezekiah the
leader of My people, 'Thus says the Lord, the God of David
your father: "I have heard your prayer, I have seen your
tears; surely I will heal you. On the third day you shall go up
to the house of the Lord. And I will add to your days fifteen
years. I will deliver you and this city from the hand of the king
of Assyria; and I will defend this city for My own sake, and for
the sake of My servant David" ' " (2 Kings 20:5-6).

On hearing the second message from God through the
Prophet Isaiah, Hezekiah asked for a sign that would assure
him the message was indeed from God. Isaiah offered to move
the shadow on the sundial ten degrees if Hezekiah would decide which direction the shadow should be moved. The king
reasoned the shadow would naturally move forward ten degrees and called for the direction to be changed. Isaiah prayed,
and God moved back the shadow. Though God had earlier
caused the sun and moon to remain in their places while Joshua
fought a battle, this is the only recorded instance where God
actually moved time back.

As God had said, Hezekiah recovered from his illness and
reigned another fifteen years in Judah. About the time of his
recovery, two things happened. First, he had a son, Manasseh, which was good news and bad news. It was good news

that the Davidic dynasty would continue, but bad news in that
Manasseh was the wickedest king the south had ever had. The
second thing that happened in Hezekiah's extended life was
that he received a delegation from Babylon. Merodach-
Baladan, king of Babylon, had heard of the sickness of the
Judean king and sent him a gift and letters. Having recovered
from a great personal crisis, Hezekiah enjoyed the attention
being given to him. In his moment of victory over the fatal
illness, he was weaker than when he had laid on his deathbed.
Pride began to overtake the king and he boasted of his immense wealth to the Babylonian delegation. He had no way of
knowing at the time that his boasting was providing the Babylonians with information that would eventually motivate them
to take Jerusalem captive (39:1-2).

Again, Isaiah was summoned by God to deliver a message
to the king of His people. God told the king of the serious
consequences of his boasting. " 'Behold, the days are coming
when all that is in your house, and what your fathers have
accumulated until this day, shall be carried to Babylon; nothing
shall be left,' says the Lord" (20:17). Though he had made a
serious error in judgment in revealing his wealth to the Babylonians, Hezekiah responded to the warning from God in humility. God responded by delaying the Babylonian Captivity
until some time after the death of the godly king.

Again Sennacherib invaded Judah, but this time the results
were different. Rather than seek peace at any price, Hezekiah
determined to fight. He led the nation to strengthen its de-
fenses and arm itself. Also, he dammed up the rivers and
brooks that might provide the invading army with fresh water.
He appointed leaders in the army of Judah and gathered the
men together in Jerusalem. There he challenged his people
before they went into battle. "Be strong and courageous; do
not be afraid not dismayed before the king of Assyria, nor
before all the multitude that is with him; for there are more
with us than with him. With him is the arm of flesh; but with us
is the Lord our God, to help us and to fight our battles"
(2 Chron. 32:7-8).

According to the Assyrian king's record, he captured forty-six walled cities and small villages without number, carrying 200,150 into captivity. The invading army surrounded Jerusalem and began a campaign designed to break the morale of Judah's army. They warned the people in the city not to trust in God to deliver them, claiming the city would fall just as others had before the Assyrian army. As Rabshakeh, the commander in chief of the army from Lachish, continued to warn Judah not to trust in God, the people of the city refused to answer the challenges. When Hezekiah realized the negative impact the continued ranting of Rabshakeh could have on his people, he asked Isaiah to pray for the nation (Isa. 36:1–37:4).

God answered the prayer of Isaiah by distracting Rabshakeh from his attack on Israel. The Assyrian general heard a rumor that his own city was being attacked in his absence and immediately took his troops to defend his city (v. 7). This removed a portion of the invading army and the constant public claims that God was incapable of defending Jerusalem, but the Assyrian army still threatened the security of Jerusalem. Sennacherib came through the Promised Land, returning from victorious battles in Egypt. He sent a letter to Hezekiah assuring him the city of Jerusalem would soon fall to the Assyrians (vv. 8-13).

On receiving the letter, Hezekiah spread it out before the Lord and prayed. He reminded the Lord of Judah's consistent commitment to Him during his reign and asked God to defend His people. God answered by first sending an encouraging message from Isaiah, assuring the king his prayer had been heard and would be answered. Then, later that night, the angel of the Lord passed through the Assyrian camp, killing 185,000 soldiers by means of a plague. When Sennacherib realized he had lost much of his army, he chose not to attack Jerusalem but rather to return in shame to Nineveh (vv. 14-38).

God continued to prosper Hezekiah during his reign. He was viewed with admiration and respect by other nations and received many gifts from other kings. Some of these gifts were given to him particularly; others were given to the temple in Jerusalem. Among the civic improvements he made during his reign was the building of an underground conduit to bring water into the city of Jerusalem. This tunnel and pool is still a popular attraction among tourists in Jerusalem today.

MANASSEH *(2 Kings 21:1-18; 2 Chron. 33:1-20)*
(697–642 B.C.)

Fifteen years after Hezekiah had recovered from what was supposed to have been a fatal illness, the godly king of Judah did die and another assumed is throne. Manasseh, the heir to his father's throne, was only twelve years old when he became king of Judah. He had been born during those years God had given Hezekiah an extension of his life. Among the kings of Judah, Manasseh holds two distinctions. First, his fifty-five-year reign was the longest of any of Judah's kings. Second, Manasseh was unquestionably the wickedest man to sit on the throne of David.

Manasseh did not share the deep personal trust in God that was so evident in the life and reign of his father. Rather, he led Judah to follow after the false gods of other lands. Not only did he restore the idol worship his father had destroyed, he introduced new gods and pagan religious practices to the people. He raised up images and built altars in the temple, practiced several forms of occult divination, and even offered his own son as a human sacrifice. "So Manasseh seduced Judah and the inhabitants of Jerusalem to do more evil than the nations whom the Lord had destroyed before the children of Israel" (2 Chron. 33:9).

God did not allow Manasseh to lead Israel into idolatry without warning him and the people of the consequences of such a course of action. Repeatedly, the Lord sent "His servants the prophets" with warnings to the wicked king and his nation, but they ignored the messages. "Moreover Manasseh shed very much innocent blood, till he had filled Jerusalem from one end to another, besides his sin with which he made Judah sin, in doing evil in the sight of the Lord" (2 Kings 21:16).

Among the prophets Manasseh is thought to have killed during his reign was Isaiah. Tradition claims Isaiah was accused of treason because his speeches were against Jerusalem and the temple. The Mishnah describes it as martyrdom. According to a Jewish tradition, the men of Manasseh found the prophet hiding in a hollow tree. The king then told his men to cut down the tree with a saw, cutting the prophet in half. Some commentators think Isaiah may be referred to in Hebrews 11:37 as an example of a man of faith who was "sawn in two."

But despite all the evil associated with the life of Manasseh, God never stopped loving him. "Now when he was in affliction, he implored the Lord his God, and humbled himself greatly before the God of his fathers, and prayed to Him; and He received his entreaty, heard his supplication, and brought him back to Jerusalem into his kingdom. Then Manasseh knew that the Lord was God" (2 Chron. 33:12-13).

Manasseh had done much to destroy what his father had accomplished spiritually in the land, and in the final years of his reign, he did what he could to correct the error of his youth. He built up the defense of Jerusalem and other important cities in Judah and reorganized the national defense by appointing captains over specific cities. Then he began to purge the land of the many foreign gods he had earlier introduced to it. He repaired the altar of the Lord and decreed that only the Lord should be worshiped in the land. He was unsuccessful in closing all the high places, but those who worshiped there worshiped the Lord rather than idols.

Because of the evil Manasseh had introduced into Judah, God raised up an enemy to discipline His people. Assyrian leaders fought against Manasseh and took him captive "with hooks" to Babylon. It was customary for the Assyrians to chain their prisoners together by placing rings or hooks through the jaw or nose of the prisoner. This appears to have been the fate of Manasseh.

JOSIAH *(2 Kings 22:1–23:30; 2 Chron. 34–35)* (640–609 B.C.)

Josiah is remembered as the last righteous king of Judah. After the two-year reign of Amon (642–640 B.C.), for thirty-one years Josiah sat on the throne of David and led the people back to God. There were two significant events during his reign which led to the last great revival in Judah before the Captivity. The first of these occurred just eight years into his reign when he was sixteen years old.

"For in the eighth year of his reign, while he was still young, he began to seek the God of his father David; and in the twelfth year he began to purge Judah and Jerusalem of the high places, the wooden images, the carved images, and the molded images" (2 Chron. 34:3). Little is known about the factors that led to the conversion of the teenage King Josiah, but several ideas have been suggested by various writers. He was no doubt aware of the consequence in the nation of the sins of his father and grandfather. He may have read of the conversion of his grandfather in the writings of Hozai (33:19) or been told of it by some member of the royal court who had been present at the time. Also, there is some indication Josiah may have been influenced spiritually by the Prophetess Huldah (34:26-28) and the Prophet Jeremiah (Jer. 22:16). As he began to realize the unique relationship his nation was to have with God, Josiah as king first made a personal commitment to God. Then, within four years of his own conversion, he began to exercise his responsibilities as king to cause his people to worship the Lord.

It was actually as an indirect result of this initial renewal in Judah that the second key event promoting spiritual renewal in the land occurred. When the land had been purged of paganism, Josiah embarked on a second phase of reform, the restoration of the temple. It was while the temple was being repaired that "Hilkiah the priest found the Book of the Law of the Lord given by Moses" (2 Chron. 34:14). It is generally agreed this book was a copy of the Book of Deuteronomy, though some argue the book included the entire Pentateuch. Some think this book may have been hidden in the temple to escape destruction during the reign of Ahaz. Others believe the book was found in the ark which had been cast aside into a storage room and had been "lost" during the apostasy which characterized much of the reigns of Manasseh and his son Amon. Since the temple had been essentially closed for seventy-five years, the rediscovery of the Book of the Law in the very place it belonged is entirely possible.

The discovery of the Law would have a profound impact on the nation. The book was brought to the king and read before him. If this book consisted only of Deuteronomy, the reading of the Law would have taken about three hours. If the book included the entire Pentateuch, the reading would have taken about ten hours. As the Word of God was read before the king, Josiah responded by tearing his clothing, a symbol of inner remorse for sin and repentance. He realized God would have to judge Judah for her sin. Through his tears he asked his men to "inquire of the Lord for me, and for those who are left in Israel and Judah, concerning the words of the book that is found; for great is the wrath of the Lord that is poured out on us, because our fathers have not kept the word of the Lord, to do according to all that is written in this book" (v. 21).

Hilkiah contacted the Prophetess Huldah who sent back a message from God for the king. The conclusion the king had come to was true: God would judge the nation for her sin. But God would also withhold His judgment until a time after the death of Josiah. When the king learned of this message from God, it served to renew his own zeal for the Lord. He gathered the nation together in Jerusalem for a public reading of the Law. After this, "the king stood in his place and made a covenant before the Lord, to follow the Lord, and to keep His commandments and His testimonies and His statutes with all his heart and all his soul, to perform the words of the covenant that were written in this book" (v. 31). The covenant made by the king was also adopted by those present that day. So effective was this second phase of the revival that all the abominations of the land were removed and Judah did not go back to its old ways throughout the reign of Josiah.

As his great-grandfather had done during a similar revival about a century earlier, Josiah led his people in the observance of the Passover. This Passover proved to be the most spectacular since the days of Samuel. About 32,600 lambs and goats and 2,500 cattle were sacrificed and roasted during this Passover celebration. All was done in accordance with the legal requirements for the observation of this feast. The celebration of the Passover was followed by the Feast of Unleavened Bread for seven days.

After this, Pharaoh Necho of Egypt marched against Carchemish. However, he was not attacking Judah. As the army of Egypt passed by Judea, Josiah went out to meet him in battle. The young king apparently assumed the Egyptians were going to also attack Judah despite Necho's claims to the contrary. Though the Egyptian Pharaoh urged Josiah not to engage in battle against them, Josiah joined his men in attacking them. In the course of the battle, the last godly king of Judah was fatally wounded. He instructed his men to get him out of the battle and back to Jerusalem. They did so, and there he died.

PERSPECTIVE

A godly man can make a bad decision. Perhaps Josiah could have lived another thirty years and made a permanent influence on his nation for righteousness. The nation mourned greatly over his death. Josiah had been a good king. He had done much to bring his people back to their God and temporarily stay the inevitable judgment coming on his nation. By the time he died, many in Judah realized the end was near.

FORTY-SIX

JEREMIAH:
The Collapsing Kings

(2 Kings 23:31–25:30; 2 Chronicles 36; Jeremiah; Lamentations)

As Judah and Jerusalem faced their final hours, God raised up a number of prophets to warn His people and call them back to Himself. Among these men of God was one who towered over all others. Jeremiah, not only was a prophet, but the prophet among prophets. He was a writing prophet, and most of what is known about him is learned in the autobiographical notations in his prophecy. But the Book of Jeremiah was not intended to be an autobiography. It is largely a collection of sermons proclaimed by him in which he happened to use a great deal of personal illustrations. As a result, it is not always easy to arrange the affairs of his life and ministry in chronological sequence.

Jeremiah was born in the city of Anathoth located about two and a half miles north of Jerusalem. He was apparently a descendant of Aaron and, therefore, part of the priestly line. At a very early age, he sensed the call of God on his life to the prophetic ministry. He was so tenderhearted and sensitive that he was reluctant to surrender to that call. Because he was so young, he felt he lacked the necessary qualifications of one involved in such a confrontational ministry. God had called him "to root out and pull down, to destroy and to throw down, to build and to plant" (Jer. 1:10). Jeremiah must have realized people would not appreciate his ministry, especially when he was so young. God had to break the pride in some when He called them, but He had to build up Jeremiah.

God called Jeremiah to serve Him just as Judah was moving into its last great revival before the Captivity. In 627 B.C., the godly king Josiah sat on the throne of David and was engaged in his initial purging of the land. Five years earlier, King Josiah had made his own commitment to God. A year prior to Jeremiah's call, the king had launched a major program of reform designed to purge Judah of the idolatry. Five years later, Jeremiah's own father would discover the lost Book of the Law in the temple and help lead the nation into revival.

Jeremiah realized his nation was in danger. God revealed to him that Jerusalem would be attacked by a power from the north. It was clear that Judah indeed deserved such judgment from God. "An astonishing and horrible thing has been committed in the land: the prophets prophesy falsely, and the priests rule by their own power; and My people love to have it so. But what will you do in the end?" (5:30-31)

As Jeremiah began preaching his message of judgment in the hopes of calling Judah and Jerusalem to repentance, he became a master in the use of the object lesson. He broke a clay pot to illustrate that God would break Judah in the coming judgment (19:1-12). He wore an oxen yoke around the city as he preached that the people would be yoked in judgment.

The ministry of Jeremiah seemed to become even more intense after the death of the revival king Josiah. Jehoahaz was selected by the people to assume the throne on the death of his father Josiah. He was twenty-three years old when he assumed the throne and only reigned three months before he was deposed by Pharaoh Necho of Egypt. Still, in those three months he earned a reputation for being an evil king. Necho took this young king with him as his prisoner and placed another son of Josiah on the throne in his place.

JEHOIAKIM *(2 Kings 23:35–24:7; 2 Chron. 36:5-8)* (609–598 B.C.)

The one whom Necho chose to sit on Judah's throne was Eliakim. But in making him king, Necho changed his name to

Jehoiakim. Both of these names are similar in meaning. Eliakim means "God is setting up." The name Jehoiakim means "Jehovah is setting up." Necho probably changed the name of this king to demonstrate his belief that Jehovah was directing him to take this course of action.

Jeremiah warned Jehoiakim he would go to Babylon in chains and die without an heir on the throne (Jer. 22:30). He announced to the nation that Nebuchadnezzar would be their captor and Babylon their home for seventy years (25:11). The people thought Jeremiah was crazy—they considered Egypt their enemy, not Babylon. Jeremiah was arrested and imprisoned for his ministry, yet he did not quit appealing to his people to repent of the sin God had to judge. While in prison, he wrote a book and gave it to his servant Baruch to read in the temple. When the scroll was seized and destroyed by the authorities, Jeremiah rewrote the same message and sent it again to be read. In addition to demonstrating the degree to which God inspired His Word, this event in the life of the prophet also illustrated the ability of God to preserve His Word.

Jehoiakim also earned a reputation for being an evil king. He introduced a taxation system to pay a tribute to the Egyptian Pharaoh. But soon there was another foreign ruler desiring tribute from the crumbling nation. When Nebuchadnezzar came against Judah, Jehoiakim switched allegiance and began paying tribute to the Babylonians. Among those taken to Babylon as a result of Nebuchadnezzar's first campaign against Jerusalem in 605 B.C. was Daniel who ministered in Babylon. Because of the immense power of Babylon, Necho and Egypt did not respond militarily to the loss of income from Judah. He had already lost a great deal of territory to the Babylonian Empire.

Three years into his new relationship with Nebuchadnezzar, Jehoiakim cut off the tribute payments. "And the Lord sent against him raiding bands of Chaldeans, bands of Syrians, bands of Moabites, and bands of the people of Ammon; He sent them against Judah to destroy it, according to the word of the Lord which He had spoken by His servants the prophets" (2 Kings 24:2). God judged Jehoiakim for shedding innocent blood by allowing invading armies to plunder the cities of Judah.

JEHOIACHIN *(2 Kings 24:8-16; 2 Chron. 36:9-10)* (597 B.C.)

On the death of Jehoiakim, his son Jehoiachin assumed the throne. Like his uncle eleven years earlier, Jehoiachin sat on the throne only three months before he was deposed by a foreign ruler. Nebuchadnezzar besieged the city of Jersualem and took a second group of Jewish leaders into captivity. Among those taken at this time was the king and his immediate family, and a young Jewish priest named Ezekiel. The Babylonian king set up one of Jehoiachin's uncles as king over the land of Judah.

ZEDEKIAH *(2 Kings 24:17–25:30; 2 Chron. 36:11-23)* (597–586 B.C.)

Nebuchadnezzar appointed the youngest son of Josiah as the last king of Judah. This king also had his named changed by a foreign power. His original name, Mattaniah, means "gift of Jehovah." This name was changed to Zedekiah meaning "Jehovah my righteousness." This change of name, however, did not represent a change of character on the part of this king. Like his brothers and nephew who had sat on the throne before him, "he also did evil in the sight of the Lord" (2 Kings 24:19). This final king of Judah sat on the throne eleven years, but during that time Judah's cup of sin filled to the point where God would no longer delay His judgment. "For because of the anger of the Lord this happened in Jerusalem and Judah, that He finally cast them out from His presence" (v. 20).

During the reign of Zedekiah, Jeremiah was again imprisoned. Zedekiah had rebelled against Babylon and was depending on Egyptian aid to defend Jersualem from the Babylonian army. But Jeremiah insisted that the king submit to Nebuchadnezzar for the sake of the nation and not trust in Egypt for their security. The prophet was arrested as a Babylonian sympathizer, but when the Egyptian aid failed to materialize, he was given a degree of liberty. For a time Zedekiah served as a vassal of Nebuchadnezzar, but then he rebelled. Nebuchadnezzar responded by leading his army against Jerusalem to deal with this problem area in his empire once and for all. For a year and a half, the army of Babylon sealed up the city of Jerusalem and placed it under siege. By the time of the end, all food supplies had been completely consumed. Finally, a portion of the wall was destroyed. Though they knew the army was surrounding the city, the king and his soldiers attempted to escape the city by night. The king was captured and tried for his rebellion. The resulting sentence was severe. Zedekiah's eyes were plucked out, leaving him blind for the rest of his days, but not before he witnessed the deaths of his sons. Then the Babylonian army went to work on the city. The temple, royal palace, and homes of Jerusalem were burned. The wall of the city was broken down. The inhabitants of the city were killed indiscriminately. Anything of value in the city was removed and taken as spoil to Babylon. Those who escaped the massacre were taken captive to Babylon. Only the poorest of the people were allowed to remain in the land to tend the vineyards and orchards. "But Judah was carried away captive to Babylon because of their unfaithfulness" (1 Chron. 9:1).

As the city fell to the army of Babylon, Jeremiah was in custody in the outer court of the prison. Though Jeremiah had long predicted the fall of Jerusalem, it was something he had desperately wished could have been avoided. He was freed. He probably sat in the mountains of Judah and watched his city burn. As he saw his city go up in smoke, he wrote the Book of Lamentations. In it he laments the destruction of the Holy City. He penned some of the most mournful lines in all of Scripture. The Lamentations of Jeremiah is an acrostic which expressed the deep sorrow the prophet felt as he viewed the destruction of his city. Yet even in the midst of his sorrow, Jeremiah expressed hope as he considered the great faithfulness of his God. "This I recall to my mind, therefore I have hope. Through the Lord's mercies we are not consumed, because His compassions fail not. They are new every morning; great is Your faithfulness. 'The Lord is my portion,' says my soul, 'therefore I hope in Him!' " (Lam. 3:21-24)

THE LAMENTATIONS OF JEREMIAH

1 Pain of Zion's fall: mourning widow
2 Plight of Zion's fall: weeping daughter
3 Purpose of Zion's fall: afflicted man
4 Pondering Zion's fall: tarnished gold
5 Plea for Zion's fate: fatherless child

Even the Babylonians misunderstood the prophesying of Jeremiah and thought of him as their ally. As a result, the prophet was allowed to live in the city even after the final deportation of captive Jews from the land. Jeremiah remained in Jerusalem, but only for a short time. After the assassination of Gedaliah, he was forced by rebels who had hidden out in the hills to go with them to Egypt. According to a Jewish legend, Jeremiah took the ark of the covenant and buried it under the temple, or buried it in the hills, or took it to Egypt. Some rabbis believe Jeremiah will return at the appearing of their Messiah and give Him the jar of hidden manna in the ark as an authenticating sign. This may have been the background behind the claim of Jesus, "I am the Bread of Life."

Jeremiah spent his remaining days in Egypt. After the fall of Jerusalem, Jeremiah continued to preach. He predicted the conquest of Egypt by Nebuchadnezzar (Jer. 43:8-13), the fall of the Philistines (chap. 47), Moabites (chap. 48), Ammon (49:1-6), Edom (vv. 7-22), Syria (vv. 23-27), Kedar and Hazor (vv. 28-33), Elam (vv. 34-39), and Babylon (chaps. 50–51). The prophet who had shed so many tears for his own people looked forward to the day when those tears of sorrow would become tears of joy as the people returned to the land and came to appreciate the faithfulness of their God.

FORTY-SEVEN

EZEKIEL:

Visions of the Glory of God

(Ezekiel)

The name Ezekiel means "the man God strengthens," and the book that carries the name of this prophet tells us little of his life. It contains mostly his messages and predictions; however, glimpses of Ezekiel's life shine through his prophecies. His father Buzi had a Gentile name, but was Jewish, of levitical descent. Perhaps the non-Jewish name of his father implies he was not a practicing priest, but Ezekiel overcame this barrier and became a priest (Ezek. 1:3). Most commentators think he was a practicing priest because of his familiarity with the temple and its practices (cf. chaps. 40–48) and because he predicts the high-priestly character of the coming Messiah, Jesus Christ.

Jehovah describes Ezekiel by using the expression "Son of man" ninety-one times in this book. It suggests he is a representative man who would receive God's message and transcend mere Judaism with a message to those in ages to come who will believe in Jesus Christ, who called Himself "Son of Man" seventy-nine times.

Ezekiel was thirty years old when he was called to be a prophet. The combination of the prophetic and priestly office is not accidental. Whereas these offices were separate, Ezekiel was transferred by God from the priestly function at the fall of Jerusalem and the collapse of the levitical offerings. But after

God's people returned from captivity, the high-priestly office gained prominence in Israel until the coming of Jesus Christ.

Ezekiel's call came in his thirtieth year (1:1), in the fifth year and on the fifth day of the fourth month of King Jehoiachin's captivity (v. 2). He got the prophetic gift (3:1ff) and continued in ministry for twenty-seven years from 593 to 571 B.C. (29:17). The fact that Ezekiel began his ministry at age thirty is not surprising. Both Jesus and John the Baptist began their ministries at age thirty. At this age the priest began his ministry (Num. 4:23, 30, 33).

Tradition suggests he was a student of Jeremiah; however, it is not found in the context of his writings. Should it be true, he would have followed the example of Jeremiah, who was also both a priest and prophet and perhaps influenced by the godly revival under Jeremiah's father.

Ezekiel was taken as a captive to Babylon after the second siege of Jerusalem in 597 B.C. He and his wife settled in a colony on the banks of the Chebar River near Babylon. He probably spent the rest of his life in ministry there. In his own evaluation of the content and emphasis of his ministry, Ezekiel simply states, "The heavens were opened and I saw visions of God" (Ezek. 1:1).

As a captive he was not in prison. He lived by the River Chebar, which was a Euphrates canal (probably dug by man) near Nippur (v. 3; 3:15). An American expedition found records in the city from a business house named "Murashu and Sons," with a number of accounts with Jewish names. The Jewish "captives" lived in their own houses (Jer. 29:5). Ezekiel probably owned his home (Ezek. 3:24). The Jews retained the rule of elders (8:1; 14:1; 20:1). So their life was not cruel; owing to the fact many did not want to return at the end of the seventy years of Captivity, their life must have been pleasant.

The Jews were "prisoners of fate" in that they lost their country, their capital city, their temple, their worship, and their independence as a nation.

Ezekiel was happily married in Babylon and perhaps had settled into reconstructed life. God revealed to him his wife, "the desire of his eyes," would die suddenly through sickness

(24:15ff), but he was commanded not to weep for her. This was a sign that Jerusalem, "the desire of Israel's eyes," would be destroyed but the Jews were not to weep for the city because God was judging sin. As with other prophets, God used a symbolic action to communicate a message. The next day Ezekiel's wife died.

Ezekiel's ministry was unique in that he was the first of the prophets to use an apocalyptic style so extensively in his writing and preaching. He saw visions and communicated them descriptively with colors, movement, and imagery. None of the Old Testament prophets used as much symbolic imagery as did Ezekiel. Like Jeremiah, he would at times resort to the use of object lessons to illustrate his messages from God. But unlike Jeremiah, the real focus of his ministry was not what God would do immediately so much as what God intended to do in the distant future. When Ezekiel saw visions in the Holy Land of Jerusalem, the commentators are not sure if God took him there physically to actually see what he described, or if he saw it in visions or dreams.

Some have suggested Ezekiel was an epileptic because he lay speechless and motionless without power of speech, a form of catalepsy (3:24ff). But that is probably not the case because he remained motionless in obedience to a direct command of God as a symbolic action. Also, Ezekiel never describes it as a disease.

Ezekiel's message was not well received by the Jews in Captivity. He describes them as being stubborn (v. 26); they had a mind harder than a rock (v. 9). The Jews perceived Ezekiel as a speaker of parables (20:49) and complained about his preaching. Ezekiel predicted the fall and destruction of Jerusalem and the temple. The false prophets said it would never fall. The Jews in Babylon, even though taken captive, believed their city could not be destroyed. They repudiated his ministry. Even when Ezekiel's prophecy proved true, they continued to reject his ministry. God summed up the people's impression of Ezekiel, "Indeed you are to them as a very lovely song of one who has a pleasant voice and can play well on an instrument; for they hear your words, but they do not do them" (33:32). Tradition suggests Ezekiel was a martyr, that his fellow exiles stoned him.

Ezekiel had a better understanding of what was taking place in Jerusalem than did most of the residents. He saw the growth of idolatry and chronicled its spread as the primary reason God had departed from His people. First, he saw "the image of jealousy" at the entrance of the temple (8:5). This was a Babylonian god that made God jealous. Then Ezekiel saw Canaanite idols on the walls of the temple (v. 10). This was followed by his vision of women weeping for the Assyrian god Tammuz (v. 14). Finally, Ezekiel saw twenty-five men turning their backs on the temple to worship the sun, the chief god of the Egyptians (v. 16). Ezekiel announced that God did not leave His people until they first left Him for the gods of the nations around them.

As life continued in Jerusalem oblivious to the spiritual crisis in the land, Ezekiel witnessed the departure of the glory of God. This was the Shekinah glory cloud that led Israel for forty years in the wilderness and came into the temple when Solomon dedicated it. First, the Shekinah glory cloud rose above the cherubim (9:3). Then it passed over the threshold of the holy of holies (10:4). Then, seemingly reluctant to leave, it hovered high above the cherubim (v. 18). The glory of God was waiting for the people to miss Jehovah or to call Him back. But the people did not call or repent. As Ezekiel finally watched it drift from above the temple over to the Mount of Olives, he was aware that most residents of the city were totally unaware of, and perhaps unconcerned with, the departure of the glory of God (11:23). "Ichabod" was written over Jerusalem.

On the tenth day of the tenth month of the ninth year (586 B.C.), Ezekiel was instructed to boil pieces of meat in a pot of water. This symbolic action predicted the destruction of Jerusalem. The people of Jerusalem were being "cooked" in judgment. God told Ezekiel, "Heap on the wood, kindle the fire; cook the meat well, mix in the spices, and let the cuts be burned up" (24:10).

News of the collapse of Jerusalem, which he had predicted,

initiated Ezekiel's message of the watchman on the wall (33:1ff). Ezekiel had been commissioned by God as a watchman over the house of Israel. Just as a city watchman would warn the inhabitants of the city of approaching danger, so Ezekiel tried to warn the residents of his city of an even more serious danger. He understood God would hold him responsible to see that the people heard and understood the message, though ultimately their response was their own responsibility (3:18-19).

By the time Ezekiel began his prophetic ministry, the end had already come. He himself was a captive in a foreign land. But he knew his people would not always remain in that land as captive. A day was coming when God would gather His people in their own land (37:1-10) and give them new life (vv. 11-28). His vision of the valley of dry bones predicts that Israel will return to the land in unbelief. They will be bones that are "very dry." When Ezekiel sees flesh come on the bones, that is a prediction of Israel's spiritual rebirth. Many Christians today believe the modern state of Israel is a partial fulfillment of the first part of Ezekiel's hope. Other Scriptures seem to suggest the second part of that hope will occur during an outpouring of the Holy Spirit immediately prior to the return of Christ.

Ezekiel did not believe Israel's trials were past in their defeat at the hands of the Babylonians. There would be other battles—some victorious, some not. Perhaps one of the most significant battles yet to be fought involving Israel is that described in Ezekiel's vision of Gog and Magog (Ezek. 38–39). According to this prophecy, there remains at least one major world conflict against the Jews yet to be fought involving nations in the regions of Russia, Europe, the Arabian Peninsula, North Africa, and Israel. Despite every indication that Israel will be greatly outnumbered in this conflict, God has already promised His people victory in this struggle.

As a priest, one of Ezekiel's greatest concerns in Babylon must have been the absence of a temple. But he knew there would someday be a renewal of temple worship. God gave Ezekiel a vision of a temple larger than any Israel has built to this day. Many conservative Bible scholars believe this will be the millennial temple and that sacrifices will be offered on a regular basis during the thousand-year reign of Christ. These sacrifices will not have the Old Testament significance, but will look back as a memorial of His sacrificial work on the cross. For Ezekiel, it was comforting to know the Shekinah glory of God he had watched depart from the temple and city of Jerusalem would someday return in greater glory than it had previously.

PERSPECTIVE

Ezekiel the priest-prophet was carried to Babylon in 597 B.C. and wrote to fellow exiles. As a watchman he was a prosecuting attorney to convince the nation of her disobedience to Jehovah and announce her judgment. He explicitly described the destruction of Jerusalem and the temple. Ezekiel used various means to deliver his message; speaking, acting, visions, symbolic actions, allegories, parables, and written messages. But God's people had gone too far.

Ezekiel saw idols in the temple and the departure of the Shekinah glory cloud. The prophetic seer described Jehovah's preparation for judgment. Then Jerusalem was destroyed. Ezekiel prophesied against those nations who plundered Israel when she was helpless.

The final portion of Ezekiel's book brought hope. He predicted the coming Messiah who would deliver Israel. He predicted Israel's return to the land and her spiritual rebirth. He predicted the rebuilding of the temple, larger and more beautiful than the one just destroyed. He predicted the land would be reallocated geographically to the twelve tribes. Finally, Ezekiel described the future city of Jerusalem with its gates and beauty. But his greatest message was that the city would be known as *Jehovah-Shammah*: "the Lord is there" (Ezek. 48:35). The Shekinah glory of God that left the old Jerusalem would reside in the New Jerusalem.

FORTY-EIGHT

DANIEL:
The Years in Babylon
(Daniel)

The fall of Jerusalem was more than a political and religious calamity. It was in the lives of those transplanted to a foreign culture also a human tragedy. Yet in the midst of this disaster, there were individuals who demonstrated their faithfulness to God in the most unusual of circumstances. One of the most influential of those taken away into the Babylonian Captivity was a prophet and prince of Judah named Daniel. His life is unique in that it spans the entire period of that Captivity. His autobiographical account of that period has long been studied for its prophetic significance, but because of the prominent position held by Daniel throughout this period, it also provides significant insights into the political affairs of two of the world's greatest empires.

But Daniel is not always remembered today as a political counselor. Beyond his ability to influence the greatest leaders of his day was his ability to influence God. He was a man of unquestioned integrity and character. A survey of his life provides ample evidence that he was a man committed to a vital walk with God. His faithfulness and life of prayer has been a challenge to Christians in the midst of trials in all ages. He is unique in Scripture in that there is no sin charged against him. He was not sinless as he confessed his sin to God (Dan. 9:4). Yet his life was so blameless that even his enemies could only find him guilty of being consistent.

Daniel was among the most educated men in the Old Testament. Perhaps only Moses and Solomon had a more thorough training than this man. He had probably received some training in Judah before the Captivity. That he was selected among the first to be taken to Babylon suggests he had already begun his education before learning the ways of the Chaldeans. When the army of Babylon returned from their first conquest of Jerusalem, Daniel was a teenager taken prisoner.

Judah had turned from God to worship idols, so God gave His people what they thought they wanted. Babylon was the home of idolatry and would be the home of God's people for seventy years. It was during this Captivity that the Jews finally sickened of idol worship. When they left Babylon, they never again worshiped idols of wood and stone. But as they arrived, they would be immediately exposed to and encouraged to participate in the worship of the Babylonian gods. In keeping with the custom of the Babylonians, the Hebrew names of Daniel and his three companions were changed to names which honored Babylonian gods rather than the God of Israel.

CHANGING THE NAMES OF DANIEL AND HIS COMPANIONS

Daniel	God is my judge	Belteshazzar	May Bel protect his life
Hananiah	Jehovah is gracious	Shadrach	Command of Aku
Mishael	Who is what God is	Meshach	Who is what Aku is
Azariah	Jehovah has helped	Abed-nego	Servant of Nebo

When Daniel and his friend arrived in Babylon, they were placed in the custody of Ashpenaz, who is described as "the master of the king's eunuchs" (1:3). The Hebrew word translated "eunuchs" is *saris* and could mean either "court officer" or "castrated one." Commentators are divided in their opinions as to what the term means in this context. Those who believe Daniel was castrated by the Babylonians note that is what this word means in Isaiah 56:3 and is consistent with the claim of the Jewish historian Josephus. Those who disagree with this conclusion note Daniel is described as having no physical blemish (Dan. 1:4) and note the word is used of Potiphar, who was a court officer and was married (Gen. 37:36). The word was translated to mean "court officer" in the Targum rendering of Isaiah 39:7.

Though Daniel found himself in a foreign culture which was hostile to his faith in God, he determined not to lower the standard of his faith. He determined God was to be obeyed in Babylon as He was to be obeyed in Judah. It was not long before that personal religious conviction was to be tried.

Daniel was given food to eat which he could not in good conscience eat. There were probably at least three reasons for Daniel's actions. First, the food did not meet the requirements of the Mosaic Law. It may have been unclean by levitical standards or may not have been prepared according to regulations. Second, there was a problem with the wine. As a prince of Judah, Daniel was aware of the consequences of those in authority using wine and other intoxicating beverages (Prov. 31:4-5). Third, there is a strong likelihood that the food offered Daniel had first been offered to Babylonian idols. Eating the food under those circumstances would amount to a recognition of the Babylonian gods.

Daniel made an appeal to Ashpenaz, requesting he be exempted from eating the food he could not in good conscience eat. God had already brought Daniel into favor with the chief eunuch, but such a request could create problems for Ashpenaz if Daniel did not enjoy the good health the others enjoyed. As he explained why he could not grant Daniel's request, Daniel made a counteroffer. He asked that he be permitted to alter his diet for ten days and then Ashpenaz could evaluate the situation more completely. John Calvin believed Daniel made this counterproposal because God had given him a special revelation. Ashpenaz agreed and fed Daniel and his three friends vegetables rather than the wine and food consumed by the others. At the end of the test period, Daniel and his companions had better complexions than those who ate the king's food. While this may have been the result of the intervention of God, it might also have been the natural consequence of a healthier diet.

God honors those who honor Him (cf. 1 Sam. 2:30). "In all matters of wisdom and understanding about which the king examined them, he found them ten times better than all the magicians and astrologers who were in all his realm" (Dan. 1:20). Though they had been instructed in the religious beliefs of the Chaldeans, their deep and abiding faith in God resulted in their being able to discern between the true and false to a greater degree than those who were themselves supportive of that belief system. For three years they had been trained in the ways of the Chaldeans, but they had not abandoned the ways of God in the process. When the time of their evaluation came about, there was no question that they excelled the rest. Daniel suddenly found himself in the court of the most powerful ruler to have ever lived. For the rest of his life, Daniel would be a counselor of kings.

Though Nebuchadnezzr had many counselors, Daniel was unique in that he had a personal relationship with Jehovah. If God wanted to communicate to Nebuchadnezzar, there could hardly have been a better spokesman than Daniel. In fact, God did want to communicate to Nebuchadnezzar and did so through dreams. But Nebuchadnezzar needed men like Daniel and his companions to model their commitment to Jehovah and explain the meaning of the dreams God gave him. Daniel had not even finished his training course before he had to reveal the meaning of the king's first dream.

SUGGESTED CHRONOLOGY OF THE EARLY YEARS OF NEBUCHADNEZZAR AND DANIEL

May–June, 605 B.C.:
   Babylonian victory over the Egyptians at Carchemish.
June–August, 605 B.C.:
   Fall of Jerusalem to Nebuchadnezzar;
   Daniel and his companions taken captive.
September 7, 605 B.C. to Nisan (March-April) 604 B.C.:
   Year of accession of Nebuchadnezzar as king; first year of Daniel's training.

Nisan (March–April) 604 B.C. to Nisan
(March–April) 603 B.C.:
    First year of the reign of Nebuchadnezzar;
    second year of Daniel's training.
Nisan (March–April) 603 B.C. to Nisan
(March–April) 602 B.C.:
    Second year of the reign of Nebuchadnezzar; third
    year of Daniel's training; also the year of
    Nebuchadnezzar's dream.

Nebuchadnezzar dreamed a series of dreams that left him deeply troubled. There was something about a particular dream that caused the king to realize it was significant. He had wondered what the future held for his kingdom and couldn't help feeling the dream was related to the answer to his question (2:29). Because of this, the king consulted several classes of wise men to secure the interpretation of the dream.

THE WISE MEN OF BABYLON

1 Magicians (scholars) *(1:20; 2:2, 10, 27; 4:7; 5:11)*
2 Astrologers (enchanters) *(1:20; 2:2, 10, 27; 4:7;*
    5:7, 11, 15)
3 Sorcerers *(2:2)*
4 Chaldeans (astrologers) *(2:2, 10; 4:7; 5:7, 11)*
5 Soothsayers *(2:27; 4:7; 5:7, 11)*

When the king had gathered his wise men before him, he announced he had dreamed a dream. He had dreamed several dreams, but there was one in particular that seemed to trouble him. That was the dream he wanted his wise men to interpret. In the past these counselors had apparently interpreted other dreams, but this time Nebuchadnezzar was calling on them to do something different. He wanted them to not only tell him the meaning of the dream, but also to tell him the dream itself.

Commentators are not in agreement as to why Nebuchadnezzar did not tell his counselors the dream. Some argue he had forgotten the dream and could not tell the dream if he had wanted to do so. This view seems to be favored by most translators of this account, including the LXX. But there is some debate over the actual meaning of the rare Chaldean word *azda*. The word is unknown outside of this account and the etymology of the term is uncertain. Though the word could mean "I have forgotten," it could also mean "I have decreed." The fact that the counselors did not try to fake the dream supports the idea the dream was remembered by the king. If this were the case, it may be that the king felt the dream was so important as to not want to risk a false interpretation. He may have concluded the one who could first discern the dream could then discern the meaning of the dream. When his wise men claimed that could not be done, he was prepared to have them killed for their incompetence.

Daniel did not apparently learn about the meeting with the king until the king's men were on their way to kill the wise men. Again Daniel appealed to his Babylonian masters for time to resolve a problem. After consulting with his friends and praying that God would give them the dream and preserve their lives, Daniel received the king's dream in a night vision. When he spoke to the king subsequently, he attributed his success to the God of heaven. His reference to the God of heaven was an obvious contrast to the wise men who worshiped the heavens themselves. Though this is a common title of God in the later passages of Scripture (Ezra 1:2; 6:10; 7:12, 21; Neh. 1:5; 2:4; Ps. 136:26), it is a title first used of God by Abraham (Gen. 24:7). He further described God as the "God of my Fathers," suggesting Daniel saw his experience with God as one of obtaining His mercy as had the fathers in Israel's past.

The dream was of a large statue which outlined the course of world history in terms of four particular kingdoms. Babylon was represented in this dream by the head of gold on the image. A second kingdom of the Medes and Persians was symbolized by a chest and arms of silver. The third kingdom of Greece was represented in the dream by a bronze belly and thighs. The fourth kingdom was Rome as pictured by iron legs and feet of iron and clay (Dan. 2:31-33, 37-40).

In keeping with his previous promise, the king rewarded Daniel. First, he honored Daniel by recognizing his God as superior to others worshiped in Babylon. Though this was not saving faith in Jehovah as the only true God, it was the first of several steps to be taken by Nebuchadnezzar toward that conclusion. Then he honored Daniel by making him a chief administrator over the wise men of Babylon. Daniel responded by requesting similar honors for his companions who had prayed with him for the revelation of the dream. They were also granted important administrative positions in the kingdom (vv. 48-49).

No sooner had Daniel's companions received this honor than they were confronted with another trial of their faith. Probably inspired by the statue in his dream, Nebuchadnezzar erected a massive statue of gold. Perhaps he was attempting to predict his kingdom would be permanent and that the others would not follow. Depending on the size of a cubit, this statue was 90 to 110 feet high. By comparison, the colossus of Rome was 105 feet high. Thought it is called an "image of gold," its immense size suggests the statue may have been overlaid with gold. It was set up in the plain of Dura. About six miles south of the ancient city of Babylon, archeologists have identified a large brick construction 45 feet square and 20 feet high. It could have been a base or pedestal for the image.

Nebuchadnezzar commanded his people to worship the statue/idol at the sounding of the music. But the recently promoted companions of Daniel, Shadrach, Meshach, and Abed-nego, refused to compromise their convictions. Those who were jealous of the positions enjoyed by these three saw to it that the king learned about their violation of his new law (3:1-2).

The Hebrews were brought in before the king to face charges. They did not try to hide their guilt but rather confessed their faith in the ability of God to deliver them from the furnace, the penalty for not obeying the law. They added, however, that even if God should for some reason choose not to deliver them, they would not alter their commitment to God (vv. 13-18).

More than one writer has noted the absence of Daniel in this situation. The Scriptures are silent on the activities of Daniel at this time and several suggestions have been made to explain his absence. He may have been sick or away from Babylon at the time these events occurred. Some have even suggested Daniel's position in the kingdom exempted him from what amounted to an oath of allegiance.

The affirmation of their faith in God did not exempt Daniel's three friends from the prescribed penalty of the law. They were bound and cast into a furnace probably not too unlike a modern limekiln. The furnace was probably fueled with oil-treated charcoal (v. 21).

When Nebuchadnezzar looked into the furnace expecting to see three charred bodies, he was surprised to see four men walking, apparently oblivious to the discomfort of the flames. The only thing damaged by the flames was the rope that had bound them. In the heat of their trial, they had been joined by the Lord Himself. Most commentators believe the fourth Man in the furnace was a Christophany (v. 26).

Nebuchadnezzar had seen one of the most magnificent displays of God's love and protection of His people; yet he was still not yet willing to make Jehovah his God. He did, however, take another step in that direction. He now concluded "there is no other God who can deliver like this" (Dan. 3:29). That statement demonstrated the power of the testimony of these three men in the midst of their trial. They had a positive influence on the king in moving him closer to an understanding of the uniqueness of Jehovah.

God had demonstrated His power to Nebuchadnezzar in a couple of very unique ways, but still the king was slow to adopt the Lord as his God. The grandeur that was Babylon caused him to be proud of his accomplishments. It was his pride that hindered him from recognizing the Lord as his King of heaven. God could only reach Nebuchadnezzar when He had demonstrated His ability in humbling the proud.

Again God gave the Babylonian king a dream only Daniel could interpret. In his dream he saw an angel calling out to cut down a tree. The nature of the dream was such that it left the king terrified (4:4). Probably because of his previous experience with Daniel in the interpreting of dreams, Nebuchadnezzar appealed to him to interpret the dream for him. Daniel had proved to be a discerning man, so much so that his wisdom had become proverbial within his lifetime (cf. Ezek. 28:3).

It did not take Daniel long at all to understand the interpretation of the dream, but what he realized left him shaken. Nebuchadnezzar was the tree that God would cut down. By this time, Daniel had probably developed a good relationship with the king, and this was the kind of thing Daniel might wish on the king's enemies, but certainly not on his friend. His final message to Nebuchadnezzar was one of impending judgment. But even as Daniel warned the king of what was about to happen to him, he appealed to the king to repent and perhaps escape the judgment of God. Unfortunately, Daniel's appeal fell on deaf ears (Dan. 3:8-27).

It was a year before the dream became the experience of the Babylonian king. He was at that time admiring the city he had built. One of Nebuchadnezzar's principle concerns had been the building of Babylon. His hanging gardens were one of the Seven Wonders of the World. It was among the most beautiful cities of the world. As one reads of the splendor of Babylon in those days, it is easy to see how the king could be consumed with pride in his accomplishment. Yet on this occasion, even as he congratulated himself for his many accomplishments, God did what He needed to do to humble the proud (vv. 28-32).

Nebuchadnezzar was apparently struck with some kind of madness which caused him to live like an animal. There are at least three kinds of madness which could account for the symptoms Nebuchadnezzar experienced and his subsequent behavior pattern. These include *Boanthropy, Lycanthropy,* and *Insania Zoanthropica.* Each of thse conditions involves a person who appears to think of himself as an animal and adopts the behaviorial patterns of that animal (v. 33).

The king remained in this mental state until he came to the place where he recognized God for who He was. Only when that occurred was his reason restored to him. He was then apparently returned to a place of influence in the kingdom and issued his testimony in the form of a proclamation throughout the land. The man who had taken the people of God as his captives eventually entered into his own personal relationship with God (vv. 34-37).

God had used Babylon as His instrument of judgment in judging His people, but Babylon could not escape their own judgment for sin. As great as the kingdom of Babylon was, it too would fall. But unlike the fall of Jerusalem, which took eighteen months, the fall of Babylon occurred in a single night. God revealed the coming judgment on the land one evening and by morning it had been accomplished.

The night Babylon fell, Belshazzar, the grandson of Nebuchadnezzar and co-regent of Babylon with his father, was hosting a feast with more than a thousand guests. Though it was not customary for women to be present on such occasions, they were present that night. The combination of wine and women at Belshazzar's feast suggests various immoral practices were taking place in the great banquet hall that evening. This was a normal part of the worship of Bel and other Babylonian deities. The festivities continued to degenerate until Belshazzar ordered that the gold and silver vessels taken from the temple in Jerusalem be brought out and used in the festivities. In the course of his feast, Belshazzar would drink toasts to the honor of Bel and the other gods of Babylon. To do so using vessels devoted to the worship of Jehovah was a challenge that could not be ignored by God. He would act in such a dramatic way as to sober the drunken guests at the feast and stress the serious nature of sin. Belshazzar had initiated the challenge and God accepted (5:1-4).

Suddenly, a hand appeared and began writing on the wall. The king immediately recognized the significance of such an event, but did not know what it meant. "Then the king's countenance changed, and his thoughts troubled him, so that the joints of his hips were loosened and his knees knocked against each other" (v. 6). In his terror, he called out for the occult counselors he had so often consulted, but they could not interpret the meaning of this sign. "Then King Belshazzar was greatly troubled, his countenance was changed, and his lords were astonished" (v. 9).

Word soon spread throughout the city of the king's dilemma. On hearing of the problem, the queen made her way to the banquet hall with advice for the troubled king. This "queen" is thought by many commentators to have been Nitocris, the daughter of Nebuchadnezzar, the wife of Nabonidus, and mother of Belshazzar. In describing Daniel's unique gifts, the queen mother used the same phrases Nebuchadnezzar had used (cf. vv. 11-12; 4:8-9, 18). This suggests she may have often heard her father speak of Daniel in this way and had probably witnessed firsthand the prophet's ability to resolve this kind of problem.

Daniel was summoned by Belshazzar and asked to interpret the writing that had appeared on the wall. As a reward, Daniel was offered the position of "the third ruler in the kingdom" (5:16). Belshazzar himself was only the second ruler, reigning with his father. Therefore, this offer would place Daniel next to the kings in power.

Normally, Belshazzar's reward would be an attractive offer. But in light of the contents of the handwriting, being third ruler of a kingdom God was about to judge did not have a great appeal to Daniel. Daniel offered to interpret the writing but urged the king to keep his reward. He began by reminding Belshazzar about God by using the title Most High God to describe Him (v. 18). The emphasis of this particular name of God is that of His possession of heaven and earth. The glory of Babylon had been given to Nebuchadnezzar by God and was about to be taken away by the same God. Then he addressed the matter of the inscription on the wall.

MENE, MENE, TEKEL, UPHARSIN

The message God had sent the Babylonians consisted of three Aramaic words. The word *mene* was repeated twice for emphasis and means " to number." The word *tekel* is based on the verb *tekal,* meaning "to weigh." The final word in this writing was a plural form of the verb *peres,* meaning "to divide." God's message to Babylon was that the kingdom had been morally evaluated by God and found lacking. As a result, the kingdom would be removed from them and given to the Medes and Persians.

Belshazzar was satisfied the message had been accurately interpreted and gave Daniel the reward he had promised him. A gold chain was placed around the prophet's neck and a royal purple robe was draped over his shoulders. A proclamation was issued making Daniel the third ruler of the nation. But his term of office would be extremely short. That same evening, a sixty-two-year-old general named Darius the Mede led his troops into the city and took control of the greatest nation on earth. Other accounts of the fall of Babylon confirm the Euphrates River had been temporarily diverted to a new channel allowing Darius and his army to enter the city underneath the wall by way of the riverbed. Because of the great size of the city, those in the outer parts were overcome before others in the center of the city even realized an invasion was taking place. According to Herodotus, the festivities continued at Belshazzar's feast as the city was conquered.

Despite the fact that Daniel had been promoted to the position of third ruler of the kingdom by the time of the fall of Babylon, Darius chose to include him in a major administrative position in his new government. The new kingdom was divided into 120 provinces with rulers responsible for the administration of each. These 120 individuals were accountable to three governors of whom Daniel was the first. "Then this Daniel distinguished himself above the governors and satraps, because an excellent spirit was in him; and the king gave thought to setting him over the whole realm" (6:3).

As is often the case, Daniel's finding favor with the new administration resulted in others becoming jealous. A group of governors and satraps conspired together in an attempt to discredit Daniel before Darius, but they were unsuccessful. His faithfulness to his superiors was beyond question. Because they could not find fault with Daniel, they chose to create a situation in which Daniel would be bound to offend his superiors.

This group suggested to King Darius the writing of a special law to demonstrate the great admiration and respect they had for their ruler. The law called for a total ban on making petitions to any god or man except the king for thirty days. It was a common practice in ancient kingdoms for people to see the head of state as a god, or at least a special messenger from the gods. When the plan was presented to the king, he liked the idea and signed it into law. The kingdom was made up of two groups of peoples, the Medes and the Persians, who didn't trust each other. Therefore, when a law was made, it couldn't be changed by either side. Hence, the law of the Medes and the Persians was ironclad.

As had been his lifelong custom, Daniel continued praying three times daily during this period. As soon as the conspirators had their evidence, they presented it to the king. Darius tried his best to have Daniel exempted somehow from the penalty of the law, but Daniel's enemies were quick to remind the king that a law in the society of the Medes and the Persians couldn't be revoked. Reluctantly, Darius commanded that Daniel be placed in the lions' den. But even as he did so, he expressed his deepest hope to Daniel. "Your God, whom you serve continually, He will deliver you" (v. 16).

When Darius went to the den of lions the next morning, Daniel was there, unharmed in any way. Daniel was released and his accusers and their families took his place in the den of lions. As they were thrown into the pit, the lions caught them in the air and tore their bodies apart.

PERSPECTIVE

Like the first foreign ruler whom Daniel had served, Darius came to recognize the uniqueness of Daniel's God. A decree was issued throughout the land calling on people to "tremble and fear before the God of Daniel. For He is the living God, and steadfast forever" (Dan. 6:26). "So this Daniel prospered in the reign of Darius and in the reign of Cyrus the Persian" (v. 28).

FORTY-NINE

FIVE LEADERS:
Their Responsiblity for the Return of the Jews

(Ezra; Haggai; Zechariah)

Jeremiah had warned the people God would send them into Captivity, but he had also promised them they would only be in Captivity seventy years (Jer. 25:11-12). As that seventy-year period came to a close, many of the Jews had become so comfortable in their new homeland they had no desire to return. Still, God would honor His Word. Among the leaders of the Gentiles, God raised up five servants to lead His people back to the land to rebuild the temple.

The five leaders were (1) Zerubbabel, who led the captives back to the land and was appointed governor; (2) Jeshua, the high priest, who came with Zerubbabel and set up the altar and reinstituted the sacrifices; (3) Cyrus, king of Persia, who signed a decree sending the Jews to their land; (4) Haggai, the prophet whose preaching motivated the completion of the construction of the temple; and (5) Zechariah, the prophet who assisted in building the temple but also predicted the coming of the Messiah who would inhabit the land and temple.

Cyrus was an unusual choice for God to call His shepherd, and one of the few predicted by name before he was born (Isa. 45:1). This Gentile leader led Persia to conquer Babylon in 539 B.C. and the next year issued his famous decree urging the Jews to return to Jerusalem. So significant was this decree in the life of God's people that it is twice recorded in the

Scriptures. "Thus says Cyrus king of Persia: 'All the kingdoms of the earth the Lord God of heaven has given me. And He has commanded me to build Him a house at Jerusalem which is in Judah. Who is there among you of all His people? May the Lord his God be with him, and let him go up!' " (2 Chron. 36:23; Ezra 1:2-3)

As one reads the biblical account of this decree without understanding the background of the times, one might come to the conclusion that Cyrus was a Gentile believer. Actually, if Cyrus did in fact believe in the Lord, he probably viewed Jehovah as a tribal deity unique to the Jews. There was a time when critical scholars disputed the likelihood that a Persian ruler would issue the kind of decree recorded in Scripture, but the discovery of "The Cylinder of Cyrus" has resolved that question. This large clay monument records a similar decree by Cyrus revealing a unique aspect of domestic policy in the Persian empire.

Cyrus apparently felt the conquered peoples of his empire were less likely to promote unrest if they were allowed to live in their homeland and maintain their religious and cultural heritage. Also, they would be productive on their farms and he could tax them. He presented himself to his people as a deliverer sent by the gods to return them to their homes. Apparently, he issued a number of decrees similar to the one affecting the Jews and, in each case, chose to identify with the god of the people involved. God used a natural movement of people to carry out His prophecy, demonstrating again how supernatural purposes were accomplished through natural means.

Zerubbabel had a Babylonian name meaning "seed of Babylon." He is identified as the son of Shealtiel (Hag. 1:14) and the son of Pedaiah (1 Chron. 3:19). Shealtiel had no children and adopted (by levirate marriage) Zerubbabel to have his rights of sonship. He was recognized as the legal heir of the throne of David (Matt. 1:12; Luke 3:27).

Zerubbabel was also Sheshbazzar (a title, not a name), who was commissioned by Cyrus to be governor of Judah. He received from Cyrus the Jews' temple vessels for sacrifice that had been in warehouses in Persia. Zerubbabel brought these to Jerusalem where the sacrifices were reintroduced. In addition to the gold, silver, and money Zerubbabel received from Cyrus, he took up an offering from prosperous Jews who were not returning. Just as contemporary Jews in the twentieth century paid for other Jews to repopulate modern Israel, the same thing happened in 536 B.C.

Jeshua, whose name was a derivative of Joshua (Jehovah saves), was the head of the levitical house who reinstituted the sacrifice, hence becoming the high priest. He had the actual oversight of building the second temple and later read the Word of God to the people, which led to a revival.

When given the opportunity to return, comparatively few Jews decided to do so. Life had become comfortable for them in the Captivity; many had roots in the community and did not want to disturb their lifestyle. Still, a number did return. In all, some 50,000 people made that first trip back to the land God had promised to Abraham. This number included about 7,000 servants.

After seventy years in a foreign land, it felt good to be going home. Some of the older members of their group could still remember Jerusalem as it had been before the fall. Others had only heard the stories of their parents and grandparents of the splendor of Solomon's temple and the royal palace. Those returning were those who had a desire to return. Now they were experiencing the fulfillment of their dreams. As they traveled from Babylon to Jerusalem, they probably talked often with each other about their feelings. From time to time, they sang individually or as a group. Fifteen psalms called "The Psalms of Ascents" are thought to have been sung by the remnant as they returned (cf. Pss. 120–134). Though at least five of these psalms had been written by former kings of Israel, some may have been composed on the journey home or even in Babylon as the remnant prepared for the journey home.

For over fifty years there had been no sacrifice in Jerusalem (since 586 B.C.). Seven months after leaving Babylon, the remnant was going to change all that. An altar was built in Jerusalem and burnt offerings were made as required by the

Law of Moses. The first of the major feasts of Israel to be celebrated by the remnant after they returned was the Feast of Tabernacles. This annual feast in the fall was given by God to remind them of the forty years Israel had dwelt in tents. Before long other special days were honored and the evening and morning offerings were being offered regularly. "But the foundation of the temple of the Lord had not yet been laid" (Ezra 3:6). There was no temple to symbolize that corporate worship was reestablished. There were no walls around Jerusalem to symbolize the nation was reconstructed.

In his decree urging the Jews to return to their homeland and build the temple, Cyrus had made a point of encouraging those Jews who chose not to return to contribute to the cause financially. The Persian king himself had contributed to the cause by returning to the prince of Judah the original vessels of the temple taken by Nebuchadnezzar. Even those who had returned had invested in the building of the temple financially. Still, the foundation of Israel's second temple would not be laid for another eight months.

"Now in the second month of the second year of their coming to the house of God at Jerusalem . . . the builders laid the foundation of the temple of the Lord" (vv. 8, 10). As the people gathered in Jerusalem that day there was much singing. The theme of their song focused on the goodness of God and His enduring mercy (cf. Ps. 136:1). It was a day of mixed emotions for those present. Some who had seen the former temple realized this second temple would not be as spectacular as that built by Solomon. They wept as they thought again of all they had lost. But for others, the building of this second temple was a step in the right direction. They shouted loudly for joy as they saw the foundation laid, anticipating it would not be long before they could worship God in the temple. Between the weeping and singing, the mourning and shouting, it was difficult to discern all that was being said and done. Those who heard the celebration in the distance heard a loud noise, but it was not clear from the noise itself what was taking place in Jerusalem. All that was certain was that something had excited the Jews (Ezra 3:8-13).

When the Jews returned to the land, they were not the only ones present. Soon the Samaritans were offering their assistance in building the temple. But Jeshua and Zerubbabel realized that the place of worship *of* the Jews should be built *by* the Jews, and so declined the offer. When the Samaritans' offer of help was turned down, they were offended and decided to do what they could to discourage the work of rebuilding. They hired counselors to argue against the project to the Persian authorities. Finally they convinced King Artaxerxes that allowing the Jews to rebuild the temple was to invite an insurrection on the part of a people with a long history of resisting foreign rulers. When a letter from Artaxerxes was received in Samaria agreeing that the Jews should be forced to cease building, the Samaritans "went up in haste to Jerusalem against the Jews, and by force of arms made them cease" (Ezra 4:23).

For sixteen years, the work on the temple ceased. Despite the fact that Cyrus, a Persian monarch, had issued an immutable decree endorsing the reconstruction of Jerusalem and the temple, the Samaritans intimidated the Jews into abandoning their noble task. The sacrifices were still offered on the altar and feasts observed with regularity, but construction was completely halted on the temple. While weeds grew among the foundation stones of the second temple, the people built their homes and developed their farms, growing accustomed to less than they had hoped for when they left Babylon to return to the land. Day after day life continued without thought of renewing the work they had begun with such zeal. Days grew into weeks and weeks into months. Then, after sixteen years, something different happened in Jerusalem.

"Then the Prophet Haggai and Zechariah the son of Iddo, prophets, prophesied to the Jews who were in Judah and Jerusalem, in the name of the God of Israel, who was over them" (5:1). Throughout the kingdom of Persia, there were many nationalistic movements beginning. For the next several years, Persian authorities would be busy dealing with one revolution after another. None of these uprisings was successful. The perceived weakness of the Persian administration did not exist. But what was taking place in Jerusalem was different than the patriotic uprisings in other parts of the kingdom.

The Prophet Haggai has been called the most successful prophet of all time; yet for all he accomplished, he is something of a mystery. One commentator affirms he was young as he began preaching; another is certain he was an old man. Some writers believe the prophet had been in Jerusalem for some time and finally spoke out in frustration at sixteen years of inactivity. Yet another claims he had only recently arrived in the city with a second group of Jews from the Babylonian Captivity. Some claimed he was a priest; another said he was not. All that can be known about the prophet with any degree of certainty is contained in the brief account of his second recorded sermon. "Then Haggai, the Lord's messenger, spoke the Lord's message to the people, saying, 'I am with you, says the Lord' " (Hag. 1:13). One suspects the prophet might have simply described himself as "nobody important with a message from the Lord." He knew much could be done for God by those who were not concerned with who got the credit.

Five times this prophet stood before the people to deliver the message that God had given him. Sometimes it was a message of rebuke designed to shake them out of their complacency into aggressive service for God. At other times, the prophet was there to encourage the faithful as they began a seemingly impossible task. The heart of his preaching is preserved in a book which bears his name. It contains only thirty-eight verses and is one of the shortest books of the Bible. But the message of Haggai did something that had never been done before. It moved a nation of apathetic Jews to build a temple to the glory of God.

HAGGAI

1	First message	Stewardship *(1:1-11)*
2	Second message	Encouragement *(vv. 12-15)*
3	Third message	Hope *(2:1-9)*
4	Fourth message	Holiness *(vv. 10-19)*
5	Fifth message	Messianic expectation *(vv. 20-23)*

Haggai was not alone in preaching to the people at this time. A contemporary of his was the Prophet Zechariah. This prophet was also concerned about the temple of God, but his preaching went beyond the immediate problem of renewing the work on the temple. He related visions, messages, and burdens from God concerning not only the temple, but also the One who would someday teach in that temple. He spoke of the coming Saviour in both His rejection and His reigning.

ZECHARIAH

---

1 Zion's sanctuary (8 Visions) *(1–6)*
2 Zion's services (4 Visions) *(7–8)*
3 Zion's saviour (2 Burdens) *(9–14)*
    A. Rejected *(9–11)*
    B. Reigning *(12–14)*

"So Zerubbabel the son of Shealtiel and Jeshua the son of Jozadak rose up and began to build the house of God which is in Jerusalem; and the prophets of God were with them, helping them" (Ezra 5:2). Of course there was still opposition to the work by neighboring peoples, but this time the Jews would not be intimidated. Again a letter was sent off to the Persian rulers, but this time the answer was different. Darius, a new ruler, called for a search of the archives to determine what had been decided earlier concerning the matter. In the process of that research, a copy of the original decree of Cyrus was found. Darius determined to enforce the terms of that initial ruling. "So the elders of the Jews built, and they prospered through the prophesying of Haggai the prophet and Zechariah the son of Iddo. And they built and finished it, according to the commandment of the God of Israel, and according to the command of Cyrus, Darius, and Artaxerxes king of Persia" (6:14).

If the beginning of the temple construction had been a cause for celebration, it was more so concerning its completion. When compared to Solomon's temple, the smaller frame building that stood in the city was rather insignificant in appearance. Years later the rabbis would lament the fact it never had the

Shekinah glory cloud of God descend on it as on the first temple. But this temple would have an even greater glory. The prophet had promised that God would not only visit it in His presence, but in His person. As the people celebrated the Passover in Jerusalem that year, they may not have comprehended the implications of Haggai's prophecy, but they rejoiced in the presence of a house of worship. "And they kept the Feast of Unleavened Bread seven days with joy; for the Lord made them joyful" (6:22).

PERSPECTIVE

For seventy years, Israel had been in Babylon as captives. But in God's timing, leaders were raised up to accomplish God's will in bringing a remnant back to the land and reestablishing religious and civic aspects of Jewish society. But some chose not to be a part of that remnant. They had grown comfortable in Babylon and were reluctant to give up their present lifestyle for something better God had in store for them. Christians today need to be careful not to be so comfortable with a materialistic lifestyle that they are unwilling to respond to the Lord's leading in their lives.

FIFTY

ESTHER:
The Saving of a Nation
(Esther)

For the Jews who chose not to return to Judah, life was good most of the time. Most had established their homes and businesses and were part of the community in which they lived. Because of the cosmopolitan character of the kingdom, it was not thought strange that these Jews chose to meet on the Sabbath and read from the Law of Moses. There was a degree of tolerance for varied religious expressions in that pluralistic society. There was, as has often been the case in societies throughout history, an undercurrent of anti-Semitism; but law and order was important to the Medes and Persians, and the physical security of the Jews did not seem to be threatened in any way. That was the case most of the time, until the day a strange decree began appearing throughout the land (Es. 3:7-15; 9:1).

What made the decree a matter of concern for the Jews was that it affected them most directly. On the thirteenth day of Adar, the people in every province of the kingdom were granted permission to kill and annihilate all the Jews and confiscate their possessions. The decree was signed by the king and that meant there was no way it could be changed. For thousands of Jews throughout the kingdom, their fate appeared settled. There seemed to be no way to prevent the inevitable. What they did not realize was that God had taken steps years earlier to stop this planned extermination of His people.

Years earlier, a young girl had been born to a Jewish couple living in or near Shushan. Shortly after her birth, both of her parents died. Her cousin, a man named Mordecai, adopted young Hadassah as his own daughter and raised her to become a beautiful young lady. Like most fathers, he wanted the best for his little girl. It might be supposed he thought of her someday marrying a leader in his community, but it is doubtful if he could have imagined the circumstances that would result in Hadassah becoming the queen of the kingdom (2:5-7).

From time to time, King Ahasuerus would entertain visiting officials from his 127 provinces. But three years into his reign, he gathered all of his leading officials together for an incredible time of celebration. For 180 days there was an exhibition of the immense wealth and splendor of the king and his kingdom. To conclude the exhibition, the king hosted a banquet lasting 7 days. The finest decorations adorned the hall, and an abundance of food and wine was available. On the seventh day of the feast, the king brought about a confrontation (1:1-8).

While the king had hosted the banquet for the men, his wife Queen Vashti had hosted a similar feast for the women in the palace. She was probably in another banquet hall with a group of women when several men arrived with a message for her. The king wanted to show off her beauty to the officials he had gathered. Normally, it was a great honor for a queen to be invited into the presence of the king, but Vashti refused to go.

Ahasuerus was furious. Not much could have been more embarrassing than to have his own wife refuse to come at his request. This was especially embarrassing in light of the recent exhibition of his splendor and the presence of so many key leaders in his kingdom. The influence of alcohol probably did not diminish his anger in any way. He knew he had to respond to this situation decisively to minimize the damage that had been done. After consultation with several of his advisors, he determined to banish Vashti from his presence and find another to replace her as queen (vv. 13-22).

A search was initiated to find a young and beautiful replacement for the queen. Many promising candidates were brought into the palace at Shushan and placed in the care of Hegai until the selection would be made. Hadassah was among those selected, but on the advice of Mordecai, she did not reveal her Jewish background. She changed her Jewish name to Esther (v. 10).

Each of the girls selected possessed a physical beauty that made her naturally attractive to men, but nothing was being taken for granted in this contest. For a complete year the women were treated with oils and perfumes to enhance their attractiveness. Only then were they brought into the presence of the king. If on that occasion he was not sufficiently impressed to remember a woman's name, that would be the last time she and the king would meet. As the selection process continued, Esther soon became the favored choice of both the king and others who met her. A feast was held to recognize the selection of the new queen and Esther began wearing the royal crown (2:17). About the time she became queen, Mordecai learned of a plot against the king and sent word by way of Esther. The conspirators were captured and hanged and the incident was duly recorded in the chronicles of the king (vv. 21-23).

Some time after the coronation of Esther, a man named Haman was promoted in the administration of the king. Because of his closeness to the king, it was customary for others to bow before him. Around the palace, such a response to Haman was commonplace. But because of his religious convictions, Mordecai refused to bow or pay him homage. Haman was infuriated at Mordecai's response. It was not enough just to get back at Mordecai for his perceived disrespect: Haman determined to annihilate the whole race of Jews to which Mordecai belonged (3:1-7).

At the palace in Shushan, Mordecai did what many Jews were doing throughout the nation. Word soon got to Esther that he was in sackcloth and mourning, so she responded by sending him more presentable clothes. Only then was Mordecai able to communicate with her concerning the danger to the Jews. He urged her to use her influence with the king to help her people, but she argued it had been a month since she had even seen the king (4:1-17).

"Then Mordecai told them to answer Esther: 'Do not think in your heart that you will escape in the king's palace any more than all the other Jews. For if you remain completely silent at this time, relief and deliverance will arise for the Jews from another place, but you and your father's house will perish. Yet who knows whether you have come to the kingdom for such a time as this?' " (vv. 13-14) In response to Mordecai's appeal, Esther agreed to risk her own life to save her people. She asked, however, that the Jews fast with her for three days before she made her appeal to the king.

When Esther entered the presence of the king, he was receptive to her coming and asked her to make her request. She simply invited the king and Haman to a private dinner she had prepared. After the meal, the king again asked her to make her request. She promised to do so if Haman and the king would return the next night for a similar dinner (5:1-8).

As Haman left the palace that night, he was happy. He considered his being invited to dinner with the king and queen among the greatest of the many honors he had received. But as he saw Mordecai at the king's gate, "he was filled with indignation." Though he had set things in motion to finally rid himself of that man, Haman could not wait. On arriving home, he shared his mixed emotions with his family and friends. They rejoiced in the favor he seemed to have found with the queen, but also understood the frustration he felt over Mordecai. They agreed the best way to deal with the problem was to have Mordecai hung on a gallows the next day; then Haman could enjoy the banquet with the king and queen. The idea made a lot of sense to Haman, "so he had the gallows made" (vv. 12-14).

The king was having a restless night and thought a boring book might help him sleep. He called on one of his servants to read "the book of the records of the chronicles." Apparently, the book did not have the desired effect. The king listened to account after account of the things that had occurred in the kingdom. Eventually the servant came to an account of the attempted coup that had been thwarted. When he heard the servant read how Mordecai had uncovered the plot against his life, he asked what kind of reward Mordecai had received. As the servant acknowledged Mordecai had not been rewarded, the king heard a commotion in an outer room (6:1-5).

Haman arrived to make a special request. He wanted to suggest the king hang Mordecai on the gallows he had prepared. But before he could make his request, the king asked Haman for his advice concerning how the king could honor a particular man he, the king, wanted to honor. Thinking the king was talking about him, Haman suggested parading the man through the streets of the city in a royal robe with royal honors. The king liked the idea and ordered Haman to do it for Mordecai (vv. 6-10).

By the time Haman had completed that assignment, he did not want to be seen in public. When he told his wife and advisors what had happened, they warned him he would fall before Mordecai since the man was a Jew. Even as they discussed the matter, men from the palace arrived to take Haman to his private dinner with the king and queen (v. 14).

Over dinner, the king again asked Esther to make her request. She did so, asking that the king act to preserve her people the Jews from the planned annihilation. When the king asked who would even presume to take such a course of action, Esther responded, "The adversary and enemy is this wicked Haman!" (7:6)

The king rose from the table in anger and stepped out into the garden, apparently to cool down. Haman, terrified of the king's wrath, began pleading for his life. As the king stepped back into the room, Haman fell across the couch where Esther was. The king interpreted what he saw as an attempted assault on Esther by Haman. Then one of the king's servants noted the presence of the gallows Haman had built to hang the man who had saved the king's life. "So they hanged Haman on the gallows that he had prepared for Mordecai" (v. 10).

The death of Haman did not insure the security of the Jews. The king was prepared to take action. Mordecai was given Haman's position in the kingdom and Esther was encouraged to write another decree in the king's name. The previous decree could not be rescinded, but the second decree called on the Jews to join together to protect their lives and property, and to take the lives and property of those who attacked them. When the day came for the two decrees to be enforced, over 75,000 enemies of the Jews fell. Following the victory, the Jews in Shushan gathered together to celebrate. The Jews still celebrate that victory today in their annual Feast of Purim.

PERSPECTIVE

The Book of Esther does not include the name of God or Jehovah. One reason was because the book was written to the Jews who remained in the Dispersion and did not return to the Holy Land. They had to learn to live where the name of Elohim and Jehovah were not mentioned. Yet the Jews of the Dispersion, like those in the Book of Esther, were influenced in several ways by God. The Jews were reminded of their Hebrew heritage, their awareness of Jehovah's presence in their lives and specifically, the constant threat of anti-Semitism among the Gentiles. God had promised Abraham there would be those who would persecute his seed, but they would be punished (Gen. 12:3).

Jewish tradition, specifically in the Talmud, asks, "Where do we get the Law in Esther?" They answer Deuteronomy 31:18, "And I will surely hide My face." Because of their sins, God hides His face from the Jews. The two contemporary Books of Ezra and Nehemiah used the divine title "the God of heaven." But in Esther the Median king is mentioned 192 times.

However, when God hides His face, He can be found by those who seek Him. There are five ruberic appearances of God's name in Esther. His name appears in acrostic in Esther 1:20; 5:4, 13; 7:7; and the fifth is the "I AM" found in 7:5. While the Jewish writers hid many different acrostics in the Hebrew text of the Psalms, the name of God is the only acrostic in Esther. Whereas the English reader may miss God's name, the readers of the Jewish Age did not. In the Masora and three other ancient manuscripts, the acrostic letters for God are written *majuscular* (larger than the rest), so the Lord stands out boldly and prominently.

Because the name of Jehovah is not apparently included, some have suggested Esther should not be in the canon of Scripture. But in no other book is the providence of God more conspicuous. To the Jews who remained in the more-lucrative Babylon, God would not forsake His covenant to His people.

FIFTY-ONE

NEHEMIAH:
The Rebuilding of the Walls
(Nehemiah)

Just because certain of the Jews chose not to return to the land of promise with the remnant did not mean they were not interested in what was taking place in Judah. From time to time groups and individuals would travel from their homes across the fertile crescent to Judah for an extended visit. When they met their fellow Jews on their return home, someone was bound to ask how things were in Judah. At times the question was asked simply to show interest in the person's trip, but more often there was a genuine desire to learn more about the land God had promised Abraham and the city David had made his capital.

This was the situation in the city of Shushan when a civil servant named Nehemiah met a group who had just returned from Judah. Naturally he asked about the situation in Jerusalem. What he learned was discouraging. He was told, "The survivors who are left from the Captivity in the province are there in great distress and reproach. The wall of Jerusalem is also broken down, and its gates are burned with fire" (Neh. 1:3). There was a temple to gather the Jews spiritually, but there was no city around which they could rally politically and nationally.

Though Nehemiah had apparently never been to Jerusalem, news of the condition of the city of David moved him deeply.

For four months Nehemiah spent time praying and fasting about the situation. So emotionally distraught was he over the news that he often mourned and wept as he prayed. He understood that the Captivity had happened to his people as a result of their sin as a nation. But he also understood God had promised to restore the nation if it repented. While he continued to serve in the royal court, he began to think of something practical he could do.

After four months, the king noticed Nehemiah looked sad one day and asked about the problem. In fear, Nehemiah briefly explained his concern about the condition of his homeland. When the king asked what he wanted done, Nehemiah explained his plan. He asked to be relieved of his duties in the palace to return and build the city wall. Further, he gave the king a list of the supplies he anticipated needing and an approximate schedule as to how long the project would take. Soon Nehemiah had his supplies and letters of passage and was on his way to Jerusalem.

Some believe this king of Persia, Artaxerxes, was the grandson of Esther and Ahasuerus (Xerxes). If this is true, the king would have some understanding of the desire of the Jews to preserve their culture and migrate back to the land promised them.

Nehemiah's first concern when he got to Jerusalem was to make a personal assessment of the condition of the walls. Three days after arriving, he took a few men with him on a tour of the walls one evening. At that time, no one in the city had been told specifically what Nehemiah intended to do. Carefully, he went from place to place to assess the damage and get a better idea of what needed to be done to rebuild the wall. Only after making his inspection did he share his burden with the officials of the city and challenge them to join him in this task. "Then they set their hands to do this good work" (2:18).

Building a wall around the city of Jerusalem was a task that could only be accomplished if many workers agreed to work together. Nehemiah gave different families different parts of the wall to build. First the rubble had to be removed so the workers could get to the walls. Then repairs were made by each worker .in the section of the wall assigned to him. Together, the people began to lay stone on stone, and a wall began to rise around the city.

Not everyone rejoiced to see the project progress. Among those who opposed the rebuilding project were two men, an Horonite named Sanballat and an Ammonite official named Tobiah. When they learned of the project, they laughed, mocking the Jews for what they intended to do. As work began, they ridiculed the idea, suggesting a wall could not be built around the city. Then as the wall began to rise, they ridiculed the quality of the wall, claiming it would fall if so much as a fox ran across it. Then as the wall approached completion, these men plotted to attack the city and create confusion.

Nehemiah led the people to continue building the wall in the face of both ridicule and threats. As each challenge faced him, he took the situation to the Lord in prayer. When it appeared an attack on the city might be a real possibility, Nehemiah had his people working with both their tools and weapons handy. They were at all times prepared for both building and battle.

But the threats of Sanballat and Tobiah were not the only problems Nehemiah encountered in rebuilding the wall. Many of the people were deeply in debt and having difficulty securing the basic necessities of life. The rulers of the people were taking advantage of the unfortunate situation and that made the problem even more severe. When Nehemiah heard of the problem, he challenged the morality of the rulers' business practices. Because he had not taxed the people as he had every right to, Nehemiah could speak to the rulers with authority. They agreed to restore the mortgaged properties back to the people and bring an end to their practice of usury.

Even as the final stages of the work were being completed, Nehemiah encountered subtle forms of opposition. First, Sanballat and Tobiah tried to distract Nehemiah from the work by inviting him to meet with them in another city. When continued attempts along this line failed, they issued a slanderous letter claiming Nehemiah was building the wall to enhance his political ambitions. On another occasion, they hired a religious leader to try to talk Nehemiah into hiding in the temple to escape a possible threat on his life. Constantly, there were letters being exchanged between Tobiah and those close to Nehemiah. Nehemiah recalled, "Also they reported his good deeds before me, and reported my words to him. And Tobiah sent letters to frighten me" (6:19).

Nehemiah persisted in the task of rebuilding the walls in spite of the varied opposition he encountered. Because the people worked together and had adopted the task as their own, the wall was completed in fifty-two days. "And it happened, when all our enemies heard of it, and all the nations around us saw these things, that they were very disheartened in their own eyes; for they perceived that this work was done by our God" (v. 16).

OPPOSITION TO THE REBUILDING OF THE WALLS

---

1 Ridicule *(4:1-3)*
2 Discouragement *(vv. 10-12)*
3 Financial bondage *(5:1-5)*
4 Subtlety *(6:1-4)*
5 Slander (vv. 5-7)
6 False Counselors *(vv. 10, 19)*

As important as the work of rebuilding the wall of Jerusalem was to the city, Nehemiah would see God do a greater work in that city before he returned to Shushan. One of those who had returned to the city of Jerusalem in a later migration from the Captivity was a scribe named Ezra. Even when the Jews were living in Captivity, Ezra had spent much time studying the Law of Moses. He was perhaps the one who best understood the Law and its implications on the lives of those who lived according to its precepts.

As the seventh month of the Jewish calendar came around, there were several feasts the people were called to gather together for in the city of Jerusalem. The first of these was the Feast of Trumpets. As the people came to Jerusalem for that feast, they gathered by the Water Gate and asked Ezra to read to them from the Law. Ezra, together with over a dozen others, agreed to read the Law and did so all morning. "So they read distinctly from the book, in the Law of God; and they gave the sense, and helped them to understand the reading" (8:8). This was more than reading the Law to the people. He explained its meaning to them. As a result of Ezra's teaching ministry, there was a revival among God's people remembered as the post-Captivity revival.

This was one of the most significant of all the revivals among the people of God in the Old Testament. Solomon had taught the criteria for revival: "If My people who are called by My name will humble themselves, and pray and seek My face, and turn from their wicked ways" (2 Chron. 7:14). Whether these were the foundation for revival or the result of revival, a number of very difficult social issues were resolved. The Jews discontinued mixed congregations (Neh. 13:1, 3) and mixed marriages (vv. 23-31). Sabbath observance was restored (vv. 15-22) and the practice of tithing was reinstituted (vv. 11-12).

Though the remnant would still need to be challenged in these and other areas in the days to come, this renewal of faith which came as the result of the preaching of Ezra may have had at least one consequence which has endured to this day. According to Jewish tradition, it was Ezra who was primarily responsible for the collecting of the books of the Old Testament canon of Scripture at this time. From this time on, the Jews would have a collection of Scripture, not isolated books.

PERSPECTIVE

By the time Nehemiah returned to Shushan, Jerusalem was a great deal different than the city he had heard about in the palace. Not only did the city have a wall, but Nehemiah had established an administration in the city in which he had great confidence. The renewal of Jerusalem had been more than physical, or even psychological and emotional. A spiritual renewal had begun among the remnant of the people of God.

FIFTY-TWO

THE END:
The Last of the Prophets
(Malachi)

God had done much for His people since He had formed that first man from the dust of the earth and placed him in the Garden east of Eden. Because of the entrance of sin into the human race, not only man but entire societies turn their back on God's revelation of Himself and defy Him that made them. Even after He chose Abraham and raised up Moses to deliver the seed of Abraham from Egypt, rebellion was far too characteristic among His people. He gave them judges and kings; then He raised up prophets to call those rulers back to Himself. Over the years there had been moments of glory in a continuum of disaster. Finally God had judged His people in Babylon and brought them back to their own land. Under the leadership of men like Ezra and Nehemiah, Haggai and Zechariah, the remnant of the people had made deep and lasting commitments to God. But again the people of God wavered in their commitment to Him. There would be yet another spokesman for God, one more appealing to the people of God.

Appropriately, the last Old Testament prophet was one known only as Malachi. The name Malachi means "my messenger" and is generally thought to be an abbreviated form of "the messenger of the Lord." He was chronologically the last of the prophets in the Old Testament account of the dealings of God with His people. Ironically, some of his message concerned John the Baptist, the one who would chronologically be the first of the prophets in the New Testament.

Malachi was raised up by God to remind Israel of His love for His people. But the love of God did not overlook the sins of the people. Because He loved them, He would confront them when they failed to obey the Law of God. Like most of the other writing prophets, Malachi concluded his message to Israel on a note of hope. God again had not abandoned His people. He predicted He would send His messenger John the Baptist to prepare the way of the Lord. The people might at times abandon their God, but their God would not abandon them.

THE MESSAGE OF MALACHI

God's love announced *(1:1-5)*
God's people denounced *(1:6–2:17)*
God's messenger promised *(3:1–4:6)*

The prophecy of Malachi is perhaps best known because he told the people they had robbed God by withholding the tithe. Even today, tithing is often misunderstood by the people of God. In his appeal to his contemporaries, Malachi stressed a number of vital truths concerning tithing which are as relevant today as they were when the prophet first preached them. First, Malachi noted that tithing is essentially a spiritual matter, not a financial matter (Mal. 3:7). Failure to tithe is a personal affront to God (v. 8). Further, God will withhold many blessings from His people if they fail to tithe (v. 9). Finally, the tithe is to be given to the storehouse (v. 10).

Many Christians mistakenly believe the tithe is simply a part of the Law. Actually, both Abraham and Jacob tithed before the giving of the Law as an expression of their personal commitment to God (Gen. 14:20, 22; 28:20-22). Under the Law, the principle was incorporated into the Law (Lev. 27:30-33) and the place of tithing was established by the Law (Deut. 12). In the New Testament, Jesus affirmed the principle (Matt. 23:23) and Paul affirmed the place (1 Cor. 16:2) of tithing.

Though it is wrong to tempt God, this is one area of our spiritual lives in which God encourages us to prove Him or test Him (Mal. 3:10). God promises to bless us abundantly if we tithe. He will reward our faith (v. 10), protect us (v. 11), and give us fruit in our life (v. 12).

In the years to come, it might indeed seem like God had abandoned His people. After Malachi there were no more Old Testament prophets. For 400 years, there would be no word from God. Though Israel was back in the land God had promised Abraham, they were clearly not in control. Their fate seemed inevitably tied to the decisions of Gentile rulers.

By the conclusion of Malachi's ministry, there were more of God's people outside of Israel than within that homeland. Called the Dispersion, those who were living among the Gentiles were for the most part doing so because they wanted to do so. They were not so much captives as colonists. But within the land there was a remnant. Though they represented only a small portion of the nation, they became the group on which much of the history of the world has focused. This was the group that had rebuilt the city of Jerusalem, complete with its temple and walls. And this was the group that had reestablished the worship of Jehovah in that temple in accordance with the prescriptions of the Law of Moses.

During the four centuries following Malachi's ministry, much happened to this struggling nation, changing various aspects of its society. The Persians continued to rule the world for another century and were fairly willing to tolerate a degree of liberty to the Jews. The high priest was given civil authority but was himself still subject to the governor of Syria. During that century, the Samaritans continued to develop their rival worship until they had built their own temple.

Then in 333 B.C., Persia fell to the third of the four kingdoms that Daniel had prophesied—the Greek Empire of Alexander the Great. Alexander himself treated the Jews favorably. When he arrived at Jerusalem, the Jewish high priest went out to Alexander and read to him from Daniel that the Greeks were predicted to rule the world, including the Jews. Alexander was so impressed that he spared the city. But as that empire broke up, Israel was ruled first by Syria, then later by Egypt (320–198 B.C.). During the Egyptian control of Israel, a large number of Jews moved to Egypt. It was there that the Old Testament was translated from Hebrew to Greek, called the Septuagint (LXX), in 285 B.C.

Then in 198 B.C., Judea was conquered by Antiochus III the Great and annexed to Syria. At that time the Holy Land was divided into five provinces: Galilee, Samaria, Judea, Trachonitis, and Perea. Initially, the Jews were still allowed to live under their own laws and were ruled by the high priest and a council. But Romans tended to interfere with the affairs of the temple and priesthood from time to time. Finally, in 170 B.C., Antiochus IV Epiphanes plundered Jerusalem, killed many of the residents, and profaned the temple. In 168 B.C., he erected an altar to Jupiter in the temple, offered a sow on the altar, and commanded the Jews to eat pork. This is characterized as the "abomination of desolation" (Dan. 8:13; Matt. 24:15).

Antiochus Epiphanes was predicted in Daniel 8:9ff as the "little horn" who persecuted the Jews and plundered the Promised Land. He is a type of "the Beast," antichrist, who will persecute the Jews in the Great Tribulation.

The excesses of Antiochus sparked a popular and patriotic revolt among the people. The revolt was begun by Mattathias Maccabee, a priest with an apparent genuine concern for the holiness of God. He led a band of Zealots into a campaign to free Israel and restore the worship of the temple in accordance with the Law of Moses. He did little more than rally enthusiasm. His son and successor Judas regained possession of Jerusalem and purified and rededicated the temple. This purification of the temple is still celebrated by Jews each December and is the only celebration of the Jews which has a historic background outside of the Old Testament (cf. John 10:22).

The Maccabean revolt was one of the most heroic in all history but failed to achieve a lasting victory against the imperial power of Rome. Judas was killed in battle but was succeeded by his brother Jonathan. Though they maintained control of a few major centers for some time, Rome soon conquered and reigned over Palestine again. By the time the Romans and Zealots met at Massada, the revolt had come to an end. For some time the Zealots continued as an underground group of freedom fighters, but they never again posed a serious threat to Rome.

The civil war in Judea came to an end with the conquest of Judea and Jerusalem by Pompey in 63 B.C. Though John Hyrcanus was given a nominal leadership role, the real ruler of Judea was Antipater. In 47 B.C., he was formally made procurator of Judea by Julius Caesar. In that role, he made his son Herod governor of Galilee.

But Rome was not without its own civil problems. News of the assassination of Caesar resulted in another outbreak of disorder in Judea. For his own security, Herod went to Rome. While there, he was appointed king of the Jews. Two years later (38 B.C.), he married the granddaughter of John Hyrcanus and appointed the Maccabean Aristobulus III as high priest. As a further gesture of goodwill to the Jews, Herod began a major restoration of the temple, which amounted to a building of a third temple. This was the temple where Jesus worshiped.

For 400 years the Jews lived and died in a changing world without a fresh revelation from God. It was inevitable that the religion of Israel would experience changes during this time. The Captivity seemed to have cured Israel of its tendency toward idolatry. It also resulted in the establishing of synagogues in every center where there were Jews. The synagogue was vastly different from the temple. Some have called the synagogue (i.e., assembly of teaching) a symbol of defeat. Whereas they met God in the temple between the seraphim when they brought a blood sacrifice, they retreated to the synagogue to learn and reinforce their sectarian identity.

During the 400 silent years, the Jews built synagogues everywhere to hear the Old Testament Scriptures read to them. During those years when there were no prophets, the vital faith of Israel became increasingly institutionalized. Whereas in the Old Testament the Jews were mostly illiterate, during the intertestamental period they became a reading people; that helped preserve Jewish identity while other cultures disappeared. Religious literature was written and revered in the synagogue until the traditions, comments, and interpretations recorded in the Talmud, Midrashim, and Cabala were considered as authoritative as the Scriptures they commented on. Sects began forming within Judaism including both the Sadducees and Pharisees.

For 400 years, God did not speak to His people. They had the record of what He had already said, but it was increasingly ignored. But one would be wrong to assume that God had abandoned His people. He was silent, but He was about to speak as loudly and clearly as He would ever speak to any people. "But when the fullness of the time had come, God sent forth His Son, born of a woman, born under the Law, to redeem those who were under the Law, that we might receive the adoption as sons" (Gal. 4:4-5). "God . . . has in these last days spoken to us by His Son" (Heb. 1:1-2).